Proud Hunters
Proud Yoopers

50 Yooper hunting stories
from Michigan's wild Upper Peninsula

By Leon E. Hank

Title Page

Published by:
Big Buck Ranch, Inc.
P.O. Box 285
Holt, MI 48842
www.proudyooper.com

Printed and Bound in Michigan
First Edition
ISBN 978-0-615-21158-951295   soft cover

Library of Congress Control Number: 2008908613

Book production by:
Sheridan Printing
Chelsea, Michigan

Cover design by:
Dan Allison, Dimondale, Michigan

Dedication

I may never write another book, so I dedicated this one to a number of special people in my life:

- My loving wife, Susan J. Sternhagen Hank, who has always supported and loved me. She allowed me the freedom to pursue the adventure that is captured in this book. I am a lucky man to have had her as my partner in life.

- My two children, Jeff and Sarah, who inspire me everyday, and who make me believe that the world will be an even better place tomorrow.

- My mother Betty J. Hurst who always encouraged and inspired me to believe that I could be anything I wanted to be.

- My father Louis E. Hank who has been my lifetime hunting partner and who gave me the spirit and passion for hunting that burns deep inside me today.

- My two sisters, Linda and Suzanne, who have both overcome tough struggles in life, and of whom I am very proud.

- All my hunting and outdoor friends who have shared adventures with me in the UP's magnificent woods, waters, marshes, and swamps.

- My associates in the Quality Deer Management Association (QDMA) who have changed my life by changing the way I hunt and manage deer.

I also wish to give special thanks to Pam Sebrink, Maria Bowerman, Michelle Myers, Dawn Garner, Dan Allison, Virginia Dorrien, Mike Jackson, Dan Timmons, Jim Culp, Wayne Roe, Joe Gawle, Larry Tibbits, Vanessa Blaxton, Linda Miller Atkinson, and my wife Susan for their help in proofing the book.

Table of Contents

Introduction

Several years ago, while talking about a hunting adventure with my son Jeff, he asked me if I had written down my favorite hunting experiences. On reflection, I knew I had no organized record for some of them. At the time, I also thought about how different my childhood had been than that of my own children. I had many unique and different experiences growing up in the rural Upper Peninsula (UP) area of Michigan than they had growing up in a southern Michigan suburban community. Following those revelations, I began writing this book about growing up in a hunting family in the UP, where my father and mother taught me about the wonders of nature and hunting. I wrote the book primarily for my two children, Jeff and Sarah Hank, so they would know about my life growing up in the UP and my lifetime of hunting adventures. Along the way, others pointed out to me that the book might have a wider appeal, especially to those who love the UP and those who love hunting.

I was also inspired to write this book after reading a book *Just One More Sunset*, that my friend, Dwaine Starr of St. Ignace, Michigan, had written. Dwaine gave me much of the encouragement I needed to write a book about my own time in the outdoors. I was further inspired when my friends Ed Spinazzola and Larry Holcomb of QDMA published books while I was writing this one.

I have hunted my entire life almost exclusively in the far northern part of Michigan called the Upper Peninsula, or the UP for short. People living in or born and raised in the UP are called "Yoopers." For a humorous contrast, people living in lower Michigan are called "Trolls," because they live "below the bridge." That's a reference to the Mackinac Bridge, the five-mile suspension bridge that connects the two peninsulas. I am proud to have been born and raised in the UP, and this book gives readers some insight into the area's unique culture, resources, history, and its people. But first and foremost, I wanted this book to vividly describe how we hunt in the land of the Yooper and how we celebrate our proud hunting heritage.

I still hunt in many of the places I write about in this book. Every fall, I make 10-15 trips from my home in Holt, Michigan, to the eastern UP. I've made these 600-mile round trips on weekends for more than 36 years – crossing the magnificent Mackinac Bridge over 1,000 times in the process.

This book is also about people who are deeply proud to be hunters. For the proud hunters in this book, hunting is much more than the killing of animals. Why am I proud to be a hunter? I am a proud hunter because hunters are truly the world's best conservationists and because we do more to protect wildlife than any other group of individuals. While I have killed around a hundred deer and hundreds of other animals and game birds, like many proud hunters, I have also spent my lifetime working to preserve wildlife and the wild places they live in - places like those in this book.

Throughout the book, I have tried to capture the emotion of being a hunter, and often that means writing about the emotions of killing a particular game animal or bird. I have also tried to portray hunters as I know them – men, women and kids who genuinely love the outdoors, who love the challenge of matching wits against the prey they seek, who enjoy carefully preparing and eating the meat of the animals they kill, and who work hard to harvest the excess animals Mother Nature has given us. It is these excess animals that hunters kill so we keep wildlife populations at a level where the available habitat can support them. Because this is a book about hunting, I need to warn you that animals do die in many chapters in this book. I write about the killing of these beautiful creatures because it is a necessary part of conservation and it is what hunters do – for themselves and for society.

I can remember when in the last decade it was considered politically incorrect to talk about hunting and killing animals. At one time, even our natural resource experts succumbed to this pressure, and they stopped calling hunters "hunters" and started calling them "cooperators." These cooperators didn't "kill" deer, they "harvested" them. To me that was a low point in celebrating the proud heritage of hunting in Michigan. At that time, it seemed to me as if some wanted us to apologize for being hunters.

I will never apologize for being a hunter and for doing the important wildlife management work that hunters perform. And I will never apologize for wanting to hunt and kill mature white-tailed deer. I will never apologize for what I do because I am a proud hunter and I am proud of our hunting heritage in Michigan and the UP. And I am glad we can again proudly call ourselves "hunters" who do humanely "kill" animals.

My hunting family and friends are people who have spent their life savings and their lifetimes preserving land that wildlife can use. They are people who dream all year long about new projects they can complete that will enhance how productive the land is for wildlife. These proud hunters freely spend their money and shed their own blood, sweat and tears laboring to improve their woodlots, marshes, swamps, and fields so they are more suitable habitat for wildlife.

My hunting friends can tell you in great detail what they have personally done to support wildlife. I am very proud of them and the work they do to support wildlife. I am proud to be one of them, a Proud Hunter, a Proud Yooper.

This is also a book about families, my Yooper family and others that I have known and loved. I grew up in a family where hunting was important – it was a way of life for us. Throughout the book, I celebrate the families that support hunting as an important part of our lifestyle and our heritage.

The early chapters in the book are stories about hunting-related adventures when I was young and growing up in the UP. Later chapters are adventures from my adult life when I experienced the UP on my weekend trips and occasional week-long vacations.

This early introduction to positive hunting experiences formed my values about life and my love for hunting and wildlife. These are important values to me that I have carried over into other parts of my adult life. They are values I try to pass on to my children and others so that we hopefully preserve the rich hunting heritage and the wildlife habitat that we have in the UP.

The book also includes some history lessons about how UP residents settled this rugged country and how they learned to survive and eek out a living in a harsh environment. While I no longer live in the UP during the work week, I am very proud of the people who make their living there. And while I am on loan to the Lower Peninsula trolls, my heart is, and always will be, in the UP. Like all Proud Yoopers, I am very proud of my roots and my UP family and friends.

At the end of each chapter, there is a valuable lesson that Proud Hunters and Proud Yoopers learned from the adventure in the chapter.

The Sault Ste. Marie area where I grew up has one of the state's largest Native American populations. Because Native American hunters (American Indians) were the first hunters in the UP, each chapter starts with a famous Native American saying. These words come from the book *Catch the Whisper of the Wind* by Cheewa James. Cheewa is a motivational speaker and writer who specializes in keeping Native American heritage and culture alive. At the Michigan Department of Transportation where I currently work, we use her materials in some of our business development work. I chose to honor our Native Americans because of their hunting skills and their love of the land.

The book also offers a hunter's perspective on the world of wildlife management decision-making and, in particular, the application of deer management principles in Michigan. Understanding and influencing how wildlife management works is something my dad likes to refer to as a diversion from hunting and engaging in "Deer Politics." In later chapters of the book, you will learn about how critical decisions are made regarding how we manage wildlife in the state of Michigan. You will also learn about the dedicated professional resource managers we have at the Michigan Department of Natural Resources (DNR). I have great admiration and respect for how we manage most wildlife species in our state, but you will also learn from this book that I think we could do a better job with our deer and wolf management practices.

Finally, I hope this book encourages you to visit and experience the UP. If you do visit us, I truly hope you will enjoy all the adventure and splendor that it holds as much as I have.

Leon E. Hank
January 2009

1

A First Hunt and a Toad Stool

What is life?
It is the flash of the firefly in the night.
It is the breath of the buffalo
in the winter time.
It is the little shadow
which runs across the grass
and loses itself in the Sunset.

-Crowfoot, Blackfoot Indian

There are few things I can remember about being age five. I can recall several adventures from my kindergarten school class at Malcolm Elementary on the west side of town on Spruce Street in Sault Ste. Marie. Beyond that, I have little recollection of that year of my life or anything prior. There is one event, however, that stands out vividly in my memory. It had such an impact on me, that it may be permanently etched in my brain. This one sacred memory from age five is the first time my dad took me hunting.

My dad didn't kill any game that day, but one lesson I learned from him has stayed with me for almost five decades. In many ways, it seems like it happened yesterday.

On this Sunday in October, my dad, mom, sister, pet dog and I left our home in Sault Ste. Marie and traveled 40 miles to my grandparents' home near Stalwart. After we had a Sunday dinner that my grandmother had prepared, dad took me with him for a quick walk across the road into the Kimberly Clark Tree Farm on the edge of the Gogemain Swamp. We were three miles west of Goetzville on M-48 where my grandfather and grandmother had lived for decades. My father had grown up in this house, and he had hunted all over this area from the time he was a small boy.

I can also remember times where I anxiously waited for my dad to come home from his hunting trips. Sometimes, he would bring home a variety of beautiful birds like ruffed grouse, sharp-tail grouse, ducks, and geese. I would watch him clean the game, and I would also watch my mom cook up a meal with the meat dad had provided.

This process of going into the field to hunt for game, bringing it home, and cooking it for a family meal was a very natural event for my family. In the eastern UP of Michigan where we lived, many of our family friends also hunted, so I grew up thinking almost all families did what my family did: we hunted for both food and sport.

Proud Hunters Proud Yoopers

On this warm October day, my dad had decided it was time to take me into the woods with him for the first time to hunt for a wonderful game bird called the ruffed grouse or "partridge" as the local Yoopers called them.

As my dad prepared for the brief hunt, I watched him and listened carefully as he explained to me all the steps we needed for our bird hunting trip. He took his gun out of the case, he loaded the gun, and he put extra shells in his shooting vest. He even showed me the back of his vest where he would put the birds if we got any. Finally, he revved up our cocker spaniel/Pekinese-mixed dog named "Peanuts" to ensure she was ready to go.

"You ready to hunt, girl? Are you ready to go get some birds?" dad asked the medium-brown, female house pet we had owned since I was born. Immediately, Peanuts got worked up into a frenzied state. Dad didn't have to ask her more than once to hunt. Despite her "mutt" status, she was a born bird dog who lived to flush partridge out of the spruce, aspen, and balsam fir thickets the birds inhabited.

In 1959 when this hunt took place, and for another 20 years, the Kimberly Clark company owned hundreds of thousands of acres of real estate throughout the Upper Peninsula. Kimberly Clark was a paper-producing company, and it owned all this land because the land provided a steady source of timber for its paper mills throughout the country. Kimberly Clark enrolled this real estate into the State of Michigan's Commercial Forest Act (CFA) property tax program. Under CFA, if the timber company allowed the public to use its land for hunting and other recreational purposes, the company got a significant break on the property taxes it owed the state. Because of the CFA, we could hunt this vast chunk of real estate just as if it were state-owned land.

There was an old logging trail leading into the Kimberly Clark property right across the road from grandpa's house, and the trail quickly branched into two old log roads, one going straight north into the heart of the Gogemain swamp and one going northwesterly along the southern edge of the big swamp.

The Gogemain swamp is one of the largest cedar swamps in the eastern UP and one of the largest winter deer yards in the area. To many, the Gogemain is a fascinating place and an ecological and environmental wonder. It was logged off in the late 1800s and early 1900s with the logs transported out of the huge swamp by railroad car five miles northeast to Raber Bay on the edge of the St. Mary's River. There were three main rail lines from Raber running into the surrounding timber-rich countryside, with one of them running right through the Gogemain and into an area called Hungry Hill on the Prentiss Bay Road – a place that would become one of my favorite hunting spots years down the road. From this main rail line, the logging laborers would relay the rail tracks into other areas after they cut the timber so they could load the logs on rail cars for transport back to the mill at Raber. After the timber was cleared, they would create another rail spur so they could cut and transport other harvested timber in the next section.

At Raber, the Mud Lake Lumber Company ran a large saw mill where they cut up and processed the logs from the Gogemain and other nearby areas. Two or three schooners at a time were anchored in Raber Bay, waiting to be loaded with the finished lumber products. There were several hundred lumberjacks and about 75 mill and yard

A First Hunt and a Toad Stool

workers who toiled in Raber during the timber heydays from 1890 to 1919, earning about $25 a month and free room and board – good wages in those days.

Many of my relatives and their neighbors would eke out a living working in and around these lumber operations. In those early days, timber was king, and for awhile, it must have seemed like the huge mature forests were never ending.

But by 1920, the massive eastern UP forests were gone, and the timber business had become a shell of what it had been. The Mud Lake Lumber Company and its many camps closed for good.

The harvesting of these once never-ending forests helped develop the eastern UP, and it encouraged people (including my family) to settle in the area.

Forty years after the Mud Lake Lumber Company cleared the Gogemain, I was about to enter one of the biggest forests in the eastern UP. By 1959, the big swamp had regenerated itself into another dense cedar swamp, more than 25 square miles in size without a single road to cross it.

While this huge swamp was still owned by private timber interests, many Michigan forests in the early 1900s were abandoned by the timber companies after they were logged, leaving the State of Michigan to reforest and manage the forest so it could be productive again. Dedicated foresters from the Department of Conservation (today's DNR) carried out this work. One of the best books written on restoring Michigan's forests after these first harvests is *Michigan's State Forests, A Century of Stewardship,* by former DNR forestry employees William B. Botti and Michael D. Moore.

I wouldn't know it at the time, but on the first hunt of my life, dad and I would be hunting just the southwestern edge of this mystical place – a place that would provide me with hundreds of adventures and a lifetime of memories.

On this trip, dad had elected to hunt the northwesterly route, and we walked about three-quarters of a mile into the woods and then came back out the same way. As we walked, dad kept explaining to me where we were likely to see partridge. He showed me how Peanuts worked in the brush while we walked down the old log trail, waiting for a clear shot as the partridge tried to escape.

Throughout the walk, dad kept emphasizing gun safety to me. He continually stressed the importance of me staying one step in back of him so that he could shoot quickly and safely if the birds flushed in front of us.

Peanuts worked her tail off on that trip, but as luck would have it, we didn't kill any birds. Even so, I really enjoyed following my dad through the woods, and I had never seen Peanuts so excited, nor had I seen her work so hard. For the first time in my life, I learned what a bond there is between a hunter and his dog, and I learned about the magic of having a dog hunt with you.

Dad had thought about how long a reasonable hunt would be for a youngster like me, and he probably estimated how long a five-year-old's patience would holdout. As a result, he had picked a turnaround spot where I would get a good feel for what a hunt is like, and yet not be bored or overly tired. Shortly before we made it to this turnaround place, I spotted something unusual.

On an old, dead aspen (or poplar) tree, there was a huge piece of fungus growing not far from the base of the tree. I ran over to the fungus and asked dad if I could have it.

Proud Hunters Proud Yoopers

Dad tried to discourage me from taking the fungus, and he explained how an item like this would be a great landmark that hunters might need in case they got lost. He explained how if we ever saw this fungus again, we would know where we were.

"It's just an old toad stool – a piece of fungus growing on this old tree," dad told me. "It grows here because the tree is dead, and soon the tree and the toad stool will rot away completely."

Wow, I thought to myself. I like the way this thing looks, and it even has a cool name like "toad stool." Now I wanted to take it home even more, and I pleaded one more time. Dad firmly said no, and we went back to hunting.

I was disappointed that I couldn't have the fungus, and I continued to look at it as we walked on by the "landmark."

A few minutes later, we had reached the turnaround, and we headed back home. Soon, on the return route, we approached the dead aspen tree with the fungus, and dad stopped and pointed to it.

"Hey, that looks like the toad stool you spotted earlier, so now we know where we are. I guess we are not lost and we must be going the right way to get home! See, I told you it was important to know about landmarks when you are hunting!"

My spirits were sky high. I had not expected to see the toad stool again, and here it was right in front of me. "Can I please have that toad stool, Dad?" I pleaded with him.

"OK, we can take it home, but then it won't be here ever again for a landmark. Can you think of something else you can use here to always remember this place?" dad asked me, trying to teach me more woods lore with this lesson.

"Dad, I don't think I will ever forget this place," I promised him as I thought about showing off the fungus to my friends in the neighborhood and at school.

With that, dad walked over to the toad stool and kicked it hard to knock it free from the tree. The fungus was huge, about a foot in diameter, and it weighed probably half what I did. Dad carried it home for me. When we arrived back at my grandparents' house, I was proud to show off the toad stool that had a brilliant creamy whitish-yellow color on the bottom with a smooth finish and a rough, deep, dark brown finish on the top. I thought it was the neatest thing I had ever owned.

I took the toad stool to school for show and tell, and I proudly pointed it out to my friends when they came over to the house. We kept the fungus for several years, and my mother used it as a door stop for our front door in the summer.

Over the years, I think I made hundreds of trips down that old Gogemain log road in pursuit of partridge, ducks, deer and bear. I probably shot about a hundred partridge in the area and dozens of ducks on some nearby ponds, and I took about 12 deer not far from where that old piece of fungus grew on the dead poplar tree. Every time I walked by that spot, I remembered the lesson a veteran hunter taught his son on his first hunt.

The old poplar tree is long rotted away, but I will never forget the toad stool nor the lesson about landmarks in the woods and how they help hunters find their way home.

Later in life I would learn just how important it was to know where you were in the Great Gogemain Swamp, and I would learn the price hunters would pay if they didn't find their way out using familiar landmarks.

A First Hunt and a Toad Stool

Decades later, as my son Jeff began to show an interest in hunting, I tried to pass on lessons to him like the landmark toad stool lesson. I secretly hoped these lessons impacted him like my dad's lesson did for me.

On this first hunt in the Great Gogemain Swamp, a Proud Hunter learned that Proud Yoopers teach young hunters survival lessons in the UP woods as early as possible and in ways that will stick with them for a lifetime.

2

BB Guns, Frogs and the "Crick"

*All living creatures and all plants
are a benefit to something...*

-Okute, Teton Sioux

In May of 1961, I got the thrill of the lifetime when I got a Daisy BB gun for my seventh birthday.

It was a model 95 Daisy that I loaded at the muzzle by turning the end of the barrel and dropping BBs into a small hole at the barrel tip. Before each shot, I had to cock the gun by using the lever action. To a seven-year-old, it was a very cool-looking and shooting gun.

The Daisy air rifle I was using was produced by a company that originally started in Plymouth, Michigan, in 1886. Clarence Hamilton, an inventor from Plymouth, developed the gun that used compressed air to propel a small lead ball. Lewis Cass Hough was the president of the company, and, history says, he was really excited after testing the gun proclaiming, "Boy, that's a daisy!"

That's where the name of the gun and the company came from, and, in 1895, the company's board of directors formally changed the name of the company to the Daisy Manufacturing Company, Inc. From that day on, the Daisy company has provided millions of BB guns to young kids like me.

In 1958, the company moved its headquarters and production plant from Plymouth, Michigan, to Rogers, Arkansas. The company is still strong today, selling BB guns in almost every country in the world.

A most important accomplishment of the company is that they have trained more than 7 million kids in gun safety and shooting education by using air rifles or "BB guns" as we Yoopers call them.

I was a lucky kid because my dad also sold Daisy BB guns in his sporting goods store in Sault Ste. Marie. Over the years, my dad estimates that he has sold over 400 BB guns to local kids.

Early on, dad told me I couldn't shoot my BB gun around the neighborhood in the city. Our shooting was confined to our weekend trips to both of my grandparent homes in the country.

On those weekends, I spent countless hours shooting that Daisy BB gun and learning about gun safety. My mother and father both taught me to be especially careful around my two sisters, Linda and Suzie, and my other cousins who would from time to time show up at grandma's home.

Over the summer, I gained confidence in using the gun, and I got to be a pretty good shot at hitting cans and bottles that we used for target practice.

BB Guns, Frogs and a "Crick"

One hot summer day, my cousin Dan Firack from nearby Detour, Michigan, and I were staying at my grandma Hank's house in Goetzville when we made a startling discovery: the small creek just west of the house was filled with frogs.

This creek began as a free-flowing spring bubbling up from the ground 150 yards southwest of my grandparents' house, and it runs across state highway M-48 through a culvert under the road. The creek also runs parallel to the state highway for a hundred yards, and then it rambles mostly straight north through the heart of the Gogemain Swamp before it empties into the South Branch of the mighty Gogemain River.

The creek (or "crick" as we called it in Yooper speak) is about four-feet wide in most places and only six to 12 inches deep. This size, however, is perfect for young boys to negotiate. As we explored the crick, we would playfully jump across it, going from one side to the other whenever the other side seemed to hold more adventure.

The water is also amazingly clear and cold. In fact, the water was so fresh, that my grandparents used it for their drinking water for years without any filtering system. The creek has a white, sandy bottom with lots of downed trees and vegetation, so it provides good cover for the small brook trout that also inhabit the creek.

What Dan and I discovered on that sunny and beautiful day is that we could hunt frogs with our BB guns for hours at a time. Sometimes my cousins Greg and Andy Dorrien would join us, and the four of us would take turns using two BB guns to harvest our frogs.

Greg and Andy were two of five sons my dad's sister Virginia Dorrien had with her husband Jack Dorrien. Jack also grew up with his family in Detour, and he and my Aunt Virginia moved to Midland after they were married. In the summertime, Greg and Andy would spend several weeks of their vacation at my grandparents.

Over several summers, the four cousins spent lots of days chasing frogs in that little creek.

We usually began our frog hunt the same way. We would start at the beginning of the creek and walk it as far as we could, carefully scanning ahead for frogs sunning themselves on the banks or lounging, partially submerged at the water's edge.

As we stalked the creek, we practiced all the skills that hunters use in hunting bigger game.

We learned that if we traveled too fast, or made too much noise, the frogs would hear us and jump into the safety of the deeper water or hide under the banks before we could get a shot.

We learned that if the frogs were spooked, they would return later if we would be patient and remain motionless and quiet. When the frogs surfaced from their hiding spots, we might get a second chance and a shot if we were prepared.

We learned that there were small frogs and big frogs, smart frogs and dumb frogs, and frogs with different colors.

We learned that there were certain features about the terrain and the habitat that attracted more frogs than in other parts of the creek. We learned that there were some places where there were almost always frogs present – places that were great "frog habitat."

We learned that if we shot too many frogs in some places, there were fewer or maybe no frogs there the next time we came back.

Proud Hunters Proud Yoopers

We learned that if we made a poor shot, we might wound the frog and finding that frog would be difficult. We learned the importance of making a clean kill when we made a choice to shoot at a frog.

In total, I spent hundreds of hours in pursuit of frogs while growing up, and, at least to me, it was quality time with my cousins that helped build my hunting skills.

In 1978, my wife and I received some terrible news. My cousin Andy Dorrien was found dead in my aunt and uncle's home in Midland from two gunshot wounds. Part of the house had been damaged as if there had been a fight. We never did learn exactly what happened, but I knew that the cousin I loved so much had died a violent death.

The incident struck our family hard, and Andy's funeral was one of the toughest funerals I have ever attended. It is so sad to lose someone so young and someone you have known for so long. As a young adult, the death of another young person, especially a close relative, is one of life's hardest realities to understand.

As we prepared to say goodbye to my cousin for the last time, all my relatives were together, sharing in our grief and reminiscing about Andy and his lust for life. All of us thought he had so much spirit and spunk. We had a hard time accepting that he was gone.

As a part of that grieving, I kept thinking about the joy that four young boys had experienced each summer, hunting frogs with BB guns along their grandpa's "crick." Life was a lot simpler then when our biggest worry was whether we'd be ready with the BB gun before the next frog jumped for cover.

Years later, my cousin Greg (one of Andy's older brothers) married Robyn Hampton, and they had a daughter they named Hope, who was close in age to my daughter Sarah. At a family reunion, Greg started telling Hope and Sarah about our frog-killing adventures from 40 years ago.

I tried to stop him.

"Greg, maybe some things little boys do as young hunters should remain their sacred secrets," I hinted to him. "Maybe our frog adventures are too graphic for our little girls."

Greg got a huge smile on his face and let out a loud laugh as he told me, "No way, Leon! I want our girls to know about all those frogs we killed as kids!"

I gave up trying to stop him, and I laughed with him as he told our young girls about what he remembered from our frog adventures. Predictably, the girls were just a bit less enthused about frog hunting than we had hoped.

After a few good laughs, we got serious for just a minute. We took time to remember Andy and the fun we had together chasing frogs and in other adventures we shared as kids. The tears flowed freely as we remembered a cousin and a brother no longer with us.

On this day, a Proud Yooper remembered the role that frogs in a crick taught him about hunting skills and quality time spent with cousins. And a Proud Yooper also learned from a cousin that Proud Hunters should not be afraid to pass on to their young daughters the pure, childhood joy of shooting frogs along the crick with your cousins.

3

A Chipmunk for a Pet

They listened to the warbling of birds
and noted the grandeur and the beauties of the forest.

- Francis Assikinack (Blackbird) Ottawa

Early in life, I learned that one of the best things in the world for young kids is playing with your cousins. While our family is not large, I am fortunate enough to have a number of cousins, and some of them live in the eastern UP.

My dad has three sisters, Charlotte Firack of Detour, Virginia Dorrien of Midland, and Lorraine Schremp of Sterling Heights and Brimley. All three girls and my dad grew up as kids in the Detour and Goetzville area of the eastern UP, and they attended the one-room Goetzville School on the corner of Tower Road and Traynor Road until high school when they went to Detour Village. My mom had only one brother, Don Westervelt. Don and his wife Betty had two kids, Leeann and Tim. Uncle Don had moved from the eastern UP to live in the Cincinnati area after he got out of the Navy.

My Aunt Charlotte had two sons, David and Dan, and a daughter, Beverly. David is four years older than I am, and Dan was born just three months before I was. As kids growing up, Dan and I got together every chance we could.

One of my favorite adventures was to visit Dan at his farm in Detour on the corner of M-48 and Ziegler's Lake Road. To me, this 120-acre parcel of land, where Dan's grandfather also lived, was pure paradise. Dan and Dave lived in the country with a small creek crossing their land (just a little bigger than Grandpa Hank's creek). They had lots of woods to explore and hunt, they had a chicken coop and several barns, and they each had a horse!

For a city kid growing in the eastern UP's metropolis of Sault Ste. Marie, I thought this little farm had it all. And could three young boys ever get in trouble on this farm!

In the summer when school was out, my parents would let me visit my Aunt Charlotte and her husband John Firack at the farm for a week at a time. Dan and I would build tree forts, sneak down to the "crick" for a secret swim, look for eggs around the chicken coop, help milk the cows, and feed treats to the horses.

David and Dan also taught me how to have manure fights in the horse pasture. That's right. We would find large quantities of round horse manure that had partially dried and hardened on the outside, but it was still soft on the inside. The best ones were about tennis ball size or smaller. Then we'd have an all-out fight with the stuff, throwing the manure balls at each other like kids playing dodge ball.

17

Proud Hunters Proud Yoopers

For nine-year-old kids with limitless energy and boundless imagination, we could make a game out of almost anything. Pelting each other with manure balls that splattered on impact was one sport we invented.

But our biggest passion was hunting birds, squirrels and especially chipmunks with our BB guns in the big hardwoods behind the barns.

The Firacks had a mature hardwood forest that was dominated by beech trees, red oaks, and sugar maples, making it the perfect habitat for squirrels and chipmunks. The beeches and oaks provided lots of hard mast as feed for animals from the beech nuts and acorns that fell all over the forest floor.

The beech trees have a remarkable smooth and soft bark. They almost beg you to carve your initials in their bark or leave some message for a future visitor. As kids, we sometimes spent hours carving our initials and writing messages in the bark of large beech trees.

Dan and I had been chasing chipmunks with our BB guns, and we had found an area of the hardwoods where they seemed to be everywhere. We weren't having much luck killing them, so we invited David to come with us. As someone four years our senior, David was a much better shot with his BB gun, and we knew odds were good we'd get some chipmunks that day, especially with more of us throwing BBs at the little rascals.

Two neighbor kids also joined us for this special adventure: Tommy and Roger Potwardowski from the next farm.

We entered the hardwoods about mid-morning, and before long, we surprised a chipmunk looking for his breakfast. The chipmunk got lucky and quickly escaped to his hidden den in the trunk of the hollow tree as we hopelessly shot our BB guns at him. After we realized we weren't going to get this chipmunk, we started talking about how much fun it would be to have a chipmunk as a pet.

That's when we hatched a plan to wound the next chipmunk we saw so we could capture him. We decided we would try to hit the chipmunk in the back leg and knock him to the ground, hopefully inflicting only minor injuries to the chipmunk.

David and Dan said they had an old bird cage in the basement, and we reasoned that we could use that as a home for our pet if we were successful in our quest.

We even talked about all the animals our grandparents and parents had as pets. Our Grandpa Hank, for example, even had a pet black bear that he and his brother Fred found and raised for a year before selling it to a visiting Detroit hunter. While that would be illegal today, it was common for Yoopers in the first half of the 20th century to keep and raise animals found in the wild.

My mom and her brother Don Westervelt had lots of pictures of a deer they had raised from a young fawn when they were teenagers. A neighbor of ours in the Soo had a garage full of wildlife he had captured, including raccoons, crows, and other birds. All this talk fueled our excitement about capturing our own animal – a first for our zoo.

As we approached the next hotspot for chipmunks, we spotted one fifteen feet off the ground on a beech limb. David took careful aim with his BB gun, and the chipmunk fell to the ground after the shot.

Danny quickly reached for the wounded chipmunk with his right hand. As he grabbed the striped little creature, it bit Dan sharply at the base of his thumb, drawing a

A Chipmunk for a Pet

small amount of blood. Danny shrieked as the chipmunk punctured his hand, but he hung on to the animal, and we wrapped it up in one of our jackets.

Quickly, we ran a quarter mile through the woods to home where we dug out the bird cage and placed our new pet in his home.

For the first time, we could examine how well our pet had survived his wound. He wasn't bleeding, but he looked somewhat aloof, probably from the shock of his injury. He didn't play around in his bird cage like we had envisioned he would.

We returned to the woods to find acorns and beech nuts so he would have food, and we even fed him some peanuts for a treat. We also made sure he had water to drink.

As we admired and nurtured the chipmunk, we started talking about trying to capture other animals. We dreamed out loud about starting our own zoo.

The Detour area, where my parents grew up and where the Firacks lived on their farm, was a sparsely settled and predominantly Polish community. In the late 1800s and early 1900s, a number of Polish immigrants came to this part of the country looking for work and a better life. My great grandfather Frank Hank was one of them, and Dan's grandfather Albert Ferck (there were four different recorded spellings of the Firack name) was also from Poland.

On our BB gun hunting trips, Dan and I would stop and see his grandfather who lived in a small farm house just west of Dan's farm on Ziegler Lake Road. Dan's father, my Uncle John, would join us sometimes, and Uncle John and his dad Albert would speak Polish to each other. Dan and I wouldn't have a clue what they were saying.

Back at home, my Uncle John would tell us about how his dad came over from Poland and how he had made his living working at the Raber sawmill and the tannery in the Sault, cutting timber in the logging camps and working construction on the Neebish Island Rock Cut and the Edison Electric Power Canal in the Sault.

My grandfather Ed Hank would explain to me later in life that one family from Poland would come over, start working here, and then send word back home that this was a good place. Other Polish immigrants would follow, hoping to find work in the lumber mills or camps or in construction.

All around the Detour, Goetzville and Raber area there were lots of Polish people who had settled here, and they had Polish-sounding names like the Zwolinski, Potwardowski, and Kiczenski families and not-so-Polish-like names like Firack and Hank.

Later that afternoon, my Aunt Charlotte went shopping at the Cedarville Drug Store. Secretly, she was worried about her youngest son and the animal bite. While at the drug store, she asked clerk Betty Smith about whether chipmunks could transmit rabies to a child through a bite.

Betty Smith told the store pharmacist John Trefry about the chipmunk bite, and he was really upset. Trefry immediately called Cedarville's Dr. Leonard DeLoff and told him about the bite.

Dr. DeLoff told the pharmacist to send my aunt right over to his office. My Aunt Charlotte made the short trip to the doctor's office where Dr. DeLoff told her he would make arrangements to have the animal tested for rabies.

Proud Hunters Proud Yoopers

Meanwhile, back at the Firack farm, the Firack's cat continuously watched the chipmunk in his cage, probably thinking of a way to have the chipmunk for lunch. The same cat had bitten my Uncle John just a few days earlier while my uncle tried to give him a worming pill.

The poor, wounded chipmunk, however, was not doing well. As the afternoon wore on, he died in his cage, with the cat watching over him.

Upon discovering the dead chipmunk and the watchful, hungry cat, my Uncle John picked up the bird cage and took it outside where he intended to feed the dead chipmunk to the cat for a treat.

Just as he was about to remove the chipmunk, my aunt pulled into the driveway and called to my Uncle John, telling him to save the chipmunk. My uncle complied and kept the dead chipmunk in a small box.

The cat, of course, was disappointed at this turn of events.

At 9 pm that evening, a Michigan State Trooper pulled into the Firack yard and told my aunt and uncle that he was there to pick up the chipmunk. He explained that the animal would be transported to Lansing where it would be tested for rabies. He told my aunt that any warm-blooded animal that bites a human could transmit rabies. If she couldn't produce the chipmunk, he told her that Danny would have to go through a series of painful rabies shots.

With all this talk about rabies, my uncle listened in fear thinking that he also might get rabies from the cat bite. He secretly pleaded with my aunt not to tell the Trooper about his cat bite.

Because the Goetzville area is a small, close knit community, eventually everyone knew the story about how the Firack boys had captured a pet chipmunk. They also knew that Danny had been bitten by the animal.

The whole event created quite a stir in our family and in the community. The five Yooper Polish boys never imagined this outcome to their BB gun escapade.

The next month, the State Police returned to tell my aunt that the rabies test was negative and that Danny would be spared the dreaded rabies shots. We were all grateful, and we vowed to never again handle a live chipmunk.

When I was growing up, I spent hundreds of hours hunting with my Daisy BB gun in the woods for small birds, chipmunks and squirrels. When I was home, I would spend hour after hour recording on little maps where I had seen the chipmunks and squirrels so I could return later to hunt them again. I was a nine-year-old kid carefully planning my next chipmunk hunt just like an adult big-game hunter today plans his next Mule deer hunt in Wyoming or an elk hunt in Colorado.

As I think back, I probably killed dozens of sparrows, black birds, chipmunks and squirrels in those days before I started hunting with a shotgun and a rifle. I learned a great deal about shooting, gun safety, different types of habitat, animal behavior, and how to hunt successfully from these early training sessions. These experiences also helped me develop the critical hunting skills I still use today.

In those days of the early 1960s, and in this rural part of the eastern UP, it was commonly accepted that little boys used their BB guns to hunt small birds, squirrels and chipmunks.

Everyone took it for granted that we were learning and preparing to hunt larger game later in life.

A Chipmunk for a Pet

In many ways, these BB gun hunts in the eastern UP are like using training wheels on a little kid's new bike.

Today, attitudes have changed significantly, and it's unfortunately not as acceptable as it once was for nine-year-olds to head to the woods to shoot chipmunks. In fact, only a small fraction of kids ever get to hunt with a BB gun as I did in my youth. I have even had well-meaning adults explain to me that kids participating in youthful hunting experiences (as I did all the time) can be "scarred for life." Some adults have told me how barbaric it is for kids to shoot chipmunks or other small animals. Some have suggested that those kids might grow up to be violent criminals later in life.

So, gee, what happened to me? Somehow, I survived these early hunting experiences, and I am even proud of them.

As I look at the future of hunting today, I am concerned about the declining numbers of hunters, particularly new youthful hunters. If hunting is to survive as we know it, we will need to encourage more of our youth to try it. We need to be recruiting new hunters, or hunting as we know in the UP and other places will be doomed. We will need innovative approaches to make hunting attractive and fun for our kids, like the adventuresome chipmunk hunts I enjoyed as a young child.

In November 2007, the Michigan Department of Natural Resources's (DNR) Budget Director, Sharon Shafer, provided me with 50 years of license data for Michigan hunters. Michigan hunters bought an all-time high number of licenses in 1992 when 1,171,721 hunters purchased a license to hunt in our state. Over the next 13 years, license sales dropped steadily almost every year until we had seen a decline of over 380,000 hunters. By 2005, only 789,244 hunters had purchased licenses, the lowest total since 1973. Clearly, if this trend continues, hunting may not have a future.

Thankfully, in 2006, the Michigan DNR got legislative approval to lower the minimum age for hunting so that youth as young as 10 years old can now legally hunt small game and deer. Across the country, states are changing their licensing laws so that more young hunters can enjoy the thrill of hunting. Many hope the new laws will reverse our rapid decline of participants in the sport. Thank goodness Michigan joined the parade.

As this book goes to press, DNR Director Becky Humphries recently told the Michigan Outdoor Writers that she favored even fewer restrictions on hunters. "Personally, I don't think there should be a minimum age. I think parents are the best judges of when their children are ready (to hunt)." This position was reported by outdoor writer Tom Carney in an article he wrote for *Woods-N-Water News* magazine, one of my favorite outdoor publications.

All we can hope for is that the DNR can continue to attract more hunters to our sport, preferably at a young age. All of us can help by providing opportunities for kids to get a chance to have a positive hunting experience early in life. Those young kids today who do get to experience the thrill of chasing chipmunks through the hardwoods with their BB guns are fortunate indeed. And maybe, because of those experiences, they will grow up to be proud, lifetime hunters.

From this boyhood chipmunk-chasing adventure, a Proud Yooper learned that Proud Hunters exercise great care when handling wounded wildlife. A Proud Yooper

Proud Hunters Proud Yoopers

also learned that Proud Hunters don't keep wildlife as pets, unless they want a rabies scare and a visit from the Michigan State Police.

4

Respect the Trophy – Respect the Law

If you do bad things
your children will follow you
and do the same.
If you want to raise good children,
be decent yourself.

-In-the-Middle, Mescalero Apache

I was about nine or ten years old when dad took me on a partridge hunt in a place the locals called "the Burning," an area five miles southwest of my grandfather's home where major fires had burned off part of the landscape decades ago. As we entered the Burning, dad took a right turn down the old log road, traveling across the state land parcels that took us south and west to a place called McAdam's swamp. Along the way, we passed the old tin shack, a nickname for an old hunting camp visible from the road on the south end. We didn't go there often, but on this beautiful October day, dad thought he might get some partridge by walking this country with our dog Peanuts.

I wasn't old enough to legally carry a shotgun, so I had my trusty Daisy BB gun with me.

Not long after we entered the heavily wooded area, Peanuts jumped up a big buck, an eight or ten pointer with a very nice symmetrical rack. Peanuts froze as the buck jumped up and stopped to look at all of us.

I had seen and read about a buck like this in the monthly *Outdoor Life* magazine my father received, but I had never seen one up close like this in the wild.

The buck looked awesome standing on the edge of a small clearing right in front of us.

I watched dad as he watched the buck. I expected him to shoot this beautiful animal.

Within seconds, the buck threw up his tail, turned away from us, and was gone into the heavy brush in two jumps.

"Dad, why didn't you shoot that deer?" I asked, almost not believing what had happened.

Proud Hunters Proud Yoopers

"Son, it's not deer season yet, so I can't legally shoot at him," dad patiently explained.

"But you could have killed the deer, couldn't you have dad?" I pressed on again.

"Yes, but, son, we don't shoot deer outside of the hunting season. We need to wait until the season opens just as we did for partridge. It is partridge season right now, and we are here to hunt partridge," he said emphatically.

"I can come back here in November with my rifle when the deer season opens, and see if I can find this buck again. That's how we hunt. There are rules for hunting, and we need to follow those rules."

In Michigan, the DNR and its governing policy board, the Michigan Natural Resources Commission (NRC), is the government agency responsible for managing Michigan's wildlife and establishing hunting rules. Later in life, I would learn just how prevalent it was to violate the DNR's hunting rules if you hunted in the UP. In fact, some would say that almost everyone violated the hunting restrictions, and some Yoopers thought it was a sport to avoid getting caught.

As I got older, I learned that many eastern UP residents freely bragged about shooting their deer outside of the season or shooting deer at night with a light. Almost everyone thought it was OK to violate game laws and avoid the State Game Wardens or conservation officers (COs as they were called).

With my inquisitiveness at a peak, dad took the time to explain to me that even our own family and many of our relatives had, at times, violated the game laws over the years. He gave me some examples, and we talked about them.

He told me that he wanted me to grow up with more respect for the game animals we hunted, especially the white-tailed deer. He emphasized that he'd like me to never shoot a deer at night, with an illegal weapon, or outside of the season.

Then he really hit home with me. He said, "What fun would it be to have to cheat to kill that deer today? I'm a good hunter, and I don't have to cheat to make sure I kill a deer. I will get a deer when the November season comes, and I will kill one legally."

He told me that he had been taught by his father (my grandfather) that it was occasionally OK to kill deer at night with a light and outside of the season. He told me that my other grandfather also occasionally killed deer illegally too. Then he told me about several of my uncles and the illegal deer they had killed. Finally, he told me about a few illegal deer he had killed, including one he had shot when he was just a few years older than me.

He explained to me that in those days, our families were poor and we needed the deer venison for food. "When we shot a deer illegally, we needed it for food," dad stressed.

"We all did it," he admitted to me. "No one thinks much about it. No one thinks it's bad to do it."

He went on to explain that our relatives would never even think of committing other crimes like stealing something or robbing a store. They would always obey those laws. But, he said, people in the UP look on the game laws differently. "They really don't think it is breaking a law to shoot a deer at night or out of season," he told me as we sat down on a fallen tree and analyzed what we had just experienced.

"There is a law that you can't jaywalk or spit on the sidewalk, and yet people do it all the time," he said. "People look at the game laws the same way."

24

Respect the Trophy – Respect the Law

In Yooper-lingo, people in the UP have a name for breaking the game laws – they call it "violating." If you practiced the acts of shooting deer outside of the season or with a light at night, you were a "violator" or a "shiner." You could brag about your violating, and most people would not turn you in nor think poorly of you. Some call the law breaking by a different name of "poaching," the more prominent term used in the lower peninsula.

In fact, being a game violator in the UP was so prevalent that one Yooper, the DNR's Sgt. John A. Walker of the western UP, has published six books about his adventures in chasing and arresting those who don't follow game laws. Walker turns many of these investigations and arrests into humorous stories like those in his books: *A Deer Gets Revenge* and *The Old School: Adventures of an Old Game Warden.* In the Walker books, he describes the outrageous and unbelievable actions people did when taking the game laws into their own hands.

Back in the Goetzville woods, I realized my dad had done something rather extraordinary on this day. Dad made a commitment that day to break the cycle of violating with me. I would be the first generation in our family to begin hunting deer legally. He made a point of trying to get me to respect deer for what they are. And he wanted me to make sure I earned my trophies the hard way – in a way that I would appreciate them.

As I think back on that day, I realize that it took a lot of courage to do what my dad did and it took an understanding of conservation, respect for wildlife, and conviction.

My dad need never wonder about what I learned that day. The lesson has stuck with me ever since, and it is one I will pass on to my children. For the sake of all our wildlife and for the future of hunting, this was a great lesson for one Yooper to pass on to another generation.

On this day, a Proud Hunter learned that Proud Yoopers respect the game laws of our state and, most important, Proud Hunters respect our wildlife and the trophies we pursue.

5

Peanuts the Wonder Dog

Every struggle, whether won or lost,
strengthens us for the next to come.

-Victorio, Mimbres Apache

In August, 1954, just three months after I was born, my parents picked up a house dog. They gave this female, half-Pekinese, half-cocker spaniel, the name of Peanuts. She was light-brown in color with a long tail and floppy ears.

Peanuts and I grew up, side by side, over the first 12 years of my life, and we were almost inseparable.

Early on in the life of Peanuts, dad discovered that she was quite a bird dog, despite her "mutt" status. In fact, Peanuts loved to hunt birds.

On top of being a great hunter, she was also a great house dog. She never, ever jumped up on the furniture or a bed, and she never had an "accident" in the house. She never bit anyone, but she was a great watch dog, barking loudly if a stranger came to the house.

Peanuts was fabulous with kids, especially with my sisters, Linda and Suzie, and me. When we had neighborhood, after-dinner baseball games in the Montgomery Wards parking lot across the street from our home, Peanuts would sit on the edge of the asphalt ball field and wait for darkness when we would head home.

On our half-mile hike to Malcolm Elementary School in the mornings, she would walk with us and then find her own way back home when we got to the school yard.

All our neighbors knew her by name, and every one of them loved Peanuts. She was a pretty-looking and gentle dog who let people pet her if she knew them. She wandered the neighborhood by the Sault Ste. Marie Memorial Hospital freely, minding her own business but chasing every bird and cat that crossed her path.

Once a year or so, my parents would find a good mate for Peanuts and breed her. Then she would have six or seven puppies, which my parents would sell for $10 each - big money in those days.

She had a cloth mattress that she used for a bed in a large basket down in our basement. At night time, she would go to the basement when my parents gave the command. When you arose in the morning, she was there to greet you with those big beautiful eyes.

In short, Peanuts was the perfect dog, especially for a hunting family like ours.

She was happy all the time but never happier than when dad would start gathering his hunting supplies. Peanuts would get excited just watching him organize his gear. He would talk to her about going hunting, and she would get incredibly excited, wagging her tail like crazy. She had a look of anticipation and excitement in her eyes that just told you how much chasing birds meant to her.

Peanuts the Wonder Dog

Over the years, I watched dad shoot dozens of partridge that Peanuts had found and flushed for him. We'd hunt with her for hours, watching her work the bushes while dad readied himself for shots at streaking ruffed grouse.

I was still in the BB gun stage in those years, not yet participating in this harvest gathering ritual, but I often saw how satisfying it was for Peanuts to be chasing these birds and being with my dad when he shot them. It was as if she knew about the teamwork they enjoyed. She found the birds and flushed them out, and dad shot them.

After every bird, dad would call her and pet her, thanking her for her great work. She loved that part of the hunt. And afterward, she would tear off into the brush looking for the next bird.

This went on for ten hunting seasons.

One day Peanuts had been gone for several hours while my parents were working outside at the fishing resort my grandmother Florence Nutting owned and operated on the Point of Frene in Raber. My mom, while coming back to the cabins to where my dad was, spotted Peanuts in the distance crossing a large field. Peanuts was holding a mature partridge (that she had caught while chasing birds in the woods) in her mouth. She walked right up to my dad and dropped the partridge at his feet. She looked up at my dad as if she had just brought him the gold medal from the Olympic Games.

This mutt of a dog, who had no training in retrieving or hunting of any kind, did every thing by instinct, almost to perfection. This much was clear: she was born to hunt birds.

In between hunting seasons, Peanuts used to love to hunt with me as I was learning my way around the woods, shooting black birds, chipmunks and squirrels. She really loved being out in the woods with me, chasing after every little bird and small animal in the forest.

In August 1966, my mom and sisters were away, and my dad was working at the family sporting goods store that we owned and operated in Sault Ste. Marie. I was home alone with Peanuts when a friend, Mark Meehan, came over. Mark, who lived on Peck Street, convinced me to go to the Krempel's Pharmacy for a new soft drink called a Cherry Coke.

This was a big thing, and I was excited about going. Cherry Cokes were the new rage in town, and I was anxious to try one. In my haste to go, I left Peanuts outside.

Mark and I came home an hour later to hear a horrifying story. As I approached our Division Street home, a neighbor kid on a bike told me that Peanuts had been hit by a car. I hurried on home, and as I approached, I could see there were neighbors all around our front porch. As I got to the porch, one of the neighbors told me that he had already called my dad to tell him about Peanuts.

I tried to piece together what had happened to Peanuts. It appeared that she had tried to follow me down Peck Street toward the downtown area, and she had crossed Ashmun Street (the main street of town), right by the bridge that crossed over the Union Carbine Power Canal. It was on Ashmun Street, right in front of the House of Bargains Furniture Store, that a car hit Peanuts, running over her back leg.

My heart was pounding furiously as I pushed past all the neighbors and ran up the stairs to the porch. There, under a bed on our enclosed porch, Peanuts was hunkered down, with her right hind leg broken off below her knee. What was left of her leg was hanging by only a piece of her fur.

She looked to be in agonizing pain, and she wouldn't let any of the neighbors near her.

She let me come to her side and pet her. As I stroked her, she whimpered softly, and I knew she was badly hurt. I had a sense that she was comforted that I was finally here with her.

As I looked at the extent of her injury, I wondered whether we would have to put her to sleep. My mom had told me about how this was done and how it was sometimes the fate of injured or old dogs. As I looked at my 12-year-old dog, I knew that Peanuts was both injured and old.

"I'm sure we are going to have to put her to sleep," I told one of the neighbors, resigning myself to the situation.

In only a matter of minutes, my dad came bursting unto the porch, and he quickly examined Peanuts.

"Dad, look how badly she's hurt," I pointed out the obvious. "Are we going to have to put her to sleep?"

Dad didn't want to answer my question, his attention consumed by the serious matter at hand.

Peanuts let dad pick her up, and he held her in his arms, cradling her carefully and talking softly to her. She seemed comforted that he was finally here too, but she was in pain as he gently handled her. My dad had his business shirt on, but he didn't seem to notice or care that he was getting blood on himself.

"Son, get in the car," dad told me firmly. "I'm going to hand Peanuts to you, and you need to carefully hold her until we get her to the veterinarian. Be very careful how you hold her and try not to touch her leg."

Then dad, thinking quickly, asked a neighbor to call Dr. Jewell, a veterinarian who lived and practiced just outside of town on Mackinaw Trail. Typically, we took Peanuts to Dr. Barber, a veterinarian in Pickford, 20 miles away.

"There's no time to get to Dr. Barber's place," dad told the neighbor. "Please call Dr. Jewell and tell him we're on our way with Peanuts. Tell him how badly she is hurt."

With that, we jumped in the car and drove off to the Hiawatha Veterinary Hospital with all the neighbors wishing us well.

In ten minutes, we were at the vets, and I overheard Dr. Jewell talking to my dad about the options. Given the age of Peanuts and the seriousness of this injury, the doctor offered to put Peanuts to sleep for a small charge.

My dad pushed back right away.

"This dog is like a member of our family," my dad explained calmly. "Can you do anything to save her?"

Dr. Jewell explained that he could amputate the leg at the top of the hip bone and Peanuts could survive on three legs. It was serious surgery, and it would require several hundred stitches to do the amputation. He also explained that this complicated surgery would cost $150.

After the surgery, Dr. Jewell cautioned, there would be no guarantee that Peanuts would live long. Getting around on three legs would be strenuous, and at her age, she might have a heart attack at any time from the strain.

Peanuts the Wonder Dog

In 1966, $150 was a lot of money to a family that only made several thousand dollars a year in earnings from our small family business.

Why would anyone spend $150 on a twelve-year-old dog with a serious injury?

On that day, my dad never hesitated, and he told the doctor to do the surgery. He asked about a payment plan so he could fund the large expenditure over time.

Dr. Jewell told my dad to come back in several days when Peanuts would be ready to come home.

Three days later, my mom, my sisters and I went to the vet hospital to pick up Peanuts and bring her home.

Mom had prepared us for the shock of what we were to see. Peanuts had the right side of her hind end completely shaved of hair. The doctor had removed her entire right leg, all the way up to her pelvis. My mom explained that the doctor had to do this so Peanuts wouldn't try to use any part of her leg to walk. Peanuts would have to learn to walk on three legs.

The doctor had needed the 200 stitches he promised to close the incision at her pelvis and he had placed a large cardboard, oval-shaped collar (called an Elizabethan collar) around her neck so she wouldn't chew on her stitches.

We would have to feed her carefully, keep her wound clean and keep her from chewing on her stitches for several weeks. We also needed to make sure she got lots of rest so she could heal up from this terrible accident and delicate surgery.

Initially, it was sad to see Peanuts look so different, but we got over that quickly as it was just great to see her and pet her again. And, boy, was Peanuts happy to see all of us, and she was really glad to get in our car and go home!

But first, the vet showed us how Peanuts could walk right now – which was not very well. Dr. Jewell explained that she needed to build up the strength in her left leg to support herself and she needed more practice to balance herself on one back leg. She needed to learn the coordination necessary to run on just one back leg. All of this would take some time.

It was possible, the doctor promised us, that Peanuts might once again walk and run almost as well as she did prior to the surgery.

Over the rest of the summer, Peanuts got stronger, and she gradually gained good mobility on three legs. She became a conversation piece almost everywhere we went. People were amazed to see the three-legged dog we had. They were even more amazed when we told them that she was 12-years old.

I always felt blessed that our first dog was a very special dog, but I didn't really appreciate how special she was until this terrible accident. Her incredible recovery taught me just what a wonder dog she really was.

At the time, the only important question on my mind was, would this Yooper wonder dog ever hunt again?

From this terrible accident, a Proud Hunter learned about the special bond that hunting dogs share with their Proud Yooper families. A Proud Yooper also learned that a Proud Hunter might spend a big share of a year's salary to make sure that a special dog could spend more time with family.

6

Library Safaris and Fred Bear

Children must learn early the beauty of generosity.
They are taught to give what they prize most,
that they may taste the happiness of giving.

- Ohiyesa, Santee Sioux

My love for hunting played out in the woods of the eastern UP, but two of the most influential acts in my youth took place in the local public library and at the local movie theatre.

In the late 1960s, my mom became a library aide for the Sault Area Public Schools at the Soo Township School, three miles outside of town on M-129. It was a job that she absolutely loved, a job where she helped kids enjoy the power of reading. So, with this background, maybe it was destiny that I would also love libraries.

Long before mom worked in a library, she would take my sister Linda and me to the public library on Saturday mornings to be a part of a reading exercise where the local librarian would read stories to all the little kids in attendance. Parts of the sessions were sometimes even broadcast on the local radio station, WSOO. After the formal story reading was done, there was time to browse the library and take books home to read.

In the late 1950s and early 1960s, there was only one public library in Sault Ste. Marie, the Bayliss Public Library. It was a huge public building to a small kid growing up in a town with few big buildings. There were even two life-size, real-looking African lions outside the library's front door. The two concrete lions looked as if they were guarding the library. I loved that the lions were standing guard at the entrance to this fine institution of knowledge where I could learn about adventures I had yet to take.

While it might have been considered a bit "nerdy" to spend your free time in a public library, I loved to read books about hunting in our public library. To find those books, I learned the Dewey Decimal System long before most kids knew such a thing existed.

And somewhere among the dozen books on hunting and African safaris, I also discovered several books about a folk hero called Robin Hood.

Those trips to the library began a new phase in my youth where I read every book I could about hunting, African safaris and Robin Hood. I just didn't read the books once; I read them over and over until I almost knew the words on the next page before I turned it.

Library Safaris and Fred Bear

Of course, all this stimulation helped form my beliefs and values that I have today about the adventures of hunting and the outdoors.

One day, I learned about the advertisements in the back of *Outdoor Life* magazine for outfitters who would take hunters into remote areas to hunt big game. There were advertisements for hunts in places like Montana, Idaho, Wyoming, Colorado, British Columbia, the Yukon, Alaska, the Northwest Territories, Newfoundland, Nova Scotia, Quebec, and, of course, Africa.

Before I was old enough to shave, I was writing letters to professional outfitters around the globe, asking how much it would cost to take my father and me on a hunting trip to Newfoundland where I told them I wanted to kill a moose with 50" antlers and a record book caribou. Most of the outfitters wrote me back and sent their brochures and literature about the hunts they offered. This only fueled the hunting appetite for a young kid in the eastern UP.

It didn't really matter that I didn't have a dime and my family couldn't afford a vacation outside of the UP on the modest income of our family business. I got a huge kick out of writing letters to these outfitters and pretending I was planning to take a hunt for every major big game animal in North America. I checked the mail every day for their responses, and I read them over and over when they came.

One day, my dad gave me the *1963 Guide to your Choice Hunting Grounds* by Ben Berg of Madison, Wisconsin. This paperback was 288 pages crammed full of hunting regulations and information about guided hunting trips in all the places I had wanted to hunt: Alaska, British Columbia, Idaho, Montana, the Yukon, and elsewhere. I read the book from cover to cover, and I kept it in a special storage box under my bed together with the letters from the outfitters I had written. In the evenings, I would pull out the book, flip through the pages, re-read the letters from the outfitters, and dream about hunting big game in all these exotic places.

To this day, I still have the Berg book, and I consider it one of my prize possessions.

As I got older, I could go to the library myself. Soon I was making regular trips there to read about this famous archer called Robin Hood. I loved reading about the adventures of a guy who hunted in the woods all day long and who could kill a deer with his bow just about anytime he wanted.

I learned about what a great shot he was with his bow and what a tough, but lovable guy he was. Those stories inspired me to practice shooting a bow and arrow and to build bows and arrows from sticks and tree limbs, just as Robin Hood had done.

Before long, I was shooting a home-made bow and hand-crafted arrows in my backyard. At about the same time, several trees in our Division Street neighborhood were missing key branches.

Out of a series of Robin Hood books, I became a huge, lifetime fan of archery and bow hunting for deer.

But the most influential event in my young hunting life may have been the night my father took me to see a movie about hunting at the Soo Theatre, our local movie house, in downtown Sault Ste. Marie.

Now, on Saturday afternoons in the 1960s, my mother Betty often gave my sister Linda and me 25 cents each for a Saturday matinee at this theatre. Mom also gave us an extra nickel for a candy bar. From these trips, I knew the theater well.

Proud Hunters Proud Yoopers

On this special occasion, my dad took me to the theater at night for an unusual event. We heard a lecturer, Fred Bear of Grayling, Michigan, talk about his hunting adventures, and we saw his outdoor film about him hunting big game all around the world.

The most intriguing part of the evening was seeing the movie of Fred Bear killing what seemed like every animal on the planet with his bow and arrow. In fact, Fred killed every animal species that I had dreamed about hunting – moose, elk, sheep, and even brown and polar bears. I remember one particular scene in the film where Fred was stalking white-tailed deer in a Michigan forest.

He had spotted a small herd of deer feeding in the distance in the middle of a hardwoods forest that looked like my cousin Dan's forest. Fred silently walked up on the herd, drew his bow, and killed a nice buck that was feeding with the herd. It all looked so easy.

I thought it was the coolest thing I had ever seen, and, for years, I believed that was probably how most hunters killed deer with a bow and arrow. From that day forward, I dreamed that I would kill a big buck with my bow like Fred Bear had in the film.

In 40 years of hunting deer in Michigan's forests, I have killed over 50 deer with a bow, but I have never killed a deer in the manner that Fred Bear did in that film – and I have never even come close.

But the film, the image of the Great Fred Bear, and his Michigan bow and arrow buck have stuck with me ever since and probably always will.

And I still hold out hope that someday I will walk through a mature hardwood forest, spot a big buck, make a careful stalk, and kill him with my bow and arrow, just as Fred did in the film.

The great Fred Bear was not a Yooper, but many Yoopers think of him as one of our own, and our admiration for this legendary, Proud Hunter runs deep.

From Fred Bear and a public library, a Proud Hunter and a Proud Yooper learned that our youth can be profoundly influenced favorably toward hunting and wonderfully entertained by good writing, good films and great public presentations on hunting.

7

Adventures with Bears

*You must speak straight
so that your words may go
as sunlight into our hearts.*

-Cochise, Chiricahua Apache

Over the years, I've had some wonderful adventures with Michigan's magnificent black bears. My fascination, respect, and even fear for them began when my mother told my sister Linda and me about a Brimley, Michigan girl who had been killed by a bear.

I can remember my mother telling us this story as if it were yesterday. I was seven years old (in 1961) and just starting to explore the woods and hunt alone with my BB gun. I think mom was worried about me wandering too far from my grandparents' house, where she feared that I might run into a real bear.

Mom told us this Brimley story so that we would stay close to the house when we were in the woods at both my grandparents' homes. "You need to be careful," my mom warned us. "A hungry bear in Brimley grabbed a little girl in her yard, dragged her off into the woods, and ate her."

My mother was a 13-year-old teenage girl herself when this little girl was brutally killed by the young black bear. I can imagine my grandmother telling my mom and her brother Don about this event.

If you wanted to scare a seven-year-old kid so that he would be careful around black bears, this was a good way to do it! My mother was extremely effective in getting my attention and ensuring that I was careful to stay away from bears when I was hunting or playing in the UP woods.

Mom continued with the story, telling Linda and me that the little girl's mother witnessed the attack and had to helplessly watch as her little girl was taken from her yard by the vicious bear and carried off into the deep woods. Mom also told us that local hunters then went after the bear and killed it. Mom told us that the brave hunters cut open the bear's stomach and confirmed that the bear had killed and eaten the little girl.

Linda and I listened in awe and horror to the graphic and largely true story, something that had happened only 20 miles from where we lived. This real life story gave us a healthy respect and fear for the black bear. Actually, the story scared us to death, and, for years, I never wanted to run into a bear unless I was with other people and carrying a big gun.

Years later, I would learn that mom had, in fact, told us the cold, hard facts about a terrible tragedy in the eastern UP.

Proud Hunters Proud Yoopers

The incident happened on July 7, 1948 to a three-year-old girl, Carol Ann Pomranky, who was playing in the backyard of her Brimley home where she lived with her mother and father. Her father worked for the U.S. Forest Service, and her mother was in the house when the attack happened. The girl's mother looked out the window where she saw the bear chasing her daughter. The girl almost made it to the door where her mother had run to help her when the bear caught the little girl. The 125-pound bear retreated to the woods with Carol where the bear killed and partially ate her.

Later that day, Alex Van Luven of Brimley used a leashed bear hound to track the bear with another volunteer helper, Wayne Weston. The two men probably startled the bear and chased it away because they found the partial remains of the little girl's body in nearby woods. While Van Luven and his hound continued to pursue the scent of the bear, Weston stayed with the girl's body. Minutes later, Weston killed the bear when it returned to its victim.

This story was widely told throughout the eastern UP and I heard it often at the Malcolm Elementary School in Sault Ste. Marie where I attended. Kids were always talking about the little girl who was eaten by the bear whenever anyone ever brought up the subject of bears. In the classroom, our teachers also warned us about the danger of bears.

The Brimley bear incident was widely written about in the UP and even nationally. In his book, *Understanding Michigan Black Bears*, the UP's Richard P. Smith of Marquette, Michigan, wrote about the infamous attack. Richard is one of the UP's most prolific authors, and he has published ten different outdoor books over the years.

Much later in life, I would learn from Richard Smith and others that while that story was true, it was a rare event that a bear would kill and eat a human being. In the last hundred years, black bears have only killed two other people in Michigan. Even so, I have never forgotten the Brimley bear story and I also learned to maintain a healthy distance from most bears.

Dad also taught me early on that we should respect the black bear, especially a mother with cubs. He also taught me to be careful of hungry bears in the spring because they haven't eaten since the previous fall, after hibernating all winter.

"Those are the bears that are dangerous," dad told me. "Never get between a mother bear and her cubs because she may attack you and stay away from ornery bears in the spring time when they are hungry."

Dad explained that most bears are scared to death of humans, and almost all of them will run away at the sight, scent or sound of us.

In early 1960s, while I was carrying my BB gun, dad and I were hunting partridge in the Burning on a big red oak ridge. It was a banner year for acorns, and the big oaks were loaded with the nutrient-rich nuts that so many deer, bears, and other animals love.

As we worked our way through a particularly thick part of the ridge, we lost sight of our dog, Peanuts. When we broke into an opening, we found Peanuts at the base of an oak tree, looking up. As we approached her, we heard an animal moving in the brush to our left.

Adventures with Bears

Dad grabbed me and whispered, "I thought I saw a bear." As he spoke, we both saw movement in the brush that sure looked like a large, black animal circling us. There was a low growl in the brush that was scary.

As our attention was drawn away from Peanuts, we heard a commotion back in her direction. We took our eyes off the black object in the bush, and then suddenly, two small bear cubs came scampering down the oak tree, dodging Peanuts as they ran at lightning speed to join their mother in the bush.

As I looked at dad, I saw a look of concern on his face. It then occurred to me that we were in the situation he had warned me to avoid. The two of us and our little dog were between a mature mother bear and her two small cubs. That was a dangerous place to be.

To ensure we weren't antagonizing the mother bear, dad had us quickly move away from the direction of the bear, giving her some space and allowing her cubs to join her. First, he had to retrieve Peanuts. While the bear cubs were about twice the size of Peanuts, she showed no hesitation to pursue them. She was determined to chase the cute, little bear cubs, which was a natural, instinctive reaction for her. Dad yelled for Peanuts and grabbed her so she wouldn't follow the small bears into the bush where the mother would almost certainly attack her (and maybe us too) in defending her young.

Dad and I, with Peanuts in tow, quickly exited the bear's domain. The bears also headed in the opposite direction once they were together. They were now safe from the hunters who had accidentally stumbled upon them in the forest. The bears could now go back to dining on acorns.

When we were safe, dad explained about the close call. He speculated that the mother had trained the cubs to climb the oaks, shake the branches and knock the acorns to the ground where the bears could feed on them. We interrupted the harvest gathering work of the bears when Peanuts got to the base of the oak tree before the cubs could get down. The mother got away more quickly than the cubs, and she likely signaled for the cubs to follow her. The mother was pacing nervously in the brush when we arrived, waiting for the cubs to figure out how to bypass our treeing wonder dog. Fortunately, everything worked out for all of us. The bears got back together, and we had a far more exciting partridge hunt than we had expected.

Most important, I had an up-close and personal experience with three real bears.

On this day, a Proud Yooper learned to give respect and some distance to a mother black bear with cubs. A Proud Hunter was also reminded again that black bears can be dangerous and unpredictable and can even take the life of another Yooper.

8

A First Duck

*A people without a history
is like wind on the buffalo grass.*

- Teton Sioux proverb

On May 13, 1966, I celebrated my twelfth birthday. One gift from my parents was a long, narrow box that they told me I had to open as the last present. When I finally opened it up, I couldn't believe it. It was a 20 gauge single shot Stevens shotgun!

"This fall, for the first time, you can legally carry a shotgun and hunt small game with me," my dad told me. "You have graduated from your BB gun. We will practice shooting and handling the shotgun this summer, and by fall, you will be ready to start hunting."

Wow, I thought. Now I am a real hunter. I have my own shotgun.

I couldn't wait to get to school and tell all the guys that I had a shotgun! Unbelievable!

When fall came, I didn't have much luck hunting partridge with dad in the first few weeks of the season. It seemed the birds were always skittish and shooting was tough, especially for a rookie with no experience. Somehow, I never got a good, clear shot, and I missed a number of birds. Dad, of course, always took out a few birds, making some incredible shots that left me admiring how he got the birds. I watched closely and tried to learn everything from him about handling a shotgun.

After a few hunts for partridge, dad asked if I thought I was ready to go try for ducks. He told me duck hunting might be even harder than partridge hunting, but he said I would enjoy it. I was a bit discouraged with my partridge experiences, but dad could have asked me to go hunting tyrannosauruses, and I would have been excited to go.

"I'm going duck hunting!" was all I could think about after he asked me.

My grandmother on my mother's side, Florence Westervelt Nutting, lived in North Raber about 10 miles from Grandma Hank. "Nanny," as I called this grandma, lived with her second husband Jess Nutting on the tip of the Pointe of Frene, one of the most easterly points of land in the mainland of the eastern UP.

This part of Raber, just south of the famous Munuscong Bay, was also fabulous duck hunting country, with its bays and marshes.

My nanny's first husband, Leon Westervelt, had settled and developed this part of Raber in the late 1940s and early 1950s. He had built the road into North Raber and the Pointe of Frene with a small bulldozer and hand tools on the road today known as Mike's Landing Road. He had moved here from Jackson Center, Ohio, where he had owned and operated a hardware store. He developed a fishing resort where the end of the road meets the St. Mary's River and the west edge of Raber Bay.

My grandpa died of a stroke in 1956 at age 42, and my grandmother remarried. Nanny sold the first resort, and then she and Jess built a second resort in the mid 1960s

A First Duck

on the tip of the Point of Frene. I guess you could say that running resorts was in my Nanny's blood. Today, both resorts are still around – businesses that have supported anglers and the local economy for more than 50 years.

My grandfather had worked long and hard to develop this part of Raber. When winter came in the early 1950s, he bought several Army "hutmuts" from the Lime Island ferry boat operator. He hauled the 12' by 12' cabin style huts one at a time on skids across the ice from Lime Island to his new resort in North Raber. Now that he had a rough road cut to the waterfront and he had a resort ready for business, he hoped the Chippewa County officials would take over and maintain the road.

This part of the eastern UP doesn't look anything like it did when my grandfather first purchased "the Point," as the locals called our settlement. In the 1950s, North Raber was a wild, remote and undeveloped place, much like it had been when the early European explorers first came here. Little by little, my grandparents developed the Point and sold off lots to other families who fell in love with North Raber and the St. Mary's River. Many of the people who bought the real estate parcels were customers who had been coming to the resorts for years. Eventually, they bought lots so they could have their own paradise on the St. Mary's River.

My grandparents were never well off, and they lived a very humble lifestyle from their resort earnings and the profits from the real estate parcels they sold. They didn't know it at the time, but they would be responsible for developing millions of dollars of real estate in the eastern UP.

In 1990, my grandmother died in a nursing home in Florida. She had been living on a small pension from her dead husband and very modest social security benefits. She had sold all her real estate holdings long before the big run up in UP real estate values. Had she held on to even a small portion of the real estate she and her two husbands once owned, she would have been a millionaire.

My parents had named me Leon Edward Hank after both my grandfathers, and I was proud to carry their names.

On a Saturday night in October 1966, my family traveled to Nanny's home in Raber to spend the night. On Sunday morning, dad had promised me we would get up before daylight and go duck hunting in the little marsh south of Nanny's house.

Now we didn't have a duck blind, boat, or decoys, or any other duck hunting equipment most hunters take for granted today. Dad explained to me that we would quietly sneak through the reeds of the marsh and jump shoot some ducks.

Dad had given me a new pair of hip boots, just the right size for a 12-year-old kid. He instructed me that I should walk slowly on the inside of the marsh, staying close to the beach in water about knee deep. He would patrol the outside of the marsh where the water was deeper. He showed me the chest waders he would use to navigate his path in waist deep water through the marsh.

We went over the safety rules again, and we talked about how we needed to know where each other was before we shot at ducks. Dad explained that most ducks we might see would jump straight up out of the marsh reeds when we flushed them. If they did that, he explained we would be safe shooting at them.

The alarm went off early for a young kid, but I was ready to go when dad called. We walked to the marsh and started our jump shoot just as dawn broke. Dad told me

Proud Hunters Proud Yoopers

again to go slowly through the marsh and to make sure I had good footing before I took my next step. He also warned me to be careful not to go over the tops of my hip boots.

We had gone about two hundred yards when a lone hen mallard exploded out of the weeds right in front of me. She was skyward bound and quacking like crazy. I shouldered the 20 gauge, drew a bead, and let go with a load of a no. 4 Winchester magnum. It also sounded as if dad shot at about the same time.

The mallard was hit hard, and she crumbled, dropping back into the weeds in front of us. I shouted out, "I got him, I got him."

Dad quickly congratulated me and got me to quit yelling so I wouldn't scare every other duck out of the marsh. "Way to go son, what a great shot! You got your first duck!"

We both waded over to the duck and admired the beautiful bird. Dad put the hen in the game bag in the back of my junior-size vest. "You are the hunter who killed this bird, and you should carry him," dad proudly told me.

I was thrilled to see and touch the duck and to feel the weight of the bird in my game bag. I was beaming about this accomplishment and this great new day.

I reloaded carefully in front of dad, and he instructed me how we would continue to work the marsh. "We are off to a great start thanks to your good shooting," he told me. "Now let's get some more ducks."

We walked another couple hundred yards, and a drake mallard took off in front of me. I pulled up the shotgun and cut loose at the bird, but it just kept on flying after my shot. A second or two later, dad's gun barked once, and the bird tumbled to the marsh.

At that moment, it occurred to me that maybe I didn't really get the first bird. Maybe I had missed that one too, and maybe the duck had died from dad's simultaneous gunshot.

We jumped some more ducks later in the morning, but they flushed way out of range.

"Black ducks," dad said to me, talking emphatically like they were something very special. "They are smarter birds and bigger birds than the mallards. They are hard to get close to. Maybe next time we'll get a crack at them."

From that day forward, I held the black duck in high esteem. I considered them a special breed of duck that required your best hunting skills.

My dad never ever mentioned to me that it was possible I might have missed on the first bird. When I asked him about it later at home, he never hesitated. "No, son," he told me, "You killed the duck. I missed the duck. Nice shooting."

Years later, I learned what an outstanding shotgun shooter my dad was. There was no way he missed the easy shot on that first mallard. At worst, I figured my dad and I killed my first duck together, and I always cherished that he let me know I killed it myself.

I have returned to this same marsh almost year to try to kill at least one duck in it by walking the marsh and jump shooting it just as my dad taught me. It is a special experience because it is the first place I hunted ducks with my dad. It is a special place where my grandparents settled and developed this rugged part of the eastern UP, making it possible for hundreds of people to have homes and cabins and to enjoy this beautiful part of the St. Mary's River and the UP.

A First Duck

Most years, I've been successful in taking at least one duck from the marsh. Every year it is a celebration just to be here where my ancestors worked so hard to eek out a living in this unforgiving land.

On this day, a Proud Hunter learned that Proud Yooper dads help their kids enjoy the thrill of navigating a big marsh and killing a first duck.

9

Close Encounter in the Burning

The birds that flew in the air
came to rest upon the earth,
and it was the final abiding place
of all things that lived and grew.

- Chief Luther Standing Bear, Teton Sioux

On a particularly nice day in early October, 1966, dad took me to the Springer Road, five miles southeast of Stalwart for a partridge hunt when I was 12 years old. We took Springer Road south of M-48 to a place where there were seven square miles of state-owned hunting land that the locals called "the Burning." The Burning got its name from the large swath of fields that cut through this wild, heavily-wooded area where forest fires had burned for days in the early 1900s.

On October 7, 1908, fires burned totally out of control all across the eastern UP. *The Detroit News Tribune* (today's *Detroit News*) reported that there were masses of flames all across the Goetzville and Detour area. The smoke was so bad, that at 1 pm in the afternoon, ships out in the St. Mary's River near Detour had to use their fog horns and anchors for safety until the smoke cleared.

Sailors on these ships reported that there was a 50 mile "Wall of Flame" from Sault Ste. Marie to Detour. *The Detroit News* reported that passing ships said the flames were 100 feet high and extended several miles back from the lake.

From Goetzville, residents told the *Detroit News* that Robert Kelly's farm of 160 acres was swept end to end and that other farmers also lost all their farm buildings to the out-of-control fires. The local Mud Lake Lumber Company lost several thousand acres of hardwoods to this ravaging fire. Fortunately, residents were able to save the small town of Goetzville.

A magical thing about forest fires is that they remarkably bring the land back to life quickly. In fact, many land managers would argue that occasional forest fires are good because they help the land replenish itself, enriching and renewing its soil. A good forest fire gets rid of years of old growth timber, accumulated brush, and layers of organic material on top of the soil. After a fire, the land quickly regenerates itself with young plants and trees. This younger, healthier forest can support substantially more wildlife than the old growth forest that burned.

Somehow, after these raging Goetzville fires, only part of the forest in the Burning area regenerated itself. A large portion of the forest remained as open fields running in a north-south direction, right through the middle of this large parcel of hunting country. The DNR built a one-lane gravel road through this part of the forest. Later, the utility company erected a power line through the area that followed much of the burned out path.

Close Encounter in the Burning

A few decades after these devastating fires, the DNR established fire towers to protect communities like Goetzville from the fires. They constructed small steel buildings that sat on top of 100 feet of tapered scaffolding that towered above all the neighboring forest. There was one such tower in Goetzville just east of where we were hunting.

The DNR assigned employees to staff the towers. Using binoculars, they were expected to spot forest fires before the fires could get out of control. As a small kid, my dad showed me this tower that was just one mile from my grandfather's home. I remember seeing someone in the tower, and I thought about how important a job it must be to be up so high in the tower watching for forest fires.

Jim Pudelko of Goetzville was one of the last DNR employees to man the towers in Michigan's forests. Jim started with the DNR in 1965 and spent time looking for forest fires from his 110 foot tower standing proudly over the Goetzville area that was spared from the raging fire in 1908.

By the late 1960s, the DNR quit staffing the towers and began relying on aerial surveys for forest fire control. By the 1980s, the DNR had sold off the fire towers for either scrap metal or to history buffs for preservation. The Goetzville tower was purchased by the adjoining landowner. The tower still stands today, one of the few remaining symbols of the DNR's fire-fighting tower history.

Some of this history about the great fires in the eastern UP and the DNR's fire fighting efforts is captured in Betty Sodders' two books, *Michigan on Fire* and *Michigan on Fire 2*. Sodders has lived in the eastern UP for a number of years, and she's written extensively about the UP, its fires, and outdoor issues. She is a regular contributor to *Woods-N-Waters News*.

By the mid 1960s, the burned out bare fields in the Burning were adjacent to heavily-wooded cover that ran for several miles. The area represented outstanding game habitat that was especially good for deer, given the tremendous amount of "edge" habitat the fires had created in the middle of the forest "cover" habitat for deer.

Years later, I would learn how important edge habitat is to the white-tailed deer, and I would learn that deer are creatures of the "edge." In fact, deer love to travel edges because edges have more food. Later in life, I would know that wildlife food sources would just explode in the area where a field meets heavy forest cover because of the sunlight that hit the ground at the field's edge. That is ideal habitat that deer and other wildlife love.

All of the hunters in our family, like many of the locals, simply referred to this large area as "the Burning." It was a popular hunting area in Goetzville because of its immense size and because it was public land open to hunting.

On this perfect morning for bird hunting, dad decided we would walk the woods on the north end of the Burning in an area he called Kelly's Swamp. This was the same farm that had burned to the ground in the great fire of 1908. Dad told me that this particular piece of property got its name because it was homesteaded years ago by the Kelly family. Their effort to farm the land apparently ended when the big forest fire roared through the area. Dad showed me a large field east of the swamp called Kelly's Field where their homestead had been. The property was also just west of a 40-acre parcel owned by the Ted Postula family of Goetzville.

Proud Hunters Proud Yoopers

We had hunted birds for about an hour when we jumped a family of partridge. Like what happens often with ruffed grouse, the seven or eight birds in this flock had scattered in all directions. Dad was confident we could pick up a few of them.

He described for me how these birds had lived together with their mother who had hatched them in late spring. She had nurtured them from the tiny birds they were when they hatched from eggs she laid in June. Today, they were almost adult-size partridge. He explained that while they stayed together as a family for now, soon they would be splitting up to form their own families, just like when kids grow up. Next spring, the young birds would look for new habitat and start new flocks of partridge.

We were in very heavy cover of thick poplars, white spruces, and evergreens at the time, a typical smorgasbord of trees in a UP conifer region. The birds had eluded us and dad thought one or more of them were hiding nearby in or under the conifer trees.

As dad showed me the habitat where these birds loved to live and feed, he pointed out to me how this place smelled. There was a particular odor to this kind of place, a place where partridge loved to hang out and feed.

"When you come to a place like this, and you can smell this scent, you know you are in good bird country," dad tutored me. "You should be ready to shoot whenever you walk into a place that smells like this."

"If you stay here for a few minutes and keep quiet, some of the partridge might just drop out of the trees," dad explained to me. "Some of them will probably return to this place they think is their home. Why don't you just rest here for a minute, and I'll swing over to the east to see if I can pick up some of the birds that flushed."

"You should get an easy shot at a partridge if he thinks we've walked away and left," dad instructed me. "I'll be back in ten minutes, and then we'll hunt the birds that flushed to the south."

I thought it was cool that my dad trusted me to stay here alone with my gun. I felt as if I were standing guard, waiting to surprise one of the unsuspecting partridge that might drop out of the thick conifers or return to its home.

Dad was gone only a couple of minutes, when I heard a twig snap.

I looked behind me in the direction dad had gone, and I saw a deer coming right toward me. Slowly, but steadily, the large doe walked almost right by me, only ten yards away.

As she quietly passed me, she kept moving as if she were on a mission. Most amazing, she never saw me even though she was so close.

The whole thing lasted less than a minute, but it was a tremendous thrill to be that close to a wild deer in the woods.

Five minutes later, dad came back from his brief jaunt. As he got close, he started explaining to me that he had jumped a few birds, but he couldn't get a shot.

I interrupted him and told him about the deer.

He asked me, "Could you have shot the deer with a bow and arrow?"

"Yes, I think I could have!" I proudly proclaimed.

"Well, then we will have to start bow hunting soon," he promised me. "Wow, you learned today what it is like to be a deer hunter!"

I did learn a great deal about the white-tailed deer in Kelly's Swamp that day. I learned that my dad, the great hunter, had not seen this deer, but the deer had probably seen my dad and apparently, managed to sneak right around him to escape. The

Close Encounter in the Burning

quietly exiting deer had, however, walked right by me, the sitting and watchful hunter, who had been patiently and quietly waiting in the woods.

On this day, in Kelly's Swamp, on the edge of the Burning, a Proud Hunter learned about the magic of the white-tailed deer and a lifetime fascination with this great creature began. And, as an added bonus, a Proud Hunter and Proud Yooper learned about the great smell of ruffed grouse habitat.

10

Double Buck Fever

*Training began with children
who were taught to sit still and enjoy it.
They were taught to use the organs of smell,
to look when there was apparently nothing to see,
and to listen intently when all seemingly was quiet.*

- Luther Standing Bear, Lakota

There is a phenomenon in deer hunting that is little understood, despite years of outdoor research. That phenomenon is called "buck fever," and it frequently strikes at young or inexperienced hunters. It has been known to also victimize older, more experienced hunters on occasion, especially when they have seen a very nice, mature buck with large antlers.

Buck fever happens when hunters see deer and take aim, preparing to shoot the quarry with either a gun or bow. Suddenly and unexpectedly, the hunter experiences so much nervousness, anxiety, or muscle tension that the hunter wildly misses the deer or cannot even take the shot. Sometimes, hunters even freeze and cannot move.

For some hunters, the experience of buck fever is so dramatic, that when it happens, they will get the shakes so badly that they actually loose control of their muscles. Others will experience such an increase in their heart rate that they will think their heart is about to jump right out of their chest. They might fear a heart attack, only to have the feeling dissipate quickly after the deer runs off. When buck fever hits, others will have their knees buckle and they can barely stand up on their two feet.

Over the years, I have known Yooper deer hunters who have experienced some or all of these symptoms. On occasion, I have had the legendary buck fever myself, but never as badly as what occurred on one of my first deer hunts.

In the fall of 1966, I also started attending a mandatory seventh grade shop class in Sault Ste. Marie. The class was taught by Sault Junior High School teacher, Mr. Ed Jacques, who was also a local contractor. On the first day of class, Mr. Jacques told us that we would have to complete one major project early in the year to get credit for our shop class. He reviewed all the possible projects we could undertake. My interest peaked when he said one of them was to build a 40-pound recurve aluminum bow from a kit we could purchase.

While other kids in the class were thinking about a wide variety of projects, my choice didn't require much thought. I picked out the bow kit right away and, together with another student, I went to work immediately building my aluminum bow.

As a young kid, I had grown up idolizing Robin Hood, and I had spent my younger days constructing bows and arrows from tree limbs I had taken from

Double Buck Fever

neighborhood trees. I loved the idea that I could build a powerful, metal bow from a kit that would transform raw pieces of aluminum into my new hunting weapon.

By early October, I had built the bow by assembling the aluminum parts, machining the limbs on lathes and with hand files, and constructing a wooden handle that I covered with dark brown and white pieces of thin leather sheathing.

Each day that I worked on this bow was a labor of love. Some days, I couldn't wait until shop class so I could get to work on that bow that I needed for the October and November archery season. After a month of hard work, the bow was finally ready for hunting.

My dad hunted with a Bear Archery bow, and we used orange-colored cedar arrows with feather fletchings. Our arrow tips were three-bladed fixed heads manufactured by Bear Archery of Grayling, Michigan, the company owned by the legendary Fred Bear, one of my idols.

In the fall of 1966, the DNR reported that there were only about 50,000 bow hunters in the whole state, and only about 2,000 of them would kill a deer that year. That means only one of every 25 hunters killed a deer with a bow. So if you killed a deer or you were even in active pursuit of a deer with a bow, you were in some pretty select company.

Today, archery hunting in Michigan has exploded, and since 1990, more than 300,000 hunters try to take a deer with a bow in our state. In 1995, the peak of the archery movement, 389,366 hunters bought an archery license, according to DNR statistician Brian Frawley and deer researcher Brent Rudolph. We've slipped some since that high point, but almost 308,000 bow hunters killed over 111,000 deer in 2005. That means one of every three bow hunters today kills a deer with archery equipment, a huge improvement over the early days when we hunted with much more crude equipment.

In the late 1960s, you hardly ever heard of anyone killing a deer with a bow. There were only a few hunters in the eastern UP who even tried bow hunting. Dad and I knew many of these hunters personally because they would come to our family sporting goods store, and we'd swap stories about our bow hunting adventures.

Some of the eastern UP bow hunters in those days were Bob and Dan Keiper (Dan would go on to be a founder and president of the Tri-County Wildlife Unlimited Association), Rob Sillers (the brother of my grade school friend Kim Sillers), Bill Elliot (a Soo businessman who also owned land in the Burning on the Springer Road), and Rick Arbic – a high school friend of mine and the starting tailback on my football team.

Because archery hunters were so rare, we were like a small fraternity in the 1960s – I just felt proud to be hunting with a bow like these guys, and I listened to everything I could about their efforts and successes, hoping to learn what I could.

On a nice October day in 1966, my shop class bow was done, and I was excited to be out on a big oak ridge in the Burning with my custom-built, homemade aluminum bow and what I thought were really cool arrows that we used for hunting.

On this day, dad would drop me off on the west side of the big oak ridge. He told me to get up on a large rock, and he found a stump for me to sit on. He told me he would be about 200 yards away near the edge of the oak ridge where there was a drop off into a more heavily wooded area below. He would be watching the top of that ridge.

We arrived in the woods several hours before dark, and after an hour, I got sleepy. I must have been comfortable because I drifted off for a few minutes. When I woke up, I was excited to see there was a lone doe 20 yards away, right in front of me. Somehow, the deer had walked right up to me, and I had not seen it.

The deer did not know I was up on the rock looking down on her, and she was leisurely chewing green leaves from a small aspen sprout.

I quickly recovered from my drowsiness, and I raised my new bow for a shot. I didn't hesitate at all. Just as I had pretended to be Robin Hood several years earlier, I pulled back the bow and confidently fired my arrow at the deer, expecting to kill it. I was as composed and prepared as I have ever been when I released the arrow at my quarry.

My arrow, however, flew harmless over the back of the deer. The deer ran off, deciding to move away from the rock with a hunter sitting on it.

As I watched the deer run away and I looked at my arrow stuck in the ground, it occurred to me that I just attempted to kill my first deer. It sunk into a twelve-year-old that I had just tried to take the life of this large animal.

As I pondered this action, I had an almost uncontrollable shaking condition in my limbs. The knees of a perfectly fit twelve-year-old kid were shaking wildly, and my arms seemed to have a life of their own too. I was absolutely trembling in a way I could not imagine. I had never felt this way in my life.

I quickly ran to tell dad. I found him sitting on the ground with his back against a large oak tree. I was so excited that I had seen and shot at a deer - I couldn't wait to tell him. Then I told him about the shakes that I had after the shot. After my walk to see him, I had calmed down. The shakes had disappeared, but I was visibly excited as I described how helpless I had felt after shooting at the deer.

Dad congratulated me on my shot at the deer. He reinforced how hard it was to kill a deer with a bow, and he wanted me to feel good about even getting a shot at the deer. He was really proud of me. Then he explained to me about the buck fever episode.

"Son, you had a case of what's called buck fever," he explained. "Lots of hunters get it. Sit here with me until dark and let's see if any more deer come out."

After my experience and the shakes, I was more than glad to sit by my dad until dark. I would have been content to just sit there until we went home, but just after I finished telling dad about the deer I had missed and the buck fever experience, a deer appeared on the edge of the clearing. The deer walked unsuspectingly right toward us.

As the deer got closer, dad whispered to me that the deer was a spikehorn buck. "Get ready to take a shot at him when he crosses in front of us and he's not looking at us," dad said in a very low voice. "Try to hit him right behind the shoulder like we talked about."

"Why don't you shoot the deer, dad?" I asked. "I will probably miss him and you could get him."

Dad assured me that I could get the deer. He said he would shoot at the deer if I were to miss.

Double Buck Fever

As the deer approached where I could shoot, I got really nervous again. I had the same buck fever shakes as I drew the bow back on the feeding buck. As I prepared to release the arrow, I couldn't help but notice how much I was shaking and how impossible it was to aim straight.

Despite this condition, I let the arrow go toward the buck and it landed way short of the deer. I was embarrassed at how poor a shot it had been, but I knew that it was the buck fever that had caused such a wimpy attempt at killing the buck. The deer looked around for a minute and then went back to feeding on acorns. That's when dad raised his bow and also released an arrow. His shot was very close barely missing the deer.

The small buck got nervous at this last arrow landing close to him. He turned his head from side to side in an excited state, and he ran back into the swamp from where he had come.

At that point, dad and I laughed about how we had three shots at deer tonight and we didn't hit anything. We also laughed about my buck fever. Dad promised me that I would overcome buck fever, and eventually I would be extremely confident as I shot at deer. He explained that I would "outgrow" this condition as I hunted more with a gun and a bow.

"You can control this emotion if you practice enough and you will," dad promised. "Many hunters get buck fever and can't shoot at deer. You still might get it if you see a really big buck, but now you know what it is, and you can work to keep it from bothering you."

"Do you still get buck fever, Dad?" I asked.

"Yes, when I see a great big buck I can get it too," dad admitted to me. "Lots of big bucks survive each year because hunters get buck fever when they see them."

As the seasons worn on, I got more and more confident with my deer hunting. I was never again plagued with a severe case of the buck fever syndrome like I was that day on the big oak ridge in the Burning– but I learned that many hunters do suffer from its symptoms and I was careful to not ever kid anyone about contracting it.

After all, Yoopers from all over the Superior State can come down with a severe case of buck fever at any time from October to December, especially if a big buck or a first deer is in their sights.

Today, our world leaders worry about SARS, Bird-Flu, and other life threatening diseases. In the UP, our biggest worry isn't these diseases, but rather those untimely cases of buck fever.

On this day on an oak ridge in the Burning, a Proud Yooper learned that Proud Hunters work hard to cure the dreaded ailment that threatens them in the fall: Buck Fever!

11

A Final Hunt for an Old Friend

A few more passing suns
will see us no more,
and our dust and bones
will mingle with these same prairies.

- Chief Plenty-Coups, Crow

In the fall of 1966, I was enjoying my first season as a shotgun hunter, and dad was teaching me everything he could about how to handle a real gun. We spent time hunting partridge and ducks, and I also got to hunt deer with my bow, but I never got to do any serious hunting with my dog, Peanuts.

Mom and dad had thought it would be best to leave Peanuts home while dad and I went on our hunting adventures. She had now recovered from her terrible car accident and the surgery that took her entire right leg.

She was getting proficient at running on three legs, and by fall, she even started chasing and terrorizing the neighborhood cats again.

Early on, we were worried that she couldn't run through the brush to hunt because she might damage her incision or tear it open. The incision would have been easily bruised by all the underbrush she would encounter chasing partridge in the heavily wooded country we hunted.

So, we thought it best to leave her home on the weekends when we went hunting.

You could tell how it hurt her spirit to leave her home. She still had the will and desire to go hunting with us, and she would work herself up into that excited state as we gathered up our gear.

Telling her she couldn't go with us was painful. You could see the disappointment in her eyes when we'd pack up, pat her on the head and tell her to "Stay here, Peanuts, and be a good girl!"

She didn't enjoy it for a second. She wanted to go with us so badly, she could taste it and we could see it in her eyes.

The last few weeks of the bird season, dad started telling me to get our gear together out of her sight or to do our preparation in secrecy so she wouldn't know we were going hunting. We got to the point where it hurt us to see her disappointment when we left without her. And we dreaded explaining it to her.

When we'd return from a hunt with some birds, she'd be at the door waiting for us, and she would be wagging her tail like crazy as we'd approach.

Dad would show her the birds and let her smell them. She would just about go crazy running around on three legs, so excited to see the hunters in their clothes, and the smell of gunpowder, birds and old hunting clothes probably brought her lots of great memories.

A Final Hunt for an Old Friend

As the season of 1966 wound down, we never did get her out to hunt, but as Christmas approached, she was really getting around well on three legs, and I began to believe that maybe she would return to the dog that she had been before the accident. Her recovery was actually quite remarkable.

The weekend before Christmas, we made a trip to the Point of Frene in Raber to visit my grandmother Florence Nutting and her husband Jess. I had been inside my grandma's house most of the day, and I was getting anxious to get outside so I could have some fun. I asked dad if he would go with me for a walk in the woods behind my grandma's place. I just wanted to go for a short hunt with my shotgun.

Dad didn't want to go. We had just finished a big Christmas dinner, and he wanted to relax in the front room.

"Do you think you could hunt safely by yourself?" he asked me. "Do you think you could take a very short walk in a big circle and come right back to the house?"

At first, I was completely surprised by dad's offer. After all, in Michigan, kids can't hunt alone without adult supervision until they are 17 years old.

I was a little unsure of myself, but I tried to not let my dad see my lack of complete confidence. I wanted the chance to go by myself and see how I could handle my shotgun without him being right there to help me.

"Yes," I told him. "I will be very careful, and I will remember all the safety rules you have taught me."

"I'm going to let you go by yourself because you know more about gun safety than most 17-year-olds," dad told me.

Right away, visions of this adventure and all the game I might bag and bring back from this hunt went running through my head.

"You probably won't see anything to shoot, but you can take a short walk and practice all the safety things you have learned. Be very careful of everything you do and how you handle your gun at all times."

I thought more about the possible game animals I might see on this adventure. It was still rabbit season, but partridge season was closed. I might see a red squirrel, but the chipmunks would be hibernating. I finally fixed my hopes that I might see a red squirrel or rabbit.

As I gathered up my gear, Peanuts was watching me and getting into that excited state again.

Dad looked at Peanuts and said to me, "You know, why don't you take Peanuts too and see how she gets around?"

Dad smiled at Peanuts and said, "Would you like to go hunting, girl?"

Peanuts just about went nuts.

My mom had been listening in on this conversation, and she also cautioned me to be very careful.

We knew a family who had killed their dog on a hunting trip as the dog chased a rabbit through the brush.

"Be very careful you don't shoot in the direction where Peanuts is," my mom warned, referring to the incident. "Make sure she's not close to the rabbit if you see one!"

Proud Hunters Proud Yoopers

The vision in my head of making a mistake and killing my beloved dog was like a bad horror movie. I vowed to myself that I would be extra careful. No rabbit would be worth taking a chance and hurting my dog.

"Take her on a short walk through the woods and let her get some exercise," dad advised.

"She has been getting around pretty well, and maybe by next year, we can take her hunting again," dad said hopefully.

With that, I headed out the back door and walked into a wooded area I knew like the back of my hand. I had hunted this woods hundreds of times with my BB gun.

But now, for the first time, I was hunting this woodlot with my single-shot Stevens shotgun and I was alone, hunting like an adult. I was in awe of this opportunity and the responsibility. On top of that, I was taking our dog on her first hunt since her accident.

It was such a perfect afternoon for a hunt. It was a nice, wintry day in the eastern UP, with several inches of fresh snow on the ground. The temperature was a moderate one in the 20s, and the sky was overcast, sometimes sunny and sometimes threatening to snow again.

Once Peanuts and I were away from the house, I felt like a king. I was on top of the world, cradling my shotgun and hunting in the snow with my dog! This was totally cool!

Not long after that, Peanuts was running around really excited, and suddenly there was an explosion of wings as two partridge flushed in front of her and flew straight away from me. I had a perfect shot at them, and I shouldered my shotgun, thinking all the while that it was not partridge season.

As the birds scattered out of range, I fired a hopeless shot in their general direction. The birds kept on flying as I knew they would.

When the birds disappeared to safer territory, I looked over at my proud, three-legged hunting dog. She was thrilled that she had found the smell of these birds and she had flushed them perfectly for me. She didn't seem to understand, though, how I could have missed them.

She gave me the look that only a dog can give a hunter that says, "How could you let me work this hard, and then you miss such an easy shot?"

I called Peanuts to my side, I gave her the biggest hug I ever had, and told her how proud I was of her for what she had done. I rubbed her head and patted and petted her, telling her what a good girl she had been. She loved every minute of it, even though there was no bird to show for her effort.

I couldn't tell her that it wasn't partridge season and I couldn't tell anyone but my family that I had shot at two partridge out of season. This would have to be a secret kept between an old dog and a young, rookie hunter.

Not killing a bird really didn't seem to matter this time. What really mattered is how happy Peanuts was to have hunted partridge again at this late point in her life and after her terrible accident.

What we experienced at that moment was nothing short of a small miracle for a twelve-year-old dog missing a hind leg and a twelve-year-old hunter, hunting alone for the first time.

She was so happy and thrilled to have been in the woods again, chasing birds and hunting with her hunter. It was like magic had happened to us. We completed our

A Final Hunt for an Old Friend

small circle through the woodlot and returned to the warm house on the edge of the St. Mary's River.

After everyone congratulated Peanuts on her first hunt after her accident, she retired to a fluffy rug in front of the roaring fire in the big stone fireplace. She sat there quietly and contently, letting the heat of the fire melt away the ice balls that had formed in her toes from her woodland adventure.

She looked at all of us as we watched her rest her tired body in front of the fire. With the fire jumping in the background, she looked so happy to have hunted again.

We returned home the next day and celebrated Christmas at our house in the Sault. Three days after Christmas, my dad had left early for work and my mom, my sisters and I were at home sleeping in on a day off during the school Christmas break.

That morning, at about 9 am, Peanuts, on her one hind leg, made the difficult ascent up our narrow stairway to my mom's second floor bedroom where she did something she had never done before.

Peanuts jumped up on my mom's bed and woke her up. My mom was startled because Peanuts knew better than to jump up on any furniture, let alone my mom's bed. This one time, Peanuts broke the rule for a reason. As my mom awoke and saw Peanuts, she immediately knew that something was wrong with her. Peanuts was shaking and she seemed unstable. She needed help.

My mom took our family pet into her arms and held her. My mom cried out to my sisters, Linda and Suzie, and me to come quickly to help her. The three kids were there in seconds, but it was too late. Peanuts died almost instantly in my mom's arms of a heart attack.

Peanuts, the dog who had been through so much medically in the last few months, somehow knew that something was terribly wrong with her. Maybe she had a sixth sense that the end was finally near. In any event, she knew that she wanted to be with us when she died.

My mom allowed us to pet Peanuts and hold her one last time, and then she took her lifeless body to our back porch. That evening, my dad buried Peanuts in our backyard.

This was a bad day; it was a day when a twelve-year-old kid lost his twelve-year-old dog, his friend, his hunting companion, and a member of our family.

In all the pain and emotion of losing a wonderful family pet and a lifetime hunting companion, I was comforted that she had four more months to live after her terrible accident, and that she had recovered enough to hunt one more time, all of this while having only three legs.

I was comforted that Peanuts had died a hunter, and that she had hunted right up until the end of her life. Most important, she had died in the loving arms of the family that had nurtured her and her love for hunting her entire life.

On this day, a Proud Yooper learned that sometimes Proud Hunters get to hunt right up to when they take their last breath, and sometimes the lucky ones even die in the arms of those who love them.

12

Snowshoe Hares and a .22 Rifle

The Ute who follows two rabbits
will perhaps catch one,
and often none.

- Dan George

At Christmas in the year 1967, I got another present from Santa in a long box. I was pretty sure it was another gun, so I couldn't wait to open it. When I did, I found a new Remington .22 caliber Model 580 Rim Fire Rifle, with a Weaver 4X power scope, mounted on top.

This single-shot, bolt action gun was my first rifle, and I was excited. I went to sleep that might dreaming about hunting in the woods with this gun.

The next weekend, my mom and dad took my sisters and me to my Grandma and Grandpa Hank's home in Stalwart. I was happy because our visit meant I could shoot my new gun and maybe even hunt with it.

In many ways, with its simple design, this new rifle was much like my single shot shotgun. It was an easy gun to use, and it was a very safe gun for a young hunter's first rifle.

In grandpa's yard, dad went over the basic safety rules with me, and he told me again about how much different a rifle is from a shotgun. He impressed upon me that the bullets from this new gun could travel more than one mile. Accordingly, I needed to be sure where I was shooting, and I needed to think even more about gun safety when I used this new weapon.

As I read the instructional warning on the side of the ammunition box, I was intrigued that the carton confirmed that these shells could really travel more than one mile. It was incredible to me that I could shoot this gun from grandpa's yard and the bullet might strike something one mile away on the Traynor Road. I was in awe of the power of this gun.

I was also impressed that this gun could shoot five different kinds of .22 caliber ammunition that we carried in our family sporting goods store. There were .22 shorts, .22 longs, .22 long rifle, .22 hollow points, and .22 fine shot shells.

Dad explained to me the similarities and differences between the different shells and how to use them. He told me we would shoot the .22 long rifle cartridges in the yard for practice and we would use the hollow point cartridges when we hunted small game.

He told me about how a hollow point bullet works and how it expands when it hits the tissue of an animal, making for a quicker and more humane killing shot. I also learned that the hollow points were similar to the bullets that hunters used for deer.

Snowshoe Hares and a .22 Rifle

We set up some targets in the yard, and I got to practice shooting the gun at them. While it was winter and cold outside, with several inches of snow on the ground, I didn't care because I was doing what I enjoyed – learning new hunting and shooting skills and using a brand new gun.

After I had demonstrated that I could shoot the gun well, dad suggested we take a short hike into Grandpa Ed's cedar swamp. "Maybe we can jump a rabbit or two and you can try out your new gun," dad told me.

"You should also be careful carrying your gun in snowy conditions like this," dad warned me. "You want to protect the end of your gun barrel so you don't get snow or ice stuck in your gun. That can blow up your gun if you shoot it with your barrel clogged."

I didn't think much about blowing up my new gun, but I was careful to not get any snow in my barrel. As I followed dad through the snow, I saw how easy it could be to get snow stuck in the end of your gun barrel as you walked through the thick brush on this edge of the mighty Gogemain swamp.

We headed southeast in the swamp, and almost immediately, we saw the unmistakable tracks of the northern snowshoe hare among the cedars in the conifer swamp. Dad showed me the tracks, and he gave me the basic lessons in how to follow them, walking slowly and looking ahead for the sitting or running rabbit that we would hopefully encounter.

He told me to take the lead, and he followed me, giving me tips on how to stalk the stealthy big snowshoes through the swamp. He told me to visualize how the rabbits would be sitting or feeding in the swamp and how they would react when they heard or saw a hunter approaching.

He taught me to look closely under branches or near brush piles where the rabbits might be sitting, hoping that we would just walk on by.

When we didn't see anything right away, he told me that we would do a brief two-man drive through the swamp. We would walk parallel to each other, staying about 30 yards apart. If we got lucky, one of us might spook a rabbit toward the other waiting hunter. He told me to be ready, and he warned me to keep him in sight as we walked through the swamp.

After we had hunted for about 15 minutes, I caught a movement to my right where dad was hunting. Sure enough, a beautiful, pure-white snowshoe hare ran from dad and stopped just in front of me, 20 yards away.

I pulled up my brand new .22 Remington and found his head in the cross-hairs of my scope. I squeezed the trigger, and the rabbit dropped right there.

At the sound of the shot, dad came to me and found me holding my big prize. I had killed my first rabbit, and I acted as if I were the happiest hunter in the whole UP! I was really tickled that I had killed something with my new gun on the first day that I had used it. This was also my first rabbit, and the first animal I had taken with a rifle. I was on cloud nine.

Dad and I returned to the house to show everyone my trophy. I had to retell the story over and over to everyone who would listen. My grandpa seemed especially proud that I had killed a rabbit with the new gun.

After we had our dinner that afternoon, I kept pestering dad to let me shoot the gun again in the yard. Dad agreed, and we set up more targets of old cans on the edge of the yard. I had collected samples of the different .22 caliber shells that I had found while exploring dad's shell container and my grandpa's gun cabinet. I was determined that I would shoot all the different varieties including the shorts, longs, long-rifles and the hollow-points that I had used on the snowshoe hare.

Some of the .22 short shells looked old, and they were a different color from the other shells. While I noticed this, I didn't know enough to be cautious about using these ancient shells.

While shooting those older looking .22 short shells, I thought one of them misfired. I later told dad that I had pulled the trigger and nothing had happened. I had ejected the shell, and I expected to find the full casing. Instead, all I found was a spent shell. I had been shooting so many shells, that I didn't really pay attention closely to the dud shell that I had taken out of the gun after the misfire.

"These shells might not be any good," I told dad.

Dad told me to quit using the older ammunition, especially if they weren't firing. He warned me that hunters and shooters need to be careful using old ammunition because they can damage guns.

I put a new looking .22 hollow point in my new rifle, and I took aim at our target. I squeezed the shot and the gun fired, but I didn't hit the target.

As I reloaded the gun, I noticed I had a big hole in the right side of the barrel, just forward of where I had been gripping the gun. I was scared, and I didn't know what to do. I was smart enough to know that this wasn't good. I showed the gun to dad, and he couldn't believe it.

"Son, you've blown a hole in the barrel. You must have had an obstruction in the barrel like the snow I was warning you about. When your bullet hit that obstruction, it couldn't push itself down the barrel, so it blew out the side of the barrel, ruining your gun."

Because we had been shooting for some time, dad knew that it wasn't the snow that had plugged my gun. He reasoned it had to have been the spent shell that had apparently misfired.

"What I think happened is that the old shell partially misfired, but it pushed the bullet up into your barrel. When you shot a second time, you hit the bullet lodged in your barrel and the second bullet blew out the side of your barrel," dad explained. "You are darn lucky son that you didn't lose part of your hand from all the force of that bullet. If you had held your hand further up the barrel, you might have lost some fingers or your hand."

Well, I was sure scared now. I had a new appreciation for the fire power of even a little rifle like a .22 caliber gun. Wow, was that a close call.

Not only did I have a sick feeling thinking about losing some of my fingers, I also felt terrible that I had ruined my brand new gun. What had been a great day so far had now turned into a very bad day. I knew that dad couldn't afford to buy me a new gun, so I accepted that I might not have a .22 rifle for years to come.

I was really sad because I knew that with more caution or experience, I could have prevented this gun disaster that seemed catastrophic at the time.

Later that week, dad packaged up my rifle with the blown-apart barrel, and he sent it back to the Remington factory with an explanation of what happened. He told me to not get my hopes up.

Snowshoe Hares and a .22 Rifle

"They will probably tell us that this is our fault and we are responsible for the damage to the gun," dad told me. "But you never know. They may have sympathy on a young guy and agree to fix your gun. We won't know unless we ask."

Several weeks later, dad came home at night and told me he had some good news. Behind his back, he was holding another long box. Inside it was a brand new Remington .22 caliber rifle – one without a blown up barrel.

"Remington decided to give you a new gun," dad told me proudly. "We should be grateful that they stood behind their product and they didn't hold us responsible. You will get a second chance with this gun."

I was ecstatic. These were great words to a 13-year-old kid.

On this day, a Proud Hunter learned about gun safety and the danger of obstructed barrels. And a Proud Yooper learned that good gun companies sometimes give big breaks to kids who make rookie mistakes.

13

Earning a Browning

It may be thought that the memory of things
may be lost with us.
We nevertheless have methods of transmitting from father to son
an account of all these things.
You will find the remembrance of them is faithfully preserved,
and our succeeding generations are made acquainted with what has passed,
that it may not be forgot as long as the earth remains.

- Kanickhungo, Iroquois

On an overcast, early October Saturday in 1969, dad and I had spent the early morning hours looking for ducks to stalk in grain fields around the Riverside Drive area, about 12 miles south of the Sault.

We had some close calls, but the ducks weren't cooperating, and as the morning wore on, it looked like we were going home empty-handed.

"We had better head back home," dad told me as we traveled in the car going north back toward the Sault. "I should get back and open up the store."

As we watched the sky and the fields for ducks and geese, dad stopped the car just before we had reached the corner of Twelve Mile Road and Riverside Drive. In a hay field near the intersection, he had spotted six mallards feeding in the short grass.

The ducks were right out in the open. While there was no way to sneak up on them in that short grass, dad pointed out a drainage ditch on the south side of the birds and another connecting ditch on their back side.

"You could sneak up on them by crawling down the two ditches," dad reasoned out loud. "If you don't spook them, when you get behind them, you should be close enough to shoot them."

"Are we going to try and get them, Dad?" I asked. I knew it would take some time, maybe an hour or more, to make this stalk, and I wasn't sure he would want to be that late getting back to work.

"Listen, I'm tired this morning," he explained. "Why don't you try to make this stalk on your own, and I'll watch you from the car. If the ducks get scared and fly away before you get close, I'll yell to you, and we can go home. Do you want to try it?"

"Well, sure I'll give it a try," I offered.

"OK, then take my gun this time," dad said. "I think you might be ready to move up to an automatic, so let's see how you do. If you get to the ducks, you'll have three shells to shoot instead of your usual one shot. Just be very careful with this gun when you are crawling through those ditches."

Earning A Browning

Wow, I was fired up now. I was going to stalk these ducks myself, crawling through two ditches and if I did the stalk right, I'd get a chance to shoot at the birds three times, just as dad did. I was in seventh heaven just thinking about this opportunity.

I could see that dad had all this confidence in me, and I was really excited about that too. So, with a few more instructions from dad about being safe with the firearm that was unfamiliar to me, I was off, sneaking and crawling down the first ditch. My main concern was keeping my head and body low enough so the ducks wouldn't be spooked until I could get within shotgun range.

My dad's gun was a state-of-the-art, Browning Automatic five shot "Light 12" model shotgun that was manufactured in Belgium. At the time, this was one of the classiest and most expensive guns that I knew about, and the most serious hunters in the area used them. Dad sold these guns in our family sporting goods business, and hunters were always coming into the store to admire these guns.

As I made my way down the ditch, I concentrated on keeping dad's beautiful gun out of the mud. I didn't want to do anything to harm this marvelous gun that I held in such high regard and that I was privileged to be using, even if only this one time.

The field I was hoping to shoot ducks in was near a farm owned by the Turner family. Randy Turner was a son in this family, and he was the starting tackle on my football team.

I remember a devastating event that happened to Randy's family while he was playing football with me. While at practice one day, he learned that his father's cattle herd had been contaminated with the animal feed that contained the toxic chemical PBB that ravaged Michigan farmers in the 1970s. The Turner farm was one of the first farms in the area forced to destroy their cattle because of the PBB contamination.

Randy is now one of the largest farmers and landowners in the eastern UP, and he is also a successful auctioneer. Each year, for about 20 years, he served as an auctioneer helping the Tri-County Wildlife Unlimited association raise money for habitat improvement and wildlife management initiatives in the eastern UP. Together with Dan Keiper, Robert and Steve Ware, Bob Ranson, Brian Harrison, and other Tri-County Wildlife volunteers, they have raised almost $250,000 to help wildlife in the eastern UP. Because of their dedication, they have developed the Tri-County organization into the largest wildlife association in the area.

As I rounded the turn and started heading north up the back side of the field to get behind the ducks, I peaked over the ditch bank once to see if the ducks were still there. They seemed content and unaware that a 15-year-old hunter with his dad's Browning was closing in on them. I hunkered down in the drainage ditch, determined to make the last 100 yards of the stalk without being seen.

It took me about 20 minutes to go that last 100 yards, and then I figured I was in a great position to shoot at the ducks. They were about 20-25 yards out from the drainage ditch where I was, so I knew I was in range for some good shooting.

I peaked up over the lip of the drainage ditch and picked out one big green-headed mallard on the ground for my first shot. I pulled the trigger of dad's gun, and I expected to see the mallard drop. Unbelievably, I missed the bird, and suddenly, six mallards flushed wildly trying to get away from the field.

Proud Hunters Proud Yoopers

I stood up this time, and I pulled to the left, trying to line up a bird. As I squeezed the trigger, the bird folded and fell to the ground. I quickly pulled back to the right, and shot again at another mallard. As if magic had happened, that bird too, fell to the ground, going down gradually, and landing almost on the road where dad and our car were waiting.

Dad had been watching me, my stalking technique, and the mallard's behavior the whole time with binoculars from the comfort of the car. Later, he would tell me how satisfying it had been to watch me stalk the birds so carefully, while using the techniques that he had taught me over the years.

As the second bird fell to the ground, dad exited the car and ran out into the field to retrieve the female mallard. I ran out into the middle of the field to get the drake mallard I had killed on the second shot.

Dad raised my bird in triumph as I also held up my beautiful, mature drake bird for him to see. We were one hundred yards apart, but I could feel the excitement we both felt for what I had accomplished.

Back in the car, on the way home, dad told me how well I had done, and he laughed, telling me that if I had used my own single shot shotgun, I wouldn't have killed any birds. "Because you were using my semi-automatic shotgun, you got two beautiful mallards," dad told me. "You should be very proud of how you handled my gun today."

About one week later, dad came home one night carrying a long, narrow box. He sat me down with my mother and asked me to open the box.

"Your mom and I want to give you an early Christmas present," dad explained to me as he handed me the box.

I eagerly opened my unexpected present to find a brand new Belgium-made, Browning Auto 5 Semi-Automatic shotgun, a gun just like my dad's gun.

"You've proven that you are ready for this bigger gun, Son," dad said proudly. "You earned this gun last week on those mallards."

On this night, somewhere in the vast UP, there was probably a more humble, a more thankful, and a more proud hunter and Yooper - but I'll never be convinced of that.

On this day, a Proud Yooper learned that sometimes Proud Hunters earn their next guns by demonstrating their hunting skills in the field and making their dads proud.

14

The Thunder of Ducks

My young men shall never work.
Men who work cannot dream;
and wisdom comes to us in dreams.

- Smohalla, Nez Perce

In the fall of 1970, at age 16, I was a junior in high school, and I played on the Sault High Blue Devils varsity football team in Sault Ste. Marie. By this time, my dad started counting on me more and more for a duck hunting partner on the weekends. He had lots of grown up friends to go with, but he regularly asked me if I wanted to join him for some early morning duck hunts.

Early in October that year, I heard a report on the WSOO radio station that lots of ducks were visiting the Sault area on the way south to their winter feeding grounds. I remember one day hearing that DNR biologists estimated there were 15,000 ducks in the Munuscong Bay area.

When I told Dad about that report, he asked me if I wanted to go in the morning and get our share of those ducks.

"Would you like to skip school and go tomorrow morning?" dad teased me.

"I'd love to go, Dad, but if I miss school, I can't practice football in the afternoon," I told him. "If I miss practice, I can't play Friday night."

"Well," dad said, looking at me with a huge grin. "You could be sick just in the morning, shoot some ducks at daylight, and be back in school long before noon. You could be there for football practice if you felt better by the afternoon."

Mom was listening in on this duck hunting strategy discussion.

My mother grew up as Betty J. Westervelt in the north Raber area of the UP before she married my dad. Mom was good friends with Raber kids: Jack and Jackie Benson, Eleanor Bender, Carol, Wilma and Web Wojnarowski, and Beatrice, Marge and Walter Wojciechowski when she was a teenager. She was also a Detour High cheerleader. She has always been known for her kind heart and her compassion and caring for others.

When I was in those difficult teenager years, my mom also had that sixth sense to know when she needed to talk to one of her kids about something or when we needed to talk to her about one of life's challenges. She had an uncanny ability to come into your room just before bedtime and strike up a conversation about something important in life that was on your mind.

Above all, my mom was a very principled and honest person. So when she heard dad and me talking about calling in sick to hunt ducks, she refused to take part in this discussion. "Your dad is signing your absence excuse for you," she warned me as she left the room. "I'm not having any part of this mischief," she said. At least there was a little bit of a grin and a smile as she walked away.

Early the next morning, with a pre-signed parent approved absence excuse in my wallet, dad and I loaded the car with our shotguns and hip boots and headed out south of Sault Ste. Marie on Shunk Road. Before daylight, we were parked near the corner of Five Mile Road and Shunk with the windows down. There were several large farms at this location with huge fields of cut wheat and lots of spilled grain on the ground. The stubble in the wheat fields was about 12" tall, perfect for sneaking up on feeding ducks. These fields belonged to Spence Shunk, a Sault Ste. Marie farmer and local retail furniture sales businessman.

As the first light of the morning came, it was incredibly peaceful and then gradually, the sounds of song birds filled the air. We sat there and listened to the birds come alive as they celebrated another day. It seemed as if hundreds of song birds were around and there were a dozen different birds calling out at any one time.

We were watching the horizon where the sun would rise in another 30 minutes. Beautiful shades of yellow, orange, red and pink streaked across the sky as daylight approached. Dad had taught me how to watch the sky just above the tree line to spot the ducks coming against the faint light in the sky.

"Look for a flock of ducks with black bodies flying in formation against the skyline," he instructed me. "Train your eye to look for them." As flocks of non-game birds flew across the skyline, dad taught me to distinguish their flight formations from the ducks.

"See those crows at 2 o'clock?" he would ask me. "See how much differently they fly than ducks?" Later, he would contrast how differently crows, seagulls, ducks and geese flew. Soon I learned to spot the fast flying forms of ducks on the horizon. After these lessons, spotting waterfowl in the early morning light was much easier.

As a large flock of mallards checked out our field on Five Mile Road and then headed south, dad fired up our Chevy Impala and began chasing the flock at 60 miles per hour.

Dad was an expert at spotting or watching game or birds out his window as he drove our vehicle down the highway, but he still needed help to keep watch over this fast moving flight.

"Keep an eye on where they are going while I keep the car on the road," dad instructed me as he gunned our family vehicle in hot pursuit of the ducks. "If they start to circle or to go down somewhere, mark the spot."

As we flew down the rural highway, we both kept an eye on the ducks. Because this flock was so huge, it wasn't hard to keep it in sight. In other years, we had chased lots of smaller flocks, so keeping watch of this one was relatively easy.

After a two-mile car chase, the ducks began circling another large grain field near the corner of Seven Mile Road and Shunk Road. This farm belonged to Gordon Andrews, one of the largest beef farmers in the Sault area. Gordon's daughter, Karen, went to high school with me and later she attended Central Michigan University with me, too.

The Andrews family had a lot of acreage to farm, and they kept a great deal of it in barley, oats, or winter wheat, three of the predominant crops that would grow in the area. In fact, it seemed to me like most serious farmers in the Sault, Brimley, Pickford,

The Thunder of Ducks

and Rudyard areas grew large fields of oats, barley, and winter wheat. Usually, they harvested the crop in late September or early October, producing 45 to 60 bushels per acre, depending on soil type.

Those farming practices made the eastern UP an outstanding food source for migrating ducks. The ducks are attracted to the Brimley Bay and the Munuscong Bay areas because they are large, protected water resting spots the birds have used for centuries on their journey south from Canada. Having the great food sources like the grain fields practically next door to the large bays made the area farms a duck hotspot for years.

Early in September, we would drive around the area and look for good fields where we thought ducks would feed once the grain was cut. Those were the areas we would watch in the early morning once the season started, where we hoped to ambush the ducks as they fed. In the case of the Andrew's Farm, we had permission to hunt the field.

Today, the farming has changed significantly in the eastern UP. Now, fewer farmers plant winter wheat or grain as they did years ago when I was a kid. Now, most farmers concentrate on a trefoil-grassy hay product that they cut two or three times a year and roll into huge round bails when the hay dries. Many farms can produce 2.5 to 3.5 tons per acre of the high quality hay. Some farmers sell their hay as far away as the Kentucky racing and breeding farms. The hay is such a high-quality product that there is even talk of marketing it overseas.

It's a lot easier and less risky to grow hay than grain, and, as a result, the area has fewer grain farmers today, a small fraction of what we had for feeding ducks in the 1960s and early 1970s. Today's hay product doesn't attract the ducks and geese like in the good old days when we had vast grain fields almost everywhere.

One day, dad and I were picking up geese we had shot in a grain field near Five Mile Road with dad's friend, Bill Ranta of the Soo. At the time, I asked about whether Chippewa County hunters like us could shoot too many ducks and geese during these intense migrations. That's when Bill turned to dad and me and said, "Leon, if we don't shoot these ducks and geese now, those rednecks in Louisiana will shoot them all winter long. We need to get our fair share right now in the week or two when the ducks and geese are here."

Following that discussion, for years, I had a grudge against anyone from Louisiana. I thought anyone from there had to be a waterfowl-shooting maniac who killed "our" ducks and geese mercilessly. It was years later in my adult life when I was working as an insurance regulator for the state of Michigan's Insurance Bureau that I met my first Louisiana native – my counterpart from the southern state.

He was such a nice guy, and I really liked working with him on national insurance committees. Still, I couldn't help but wonder whether he hunted ducks, and, once I got to know him well, I couldn't wait to tell him how for years I thought everyone from Louisiana was a duck hunting redneck that Bill Ranta had warned me about.

"Ya, I shoot a few of your ducks," he told me one day, smiling from ear to ear.

As our current huge flock of ducks circled the Andrews' grain field, dad started to get confident.

"Uh, oh," he grunted enthusiastically. "It looks like we can get them here!" He was excited because this huge flock had joined other flocks in this large, freshly-cut grain field. As we tried to size up how we would approach the birds, more and more ducks just kept circling the field and dropping in to feed.

It looked to me like there were mallards, blacks, and other ducks everywhere. As we watched them land several hundred yards out in the middle of this grain field, other ducks kept coming in from all directions to feed.

"There must be thousands of them in that field," dad summed up for me. "And this is a perfect setup!" We took a quick drive around to the other side of the field to ensure we knew the layout well. Dad checked over every detail carefully with binoculars as he planned our approach.

Then he began to quickly assemble his gear and uncase his gun after he parked the car.

In a low voice, he gave me detailed instructions about how we would sneak up on the ducks. First, we would stay behind a fence line to the east of the birds in the higher grass of an adjacent hay field. We could sneak out to that point in a crouched position, but dad warned me not to stand up.

"Keep your butt and head down at all times," he warned. "Stay behind me and do as I do."

When we were directly east of the birds, we would begin crawling toward the ducks on our bellies, carefully sliding under the barb-wired fence and then slipping quietly through the grain stubble until we were in range of the birds.

"We will have to crawl about 80 yards through the grain to get good shooting," dad said, assessing the situation carefully. "You will need to be very careful crawling under the fence with your gun," he warned. "Don't blow my head off," he teased.

That was a standard warning and caution that he gave me often in my youth. I came to expect it and appreciate it.

"When we get close, I will give you the signal to shoot. If the ducks get up early before we are ready, start shooting if you think the birds are in range and empty your gun."

I was primed because this did look like a good setup. We had tried crawling out on ducks and geese earlier in the season where we had little cover, and it was tough getting close to the birds. This layout looked as if we could get really close before the ducks might see us. This did look like a great ambush about to unfold.

Dad's last quiet instruction to me was important.

"If we get close and the ducks haven't flushed, be prepared to see lots of ducks in the air at one time. It will be difficult to concentrate on shooting just one duck, but that is what you must force yourself to do. Discipline yourself to focus on killing just one duck at a time and resist the temptation to shoot at the entire flock! Don't flock shoot!"

"Trust me on this," dad continued. "If you try to shoot at the whole flock, as hard as it is to believe, you might miss all the ducks. On the other hand, if you concentrate on getting a good bead on just one close duck, you might find that you will kill two or three with every shot!"

I didn't need to be any more pumped up, but that did it anyway. I was ready to roll.

The Thunder of Ducks

Getting through the hayfield was easy, and before long, dad and I were on our bellies, carefully making our way under the barb-wired fence. If we could just get out into this grain field without the ducks spotting us, we would have great shooting.

My heart was pounding with each movement I made sliding on my belly, as I cradled my Browning 12 gauge semi-automatic shotgun in my hands. I was careful to keep the barrel end away from dad as he led the way across the field toward the unsuspecting ducks.

When I looked back toward the barbed wired fence, I knew we had closed the gap and we were in shooting range. Each time I poked my head up, I could see the heads of ducks all across the field just 20-30 yards away. I knew the time was drawing near.

Soon, dad carefully motioned for me to crawl up beside him. He whispered to me to get ready to shoot on "three." His final words were, "Remember to pick out one duck – don't flock shoot!"

"One, two, three," he whispered with an intense look on his face. On three, we both stood up on one knee and shouldered our shotguns. Upon rising from our hidden, prone positions, maybe a hundred or so ducks closest to us exploded into flight, and dad and I took our first shot.

At the sound of those first shots, all the ducks in the field jumped into the air, and there was an explosion of sound from flapping wings and quacking ducks like I had never heard in my life. It almost seemed as if the sky and the air around me was just black with ducks as they did everything they could to get away from the intruding hunters.

As I looked at the flock, it looked like a solid wall of ducks. The sound of them quacking and flapping their wings so close to us was almost as loud as a bolt of thunder. It was almost deafening. It was an incredibly intense sensation.

Dad had also taught me to make sure we each shot at a different side of the flock. He would take the right side of the flock, and I would take the left side. That practice, he told me, would help us get more ducks and ensure we weren't shooting at the same ones.

As the ducks made their exit, I tried to concentrate on getting a bead on just one close duck. It was tough because it seemed as if there were ducks everywhere. After my first shot, I saw two ducks fall and then, in my excitement, I did the unthinkable: I just fired away at all the swirling ducks. I was flock shooting!

Just as dad predicted, I am not sure I hit anything with my second shot. If I did, it was an accident.

Remembering who I had to ride home with, I concentrated on my third and final shot, and it seemed like several more ducks again fell out of the sky as I touched off the shot. I looked over at dad in time to see him drop two ducks with his last shot.

As we stood there with our empty guns and our barrels smoking, we watched the huge flock of ducks take to the sky and head back north, probably to their evening watering spot or to another field they thought was safer. Some smaller flocks even circled the field several times at a safe distance to see what all the excitement was about.

"Now that was fun," dad snickered to me as the birds disappeared out of sight. "How many did you get?"

Proud Hunters Proud Yoopers

"I don't know, but I think we got quite a few," I responded. I didn't dare tell him that I was flock shooting on at least one shot.

"Yup, we got a bunch. Some of them are crippled, so let's run them down before they hide on us in this stubble," dad warned.

By the time we stuffed ducks into each other's game bag, we were loaded down with about all the ducks we could carry.

"We got our limit or close to it, so let's go home and give these birds a rest for a day," dad said to me. "And we can get you back to school at a reasonable hour too," he chuckled.

As we drove back to town, I thought about the 15,000 ducks the radio station said would be in the area. "They must have all been in the Andrews' field today," I thought to myself.

"Dad, how many ducks do you think were in that field today?" I ask.

"I don't know son, but it had to be several thousand," dad said. "I don't think I've ever been that close to that many ducks before. That's some of the best shooting at ducks I've ever had."

An hour later, dad dropped me off at school. I turned in my absence excuse while trying to pretend I had been feeling ill all morning.

As I suited up for football practice later that afternoon, I thought about the morning I had with my dad in the grain field.

With any luck, this Yooper would be getting sick a few more times before the ducks headed south for winter.

On this day, a Proud Yooper learned that sometimes Proud Hunters might bend the sick leave rules a bit during the fall waterfowl migration so they can experience the incredible thunder of ducks.

15

"Aye? What did you say?"

The Indian believes profoundly in silence –
the sign of a perfect equilibrium.
Silence is the absolute poise or balance
of body, mind and spirit.

- Ohiyesa, Santee Sioux

While my grandfather Ed Hank was in his 80s and 90s, he was famous around our family for his hearing loss and his greeting to people. When he saw someone, he usually let him or her speak first. Then, often his first words back to the person were, "Aye? What did you say? You will have to speak up. I can't hear you!"

Like many laborers, grandpa had worked around lots of loud machinery for the Chippewa County Road Commission for many years. Like many laborers and hunters in the early 20th century, he never used ear protection when he worked, hunted or shot a firearm. Consequently, it wasn't surprising later in life when he had a hard time hearing people. His hearing got so bad that he depended on hearing aides to hear normal conversation.

The chance of hearing loss among Yooper hunters was fairly good, and dad and I were victims too, although not in the usual way.

On a Saturday morning in late October 1971, dad and I were driving down Nine Mile Road near the intersection of Riverside Drive, just six miles south of the Sault Ste. Marie city limits. As we approached the intersection, we noticed a flock of about 25 sharp-tailed grouse fly across the road into a large hay field.

While we were looking for flocks of ducks and snow geese, these birds looked like they would be easy to stalk. We decided to go after them.

The sharp-tailed grouse is one of the rarest gamebirds in Michigan. While the bird is common in the western and central plains of the United States, the bird has sustainable populations in only several scattered parts of Michigan, with the eastern UP area just south of the Sault as one of the bird's strongholds. There are also sharptails in large openings and farm fields around Brimley, Rudyard, Pickford, Stalwart, Raco and even Neebish Island.

Because the birds only inhabit small areas of Michigan, the Michigan DNR carefully regulates the harvest of the birds, establishing a short season and generally only allowing hunters to take one or two birds per day.

I always felt fortunate that in the eastern UP, we were blessed enough to have this special bird and we could hunt him too. Unlike the ruffed grouse that lives in the forest, sharptails like the open fields similar to the common southern Michigan pheasant. I also loved that sharptails made a cackling noise like a pheasant just before they flushed.

The sharp-tailed grouse has beautiful shades of both light and dark brown feathers that cover his head, back and chest. His belly is graced with long white feathers that have gorgeous flecks of brown on them. As the name depicts, the bird has a sharp, pointed tail that differs significantly from the ruffed grouse tail which fans out.

In the springtime, the male sharptail puts on one of the most interesting courtship rituals ever seen in the wild. In fact, it is one of the coolest displays I have ever seen any creature perform. The birds actually dance in a way that that is just awesome while they try to entice a female to breed. In some locations, watching this mating ritual in the spring is something bird watchers and wildlife enthusiasts wait for all year.

On top of that, the way the bird flies is also most impressive. As a teenager, I loved to watch a flock of the birds seem to float over the large fields south of the Sault, flying rapidly, but continually alternating this flight with short periods when they would appear to just glide away from you. Then, almost in unison, the birds would pump their wings several times to maintain good speed and then glide again in perfect formation, riding the air currents like a glider plane until they were out of sight.

As we approached the field where the birds had landed, dad stopped the car and we quickly loaded our Browning shotguns for the stalk. I could see dad was sizing up our strategy as I quickly threw three shells in the gun. Soon, he was signaling me to stay behind him as we crouched down, running toward the birds through high grass until we hit the edge of the field.

I knew this drill well. As we got to the shorter cut hay field, we began to crawl on our bellies to where the birds had gone down. I was right behind dad, following his movement, trying to keep my head down. I knew he would signal me when it was time to shoot.

After a short stalk through the medium-length grass, dad motioned me to come up beside him. He gave me the "Let's shoot on three" instruction, and he began counting.

As he got close to three, he stood up on one knee, and the birds exploded into flight, going off in all directions, trying to escape the hunters who had surprised them so suddenly. We both started shooting, and there were feathers falling as shotgun blasts shattered the morning stillness.

I had been shooting at the left side of the flock. On my third shot, I swung on a bird that crossed from left to right towards dad. I ended up swinging my automatic shotgun right by dad's head as he crouched in the field in front of me, and I fired the third shot almost directly over his head, just inches away from his left ear.

"Geez, son, are you watching where you are shooting?" dad asked me as I kept my eyes on the last sharptail I had pulled on.

"Dad, I think I hit that bird. I think he went down about 400 yards over there," I told him, appearing to be totally focused on the bird and not on the safety warning I was about to get.

"Son, did you hear what I said?" dad questioned me. "You need to be careful when we are shooting close to each other like this. You almost blew my head off with that last shot. I could feel the shot go right over my head, and I can't hear a darn thing, you shot so close to my ear."

"Aye? What did you say?"

"Wow, Dad, I am sorry," I explained. "I didn't realize I was shooting that close to you. I guess I got too excited shooting at all these birds."

For a minute, in the middle of a hay field, with spent shotgun shells littering the ground around us and dead birds 30 yards away, dad and I forgot everything else and we debriefed on what had happened and how dangerous it was.

It was probably obvious that I was feeling bad that I had not been very careful.

When the safety lesson was over, dad gave me a big hug and we celebrated the great shooting we had on the sharptails. We set out to retrieve our birds, and we had our limit when I found the last one, dead as a doornail, 400 yards away at the far end of the field.

As we walked across the big hay field, we talked over and over about the great wing shooting we had that morning on the sharptails – this magical bird that only inhabits a few rare spots in all of Michigan.

And we marveled at how much tougher this game bird was over the ruffed grouse.

"Isn't it amazing how much lead that bird took before he went down?" dad asked me as we carried the birds to the car. "You pounded that bird, filling his body with lead. He had to be almost dead while he was flying 300 yards out there. He glided another 100 yards until he piled up. These birds are sure a lot tougher than partridge."

For the next couple of days, dad kept reminding me that he had a constant ringing in his ears and that he was having a hard time hearing. After that round of sharptail grouse shooting, his hearing was never the same.

But several years later, he got a chance to get me back.

In October 1973, my mom's brother Don Westervelt, who had grown up in the eastern UP, came to visit us and hunt for a week. Uncle Don lived in Hamilton County, Ohio, where he was a deputy sheriff. I loved to hunt with Uncle Don and hear his stories about hunting because he was such a colorful character. He had the greatest laugh, and he could take any average tale and spin it into something that would make you laugh until your sides hurt. He was that kind of a guy.

On this trip, Uncle Don had been duck hunting on the Pointe of Frene, on the tip of the peninsula that guarded the opening to the marsh where I had killed my first duck. Don had hunted this marsh and the surrounding countryside for years as a kid, so he really loved to come back and hunt the old spots again.

On this cold, rainy, and stormy day, we sat out in a duck blind and watched only a few ducks fly by our decoys, all of them out of range. After several hours of sitting in terrible weather conditions and the waves of the St. Mary's River getting dangerously high, we decided to call it quits.

We fired up the motor on the 16-foot boat and proceeded to pick up the decoys. Uncle Don was driving the boat from the rear, dad was in the middle of the boat, and I occupied the front. As we battled the fierce waves and driving rain, we were struggling to collect the decoys. When we had collected almost all of them, two bluebill ducks swung over us and landed right outside of the last few decoys in our set.

I watched the ducks carefully as I heard the older generation working the actions of their shotguns, loading up with no. 4 magnums, the standard duck shell of the day.

"Better hurry up," I whispered quietly. "They are really nervous and about to get up!" I warned.

Proud Hunters Proud Yoopers

In the next few seconds, the ducks jumped up and Uncle Don blasted away at them from the rear of the boat. During the whole event, I never reached for my gun, figuring that dad and Uncle Don would easily kill the two ducks. As I predicted, Uncle Don took the first duck, but it took all his shells to get him. That left dad to kill the second duck, which had now reversed directions. This lone duck was heading north, back up the St. Mary's River and flying right in front of me.

As the second surviving duck flew swiftly to escape, dad swung his Browning from right to left, following the path of the duck and pulling his gun closer toward me.

I was idly watching the last duck and not focused on the shooting hunters seated behind me in the rocking boat.

With no warning, I heard an enormous blast from dad's gun, and I felt the spray of the shotgun pellets go racing by my face. It felt as if the air entirely pulled away from my face caused by the force of the shot blasting through the air. The shot came so close that I was grabbing my face, feeling it for damage. I was certain that I had been shot in the face or head. My ears were ringing so loudly that I couldn't hear a thing. For a few seconds, it was as if my senses were dead.

I screamed out a loud shriek, which scared both dad and Uncle Don.

"What's wrong?" dad asked in a concern voice. He had pulled down his gun to check on me as the lone duck escaped unharmed.

"I thought you shot me!" I yelled back to him.

"What the hell is going on?" my Uncle Don yelled out to both of us. "Are you guys OK? Neither one of those two ducks is worth killing each other over," he quipped. "I think they were fish ducks anyway – I would have hit both of them if they had been mallards or if it would have kept you two from shooting each other."

It was classic humor from my Uncle Don that I didn't appreciate at the time, but I do today.

I took several seconds to calm my nerves while dad made sure I was all right.

"I may have shot closer to you than I thought, but I was sure the muzzle was far enough away that you weren't in any harm," dad explained. "I guess the end of the barrel was closer to your face than I knew."

"Wow, that was a bizarre feeling," I told them. "For a second, I felt like I had been shot in the face. Everything went numb on me. It was really weird."

Except for a ringing in my ears, I was OK. We took another minute to let the excitement and tension die down. We laughed again over the two stupid ducks that landed in our decoys while we were picking them up. We'd been out all day and not a single other duck would come close to the decoys.

Now I knew how dad had felt that day in the sharptail field when I shot right over his head. Sometime later, I would have my hearing tested, and I would learn that I had a significant hearing loss in my right ear. The doctor would explain to me that I had lost the ability to hear the tone range of a woman's soft voice. Now there's a convenient excuse I could use for the rest of my life. After those tests, three generations of the Hank family could now ask the question, "Aye? What did you say?"

From these two adventures, a Proud Hunter learned the importance of always knowing where your hunting partner is when you pull the trigger. And, on this day, a couple of Proud Yoopers also learned that you can lose your hearing when the wing shooting gets intense and you shoot too close to your partner's ear.

16

A Coyote and a Hulbert Button Buck

I have received much.
I am willing to give much in return…
there must be a giving back for what one receives.

-Sevenka Qoyawayma, Hopi

By late November 1971, dad and I hadn't had any luck killing a deer. So, in the final days of rifle season, we were still hunting hard in the big woods of Hungry Hill, one mile east of Clara's Gultch, where the Beavertail Creek crosses the Prentiss Bay Road.

On this day, dad and I hiked deep into the remote Hungry Hill countryside to where there are several big rocks, one of them the size of a small house. We made a comfortable seat on top of this big rock in a section of maple hardwoods. From this vantage point, I could see almost all the way across the hardwood forest. Dad had selected a spot about 300 yards east of me in more heavily forested terrain.

Grandpa Ed was having difficulty making this long hike into the woods with us, so he chose to stay closer to the road, near where we parked the Bronco.

Dad and I had seen several deer in the big hardwoods earlier in the season, but we couldn't put antlers on them, so we hadn't taken a shot.

This was our last day of rifle season to hunt, so we were hoping we would see something to shoot. As the late afternoon wore on, it started to look like the rifle season would end without us firing so much as a single shot.

As the sun sank behind me on the horizon, I saw a movement 100 yards away in the hardwoods. With light snow on the ground, I was able to quickly pick up that this was a lone coyote crossing the big hardwoods. She was probably just starting her evening hunt.

I raised my .30/06 Remington Model 721 bolt action rifle and put the crosshairs of my scope on the animal's shoulder. As the coyote stopped in the hardwoods to check things out, I slowly squeezed the trigger. At the sound of the rifle shot, the coyote disappeared from sight.

It had been an extremely calm and quiet evening, so the boom of that rifle blast echoing across the hardwoods must have sounded like a cannon to dad. He came running over immediately, anticipating that I had taken a buck.

"Did you get him?" he yelled out as he approached me. "Tell me that you got him!"

"I got something straight ahead of you," I responded. "Coyote – be careful because I think he's still alive."

Proud Hunters Proud Yoopers

Dad easily picked up the coyote's tracks in the snow, and he found the dead coyote at the end of them. I had dropped her right where I shot her, with a perfect shot of a 180 grain Winchester Silvertip bullet slicing through her shoulders. The coyote was a young female, and she died almost immediately from the clean, killing shot.

I had never seen or killed a coyote before so I was really excited. I jumped off the big rock and ran over to dad to see my trophy. I was thrilled to have killed a coyote.

Rather than carry the 30-pound animal more than a mile to the road, dad suggested we pick an eight-foot pole and tie the coyote's front and hind feet to each end of the pole. We would transport the coyote out of the woods by resting the ends of the pole on our shoulders, with dad in the lead and me following him at the back end of the pole. The coyote was swinging between us, and we hardly noticed her weight on our shoulders. It was a really easy way to get her out of the deep woods.

As we approached the road after our one-mile hike, grandpa was waiting anxiously for us. He had heard the shot, and he suspected we had gotten something given how long we were taking to get out of the woods.

When he saw us, he hit us with his flashlight beam, which revealed us carrying the small, brown animal. "Oh my," he exclaimed. "That's a really small one. Maybe you should have let that little deer live."

He was, of course, thinking we had shot a small fawn on the last day of the season, probably out of frustration.

"Grandpa, it's a coyote and I got him right at dark," I told him proudly.

"Well, that's great, you got a coyote," grandpa said in a congratulatory way, correcting his misidentification of my trophy.

"Yah, he made a nice 100-yard shot clean across the hardwoods to get her," dad told grandpa.

From the age of 12, I had been practicing taxidermy work on various animals that dad and I had killed or that other hunters had given me. I had taken a popular correspondence course with the Northwestern School of Taxidermy out of Omaha, Nebraska. The company advertised its program in all the outdoor magazines like *Outdoor Life,* and I paid them my tuition money, using birthday and Christmas money I had saved. I read and practiced the techniques they recommended in their ten lesson course until I knew how to do most basic taxidermy skills on common game animals, birds and fish. At the end of lesson ten, I got my official Northwestern School of Taxidermy certificate, which was proudly displayed on my bedroom wall for many years.

Now I had my first real trophy of my own to mount. I set off right away to tan the hide of the coyote.

The State of Michigan also paid a $15 bounty to anyone killing a male coyote and $20 for a female coyote. Dad and I took my coyote to the Conservation Department's office on Ashmun Street in the Sault to collect my bounty reward. I also got an official receipt for disposing of a coyote. I used the bounty money to buy more taxidermy supplies.

While I didn't get a deer, I was on cloud nine over the successful hunt for the elusive animal that some Yoopers called the "brush wolf" or coyote. For years, the tanned coyote hide would be my finest trophy.

A Coyote and a Hulbert Button Buck

Later the next month of December, dad and I spent more days on the weekends trying to get a deer with our bows in archery season. We hunted in Hungry Hill, at grandpa's near the Gogemain, and around the Burning, but we had no luck and no close chances at deer.

On December 29, the third to the last day of the bow season, dad asked me if I wanted to go an hour west of the Sault to Hulbert, Michigan, to hunt in a big deer yard there. He told me his friend, Ken Fazarri, the editor of the *Sault Evening News*, also would go with us. Based on dad's description, it sounded like a good opportunity, and we had nothing to lose.

The next day, the three of us drove in the early morning darkness to Hulbert, Michigan so we could start hunting for deer near daylight. Neither dad nor Ken knew exactly where we should go. They had only a general idea of where there were good spots to hunt from vague descriptions other bow hunters suggested to them while they visited our sporting goods store.

Our store on the main street of Sault Ste. Marie was often the gathering place for local hunters to stop and swap stories about their hunting success. Ken was a regular, daily visitor who worked just one block away. During the day, he would stop in to see dad, and they would shoot the breeze about hunting and fishing adventures.

Dozens of other hunters would come by too, some of them regulars. Some wouldn't come to buy anything, but they just enjoyed hanging around the store and talking about hunting. Some of these guys were seeing lots of deer at Hulbert where the deer were beginning to "yard" up, migrating to the area from miles around.

Right near daylight, we arrived just west and south of Hulbert where dad determined would be a good place to go for a walk. He explained that we would move slowly through the woods, spaced out 100 yards apart. If we got lucky, we might drive a deer to one another.

We had never yet been successful at this two-or-three-man driving technique with our bows, but this approach sounded like a reasonable plan. We took off into the big swampy area with dad on my left and Ken on my right. We had agreed that we would hook up when we got to the middle of the swamp and regroup.

Right away, I saw lots of deer tracks, far more than we had been seeing in the Stalwart and Goetzville area. After about 15 minutes, I had lost track of both dad and Ken, and I was moving slowly through the swamp alone, looking ahead for signs of deer. It was so quiet; it almost seemed as if I were hunting on my own.

Suddenly, I spotted a deer running from where I thought dad had last been. At first, I thought the deer was running away from me. Then I realized the deer was coming right toward me, probably because dad had jumped him.

I froze in my location as I watched the deer run and jump closer and closer. Incredibly, the deer looked like it was going to run right by me. When the deer got 10 yards away, I thought it might run me over. As I raised my bow, the startled deer tried to stop, turning broadside for a few brief seconds.

I hurriedly drew the bow back and released an arrow toward the deer that was almost right on top of me. The arrow struck the deer square in the middle of the deer's hind quarter. The deer ran off with the arrow sticking out of its leg. While I was excited to have finally hit a deer with an arrow, I was also just about sick over the poor shot I had made at this animal.

71

Proud Hunters Proud Yoopers

I had missed several deer with my bow in six years of hunting, but I had never killed a deer yet. I yelled for dad and in a few minutes he joined me. I told him the story, and he calmed me down by telling me that sometimes hunters kill deer with bad shots, if they are lucky.

"Let's track the deer and see how much damage your arrow did," he explained.

As we moved thirty yards away from where I had shot the deer, dad showed me the large blood spots in the snow where the deer ran.

"I think you cut a major vein because this deer is bleeding really well," he said. "If this continues, we'll get this deer."

In the next fifty yards, the snow was covered with blood, and now dad was certain the deer would die. "It's a matter of time, Son, before we catch up with your deer," the veteran deer tracker explained to the novice.

Sure enough, just twenty yards ahead was my deer with an arrow in its hind quarter - dead in the snow. Death had been quick for the animal as it lost a huge amount of blood in a short period of time.

"Congratulations, son, you have your first deer, and it's a button buck," dad announced, showing me the small "button" antlers on top of the young, male fawn's head.

As we waited for Ken to join us, dad and I talked about how I got the shot. Dad was certain that he had jumped a number of feeding or bedding deer. This deer was most likely one of them. He was running away from dad when he happened to run into me. Dad stressed how hunters can work like a team in these mini-deer drives, chasing the deer to each other where the waiting hunter can get a shot.

In many ways, this deer had behaved just like the big doe that I had seen near Kelly's field on the Burning early in my hunting career.

I knew that I had been lucky on this deer. Dad explained that I had hit the major artery that carries blood through the deer's hind leg. Severing that artery with my sharp arrow had turned a bad shot into a successful hunt. But following that kill, I vowed that I would practice regularly so that I minimized the chances I would wound deer with a bow. I never wanted to hit a deer in the hind leg again.

Soon, Ken joined up with us and he too, congratulated me on taking my first deer. "That's great, kid, that you got your first deer with a bow," he told me. "Not many hunters can say they did that this year."

For the first time, I got to clean out my own deer with my own knife. I also got to put my own tag on a deer. The fact that I had made a bad shot on this deer had all but disappeared from my mind. I was very proud of the deer I had shot.

We dragged the deer to Ken's Bronco and loaded it up. We hunted for a few more hours, seeing several more deer, but without Ken or dad getting any shots. We then returned to the Sault.

When I went back to school following the Christmas break, I was fired up to tell my bow hunting friends that I had killed a deer with my bow. Rick Arbic, the star tailback on my football team, listened the most intensely to my story, and then he retold how he had taken a small deer with another shot he considered just as lucky as mine.

For me, it was great to be swapping my own real deer stories with young friends who were hunters. I had a ball retelling the story to anyone who would listen.

A Coyote and a Hulbert Button Buck

I had now learned how to kill a deer with a bow, even if this first kill wasn't a perfect one. After six years of trying, I was now a successful bow hunter. In the decades that would follow, I would never hunt in the Hulbert area again, but I would be fortunate enough to take a UP deer with a bow almost every year.

And the many lessons I learned in the Hulbert swamp that December day on my first deer kill would help prepare me for many future successful deer hunts.

On this day, in a snow-filled Hulbert swamp, a Proud Yooper learned that sometimes Proud Hunters can have a successful hunt even on the last days of the season and even after making a bad shot.

17

So you hunt on Christmas Day?

Love songs are dangerous.
If a man gets to singing them
we send for the medicine man
to treat him and make him stop.

- anonymous, Papago

In the fall of 1972, I left Sault Ste. Marie to attend Central Michigan University in Mt. Pleasant, Michigan.   At the university, I studied finance, economics and journalism, and I ran on the CMU track team.   Leaving the UP was a difficult decision for me because I loved the area so much and it was where my roots were.   Most important, I had anxiety about leaving the UP because I thought I would be giving up the quality hunting experiences that I loved so much.

Like many young UP residents of the time, I struggled with what I would do for a living now that I was becoming a young adult.   My parents helped make some of those difficult decisions, telling me from day one that I would attend college somewhere when the time came.   They always stressed to me the importance of education, and they drilled into me how a good college education would help me acquire a better paying job and lifestyle.

Both my parents were 1953 graduates of Detour High School.   They married right after they graduated by eloping to Indiana.   At the time, my dad was still 17 years old.   His parents weren't too keen on his getting married.   In Michigan, a person under age 18 couldn't get legally married without a parent's permission.   One day, the two of them took a short vacation to Indiana where they were able to get married.   After staying in Indiana for a day, they did call their parents, and all but Grandpa Hank traveled to Indiana for the wedding.

Neither one of my parents had the chance to go to college.   From the time we were little kids, the two of them talked to my two sisters and me about the importance of a college education.   They were determined that their own kids would go to college, no matter how rough a struggle paying for college might be.

"Of course, you can stay here and work in the store (our family business)," my mom would tell me.   "But you should go to college and learn about other things in life. The more you learn in college, the more options you will have in life."

My mother and father were convincing that I should not be afraid to go pursue my dreams somewhere outside the UP if I had the opportunity.

For generations, Yoopers all across the UP have worried about the loss of their young kids to other parts of the country, especially the lower peninsula of Michigan and Wisconsin.   With the UP's high unemployment rate and an undiversified seasonal economy, there are often not enough jobs nor opportunities for many UP kids to make

So you hunt on Christmas Day?

a living in their home area. As a result, far too often, young UP adults pursue educational and job opportunities outside the UP. Sometimes, they get chances to come back, but more often, they move away, living their lives and making their homes outside of the UP.

This trend is a tremendous concern to UP residents and a significant challenge to business, community, and economic development leaders. These leaders ask themselves tough questions: How can we create more opportunities for our youth? Can we preserve the uniqueness of the UP culture if so many of our youth move away?

I thought long and hard about these issues and my career and educational goals in the early 1970s. Should I leave the UP for other opportunities or should I stay here? After all, there was a very good local college, Lake Superior State College (later to be called Lake Superior State University – LSSU), right in my backyard. I wouldn't have to leave the UP if I didn't want to.

At the time, just after the end of the Vietnam War and in the turmoil of the early 1970s, it wasn't an easy decision.

To complicate matters, I had become a good track and field sprinter and middle distance runner in high school, winning the UP track championships in the 440 yard dash and the 880 yard run my senior year at Sault High. Several colleges with good track programs showed an interest in me, including Central Michigan University (CMU) in Mt. Pleasant, where one coach worked hard to convince me that CMU was the place for me.

The coach, Don Sazima, of Shepard, Michigan, was a Bowling Green State University alumnus where he had made it to the U. S. Olympic Trials in the sprints. He had also coached the Ethiopian Olympic track team, including the two-time Olympic Marathon champion, Abebe Bikila. In addition, one of my favorite football coaches, Escanaba native Ralph Sarnowski, had been a really good football player at CMU, and he was encouraging me to consider CMU. My high school track coach, Roger Wahl, had run college track at Northern Michigan University in Marquette, and he also encouraged me to give CMU a try. Coach Wahl lived in Goetzville, just three miles west of my grandparents. He was an outstanding track coach who had turned us into a respectable track and field program, and he was a top-notch deer hunter to boot. As a bonus, he hunted in the remote country of Hungry Hill just a mile or two north of where dad and I hunted in a spot the locals called "Birch Hill."

By my senior year, I had learned to love to run almost as much as I loved hunting, and I wanted to compete in track and field at the college level where I could find out how good I was.

The opportunity to train at an indoor winter facility and the chance to work with a former Olympic coach at CMU ended up being too hard to turn down. After considering my limited options, I decided to take the plunge by leaving the UP and attending CMU. It was a scary and gutsy decision for a 17-year-old kid who had rarely ever been outside of the UP.

Even as I moved to CMU, I was still concerned about how I would maintain my hunting interests while I was 240 miles away from home in Mt. Pleasant. I quickly learned, however, that I could find rides home every weekend in the fall with other CMU students. That meant I could still hunt with my dad on the weekends in my beloved UP.

Proud Hunters Proud Yoopers

These road trips became my first long treks home on weekends – trips that I would continue for more than 35 years.

Near the end of my sophomore year at CMU, I began dating Susan Sternhagen from Saginaw, Michigan. She was also a sophomore, and she was studying to be a secondary school English teacher.

We had been dating regularly when we temporarily left CMU for the 1974 three-week Christmas break. Susan returned to her family's home in Saginaw, and I returned to our home on Sun Glo Drive just outside of the Soo.

While we were separated for the holidays, we were writing and calling each other just about every other day.

When Christmas day came, I celebrated the day with my dad, mom and two sisters as we did every year. We got up early in the morning and opened our presents. Shortly after noon, we had a big dinner that my mom had prepared.

Because my dad was self-employed as the owner and operator of our family sporting goods business, he rarely got a day off. Because he wouldn't be open for Christmas, this was one of his rare, true "holidays."

At this time of the year, the deer were migrating across the eastern UP to their favorite deer yards where they would spend the winter in one of several large cedar swamps in the area. The deer are more concentrated this time of year than they usually are, and there were just a few days left in the archery deer season before it ended on Dec. 31. Dad and I were looking for chances to hunt the Gogemain Swamp deer yard near Grandpa Ed's place one more time before the season ended.

Dad had it all worked out with mom that he and I would be able to leave the house in the early afternoon on Christmas Day so we could bow hunt the last few hours before dark. Our whole Christmas Day schedule was built around us sneaking out late in the day for the evening hunt.

Just as dad and I were about to leave the house for the deer hunt, the telephone rang and it was Susan, calling from Saginaw to wish me and my family a Merry Christmas.

"Wow," I told her. "You are lucky to catch us. The Bronco is loaded, and we were just walking out the door to go deer hunting. I was planning to call you later this evening after we got back. Merry Christmas!"

My girlfriend was just a little taken back by my explanation. There was a long pause on the telephone.

"You are going hunting on Christmas Day?" Susan asked incredulously. "Don't tell me you hunt on Christmas Day, too?"

For a moment, I wasn't sure how to answer the question, so then without thinking, I just blurted out, "Sure, doesn't everyone hunt on Christmas Day?"

After I gathered my thoughts, I explained the whole situation, and I think I made Susan feel just a little bit better. Still, she must have thought long and hard about a Yooper family that arranged its Christmas schedule around deer hunting. I think she wondered just a bit about my sanity and the sanity of Yooper hunters in general.

If my girlfriend ever doubted that I was a serious deer hunter, I think that issue was answered on this day. On Christmas day, she knew she was dating a Proud Hunter and a Proud Yooper.

So you hunt on Christmas Day?

On this special day, I also learned that sometimes Proud Hunters and Proud Yoopers, and their hunting lifestyles, are supported by terrific friends, family members, spouses, and girlfriends. And sometimes, young Proud Hunters also marry these girls.

18

Benny and the Stolen Buck

A man ought to
desire that which is genuine
instead of that which is artificial.

-Okute, Teton Sioux

This is a story about a special Yooper buck that my cousin Benny Hank shot deep in the big woods of the UP. It wasn't a big buck. In fact, it was a relatively small buck. But what the Hank family had to do to get this buck was rather remarkable and that makes this buck a very special one.

But first, how did families like the Hank family get to this country and what attracted them to settle in the eastern UP?

The first person from the Hank family to come to the United States and live in Michigan was my great grandfather's brother, a man named John Jacob Hank, who was born in Kozainia, Poland, in 1865. In 1891, he emigrated to the U.S., where he settled in the Goetzville area after he married Mary Traynor. There were lots of Polish people already living in the area, and that attracted others from Poland to settle in Goetzville or nearby. Some of the Traynor family settled just west of Goetzville on Traynor Road where several Traynor families still live to this day.

My great grandfather was named Frank Hank, and he was John Jacob Hank's brother. He emigrated to the eastern UP from Poland around 1904 with his wife Apalonia.

John and Frank's father, my great, great grandfather, was Jacob Hank. All we know about Jacob is that he worked in a basket factory in Poland. We believe he was born and died in Poland, never making it to America. His two sons, however, moved to the U.S., seeking a better life, and they both eventually ended up living in the Goetzville area, near the Traynors.

Frank and Apalonia Hank had two sons, my Grandfather Edward and his younger brother, Fred, or Uncle Fred as dad and I called him. Frank and Apalonia had a farm and also a sawmill on the corner of Traynor and Taylor Lake Roads, just two miles directly west of Goetzville, where they raised my grandpa and Uncle Fred.

Uncle Fred married Caroline Yegal, and they had two kids, a son named Benny and a daughter named Francis. Fred and Caroline lived in the same house that Fred's father (Frank and Apalonia Hank) built on the property. Benny built a home next door to his parents when he married Francis LaPoint. Fred worked as a welder for the Cedarville limestone quarry, and Benny also worked there.

I always thought Benny had a cool job because he got to drive the locomotive, hauling limestone from the Cedarville open quarry pit to the anchored Great Lakes

Benny and the Stolen Buck

freighters on the extreme north edge of Lake Huron, just east of Cedarville. The Cedarville quarry pit (the "Quarry" as the locals called it) is located just one to two miles from my favorite hunting spots in Hungry Hill, off the Prentiss Bay Road and north of M-134.

As complicated as this genealogy lesson is, I owe my eastern UP hunting experiences to John and Frank Hank. If they had not taken the bold step to come from Poland to this harsh environment, I would not have grown up in the UP, and I would have never learned to hunt the eastern UP as I have enjoyed for almost 50 years.

Now I've been told that my family takes its hunting way too seriously and that we are on the verge of being fanatical about hunting. If that's the case, then my relatives Fred, Caroline and Benny are worse off, because they take their deer hunting to an even greater extreme.

In any case, neither Hank family will win any awards from PETA this year.

At no time was the seriousness of our hunting more obvious than in the early part of a new rifle season in November, 1976.

Grandpa Ed, dad and I were splitting our hunting in the Springer Road area (around the Burning) where we had hunted for years and in the Hungry Hill area off Prentiss Bay Road, where we were now hunting much more frequently. Fred, Benny and Caroline were hunting several miles south of us in another remote part of the Springer Road network, in an area the locals called "Frog Pond."

Frog Pond is actually labeled Fulmer Lake in the official plat books and topographical maps. It sits in the middle of remote country that was tough to get to and was surrounded by three or four miles of state land without any roads crisscrossing them. Back in the mid 1970s, that meant it was tough to get close to this country, let alone hunt it from daylight to dark.

The long and rugged hike into and out of this country took a heavy toll on hunters. It took a lot of effort and energy to get to and return from Frog Pond. Once you were there, your reward was that you were unlikely to see many other hunters, and the odds of seeing a big buck were good.

This is the way Fred, Caroline and Benny liked it. They didn't seem to mind the rigors of getting to and from Frog Pond, and they hunted this country hard everyday, all season long from daylight to dark. And they liked being off alone in an area we liked to call a "big woods."

Few hunters in the whole UP made the effort to hunt so hard, and I admired them for their dedication.

Sometimes they were rewarded with huge deer, deer that lived alone in the remote country for years, where they could age and develop big antlers.

In 1979, Aunt Caroline would take one, well-placed shot at a huge buck making a scrape near her seat. The gigantic typical twelve point buck, with a 22.3 inch inside spread, would score 166.3 Boone and Crocket points, the state record for a woman in Michigan. Caroline would proudly hold this state record for a number of years.

Benny and Fred were also frequently killing big bucks, usually nice eight and ten pointers.

But it was a small buck in 1976 that got all of our blood pumping the hardest.

Because my grandfather and his brother only lived two miles apart, they called each other each night during the season, usually after supper and just before turning in

Proud Hunters Proud Yoopers

for bed. They would discuss the day's hunt and what they had seen, exchanging thoughts on everything from the weather to deer movements.

On this one particular night, Fred had been complaining to my grandfather about how there were more guys than usual in their area. There was a camp party staying in tents in the area, and two other Detroit area hunters were in the area too. These outsiders had learned to get here by coming north from M-134. The Cedarville-based Dutcher family had previously guided these hunters into the area, and now they were hunting here on their own.

Occasionally, moose from Canada's St. Joseph Island crossed on the ice or swam across the St. Mary's River shipping channel to make their home in the eastern UP. While they were relatively rare, we periodically would see one or see their tracks.

In mid-November 1976, someone had illegally shot a cow moose near Frog Pond. The local conservation officers and State Police troopers were in the area investigating the kill.

Benny had some luck this day. He had shot a small spikehorn back farther in the bush than where he usually hunts. Benny had picked up the trail of a wounded buck in the snow, and the deer took him toward Little Trout Lake. After a long stalk, Benny caught up to the buck and killed him. Benny had been under the weather, nursing an ear infection, and he was a long way from Fred's Jeep. After dragging the deer half way out of the woods, Benny hid the deer under a large spruce tree. His plan was to drag the deer the rest of the way in several days, probably with some help from us. Given that he was so far back in the woods, he assumed his deer would be safe for a day or two.

The next night, however, our nightly phone call from Benny was frantic. Someone had stolen his deer from under the spruce tree, and he and Fred were certain it was the two Detroit-area hunters. They didn't know, however, how they would prove it.

Benny had followed the drag marks in the snow past the tenting party where there was a four-point buck hanging in their camp. After he verified that they did not have his buck, he asked if they knew who had dragged a deer through this area. The hunters identified two Detroit-area hunters staying in Detour as the guys.

Fred and Benny had passed this information on to area State Police Trooper Stemic, and he assured them that he would conduct a thorough investigation. Fred and Benny encouraged the trooper to get with the Detroit-area hunters right away because they suspected the downstate hunters would close up camp quickly and head back to Detroit.

The trooper started the investigation right away, but he confirmed to Fred and Benny that the Detroit hunters had denied they took Benny's spike.

Interestingly, however, is that the Detroit hunters did show the trooper a single set of antlers from a spike buck they had allegedly killed. While they had claimed to have just killed the deer, they had boiled the skull of the spike clean without as much as a speck of tissue on it.

The hunters also showed the trooper the wrapped packages of meat from the deer they had killed. Interestingly, however, is that there were no signs of the hide, head, bones or anything else from the kill. The hunters had neatly gift wrapped the deer in freezer paper, and they were just about to go home to Detroit.

Benny and the Stolen Buck

Fred and Benny begged the trooper to get the Detroit hunters to tell them where they had dumped the remains of the deer they supposedly killed. Benny was especially interested in seeing the head of the buck these guys had taken.

Just before the hunters were leaving, the trooper prevailed on one of the hunters to take him to where they had disposed of the deer's remains. First, the hunter took the trooper to the Detour dump where the hunter looked around the dump and proclaimed that it looked like they wouldn't be able to find the remains. The trooper got angry with the hunter and told him to quit playing games and take him to where they had really dumped the deer's remains. The hunter, who had been staying at the John Steele cabins in Detour, then promptly took the trooper to the Detour State Park on the M-134 Scenic Highway just west of Detour. Here the hunter retrieved a sack of deer remains from a park trash barrel.

The hunter and the trooper returned with the head of the deer to Goetzville where they reunited with the second Detroit hunter and Uncle Fred. Benny was unable to attend this meeting because he had been called into work at the Cedarville quarry.

When the hunters again insisted that they had killed the deer and that they had not stolen Benny's buck, the trooper examined the head of the deer.

As the four men stood around looking at the dead buck's head, the trooper noticed that both ears of the deer had been notched with a small "V." When the trooper mentioned the notched ears, the second hunter announced that he always notched both ears of his deer. At that instant, Fred pulled out a furry "V" shaped piece of a deer's ear that Benny had carefully cut and removed from the base of his buck's ear. The trooper put the "V" into the "V" shaped notch at the base of the deer's ear and announced that it appeared to be a perfect fit.

At that point, the Detroit hunters panicked, and one of them shouted out again that he always notched his deer the same way as Fred claimed Benny had done.

The trooper calmly told the Detroit hunters that the Marquette State Police lab could confirm whether Benny's piece of the ear matched the deer. He promised the hunters that they could be here in 3-4 hours to ascertain if the Hanks had the same tissue as the Detroit hunters had claimed to have killed. The trooper told the Detroit hunters that, if they were guilty, they would have to pay for that lab test procedure on top of their fines.

He asked them if they wanted to confess to stealing Benny Hank's deer.

Now this incident happened long before the days where we have three *CSI* television shows a week showing elaborate scientific evidence testing and long before DNA testing was a commonly understood household term.

Even so, the Detroit hunters took a minute to think hard about the scientific evidence that could prove they were lying. After some reflection, they figured out that the game was up and that they would have a tough time beating this rap. After a private discussion, they came back to the trooper, and they admitted that they had stolen the buck, cut it up quickly, cut off the antlers, boiled the antlers clean, and then disposed of all evidence of the deer other than the antlers and the wrapped meat.

The guilty hunters moved closer to the trooper and moved away from my Uncle Fred. As my Uncle Fred reached inside his pocket for a lighter to relight his pipe, one of the deer thieves asked the trooper if Fred had a gun with him.

Proud Hunters Proud Yoopers

The trooper could have given the thieves some comfort, but he didn't. Instead, he let the Detroit-area hunters sweat it out a bit.

"I never searched Mr. Hank, so I don't know if he's got a gun in his pocket or not," warned the trooper. "You know, people in the UP take their deer hunting seriously, and they don't take kindly to people who steal their deer."

The trooper was undoubtedly a Proud Yooper and Proud Hunter himself.

Those unsolicited words of support drove fear into the hearts of the thieves. Fred, who was unarmed at the time, didn't do anything to give them any comfort. In fact, the thieves had no idea just how angry Fred was with them.

After several days of this high anxiety, the Hanks were finally going to get their buck back.

All of this surveillance activity forced Fred, Benny and Caroline to miss some of their precious hunting. Normally, that would be unacceptable. But in this case, they were so angry to think another man would steal someone else's deer, they were determined to see justice prevail, no matter what the cost.

Following these events, grandpa, dad and I went to Fred and Caroline's house after supper one night to hear the whole story first hand. Benny was also there.

Fred was usually a man of few words, but on this night, he told the story from beginning to end, and I remember how captivating it was to hear it.

Fred told the story in one of the most dramatic ways I think I've ever heard a story told. He sat at the head of the kitchen table, with his pipe in the side of his mouth. We surrounded him with keen interest, hanging on his every word, as he started the story. At times, he got a little clarifying help from Benny and sometimes Aunt Caroline. Eventually, he got to the work of the state trooper.

Now Fred didn't usually praise law enforcement officers, but he did this time. He was grateful that Trooper Stemic was so persistent and cagey with these guys. Fred was also grateful that his son had the foresight to think to notch his deer so discretely as Benny had done. Fred was also happy that he had been able to keep the notched "V" hidden until the final, defining moment.

The whole thing had worked out incredibly well when it could have easily ended with the Detroit hunters going back to Detroit with Benny's buck and no evidence to stop them. Everyone would have known they were guilty, but no one could have conclusively proven it.

It was as if the Polish and Yooper gods were looking out the for the Hank hunters on this day. And they brought justice to the UP against the sinful Detroit guys who had a far different set of values. As Fred said, it was as if they were guys with no regard for the importance of a man's deer.

"Can you imagine stealing someone else's deer?" Fred yelled out so loudly in a booming voice that it felt as if he shook the whole house.

Near the end of the story, I learned just how important a Yooper's hard-earned deer is to him.

Fred told us in no uncertain terms, "I have never wanted to kill another man since I returned from Japan (where he was in the heat of battle during World War II). But it was a good thing that I wasn't alone with these guys, because I think I know what I would have done to them."

Benny and the Stolen Buck

Fred just sat there and looked off into space, thinking about what he had just said. You could just see the anger in his eyes, and you could feel the tension in the room.

When I looked into the eyes of my Uncle Fred, there was no doubt in my mind what he would have done to those guys.

I thought to myself, "Those guys are really lucky they didn't run into my Uncle Fred after he knew what they did!"

After holding the evidence for some time, Benny eventually got his deer antlers and his wrapped and frozen venison.

The Detroit boys got a mild sentence of a $100 fine for larceny of a deer from the judge for their guilty plea. As far as I know, they never returned to hunt the "Frog Pond" again. And they certainly had the common sense to never cross my Uncle Fred a second time.

If they never do show their faces in the eastern UP again, well, that's just fine with Fred, Caroline and Benny.

On this day, a Proud Yooper learned that no Yooper hunter should ever leave a deer in the woods overnight without taking a notch out of the deer's ear! And, on this day, Proud Hunters learned that sometimes a hard-working and crafty state trooper might go the extra mile to help a Proud Yooper retrieve a stolen buck.

19

Bears at Point Blank Range

I am particularly fond of the little groves of oak trees.
I love to look at them
because they endure the wintry storm
and the summer's heat,
And – not unlike ourselves – seem to flourish by them.

- Sitting Bull, Hunkpapa Sioux

In the late spring of 1975, I had just finished my junior year at CMU, when a friend of mine from Lansing asked me to join him on a black bear hunt in Canada. I had never hunted outside of Michigan, so this was a big event. Dave Powell, an avid hunter I had met at CMU, told me we would be hunting near Ranger Lake, Ontario with his father, Dr. Gerald Powell, a practicing physician in the Lansing area (and later Houghton Lake), and his brothers, Stewart and Andy.

Today, Dave is a lumber broker in Okemos who also runs a 120-acre family hunting club in the North East Michigan club country area near Alpena. He's killed some very nice whitetails over the last 20 years and some nice bears, too. During our 1975 bear hunt, Dave taught me lots of tips and techniques about how to bait bears successfully as we ran a 20-mile bear bait line west and east of Ranger Lake. Over the years, I have used Dave's baiting techniques, and I have developed a few new ones to take a number of bears in both Ontario and the UP.

To get to the Ranger Lake area, Dave and his family met me in the Sault with their RV, and I followed them in dad's Bronco. We drove about four hours to get to the spot we wanted to camp, only to find that another party from the Lansing area was already in our site. When Doc Powell talked to the hunters, it turned out that he knew a mutual friend of theirs, someone who had directed them to this place. We swapped some stories over a Canadian beer while the hunters were packing up to leave. As a favor to Doc Powell, the hunters told us about an active bear bait they had just two miles away.

"The bear has been hitting the bait about every other day, but he usually comes late at night, so we haven't seen him yet," explained the leader. "We've put in a full week watching the bait, with no luck. He must be a nocturnal bear. If you've got a week, maybe you will get him."

I didn't have as much experience as these guys did hunting bears, but I wasn't optimistic we would get this particular bear.

As these hunters packed up and left, we took over their camp site along a beautiful trout stream, and we prepared for our hunt. After we unpacked, we loaded up the Bronco with supplies, and we began the hard work of putting out bear bait in remote locations over a 20-mile stretch of this big, majestic country.

Bears at Point Blank Range

The countryside, south of Chapleau, Ontario, where we hunted, was absolutely stunning. There was a beautiful river, creek or lake around almost every turn, and the terrain was hilly and steep, with gorgeous cliffs and rock outcroppings everywhere. As flat as the eastern UP is, this was quite a change for me.

Selecting locations for the bear baits and hauling the meat and bread into the bush was an exhausting experience. We did this for two days straight, hoping to get a number of bears working our baits in several locations.

On the second day, we noticed that a bear had again hit the old bait that the Lansing hunters had told us about.

"One of us should sit here tonight," Doc Powell said matter-of-factly as we looked over the site. With hopes running high that we had a bear likely to come here, we looked over the blind the other hunters had used. That's when Doc told us to move the bait to another location further away from the blind and to move the blind closer to where the bait had been.

The Powell family graciously let me hunt this spot that evening. At 6 pm, Dave and his dad dropped me off at the site. They promised to return at dark, which would be around 9 pm.

I settled into the ground blind with my Remington .30/06 rifle cradled across my lap, expecting a long evening with no action. "This bear comes after dark every night, so I'll probably sit here for three hours and see nothing," I thought to myself as I tried to get comfortable. I brought four shells with me, and I loaded them in the rifle.

I had only been in the stand about 30 minutes when I heard a sound behind me. When I slowly turned around, I saw a good-sized bear walking almost right behind me. He was circling the little clearing I was watching.

I was totally pumped that I had seen a bear this early in our hunt, and my heart was pounding as I lost sight of the bear that I knew was almost on top of me. It was a little tense for a few seconds while I couldn't see the bear, but soon, he turned into the clearing I was watching. He was only about 10 feet away. The bear moved steadily toward the location where the bait had been. Soon, he was right on top of me, walking right by me, just feet away.

When I put the scope on him, he was so close that all I could see in the scope was black hair. I centered the scope in what I thought was the middle of his shoulder, and I fired. The bear jumped straight up in the air and landed almost right at my feet. He was growling and thrashing around almost on top of me. I quickly bolted the gun and fired at him. I bolted it again and fired a third time. Then it occurred to me that I only had one shell left. I told myself to wait and not shoot my last shot at the bear until he came after me.

Within another minute, the bear expired, dying almost right in front of me, only about three feet away. When I dressed out the bear, I learned that I had missed him once at point blank range while he was thrashing at my feet and I had hit him in the rear end with the other shot. My first shot had been the fatal shot. I couldn't believe that I had missed the bear with one shot, but that's hunting and that's how excited, nervous and scared I must have been.

When I returned to the UP and told my dad this story, he gave me a new challenge. "Son, you could hunt another 50 years and never have anything more exciting than that happen to you while rifle hunting for bears. I can't imagine any other adventure with a rifle to top that experience. Maybe you should hunt bears with a bow from now on for the challenge of it."

At the time, almost no one in Michigan hunted bears with a bow, but following that challenge from dad, I began pursuing black bears vigorously with a bow and arrow. Over the years, I've taken four nice bears with a bow and had dozens of memorable encounters with this great animal that roams the UP forests and swamps.

In the early 1980s, I was hunting Hungry Hill for deer near Brad's Marsh. I didn't have a bear tag and neither did dad, but we were sure there was a big buck hanging around the ridges that surround the big marsh. We were hauling in about 50-pound pack sacks of apples for deer bait every trip we made into the big country. We hoped these apples would increase our odds that we would see the big buck. In those days, that much bait was legal, and it was about all we could carry in one trip.

At my favorite bow seat, something was eating my apples like crazy, and yet, by the third week of October, I hadn't seen a single deer there. That's when I surmised that the deer were avoiding my stand on the weekends and probably hitting the apples hard on Mondays, Tuesdays and Wednesdays when dad and I were not hunting. I decided to stay late on a Monday night to see if I could trick up the big buck that I thought was eluding me.

About 30 minutes before dark, I heard a crunch, and then I heard a grunting noise that sounded like a rutting buck. "Oh, it's a big buck coming," I told myself. As the noise approached my stand, I was sure that I could hear two deer grunting. It also sounded as if they were communicating with each other.

"Oh, that's got to be two big bucks coming to these apples," I excitedly reassured myself. Then I was sure that I could hear a distinct third animal making a grunting sound. I was really confused now, because I could hear multiple animals walking almost right underneath my stand as they approached the apples from directly behind me.

In another minute, a large female black bear walked right under my tree and waddled out to the pile of apples I had placed in a small clearing. While female black bears are much smaller than mature male bears, this female was huge. Following her into the opening was not one, not two, but three little bear cubs, probably weighing about 40 pounds each. They looked so tiny compared to their mother.

I stayed as still as I possibly could, perched just 20 feet high in a white pine tree above the four bears, and for the next twenty minutes, I watched an incredible show.

The mother never left the pile of apples. She munched on apples the entire time, eating most of the whole 50 pounds herself. Periodically, one or more cubs would join her and eat an apple or two. Then a bear cub would walk over to another sibling, and the two of them would start playing around. They would climb on top of each other, wrestle each other and just roll around together, having fun and seeming to tease, taunt and play with each other.

Of all my years in the woods spent watching wildlife, this was one of my greatest moments. I had never seen a black bear mother with triplets before, and I had never seen bears clown around with each other as these bears did. I had also never seen a mother bear gorge herself like this hungry mother. The whole experience was just remarkable and wildly entertaining.

Bears at Point Blank Range

While I watched the four bears play with each other and eat apples, I was kicking myself because I had left my 35mm camera on the kitchen table at Grandpa Ed's house. With that camera, I could have captured some fantastic pictures of this unusual event. As it was, I would have to remember this event in my brain.

As darkness started to creep in, I was getting sore from sitting so still in my tree stand. I shifted my weight in my seat to get more comfortable, making a small noise as I moved. Immediately, the mother bear spotted me in the seat above her, and she became nervous. She began grunting, and the three little bears quit their escapades and came to attention.

In a matter of seconds, the four bears disappeared into the brush and were gone. While I hunted Hungry Hill and this seat hard for the next few weeks, I never saw the bears again, and I never saw any deer at this site either. Dad speculated that the mother bear had left so much scent at this location that she had spooked the deer so that they wouldn't come near the place. If that happened, it would explain why I never saw a deer there. In any event, it was a great experience to see those bears and observe their behavior. I shall forever cherish that evening just as much as the hair-raising hunt where I killed the Canadian bear at point-blank range.

As I left the woods that evening, I sang a song as loudly as I could just in case the bears were still in the area.

On these two days, a Proud Hunter learned just how much fun it can be to have big black bears show up unexpectedly at point-blank range. And on this day, a Proud Yooper learned how many apples a mother bear of three can eat as she prepares her family for winter's hibernation.

20

The Bedsprings Hunt

Which of these is the wisest and happiest –
he who labors without ceasing and only obtains,
with great trouble, enough to live on,
or he who rests in comfort and finds all that he needs
in the pleasure of hunting and fishing?

- Micmac Chief

It was November 15th, 1981, the opening day of gun season for deer. I hadn't hunted or scouted as much as I had in prior years, and I wasn't quite sure where I might find a buck. I didn't feel like I was as prepared for the gun season as I should have been. As a result, I was depending heavily on my dad for guidance on where to get a buck this year.

Dad had been bow hunting regularly during the fall, and he had made a few long trips into our favorite country, the deep woods of Hungry Hill. Hungry Hill was west of the Prentiss Bay Road, near its southern end, just north of M-134, about ten miles east of Cedarville. We entered the woods from the road at a creek flowing out of a large beaver dam the locals called "Clara's Gultch." We drove our old Ford Bronco as far as we dared into the woods in a westerly direction down an old log road. From there, we hiked in on foot another one and one-half miles to what seemed like a desolate place.

Hungry Hill is dead smack in the middle of one of the most remote areas of the eastern UP. I loved to hunt this vast country. There were no roads into these big ridges we would hunt that day, and we were about 2 miles from the nearest gravel road and three or four miles from other paved roads. In these days before ATVs were common, almost no one came in this far to hunt given how difficult a journey it was. That was OK with me, and I liked being here in the deep woods alone with only my dad nearby. Even though all this land was state owned, it seemed as if it were our own private paradise to hunt.

We knew of one hunter who backpacked into this area and stayed overnight for several days, camping out in an old logger's shack somewhere north and west of where we hunted. His name was Dave St. Onge of Cedarville, and, occasionally, he would come to my dad's sporting goods store in the Sault. Dave and dad would swap stories about deer they had seen and killed in this big country that we both hunted.

Years ago, there were old log camps here on this big vast stretch of state land. There was one place where an old logger's cabin had long since disintegrated, but the bed frame from the cabin's bedroom was still there, mostly intact, with medium-sized trees growing up through the bed frame. It was a strange sight, and my grandpa called the place the "Bed Springs." Like Clara's Gultch, the Burning, Sandridge, and Hungry Hill, the names from these places were second nature to my dad and grandpa. They

The Bedsprings Hunt

had heard about these places all their lives, and they knew stories about them. The names were new and intriguing to me.

I tried to imagine the lumberjacks working this remote area at the turn of the century when they logged off the big white pine trees, hardwood maples, and mature cedar swamps. Many of these loggers came from Poland and other eastern European countries to find a better life here. What they found in these logging camps was a very hard way of life. My grandpa would tell me that they lived in the woods most of the year where they performed dangerous work all day long. They worked long, hard hours doing physically demanding manual labor, while fighting awful swarms of mosquitoes and flies. And they did it all for about a dollar a day. Some of these legendary lumbermen no doubt slept in the cabin and bed frame we now called the "Bedsprings."

On this quiet, crisp opening morning, dad and I would be hunting not far from the Bed Springs.

Dad had been watching for rubs and scrapes earlier this fall, and he had a hunch about where the bucks might be seen on this morning.

In those days, we didn't have well-built, state-of-the-art deer blinds. When we found a good-looking spot, we would select a solid tree on a ridge or a large rock to sit on, and we would wait there for deer to pass through. We sat right out in the open with no roof over our heads. You needed to react quickly when you saw the deer, resting your elbows on your knees to steady your rifle for the shot.

The country was a mix of poplars, spruce, and evergreens, occasionally broken up by maple hardwoods and a few pines thrown in. Some of the country was fairly open, and you could see 100 yards in places – not a common view in the eastern UP. In other places, the cover was thick and dense, making it difficult to see or shoot at a deer – more typical cover for our part of the world.

As we approached the ridge in the dark where dad wanted to hunt, he gave me clear instructions: Go down the ridge east about 100 yards and sit down at a big spruce, watching the draw below the ridge. Dad said he would head west and north, until he found a huge rock where he watched last year. We would be about 500 yards apart, and we would be able to hear each other shoot if we got lucky.

I followed dad's instructions to the letter as best I could in the darkness. I paced off 80 steps from where he left me, and I began looking for a spruce tree with my flashlight. There was one right ahead, and I figured this was where dad had wanted me to be. I liked this spot. It was fairly open, and I could see quite a reasonable distance in some directions. There was good cover, and it looked like deer had been traveling this ridge, crossing it regularly based on runways and tracks that I could see in the dark.

I found several small pieces of old stumps I could sit on, and I placed them under the spruce tree for a seat. To make myself even more comfortable, I pulled out my seat cushion, a red "Hot Seat," so I would stay dry and warm. Hot Seats were the rage in those days, and we sold lots of them in our sporting goods store. I never took the time to learn how they worked, but they sure helped you stay warm and dry. They made sitting on a deer stump much more comfortable.

It was an incredibly quiet morning, as still as any one opener I could remember. There was no snow, but it was cool, probably near 35 degrees. It had been dry, so I visualized that I would hear deer walking in the crunchy leaves if they came close. I loved this kind of opening day morning. It seemed like a magical morning as the birds around me started to wake up, and all the creatures in the woods anticipated a new day.

In a few minutes, the darkness slowly disappeared, and the morning dawn began to show itself. Gradually, I began to make out the terrain, and I liked the view and location. I kept telling myself, this should be a good spot.

For the first hour of daylight, I didn't see any deer nor was there any shooting. I mean there wasn't a shot fired anywhere close. I had expected a lot of shooting out by the road where I knew there was an army of hunters, and, instead, it was like the deer had left the county.

"If I get lucky, maybe I can kill the first buck of the morning," I told myself over and over to keep my spirits and hopes high. Soon, there was a lone shot way off in the distance. "Well, I'm not going to get the first buck today," I sighed.

And then the stillness was shattered by the incredibly loud sound of deer running very fast and close to me. It sounded so loud, I was sure the deer had to be right on top of me, but I couldn't see a thing for what seemed like an eternity. It was so frustrating. I could hear deer running hard across the ridge somewhere to my right, but I couldn't see so much as a single hair.

Then, suddenly, a deer streaked across the ridge 70 yards to my right. I quickly threw up the Remington Model 721 .30/06 bolt action and tried to see antlers in the scope. The deer passed through so quickly, I wasn't even sure what it was. "Wow," I thought. "That could have been a buck and I wouldn't have known it."

About 20 seconds later, as I was regrouping myself, a second deer flashed through the same place running just as hard as the first deer. I couldn't get the scope on this deer very well either, but I got a better look than I had at the first deer. I couldn't figure out why the deer were running so fast. I hadn't heard any shots fired close by. Had they been scared by another hunter? Was a pack of coyotes chasing them?

Another 20 seconds passed, and as I pondered how I had just missed an opportunity at these two deer that had come so close to my seat, I heard a third deer running. This time I was ready with the gun up and watching the opening where the first two deer had crossed. I had been straining hard to see small antlers on the first two deer and had seen none. I imagined that they might have been small bucks, and I just had not seen their small racks.

When the third deer crossed the ridge at Mach-1 speed like the other two, I was ready, and I was shocked because I immediately saw his head gear. There was no straining to see spikes on this guy. He had a nice rack well above his ears. There was no question this was a nice buck. I focused hard on getting him in the cross hairs, and I squeezed the trigger.

At first, the big buck seemed to be unfazed by my bullet and the loud sound of it streaking by him, but he got nervous about all that commotion, and he stopped for just an instant. That gave me time to work the bolt and send another bullet his way. This time, I hit him and he stumbled. I worked the bolt on the old .30/06 one more time and sent one more bullet at him as he ran away, just as he was disappearing over the ridge. This time he went down hard and fell out of sight on the other side of the ridge.

I raced over to him, and he expired just as I got there. I raised his antlers in triumph and said a quick prayer of thanks for the beautiful buck. He was a good buck

The Bedsprings Hunt

with a 15" spread and two six-inch G-2 tines. He had no brow tines and just six total points, but he was a beautiful buck to me, my largest ever with a rifle.

He was also the first buck I had killed on the run. Other deer I had shot had been standing, easy shots. Somehow, I felt as if I had earned this deer because I had used lots of hunting and shooting skills to get him. He could have so easily streaked by me like the first two deer.

As these thoughts raced through my mind, one of the first two deer came back to the scene to see what had happened. It was a large doe. Upon seeing me standing over the dead buck, she whirled and ran back into the thicket from where she had been leading the buck.

It all made sense now. The big buck had been chasing one of the two does who was probably coming into her estrous cycle. They were running hard because that was a part of their courtship. The doe was playing with the buck and probably romancing him a bit. She also might not have been ready to breed just yet, and so she needed to stay away from her romantic suitor. The buck may have been chasing her, encouraging her to mate. In any case, this was a sign that the mating ritual was in full swing.

As the doe ran off, I also thanked her for bringing the big buck by me.

I began to field dress the deer when I saw and heard dad coming over the ridge.

"Did you get one?" he asked me.

I held up the antlers and watched the excitement race across his face as he saw the big buck. "You did well, young man! You are exactly where I told you to be, and you got a big buck right here! Good thing you went right where I told you to go!" He had a huge smile, and I could tell he was just as proud of my buck as I was.

He gave me a big hug, congratulating me as we finished field dressing the deer. I retold the story several times, and dad confirmed that the buck was chasing one of the two does, probably trying to mate with her before she was ready.

We hunted until dark without seeing any other bucks. As darkness fell, we began dragging out the big buck one and one-half miles back to our Bronco. It was one of the most physically demanding things I have done, and I was exhausted, but it was also pure pleasure to finally load the buck into the truck. It was the end of a great opening day.

In all my years of hunting, this was one of the most satisfying hunts ever. This buck wouldn't be a "trophy" buck to most hunters, but he will always be one to me.

On this day, a young Proud Hunter learned to closely follow the instructions of your hunting partner because that might lead a Proud Yooper to the biggest buck of your life.

21

Bag Limits by 10 AM

And the bird song,
and the people's song,
and the song of life
will become one.

- Song of the Long Hair Kachinas, Hopi

In October 1983, I made a late night journey to the UP to hunt with dad. I had gotten a very late start leaving Holt, and I didn't arrive in Sault Ste. Marie until after 2 a.m. When I got to dad's place, he told me to plan on only getting a few hours sleep. He said we would get up at 5 a.m. because he had geese located on a Brimley grain field. We would need to set up the decoys before daylight to get them.

It seemed as if I had just fallen asleep when dad woke me. We ate a light breakfast, and before long, we were riding in his Bronco, headed to Brimley, about 20 miles west of the Soo. When we arrived, we quickly went about transporting our decoys and guns to the far north end of a large grain field where dad had spotted the geese feeding the last few days. We used our flashlights and the light of the star-filled sky to make sure our goose set up looked perfect.

It was still dark outside when car headlights came down the road and stopped at the field. In a matter of minutes, another set of hunters with flashlights were hurrying across the field in the dark. They set up on both sides of the field just outside our decoys, south of our position.

Dad and I were angry that these hunters had the nerve to set up right along side us. Depending on how the geese approached the field, the encroaching hunters might also have us cut off. What had seemed like a great goose set up just minutes earlier now had us wondering whether this trip might now be ruined.

When the first rays of light began gradually appearing across the skyline, there were five or six coyotes howling just north of us in the woods. They were probably finishing up a night of hard hunting, and they were very vocal, telling everyone they were in the area. Their howling and yapping lasted less than a minute, but it was a very cool way to greet the morning.

In a few more minutes, just after daybreak, we were treated to another great early morning experience that is unique in the eastern UP. With a gorgeous sunrise in the background, there were about a dozen sharp-tailed grouse working the field. They were running and jumping all around our decoys and making the vocal noises that only sharptails can make.

For those few minutes, we were thoroughly entertained by the sharptails, but then they got nervous about the big fake birds in their field, and the hunters hunkered down on the sidelines. Soon, they became very vocal, with their nervous clucks, and then, almost on cue, they grouped up and flew away to a safer place.

Bag Limits by 10 AM

In a few minutes, the large flock of Canadians sounded off as they approached our field. I love this goose music. My heartbeat increased as I anticipated the excitement. Unfortunately for dad and me, the birds circled once and then came in high over the other hunters. Those hunters couldn't resist the big birds, who were too far away, and they skybusted at them, not killing any, but ensuring that the birds wouldn't be back anytime soon. In an instant, our geese were headed to an unknown safer location and our morning hunt, that dad had so carefully planned, was ruined.

Dad was thoroughly disgusted. We picked up our decoys in a hurry as he yelled out cuss words at the other hunters as we departed. We were fortunate that there wasn't a fist fight, but soon dad and I were back in the Bronco. He was determined to find another flock of geese.

We headed toward Rudyard where he had seen other geese. Just south of town, in a huge grain field, we found a large flock of Canadians about 100 yards from a back woodlot.

Dad sized up the field and asked me if I would like to make a long stalk through the woods east of the birds until I was directly south of them. Then, he explained, I should crawl out toward the birds from the woods, and flush them to dad who would try to crawl out to them from the north.

"If we get them in between us, then one of us, and maybe both of us, should get some good shooting," he predicted. It sounded like a good plan. We didn't have anything else lined up, so I grabbed my gun, heading through the woods, out of sight of the geese.

I had about a half-mile stalk through the woods before I would be close to the geese. As I started off through the unfamiliar woods, I immediately came upon a small pond with some flooded timber. The pond was loaded with beautifully colored wood ducks, one of Michigan's most gorgeous birds. As I approached the pond, the woodies exploded and went airborne from their secluded location. I had mixed emotions about shooting them, anticipating that I would scare up the geese and ruin the planned hunt, if I did. That would ruin the hunt for dad and would have been a selfish act.

But, as I let the woodies go, I thought about how much I wanted a mounted wood duck. I had a perfect chance to get one, but I turned it down for a chance to ambush some geese. I thought about the old rule dad had taught me when we hunted ducks and partridge together on the edge of rivers or in beaver ponds: "one bird in the hand is always better than two in the bush."

I watched the wood ducks escape from their secret place. I could only hope the geese in the big grain field would cooperate. A half hour later, I was in position to start crawling on the unsuspecting flock of Canadian geese. I was confident that dad would be in position, and it looked as if I could get close to the geese, too.

As I wiggled my way on my belly across the field, I quickly closed the distance between the sentinel geese, who were watching for danger on the outskirts of the flock. I was thinking about pulling up on the birds when they flushed and began honking like crazy.

I was drawing a bead on one bird when I heard another shot, and I was confident dad was nearby shooting at the flock from the other side. I dropped one bird and missed the others, but dad had gotten one bird, too.

Proud Hunters Proud Yoopers

Dad gave me a "nice job son" yell as he walked toward me holding his goose. "You pushed them right to me, and I had great shooting. I was waiting for you to shoot first, but when they flushed, I figured I better throw some lead at them," he said.

We quickly swapped stories, and I told dad about the wood ducks. He was impressed that I had seen them, but he was surprised I had not shot one. "I know how much you want to get a wood duck," he said. "I wouldn't have blamed you if you had taken one. We can get these geese again, but chances at wood ducks are rare."

At that point, dad suggested that I run to the Bronco, retrieve the goose decoys and we try this field some more. "There were lots of ducks in the field too, and maybe we can get some of them to come back."

We were running out of time and options, so this sounded like a good plan. I hustled to the Bronco and before long, I was hiding in an unplowed section of the field where there was just enough brush to conceal me. Dad selected a spot along the woodlot where I had entered the field.

In a matter of minutes, there were geese honking again, and they were on their way to our field. Before they got to us, a flock of mallards circled the field, dropping in around our decoys just as the geese arrived.

When the geese swung over dad, he pounded them with his Browning, turning the birds toward me. I also shot at the fleeting geese, dropping another bird. Meanwhile, the ducks got scared and flushed toward dad, with him dropping two birds, turning them back toward me. I had reloaded two shells and dropped a big drake mallard.

I heard dad yell out, "Wow, that was great shooting," as he hoisted his collection of geese and ducks in the air for me to see. I was chasing down a wounded goose, while holding my mallard and gun in my other hand. As I retrieved my game, dad had started walking toward me.

We were now alone in the middle of this huge grain field on a Saturday morning. As dad got close to me, he said something I immediately knew I would always remember and cherish. He said, "Son, do you realize that some guys pay big money and travel across the country just to hunt like this once a year? Not many guys can have adventures hunting like you and I do every weekend."

I had just started to think about that profound statement when we heard more geese on the horizon.

"There are more geese and ducks coming," dad excitedly stated. "Let's get down and see if we can get our limit this time."

I was still breathing hard from hustling back to my makeshift blind and hiding my stash of ducks and geese when a flock of honkers circled again. We stayed hidden in our seats because there were hundreds of mallards and other puddle ducks circling the field too. Our Brownings barked again, and we collected our last ducks that made up our daily bag limits.

As we walked to the Bronco, we were each proudly holding an impressive display of geese and ducks taken from a field we had not intended to hunt. It was a day when we had to improvise and come up with a Plan B. This alternative plan had worked to perfection, and we were about as proud as any two hunters could be. We were really pleased that we had done so well after a lousy start in the morning.

The incredible thing was that dad would be back in town by a reasonable time to open up his business, a business that caters to hunters and fishermen. Waterfowl

Bag Limits by 10 AM

hunters would come to visit and shop in our store the rest of the day, and our story of the morning hunt would be told over and over again to other hunters who would marvel at our success, our good luck and maybe even a little bit of skillful team work between two long-time hunting partners.

On Sunday night, I made another long, tiring 300-mile drive from my homeland in the eastern UP back to the Lansing area. Along the way, I thought long and hard about the words my dad had said to me in the grain field.

His words were etched in my mind – words that celebrated two long-time hunting partners, a father-son team who had already hunted so long together. The words of "not many guys can have adventures hunting like you and I do every weekend," resonated in my mind.

On this day, a Proud Hunter made a commitment that he would return to the UP as often as he could during the hunting season to make sure he hunted as much as possible with another Proud Yooper, his father and lifetime hunting partner.

22

The Incredible Seven Pointer

In you, as in all men,
are natural powers.
You have a will.
Learn to use it.
Make it work for you.

- Legendary Dwarf Chief, Crow

All across the UP, there are some white-tailed deer that have an incredible will to live, and occasionally hunters get to experience that up close and personal. This is the story of one such Yooper buck and the signs he left for only the most persistent hunters to find.

On opening day in 1984, dad had constructed a blind on the new snowmobile trail that had been partially cut across Hungry Hill. He was overlooking almost two hundred yards of prime deer habitat about as far from any road as you could get.

I had decided to hunt about 600 yards south of him in a spot I had watched for years – a good spot between two ridges where deer seem to cross.

As the season opened, there were slightly more shots than usual, and it sounded as if dad may have had some action. Despite all these shots in the area, I hadn't seen a thing. By 10:30 a.m., I took a walk to see dad, hoping he had a buck.

As I approached dad, I could see him looking straight away from me, intensely staring down the snowmobile trail. He was so closely watching the trail, that he didn't even see or hear me until I was almost on top of him.

"Who is doing all that shooting?" I asked him after he finally spotted me.

Dad shook his head in disgust and then asked me, "Can you shoot?"

"What do you mean, can I shoot?" I asked him with a puzzled look.

"Well, I've had three chances at big bucks in this new spot, and I don't think I got any of them," dad said in a dejected tone. "I should probably put you here in case one of those big guys comes back."

"What happened?" I asked, knowing there was more to the story.

Dad told me about two bucks who had sneaked by him. He didn't see the first buck until it was going into the brush behind him. The second one was running, and dad took a quick shot, missing the deer cleanly. Then he started a long story about the third buck that came out on the snowmobile trail about as far away as dad could see. It was a buck with a high rack and long tines. Dad had to shoot quickly on this buck too, but he was certain he had hit him.

"I know I either clipped or hit that deer because he went right down when I shot, but then he got right back up. He ran hard into the thick spruce timber. I have looked everywhere, but I can't find any blood," dad said. "Why don't you go down there and

The Incredible Seven Pointer

see if you can find any sign of the hit? I'll stay here and line you up where the deer was when I shot."

"Gosh, Dad, it sounds as if you had to have hit the deer, so let me see if an extra pair of eyes helps," I told him. "If you knocked him down, we should find him."

I hiked down the line at a brisk pace to where dad described he last saw the deer. When I got to where he told me to go, I could tell he was signaling me to go farther. When I went another 20 yards, dad was waving his arms wildly. I took that signal to mean that I was standing where the deer was when he shot.

I scanned the area thoroughly, but there was no blood or sign that a big buck had traveled through this area. As I was about to leave, I caught sight of one small piece of red meat that looked like a piece of hamburger about the size of an eraser on top of a pencil. I now knew that dad had hit the deer, but this evidence didn't look good for recovering the buck. I wasn't optimistic we would ever find the deer. On the contrary, it did look as if dad may have just clipped the deer with a non-fatal shot.

Dad joined me as quickly as he could. We made plans to walk in circles to the north where the deer had run after the shot, hoping we would pick up a blood trail somewhere. For 90 minutes, we combed a 200-yard square where the deer should have crossed. Unfortunately, we never saw so much as a single speck of blood. Intuition told us that this was hopeless, and that we should quit. After all, it was opening day, and we were losing valuable hunting time, decreasing our odds of seeing another buck.

Despite the long odds, dad suggested we go deeper into the spruce thicket on the chance that we would see some sign farther from where he had shot the deer. I thought this was hopeless too, and a waste of time. But when you have wounded a big buck, you always hold out some hope you will find him.

As I walked deeper into the heavy cover, with dad walking parallel to me on the east side, I saw small specks of blood on a deer runway. I signaled dad that I had found something. Our spirits were immediately raised as dad looked ahead to find even more blood.

"Good work, Son, we are on him," dad said. "Good thing you found that speck on the trail so we didn't give up too easily. But I still can't figure out where I hit the deer so that he wouldn't bleed until now. He covered a lot of ground before he shed his first drop of blood."

Sometimes when tracking a deer, the deer bleeds well for 100 yards and then gradually, the wound coagulates, stopping the bleeding. This deer was the opposite. He had not bled for the first two hundred yards, and now he was bleeding more every step he took.

After a few minutes on the blood trail, the blood was pouring out of the deer like I had never seen. As we walked down the runway, I stopped dad and asked him, "How much longer can this deer go on? I've never seen an animal bleed like this."

"This is one tough buck who refuses to die," dad explained. "He's running hard with an incredible will to live. He knows he's trying to get away from danger, and he is running on adrenaline."

In another minute dad looked ahead and thrust his arm in the air. "Here he is, we got him," he said in an excited tone.

When we got to the deer, we first examined his beautiful rack of seven points. Like some of the Hungry Hill bucks, he had a narrow, high rack with long tines, and he

Proud Hunters Proud Yoopers

was missing his brow tines. As a result, he had a large, typical ten-point frame without three of the points. He was a beautiful buck and very special trophy to dad and me.

Next, we looked over where the deer had been hit. Dad had shot him through the throat area, cutting a major vein in the process. The shock of the bullet had knocked the deer down, but it didn't do any immediate damage to the animal until it got several hundred yards away. Then the bleeding was severe, and the deer quickly bled to death while he was running away.

We weren't sure why the deer didn't bleed sooner, but we were grateful that we were able to piece together enough clues to stay on task and find the mortally wounded buck. Dad decided on the spot that this was a special deer - one that he would have mounted.

He had made a 175-yard shot at a running whitetail buck in heavy timber, making a skillful, killing shot, and maybe using just a bit of luck, too.

"You weren't trying to shoot this big buck in the throat were you?" I teased dad.

"No," he said with a twinkle in his eye. "I must have been leading him just a little too much."

As we dragged the huge buck out of the tangled thicket, dad was thrilled that we had found the deer. He was incredibly proud of this buck. As we strained to pull the big-bodied deer over a number of spruce deadfalls, dad spoke over and over about how other hunters would have given up on the deer and never recovered him.

When dad got the mounted deer head back from taxidermist Randy Desormeau of Barbeau, we hung him in our family sporting goods business. Every time I look at the deer, I think about a flash shot at a fleeting buck on Hungry Hill. I also think about the luck and skill of finding a big buck who had been shot through the throat, and who didn't bleed for several hundred yards. I remember an amazing animal with an incredible will to live who kept running hard until he bled to death in a maze of white and black spruces. And I remember two stubborn hunters who wouldn't give up tracking this whitetail despite the evidence that they should.

On this day, a Proud Hunter learned that dedicated deer hunters don't easily give up on deer they think they may have hit. On this day, I also learned that stubborn Proud Yoopers almost always find their deer if the Good Lord gives them a few clues.

23

Geese in the Barley

Our bodies bathed in air,
and breathing was not only
conducted through nose
and lungs, but with
the entire body...
Bodies were nourished
not only by food...
wind, rain and sun
also nourished.

- Luther Standing Bear, Lakota

The 1980s rock band Guns'N'Roses released a song called *November Rain*. In the song, the band's lead singer, Axel Rose, sings about being out in a cold, November rain, as if it is something very dreary and uncomfortable, and something that should be avoided. Whenever I am hunting on a cold, wet November day, I always think about this song.

When I recall a certain November 1984 goose hunt, I also remember the *November Rain* song.

On this day, dad and I returned soaking wet and freezing cold, from a morning bow hunt on Hungry Hill. I remember this was one of the most miserable days I had ever experienced.

It was early November and it should have been a good day to be bow hunting, given that this is the peak of the deer rut. Instead, there was a steady downpour while we were on stand. It seemed as if it had been raining all morning long. The temperature was just above freezing and the wind was blowing fairly hard, driving the heavy rain almost sideways. It was miserable to be outside for a few minutes, even in rain gear. We had been out all morning, sitting in uncovered tree stands. Despite our rain gear, we were soaked to the bone. I was anxious to get home to Grandpa Ed's place where we could dry out and get into some warm clothes.

As we drove by the Patrick farm on the corner of Traynor and Springer roads, dad spotted a flock of geese feeding in the middle of a 160-acre barley field that Augie Patrick had planted and harvested earlier in the fall.

"You know, we are already as wet and cold as we could be," dad said to me. "Would you be interested in trying to get some of those geese in this crazy weather?"

"They would be really hard to get Dad," I said in a very doubting tone, trying to discourage dad from thinking about spending any more time in this nasty weather. "The grain has been cut short. There's only six inches of stubble in the field and the geese are way out in the open. There's no cover to protect us."

Proud Hunters Proud Yoopers

"Yes, that's true, but I know how we could get them if you want to try a little experiment," dad suggested.

"I don't see how we could get them, dad," I reasoned. "They will spot us a mile away and they will be gone before we ever get close."

"Listen, you know we have seen these geese fly out of this field a number of times. They always fly lengthwise down the middle of the field, going straight east toward the pond," he said. "I am sure if one of us pushes them from the west, they will fly right through that opening in the tree line toward the pond. One of us could be there waiting to ambush them. We should get good shooting if they don't fly through too high."

"The pond" was a reference to Sam Taylor Lake, a small lake and boggy marsh that allegedly had no solid bottom. Just like Ziegler Lake, four miles southeast of here, the pond was said to have a lake bottom just like "quick sand." According to eastern UP legend, if you tried to walk into either lake, the boggy bottom would take you to the center of the earth.

I never doubted the accuracy or authenticity of the bog legend. I was in fear and awe of the "quicksand" that was at the bottom of these two bodies of water.

The John O'Polka family owned Taylor Lake and it was just two miles east of the Patrick farm (and two miles west of Goetzville). We knew this flock of geese spent their summers and fall on the O'Polka pond where they were safe from hunters because the O'Polka's protected the geese from hunting. Besides, who would be crazy enough to try to hunt geese in a bottomless bog?

For the plan at hand, I knew dad was right. The geese, when scared up, would head directly to their safe haven on Sam Taylor Lake. I knew, in theory, his plan should work.

"Well, we can try it if you'd like," I said, trying to not sound too excited about the prospect. "But, we don't have permission to hunt the field."

"I'll drop you off at the farm house. You ask Mr. Patrick for permission to hunt," dad told me. "Tell him who your grandfather is, so he knows you."

I wasn't looking forward to this, because Mr. Patrick had told us earlier in the year that we couldn't hunt the field. He had other hunters using the field with their decoy spreads, and he wasn't allowing anyone else to hunt. I wasn't sure he'd let us hunt now, but it was worth a chance.

When I went to the door, Mr. Patrick was hesitant at first to grant permission, but after we talked for a minute, he became more receptive.

"You mean, you really do want to hunt those geese in this weather?" he asked me. "If and your dad are that crazy, I guess I should let you go. I don't normally let guys other than my relatives hunt, but go ahead and have some fun today."

With that, I thanked Mr. Patrick and I headed back to the Bronco. Dad and I started planning the impossible stalk.

He volunteered to go after the geese on his belly, trying to crawl up close enough to them where he might get a shot. I knew the field would be filled with water and I knew it would be a wet, cold crawl. He probably wouldn't even get close to the geese. We both agreed odds were low that he'd get anywhere close enough for him to get a shot. For all practical purposes, he was merely trying to drive the geese to me.

Geese in the Barley

And, it was a long way to the geese. They were in the middle of a huge, 160 acre field without any cover except for the grain stubble.

Dad never hesitated to do the dirty job. He gave me the easier task of waiting for the geese near the opening in the tree line.

He gave me explicit instructions to go down the fence row, keeping out of sight of the birds at all times. When I hit the fence row, where there was an opening in the tree line, I was to carefully crawl out in the field toward the geese, and get ready to shoot after dad flushed them.

The plan for me was to go out into the field just a short distance to try to cut down the chances that the birds might be flying too high when they went by me. My goal was to be sure that I minimized the odds of being out of range by the time they climbed to their typical flying altitude.

It sounded like a good plan. I knew from experience that geese and ducks both flew lower to the ground when the weather was so nasty like this. When they took to flight, they didn't tend to fly so high, and that usually made for better shooting at them on bad weather days.

I was feeling a little guilty about this plan because clearly dad had to do the more difficult and strenuous job.

As I crawled out to my waiting position, I was already soaked with a new layer of cold, wet rain. It was physically taxing on me to stay low to the ground as I crawled toward the geese. During the crawl, I concentrated on keeping my six-foot frame from appearing above the height of the barley stubble.

All the time I was trying to get into position, I kept scanning the horizon across the grain field, looking for a sign of an almost 50-year-old guy crawling out on a flock of unsuspecting geese.

I was sure I would be able to see dad's head periodically poke up above the grain or I'd see parts of his body twisting along the wet ground as he slithered through the mud puddles toward the birds.

I thought about how much physical labor it had been for me to crawl this short distance. I was 30 years old, an active runner and weight lifter, and in relatively good physical condition. This was hard work for me.

I couldn't quit thinking about how hard my 48-year-old dad had to be working, and how cold and wet he had to be.

Every few minutes, I would slowly and carefully lift my head up to look at the geese feeding 300-400 yards away. They looked content and unalarmed.

For more than an hour, I waited in the driving rain and pounding wind for something to happen, but nothing did.

No matter how hard I strained to see some sign of my dad, he was no where to be seen.

It seemed like I was in a time warp, with no sense of when I would get out of this cold, wet, driving rain storm. I started to think about how nice it would be to get up from this cold, hard ground I hugged so closely.

I was beginning to think that maybe dad had changed his mind and returned to the Bronco to do something else. Maybe he had realized that this was an impossible mission. Maybe he had called off the attempted ambush.

Proud Hunters Proud Yoopers

I started thinking again that I should be back at my grandfather's house, wringing the rain water out of my clothes, and taking a hot bath.

Suddenly, there was one shotgun blast, the sound greatly muffled by the falling rain. Instantly, there were about two dozen geese madly scrambling to get airborne. They were flying down the middle of the field, honking like mad, coming right at me.

While the birds would have normally been climbing for more altitude, on this nasty day, as predicted by my hunting partner, they clung low to the ground.

As I readied myself mentally for the coming excitement, I thought about how perfect this looked. The birds were coming directly at me, and it looked like they would fly right over me.

I kept my head low. I resisted the chance to try to get ready. I convinced myself that I would jump up and shoot in one smooth motion when the time was right. I clenched my Browning tightly in the palms of my hands as I waited for the perfect moment.

I loved the sight of big geese flying in formation right over you, especially during hunting season! My heart pounded furiously as the birds drew closer. I still secretly feared that maybe they would see me lying flat against the ground and they would flare up out of range right at the last minute. That thought kept me focused on staying as motionless as I could.

Finally, the moment of truth was at hand. I jumped up from my hiding place in the barley stubble. The birds instantly reacted, and began climbing straight up for altitude.

But it was too late. The birds were right on top of me and it was almost perfect goose shooting. Incredibly, I missed everything on my first shot, but a goose fell hard on the second shot and another went down on the third shot.

I raced toward the two birds to find that both of them were dead when I got there. I looked back across the field where my dad was holding up one goose.

I triumphantly hoisted up my two birds in one hand and I thrust my wet Browning up in the air with the other hand.

As the geese continued honking and flying directly toward Taylor Lake, I proudly saluted my partner for the remarkable stalk that he had made and for so perfectly predicting how these geese would react to his attack plan.

We were more than 400 yards apart on this massive eastern UP grain field, and yet, we each knew that the other one was smiling from ear-to-ear. We knew how extremely proud we were of the incredible hunt we had just experienced.

This was one of those moments that hunting partners live for.

Dad gave me a big wave, signaling that we would meet on the road.

It was time to gather up our birds and go home to grandpa's house to celebrate this great day.

Ten minutes later, the Bronco was coming down the road to pick me up along with my two birds. Dad and I high-fived each other, and told our stories over and over.

Dad said that once he got out into the middle of the field, he thought there was more cover than we had originally expected. The closer he got to the birds, the more confident he got that he could get close enough to shoot.

"I watched the two sentinel birds carefully. They never seemed alarmed that I was getting closer to them," dad explained. "They weren't doing their jobs honestly, and

Geese in the Barley

they were feeding too much. When they would put their heads down to feed, I would inch a little closer."

Eventually, dad thought one close bird had spotted him, so he shot that bird. He pulled on the rest of the flock as they got up to leave, but his gun had jammed. It wouldn't chamber a second shotgun shell. Dad had gotten mud stuck in the action of his shotgun as he crawled across the big, muddy field, and that made his gun malfunction.

All he could do after that was watch the flock of birds get up and fly down the middle of the barley field just as he had predicted.

And just as I had not been able to see him in his stalk, he had no idea where I was, but he was hopeful that I would be where he wanted me.

He was able to see me pop up and shoot at the geese. He saw the two birds drop from the flock after I fired.

As we loaded up the birds and put away our gear, we thought about what a great hunt this had been, and what a remarkable amount of teamwork we had experienced. We also talked about how knowing the behavior of the geese had benefited us. Clearly, scouting earlier in the year had increased our chance of success.

Later that night, I made my 300-mile drive home to Holt, just south of Lansing. On this five-hour trip, there is lots of time to think about things.

On this trip, all I could think about was how remarkable a hunter my dad was. I couldn't imagine that there were many 50-year-old guys in the whole state of Michigan who could do what he did today.

I thought to myself that my dad must be one of the best darn goose hunters in the whole eastern UP. When he was younger, some of his friends had told me that. Now I had experienced it for myself.

On this day, a Proud Yooper learned how important the power of teamwork can be and how satisfying the rewards are among Proud Hunters who hunt together successfully, even when the cold November rain pounds down on you.

24

The Barstool Buck

You must teach your children
that the ground beneath their feet
is the ashes of our grandfathers.
So that they will respect the land,
tell your children that the earth is rich
with the lives of our kin.
Teach your children
what we have taught our children,
that the earth is our mother.

- Interpretation of Duwamish thought

In the late 1970s, an entertainment band called Da Yoopers became a state-wide icon for its catchy tunes about life in the UP. One of their most famous songs was called *the Second Week of Deer Camp*. The song has lived on in deer camps for decades following its release by the band.

In the song, Da Yoopers sing hilarious lyrics about the low chances of actually killing a buck and the high probability of doing some serious drinking in a Yooper deer camp during the slow, second week of the rifle deer season.

The reality is that most deer in Michigan are killed during the first two or three days. Sometimes 70-80% of the total rifle kill is taken during these intense three days, leaving slim pickings for Yoopers hunting later in the season. By the second week, most of the year's harvested deer are already dead, and those that survive are usually very smart, very lucky or both. In any case, they are difficult to kill. Despite those odds, I have always loved to hunt the second week of deer season.

In November 1986, I followed my usual routine by having Thanksgiving Day dinner at my in-laws, Mel and Ginny Sternhagen, of Saginaw. On Thursday afternoon, I had another great dinner prepared by Ginny and Mel's mother, Helen Sternhagen. Early the next morning, I loaded up my 1975 light-blue International Scout and headed for the eastern UP. There were only a few more days in the rifle season, and I was determined to see if I could get a big buck somewhere on Hungry Hill during the infamous second week of deer season.

Dad had hunted on Thanksgiving Day, and he gave me a telephone scouting report. He hadn't seen a buck, but he was optimistic that we might see something this last weekend of the season. There were lots of tracks in the fresh snow, and he had seen at least one big track.

I crossed the Big Mac Bridge at about 1 pm and cruised through the downtown metropolis of Goetzville just before 2 pm. Now in Goetzville, there isn't even a stop light, but there is a post office, a gas station and the Goetzville Bar and Store. My

The Barstool Buck

Uncle John Firack's brother, Ted Fireck and his wife Helena, ran the Goetzville Bar and Store in those days.

That's not a misprint: even the two Firack brothers didn't spell their last names the same. That's something I never really understood. To make matters even more confusing, two other Firack relatives had two other spellings for the same last name from the same family.

The Goetzville Bar sits about 25 feet off the M-48 state two-lane highway. So, as I passed by at 55 MPH, I could almost make out the faces of the customers sitting at the bar. I could also see the few cars parallel parked on the roadway shoulder in front of the bar. One of the cars looked like the car my cousin Dan Firack drove.

For a fleeting second, I thought about stopping to see if Dan was there. If he were there, I could buy him a quick, cold beer. I hesitated slightly, but then thinking about the long trip into Hungry Hill, I put my foot back on the gas. In two minutes, I arrived at my Grandpa Ed's place, where I changed clothes, dropped off some gear, and made plans for the evening hunt.

As I was about to leave, Dan pulled into the driveway. As I suspected, he had been sitting at the bar in Goetzville with his friends when he saw my Scout go by. He had jumped in his car and followed me to grandpa's house.

"Can I go hunt with you today?" Dan asked. "I've got all my gear right here in the car."

Now we hadn't hunted together in years, so I was a bit surprised by his request. Knowing that dad wouldn't be out today, I said, "Sure, I'd be glad for the company, and you can sit in my seat. I'll sit where dad sits."

With that game plan, we headed into the big country of Hungry Hill, driving the Scout as far as we dared and then hiking into our seats on the snowmobile trail, one and one-half miles away.

We arrived at the seats just about 3:30 pm, so I knew we would only have the last two hours to hunt. It was a nice day, with several inches of snow on the ground, only slightly overcast skies, a temperature of about 25, and so little wind it seemed as if you could hear a pin drop.

I was about 300 yards west of Dan. I would be able to hear him shoot if he saw something.

As the afternoon passed, I saw only one doe cross the 200-yard line I was watching.

Right at 5pm, I heard one slightly close, but muffled shot. I thought it might have been Dan, but I wasn't sure. Because there were only 30 minutes of daylight left and this was the best time of the day to hunt, I stayed put and resisted the urge to go see if he had shot.

Several minutes later, I heard a man walking down the snowmobile trail behind me. Soon, Dan showed up at my seat.

"Lee, I got one," Dan told me in a rather casual statement.

"Well, that's great. I thought that shot might have been you," I said with some excitement. "How big is he?"

"An eight-pointer," he answered, still not showing too much excitement. "I dropped him right on the trail, just 50 yards from the stand. I didn't bring a knife today. Can you come and help me clean him out?"

Proud Hunters Proud Yoopers

Normally, I would have suggested he go back to his seat so I could hunt the last few minutes, but I was curious as to how big this buck was. So, I gave up the last few minutes of the magical time of day I called the "witching hour," and I went with Dan to clean the deer.

Given how calm Dan had been about the whole incident, I thought he had shot a small or medium-sized eight pointer. He hadn't killed a deer in years, and I couldn't remember him ever killing a buck of any size. I thought any buck he killed would have gotten him quite excited.

When I got there, I couldn't believe it. This was a huge buck both in body size and antlers. It was one of the nicest bucks I had ever seen killed in the eastern UP.

I gave Dan a hard pat on the back and big bear hug to congratulate him on this outstanding trophy.

"Wow, Danny! This is a beautiful buck!" I said to him, still in amazement. "You did well to get this big rascal!"

The buck had a perfectly symmetrical rack, with 10 inch long G-2 tines and eight long points. He also had an 18-inch spread. Years later, we would have the buck scored and he was a 130-inch class buck, making him one of the top 200 of all time ever killed in Chippewa County. Randy Desormeau of Barbeau would do the taxidermy work on this buck too, and Dan would display the buck in the front room of the Firack's home.

I was overwhelmed by this beautiful buck that I had never seen even though I had been hunting this seat and this general area for almost two months. I thought about how many hours I had spent in this rugged country looking for a buck like this and then my cousin comes here for the first time, and he kills a Commemorative Bucks of Michigan record book buck in two hours.

That's the magic of the Whitetail and the magic of deer hunting.

I tried to imagine how many times this buck may have seen me first and how he must have skirted around me to avoid being killed.

I thought about the freak events that had happened to bring Dan and me together on this day to enjoy this special moment. If I hadn't left Saginaw when I had, if I hadn't slowed down when I went by the bar, if Dan hadn't seen me from the barstool, none of this would have happened.

I thought about the low odds of killing any deer the second week of deer season. I also thought about the even lower odds of killing a beautiful buck like this one.

I thought about my grandmother Mary Hank and what a special person she had been to both Dan and me. We had stayed with her often when we were little kids, and she let us hunt frogs, birds and squirrels all over her 40 acres. She had played a big role in our development as hunters, and she had helped nurture the desire in us to be hunters. She had passed away five years ago, and I still missed her dearly.

When Dan and I had first started hunting deer as 14-year-old kids, grandma had been a key part of getting us together. As we gathered each morning before the hunt, she prepared a huge breakfast for us, packed us big lunches, and had a warm supper ready for us each evening. She did everything she could to support us in our hunting experiences. On our first few deer drives, she even sat right with us.

She was a strong Christian woman and before each breakfast, she said a prayer wishing us safety in the woods.

The Barstool Buck

She ended every breakfast prayer with these words: "And we pray, dear Lord, that it would be thy will that the men would get a deer today."

As Dan and I finished cleaning out the deer and we started the long drag back to the Scout, I told Dan how proud Grandma Hank would be of us today.

I then looked up to the heavens, and I knew my grandmother was smiling down on two of her grandchildren.

I said a silent prayer to her thanking her for all she had done to prepare Dan and me for this day, and I told her how much I missed her.

This whole event solidified for me the magic, the adventure, the wild spirit, and the mystique of hunting this majestic creature we call the whitetail.

On this day, two Proud Hunters learned that sometimes you can kill a big buck in the second week of deer season. And on this day, two Proud Yoopers learned that sometimes, to kill a big buck in the second week of deer season, you just have to get off the barstool.

25

A Yooper Goes on Oprah

It is well to be good to our women
in the strength of our manhood
because we must sit under their hands
at both ends of our lives.

-He Dog, Oglala Sioux

My wife Susan was an early Oprah supporter, who began watching Oprah's show when it first was shown on network television in the mid-eighties. For some time, she had wanted to see her show in person. In the summer of 1988, I had to go to Chicago on a business trip. I was working as the Chief Examiner for the Michigan Insurance Bureau, where my job was to regulate the 1,600 insurance companies that did business in the state of Michigan, ensuring that they were financially solvent. My most important responsibility was to be certain the insurers could pay their bills and fulfill their promises of providing insurance coverage to Michigan citizens.

I worked with a staff of 40 dedicated auditors and financial analysts who monitored these insurance companies. In Chicago, I was joining my peers from the other 49 states at the National Association of Insurance Commissioners quarterly meeting. At these meetings, we worked together to establish accounting standards that insurance companies had to follow.

You might say it was the kind of meeting that only a financial geek from the UP could get excited about.

Oprah Winfrey was doing her daily television show from a studio in downtown Chicago close to where I would be staying.

When Susan learned that I was going to Chicago and staying near the Oprah show, she asked to go with me, and she started calling to get tickets. She quickly learned that these tickets were not easy to get. Officials working the show told her that they only gave tickets to people who had something in common with the show's topic on that day.

Susan tried several times to get tickets to the show, but nothing seemed to work out. She and I left for Chicago, and she had no tickets lined up. After arriving in Chicago, she continued to call the show, asking about tickets.

Each day, she would tell me how show officials had asked her questions about the show's topic, and how she somehow didn't seem to meet the criteria for tickets. One day's topic was witchcraft, which was not up my wife's alley, and another day's topic was the summer's current movies. As the mother of two young children, Susan had not exactly had much time to spend relaxing in a movie theater and taking in new

A Yooper Goes on Oprah

releases. Consequently, she was getting desperate knowing that time was running out to get a ticket.

Near the end of the trip, I told Susan that she was being too honest with the Oprah people. When they would call her and ask if she knew anything about "witchcraft" or the latest summer movies, she would tell them she didn't know much about the topic.

"You should tell them a little white lie, and maybe you could get tickets to the show," I told her after she told me another story about getting rejected for tickets.

In the late afternoon of our next-to-the-last day, Susan was out shopping when the Oprah show officials called our hotel room. An Oprah representative asked me if Susan had any connection to a show topic about "wives who live with husbands who are always away from home pursuing their hobbies."

I laughed out loud and ensured the Oprah official that Susan would be perfect for the show because I was her husband. I told them I spent all my free time hunting 300 miles from our home. I also told the officials that I could make the show, too. The show official told me to have Susan call them when she returned.

When Susan got back to the room, she called the studio and confirmed that she could relate well to the topic. This time the official agreed, and he promised her two tickets.

The following day, we had a date for the filming of Oprah's next show. I made arrangements to take time off from work so I could attend the show.

When we arrived at the studio, we were all excited about seeing the show. That's when we got another surprise. "We've overbooked on tickets, and many of you will have to watch the program on TV from our lobby," an Oprah official told a huge gathering of disappointed fans holding tickets they thought would get them into the studio.

The officials ushered us into a huge room where they began discussing today's topic for the show – husbands who spend too much time away from their wives while they pursued their hobbies.

The officials were actually working the audience into a frenzied state for the show, and getting people both excited and agitated about the topic. In the process, people were getting really pumped up about the show. When someone in the audience voluntarily spoke up about the subject – and if the Oprah officials liked what they heard – they were giving those people passes to get into the studio.

Susan and I sat quietly in the huge crowd of people, and listened as a dwindling number of people were selected to be a part of the studio audience. It occurred to me that we were not likely to get into the studio if we didn't do something drastic to get the attention of the Oprah officials. I pleaded with Susan to speak up and tell the crowd why she should be in the audience while there were still a few seats left. Susan whispered to me that she didn't want to say anything.

If she didn't speak up, I was fearful, we'd be close to the studio all morning, but we'd never really get on the set with Oprah.

Suddenly, the Yooper instincts in me took over, and I boldly stood up and shouted that married men should be free to spend time on their hobbies. I proudly and defiantly said that we need our space to pursue the things we enjoy in life. For even more effect, I firmly stated that good wives should appreciate that men have these needs, and that wives should be supportive of the consuming hobbies that men have.

Proud Hunters Proud Yoopers

While I was trying to be dramatic and just a little wacky, I was also trying not to laugh because I was acting out this role only so we could get the attention of the Oprah helpers.

As I was speaking about the rights of husbands, Susan stood up, interrupted me, and gave her view of the subject, which not surprisingly, was different than mine.

Before I knew it, an Oprah official signaled us to come with him. On the way to the studio, he asked if we were comfortable talking with Oprah live on the show about the subject. Susan and I looked at each other in amazement, and assured him we could. Then he took us to the front of the audience, and sat us on the aisle seats. "Oprah may talk to you early on in the show, so please be ready," he told us.

As he left, I turned to Susan and said, "Hey, we're in. Can you believe it?"

Susan gave me a look. "I can't believe you did that," she said, "but thank you!"

I winked at her and said, "You're welcome!"

We now had great seats right in front of the main stage where Oprah and her guests would be super close to us. We were really pumped up as the stage crew gave us the final instructions for the show.

As the show began, Oprah came on stage. She asked the audience: "Do you have a husband who has turned a night out with the boys into every night of the week? Are you sick of husbands who won't come home? Then talk to angry wives and their never-at-home husbands!"

Oprah then introduced two couples on the stage who had this situation in their marriages. One husband spent all his spare time playing softball six nights a week. His pregnant wife told the audience that when he was home, he spent his time figuring out line-ups and computing batting averages and RBIs rather than helping with the chores.

The second husband spent all his free time playing sports and going to the bar afterwards with his team until 3 am. He rarely helped with their kids or household chores.

After Oprah talked with them and set the program for the day, she came out in the audience. The first person she talked to was the wife of a Proud Yooper.

Neither Susan nor I could believe it as Oprah walked right up to us, put the microphone in front of Susan, and asked her, "Is this something you can relate to?"

Susan stood up and told Oprah, "My husband is the Great, White Hunter. He says it's a short season. I don't see it that way. From September through January, he's gone every weekend, the whole weekend, and he is 250 miles away. He also takes a week to a week and a half off. We have two small children."

Oprah interrupted Susan and put the microphone in front of me. "Great White Hunter, do stand up."

All of a sudden, I was on the spot. What do I do? Do I rant and rave as I did in the studio before the show? I'm on national television. I'm here in Chicago representing the state of Michigan on serious government business. I decided that I had to be much more reserved than I had been in the pre-show, hype-us-up exercise.

"There are a lot of time pressures," I told Oprah and her audience. "You try to balance a number of things, you try to find time for everything. It's always a juggling act. I spend time with my children, spend time with my wife, spend time for yourself."

A Yooper Goes on Oprah

I felt like I was rambling and not making any sense. I was hoping I wasn't making a fool of myself and my spouse. Then I said something that went the other way from my earlier ravings in the studio.

"I am probably fortunate that I have an understanding wife who has put up with this, this long." To my amazement, the audience gave my comment a soft and affectionate groan of approval, and they applauded.

Oh my gosh, we had pulled it off! I couldn't believe how well this had turned out. Not only had we beaten the odds and gotten in the studio to see the show in person, but we were on the program as well! It was an incredible event in an incredible day!

After the show, we got to meet and talk with Oprah, her staff, and the other audience members. The whole day was quite an experience. Susan was really pleased.

On this day, a Proud Hunter learned that sometimes we can get our wives on popular television shows, and sometimes, if we act just a little crazy, Proud Yoopers might even get a chance to defend, on national television, the sport we love.

26

Hungry Hill's Sneaky Little Buck

Some need a series of defeats
before developing the strength and courage
to win a victory.

-Victorio, Mimbres Apache

The opening day of rifle season in 1988 was a day of little action for me. For all the deer there were supposed to be this year, I didn't see much from my comfortable blind in what I hoped would be my Hungry Hill hotspot.

DNR deer management experts had predicted that there would be almost 2 million deer in Michigan's woods this year. They characterized the herd as being at its largest point ever in modern history and they predicted a record harvest by hunters.

For the first time in almost seventy years, Michigan hunters would be allowed to legally kill four bucks each in an effort to try to trim down this huge deer herd.

Throughout the day, I sure wasn't seeing my share of them. As the long day in my blind was just about to close, I hadn't seen a buck yet, and neither had dad from his seat just 300 yards west of me.

I had been hunting this particular blind since about 1985 after the DNR and the local snowmobile association had cut a 20-foot-wide snowmobile trail clean through this country from the U.S. Steel limestone quarry east of Cedarville to the Prentiss Bay Road.

The entire snowmobile trail ran from Cedarville to Detour. It was intended as an economic development project for the local area. Snowmobiles were becoming big business in Michigan and organized trail rides were rapidly gaining in popularity, too.

A chance to ride a snowmobile on a professionally-groomed trail through some of the most remote and scenic parts of the eastern UP might bring lots of winter tourists and their snowmobiles to the area. For those business reasons, the DNR and the local snowmobile association partnered on this project to build the long trail.

In the summer and early fall of the mid-1980s, they cut this trail though the heart of some of Hungry Hill's most rugged country. Jim Crawford, a long-time Stalwart resident, had marked much of the snowmobile trail for cutting. I saw him in the woods one day as he was laying out the next section of the trail. On that day, I convinced Jim to move the trail slightly to the southeast so that he wouldn't run the trail right down one of the better deer runways in the area.

When I showed Jim the area where the deer traveled frequently and where we watched for deer during the rifle season, he was willing to move the trail to accommodate a fellow hunter. I thought this was a small victory, and I thought that his good gesture had preserved a small piece of the wildness that is Hungry Hill.

Hungry Hill's Sneaky Little Buck

As an economic development project, this trail made perfect sense. For the die-hard snowmobile enthusiasts, it is a scenic trail through a beautiful part of one of the eastern UP's most isolated areas. As I surveyed the trail one day, I imagined that future trail riders would think they were in snowmobile heaven as they passed through this place.

Dad and I, however, had mixed emotions about the trail. We were certain this trail would bring more hunters into Hungry Hill. We also believed it could reduce the quality of the hunting we had become accustomed to. What was formerly a nine-square-mile piece of road-less country, now had a really good trail running right down the center of our favorite hunting land.

We decided we would hunt right on the snowmobile trail, building natural blinds on the trail so other hunters would know we would be here. We decided we would try to make the best of the snowmobile trail.

As dusk came to Hungry Hill on opening day in 1988, I knew the witching hour was upon me, that magical time when it seems that deer really move. It is the time that all serious hunters relish and cherish.

And then, just like magic, a good-sized deer stepped out of the heavy cover, slowly walking across the far west end of the line I watched. Within five seconds, the deer crossed the line and headed north back into heavy cover.

I reacted quickly to get the deer in my scope, checking to see if it had antlers.

Even with only seconds to bring my gun up and check the deer's head, I was fairly confident the deer was a large doe. Without a 7X power scope, I could barely see the deer let alone see small antlers, if they were there. After looking through the scope, my instincts and experience told me that the deer was a doe, and I didn't shoot.

I lowered the gun and prepared myself for what I thought could happen next. I knew this drill well. I watched the line intensely knowing that a mature doe probably wasn't alone. I knew odds were good that a buck might be following this doe if she were in heat or, more likely, she could have one or two fawns with her, if she were not in heat.

As I watched the trail for another deer to cross, it got darker and darker. My hopes of seeing another deer cross the end of the trail started to fade almost as fast as the remaining daylight.

To make things interesting, I silently kidded myself that a big buck would be following this lone doe, knowing that with each passing second, odds of that happening were going down dramatically.

Suddenly it happened. Another deer appeared on the trail crossing exactly where the doe had crossed. Before I could even get my gun up, I was certain this deer was a small fawn slowly following behind its mother.

"That's a tiny deer, much smaller than the doe, so it's got to be a fawn," I told myself as I raised the gun quickly to check just to be sure.

I had only another second or two before this animal moved across the line and faded into the heavy timber on the other side.

When I got the gun shouldered and the scope on the deer's head, I almost did a double take. The deer had a big rack with high, white tines.

"Holy smokes," I thought. "That's a huge rack on that small deer!"

Proud Hunters Proud Yoopers

I quickly pulled the crosshairs onto the deer's chest, and then I pulled back up to the top of his shoulder to compensate for the long, 150-yard shot. I squeezed off the shot just as I had on dozens of other deer. I was confident that I had hit the buck, but in the fading light, I lost sight of him at the shot.

I raced up to the bottom of the ridge where he and the doe had just crossed, expecting to see blood or hair from the buck. Maybe I would find him close by, just off the side of the snowmobile trail.

Instead, I found nothing. There were no clues about what had happened to the deer.

Soon, it was dark, and I saw the light of dad's flashlight moving rapidly down the snowmobile trail coming toward me.

"Did you get him?" he asked, almost out of breath. "You shot pretty late. Are you sure you were on him? How big was he?"

I nervously told him the story, stressing the part about the deer looking like a small fawn and yet having a huge rack.

Dad was worried that I had held too high for the shot. "You've never shot a deer over 100 yards. What made you think you'd have to hold so high? I think you may have shot over the top of him!"

In the darkness, we looked with our flashlights for some visible sign that I had hit the deer. There was nothing.

"Son, you sighted in your gun for 100 yards. I don't think your bullet drops more than a couple inches at 150 yards," dad told me. "I think you just plain missed him. You probably should have just held the crosshairs on him like all the other deer you've killed, and you would have gotten him."

As we started the 45-minute walk out of the woods, dad tried to make me feel better about my missed opportunity.

"I think you just scared the daylights out of him," dad kidded me. "I was packing up my gear to leave when I heard you shoot. I came right away because you've never missed a deer with that rifle, and so I was sure you had gotten something."

I couldn't sleep all night thinking about the big buck, and by then I was actually hoping I had entirely missed him. I hoped I had not wounded him. My biggest fear now was that I had hit him in a non-vital area. I worried he would go off and die somewhere, never to be found.

Dad and I looked for several hours the next morning in the daylight, and there just wasn't a trace of the big buck.

I resigned myself that I had probably missed the buck of a lifetime in my haste to shoot. Later in the season, I tried several 150 yards shots from a bench rest. I learned that my bullet didn't drop much, at least not the six to eight inches I had planned for.

"You always seem to hit deer high anyway," dad reasoned with me one day. "Most deer you kill are hit a bit higher than where you aimed, so I think you pull up naturally just a bit when you shoot at deer. If that's what you did on this big buck, then it's likely you shot right over the deer's back."

Then dad gave me hope. "Keep your spirits up. Maybe we will see that big buck again."

Hungry Hill's Sneaky Little Buck

We hunted hard the rest of the season, but we never saw the little deer with the huge antlers again. I checked at local camps and with other hunters I knew. By the end of the season, no one claimed to have killed or seen a buck like the one I described.

I thought a lot about how magnificent this buck's antlers looked to me in my scope. They were unique in shape and character. He had a high rack with a number of long tines. I didn't think I would ever forget how impressive his rack looked to me and how surprised I was that this little deer could have such a great set of antlers.

Deep down inside, I wasn't sure that the big buck was alive. I thought there was some chance I may have hit him, and that maybe he was dead.

After the season ended, it occurred to me that maybe this magnificent buck was now just a whole lot smarter because of our opening day encounter. It occurred to me that maybe I would have to work harder than ever to see him again if he were alive.

On this day, a Proud Hunter learned that sometimes big bucks have small bodies, and a Proud Yooper learned the importance of knowing exactly where your rifle shoots for all reasonable distances you might encounter in the Yooper forest.

27

Déjà vu with the Sneaky Little Buck

Whenever, in the course of the daily hunt
the red hunter comes upon a scene
that is strikingly beautiful or sublime
-a black thundercloud
the rainbow's glowing arch above the mountain,
a white waterfall in the heart of a green gorge,
a vast prairie tinged with the blood-red of sunset
-he pauses for an instant in the attitude of worship.

-Ohiyesa, Santee Sioux

Dad and I hunted hard the entire 1989 season, spending much of our time in the big woods of Hungry Hill. We also hunted regularly in the Gogemain Swamp, putting in over a hundred hours in our deer stands in both bow and rifle seasons.

In one sense, it was a magical time to be a deer hunter because there were deer everywhere in Michigan. The deer herd had exploded to near 2 million animals, and, for the second year in a row, the DNR had liberalized licenses to where you could again legally kill four bucks. You could also get doe permits to shoot antlerless deer in most parts of the state.

On opening day of rifle season, I had seen three small bucks before noon from my cozy little hut on the snowmobile trail running through Hungry Hill. I took one of them and tagged him early in the day. Now I waited for a bigger buck before using my last tag.

Dad passed up lots of small bucks that year too, and this was the start of him letting little bucks go so they could grow up into bigger bucks. In the late 80s and early 1990s, he stopped shooting some yearling bucks, and sometimes he waited patiently for a nicer buck with a decent rack.

We hunted hard, putting in daylight to dark hours in our seats, each day for most of the entire season. Neither of us had killed a big buck in several years, and we talked often of when we might get the next nice one.

Throughout the whole bow season and right to the end of the rifle season, we never saw any sign of the sneaky little buck I had missed the previous year. While I often thought about seeing him early in the season, as the year had worn on, I became more convinced that I had fatally wounded him. I was now sure that he had run off and died.

There was just no sign of him nor any sightings of him to give me hope that he had survived.

After Thanksgiving, I made my traditional last trip to the eastern UP to hunt the last three days of the gun season. I always enjoyed this hunt, but I knew the success

Déjà vu with the Sneaky Little Buck

rate was not good. I knew that by this point of the season, most of the bucks were dead.

Those bucks that are still alive are very lucky, very smart, or both. Many of them are nocturnal deer – deer that had learned to remain hidden all day long inside thickets where a hunter could not easily penetrate. They only moved and did their feeding after dark.

That is how they survived.

On this holiday weekend, I hunted all day Friday on Hungry Hill with almost no action. I had a doe and fawn come to some apples by my seat, but after all day in the stand with little action, I decided that Saturday would be my last day to hunt Hungry Hill. I called dad Friday night from grandpa's house after the day's unsuccessful hunt. I told him I'd give Hungry Hill one more day.

Dad told me he would come out to Grandpa Ed's place, where I was staying, on Saturday night. He also said he would bring his friend Ronnie Kaye from Sault Ste. Marie, Ontario. Dad suggested we hunt the Gogemain on Sunday, the last day of the season for us.

On Saturday morning, I was running a bit later than usual in getting ready to hit Hungry Hill before opening light. In my haste to get ready, I accidentally left my lunch in grandpa's refrigerator.

When I got to my stand on the snowmobile trail, I learned that I would either have to go without food all day or leave early to get something to eat.

The morning hunt from my stand was uneventful as I saw only one small doe. Around lunch time, I decided to take a walk up to dad's seat to see if there had been any more activity around his place.

As I walked down the snowmobile trail toward the end of his shooting lane, I saw a huge track in the snow, crossing 100 yards from his seat. The track was going north into the big country where there were no roads for miles.

With no lunch to eat and no particular plan for this day, I decided I would take off after this big track to see if I could jump the deer. After all, I had the whole afternoon to kill, and I needed to do something to keep my mind off my growling stomach.

Based on the sheer size of this track, I was almost certain it had to be a mature buck. I hadn't seen a track this big all season.

I took the track through rugged country, climbing over lots of deadfalls and navigating ridge after ridge, swamp after swamp, and marsh after marsh. It was typical Hungry Hill country – big and vast, with lots of heavy cover.

As I tracked the big deer, I had no idea where I was most of the time. While I knew some of this country, much of it looks the same and much of it is so different. As I headed off into no-mans-land, I felt a little like a French trapper or British explorer. I was exploring big, vast country that few people had ever seen. I fantasized that I was just like one of the first white men from Europe who crossed this vast land several hundred years ago, admiring the big timber filling the ridges and the abundance of wildlife in this wild and unspoiled place.

It was both exciting and scary to be headed into country I didn't know that well. I made up my mind that I would go wherever this deer took me. I thought I might learn more about his habits if I could stick with him for awhile.

Proud Hunters Proud Yoopers

I had a trusty compass to guide me, and I knew I could always come back to the snowmobile trail if I got lost. With that as a plan, I kept after the big deer for an afternoon adventure.

The big-footed deer headed mostly straight north, and I followed him without incident for about one and a half hours. Then, as I started to ascend into a swampy area where I suspected I might find him bedded, a deer jumped up and exited out ahead of me. As often happens when tracking a big buck like this one, I only caught a flash of him running hard, and I couldn't see his head. In a split second, he was gone, and now he knew I was after him.

I stayed on the track for about two more hours. I jumped a deer one more time that I thought might have been him. I couldn't be sure because there were a number of tracks in the area and I wasn't sure which track had been the deer I had spooked.

Eventually, I had trouble following the track in a heavily traveled deer area, and I got off the track. I gave up and headed back south to the snowmobile trail. It took about another hour to come back to where I had started. I estimated I had gone about two to three miles through some rough country while slowly tracking and watching for the big buck in my early afternoon adventure.

As I got back to the trail, I was exhausted, hungry, and damp from perspiring while on my extensive chase. I knew it would be a long couple of hours until dark. It occurred to me that I could go to Grandpa Hank's home now and get something to eat.

I was just about to decide to go home and give up on Hungry Hill when I came across the huge track again, crossing the snowmobile trail going south.

Maybe, just maybe, the big buck I was after had circled after I last jumped him, and he headed back south to one of his secret hiding spots the other side of dad's deer blind. Or maybe, I had pushed another big buck from his hiding spot.

At that point, I made up my mind I would stick it out at dad's seat until dark just in case the big guy moved again and went back north where I had chased him all afternoon. I didn't think the odds were good of that happening, but then I'd see a fresh, big track cross twice by dad's seat. I had also chased one big deer all over Hungry Hill much of the day.

What did I had to lose by sitting my tired, cold, hungry body down and resting here until the sun set? I didn't really have a better plan than to wait it out here.

As I settled into dad's seat, I put my packsack and excess gear outside of his small blind so I'd have more room. I checked the packsack one more time for any food. There was none, and I was now famished.

For the next hour, I thought about people who go days and weeks without eating food. I thought about how weak I was and how miserable I felt just because I hadn't had my noon meal. Somehow, that made me feel a little better knowing that others suffer a lot more than the minor inconvenience I was experiencing.

At 4:00 pm, a single, mature doe crossed dad's shooting lane, and I excitedly watched her make her way through the heavy timber of Hungry Hill, going in a northeasterly direction. Maybe the big buck would be behind her.

She was all I was to see after my long hike. The time passed slowly, and I never saw another deer. Soon, darkness started to settle in. I looked at my watch and told myself I would stick it out five more minutes.

Déjà vu with the Sneaky Little Buck

After three minutes, I started thinking about the big spaghetti dinner with juicy and spicy meatballs we would have when dad and Ronnie came. The thought of that food made me decide to pack it up, calling it a day.

I stepped outside of dad's seat and began packing up my gear, placing it in my packsack. I rested my gun against a large cedar tree near the deer blind.

As I put the last piece of gear in the packsack, I looked down the shooting lane one last time. To my amazement, I spotted a deer standing in the middle of the lane about 100 yards away.

The small deer had already seen me and was watching my every move. The deer looked so small compared to the big doe I had seen earlier that I was sure it was a fawn.

To be absolutely certain, I needed to look at it with my scope. The problem was I couldn't reach my gun. It was three steps away, leaning against the cedar tree. In very slow motion steps, I moved over to the cedar tree where the rifle was resting. I slowly brought the gun up to my shoulder. The deer watched my every move but never moved a muscle. The deer stood motionless, fixated on me, like a statute. It looked like it could bolt into the thick timber at any second.

I nervously put the scope on the deer's head and my jaw dropped. It looked as if this little deer had a huge rack way above his ears!

I put the gun down and turned up the power of my Redfield 2X to 7X variable scope to seven power. I looked again at the deer, and now I was shaking because it looked even clearer that this was a huge buck staring at me.

For a fleeting second, I wondered whether I could be imagining those big antlers on this small deer. After all, it was a rare occurrence to see a huge rack of antlers and I'd been in the woods all day without any food. I was tired, cold, rundown, and incredibly hungry. I wanted to see a big buck so badly. Could I be hallucinating?

I looked again to make sure this was a buck. Because I was sure this was a big buck, I quickly tried to put the crosshairs on the deer's chest. I was standing up outside of the blind, and I didn't have any comfortable rest to shoot from. I would have to shoot offhand at the deer.

By now, I was shaking so badly, I couldn't even hold the gun on the deer. I had a minor case of buck fever that I was working hard to control. Because of the buck fever, I knew odds were low I could hit the deer. I feared more than ever I would wound another big buck like last year.

I slowly dropped to one knee and leaned against the cedar tree for a rest. I could tell that I was steadier than I had been, and I looked one more time at the deer's head. This had to be a huge buck – I couldn't be dreaming this. I took a deep breath and said a quick prayer. I put the crosshairs on the buck's chest, and I tried to squeeze the trigger gently.

At the sound of the shot, the little deer crumpled right on the trail. The deer was down.

I went racing down the snowmobile trail as fast as I could run while cradling a Remington Model 742 .30/06 caliber semi-automatic rifle.

On the way down the trail, it flashed through my mind again that maybe I had imagined those antlers and maybe I had killed a small fawn. Oh, my gosh, I thought to myself. I don't even have a doe permit! I thought about what I would do if I had made such a horrible mistake.

On the more optimistic side, I also thought how this deer looked exactly like the big buck I had missed on opening day the previous year. I was gaining confidence that I might have taken the sneaky little buck I had missed earlier.

The deer had fallen back into a small impression, so I couldn't see him until I was right on top of him. When I got there, I was stunned. I had not made a mistake. This was a fabulous buck with a dazzling set of antlers, and I had made a perfect shot, killing him almost instantly.

I hoisted up his huge rack! I bent down on my knee to hold the rack in both hands. Unbelievable! He was a buck with a beautiful rack, the biggest I had ever killed by far!

For a brief moment, I was overwhelmed by the sheer joy and incredible sense of accomplishment.

This was a moment to savor. This is what being a hunter is all about. This is what hunters dream about, and, in part, what we live for.

I couldn't believe the emotions I had experienced all day. What a rollercoaster ride I had been on today. From seeing few deer all day, to seeing the track of a huge deer, to the long tracking exercise, and then seeing this beautiful deer at the end of my last day here, just as I was packing up to leave.

I couldn't believe the incredible combination of pure luck and hunting skill it had taken to get this deer. Wow!

I slowly counted the buck's 11 long tines. I admired his huge forked 10" G-2 tines. What a beautiful buck with a rack of such character. The tops of his long tines were pure white, and the bases were very dark brown, probably from rubbing on cedars. He even had a small hole in the right side of his main beam. This was a rack that most hunters would describe as having "character." What a magnificent animal I had killed and what a long and challenging hunt it had been to get him.

I brought down my other knee, and I prayed right beside the buck, thanking the Lord for allowing me to take such a great creature in such a dramatic and satisfying hunt.

I cleaned out the deer, and I wrapped my hunting shirt around him, hoping the human smell might keep the coyotes away until I could come back to get him out.

As I made my long walk out of Hungry Hill in the dark of a cold night, I relived the last shot at dusk over and over in my mind, enjoying the thrill of those few seconds again and again.

When I arrived at grandpa's home, dad and Ronnie came out to meet me.

"You are really late, so I assume you got something," dad said excitedly as he greeted me. "Do we have to go drag one out of the woods tonight?"

I quickly told them the story of the 11 pointer. The spaghetti dinner was on the table and ready to go. They were so excited, they didn't even want to eat first.

"Let's get the deer now, and we can eat later," Ronnie said in all seriousness.

"I need to eat something," I proclaimed. We decided to wolf down the spaghetti dinner as fast as we could. Then we made the long trip back into Hungry Hill in the dark to drag out my trophy.

At noon, the next day, we skinned out the sneaky little buck of Hungry Hill.

Déjà vu with the Sneaky Little Buck

"Wow, there isn't an ounce of fat on this guy," Ronnie remarked as we pulled the skin off the deer. "He's smaller than most of the does we kill. I think he's been running does for the last six weeks and not eating a thing. How does a small deer like this grow such nice antlers?"

Dad and I later decided that this was indeed the small deer with the big antlers that I had missed the previous year. There were just too many similarities for it to be anything else.

Ironically, I had only seen him twice despite hunting hundreds of hours in his backyard, and both times were right near the end of the day.

"He is probably a nocturnal deer who rarely ventured out in the daylight," dad reasoned. "He might have made it through another hunting season if you had left one minute earlier!"

This buck was the first buck I had wanted to have mounted so I took him to Randy Desormeau, the eastern UP's most famous taxidermist. Randy lives and runs his taxidermy business near the corner of Fifteen Mile Road and M-129, about half way between the Sault and Pickford. He has won some of the country's top honors for recreating natural-looking mounts.

Randy aged the big buck for me at four-and-one-half-years-old, making him a three-and-one-half-year-old when I missed him on opening day in 1988.

The taxidermy work that Randy did was superb. I have spent hours over the years admiring this trophy, and reliving the special hunts I had in search of a magnificent animal like this guy.

In 1999, I had my good friend and hunting companion, Mike Jackson of DeWitt, score the big buck. Mike told me that the antlers scored just under 125 as a typical whitetail rack and just under 150 as a non-typical, making him not quite big enough to be listed in Commemorative Bucks of Michigan's record books.

"If you knock off those forked tines, you'd be in the book for sure," Mike kidded me one day. "You get some significant deductions for them. Those forks are keeping you out of the record book."

"That's OK," I told him. "I like him the way he is. Those forked tines show great character. I don't need to be in the record book that badly!"

In all my years of hunting, the sneaky little buck of Hungry Hill has been one of my top trophies and one of the most special deer I have ever killed.

On this night, a sneaky little buck taught Proud Hunters and Proud Yoopers to be patient when hunting, to never give up early, and to always believe that you can kill a big buck right up to the last minute of the season.

28

Life and Death in the Forest

A brave man dies but once –
Cowards are always dying.

- Moanahonga, Iowa

On a nice October afternoon in the late 1980s, I headed into Hungry Hill to bow hunt for deer in a small clearing just west of a place my grandfather liked to call Brad's Marsh. The sun was shining, there was a mild, gentle breeze, and it was a warm day, with the temperature near 50 degrees. It was an almost perfect day to be in the woods.

Brad's Marsh is a large 40-50 acre marsh that is intersected by the Mackinaw-Chippewa County line, and it lies one mile west of where Clara's Gultch crosses the Prentiss Bay Road, just one mile north of M-134.

My grandfather swears that years ago (probably in the 1930s and 40s), local farmers came into this remote area and took hay from part of this big marsh when the water level would go down in the summer time.

Of course I believed him, but it always seemed like an incredible amount of work just to get a few acres of hay. When I challenged grandpa on the sanity of coming to this remote place to harvest hay, he would very nonchalantly insist that is just what some farmers did. He told me they gathered the hay by hand with large sickles and rakes. One of them was named Brad, and that's how the marsh got its name.

From other historical accounts, I learned that there were some droughts in these years, and that may have been when farmers needed the hay from this remote marsh to feed their livestock.

Today, only beavers and waterfowl occupy this large marsh that holds lots of water. From the northwest edge, you can see a large beaver house out in the middle of the marsh. There is also high, light brown grass that covers most of the marsh other than a small strip in the middle where the deeper, open water attracts local ducks and other migrating waterfowl.

The previous April, I was in the same woods looking for antler sheds. I happened to be at the west end of the big marsh right at dusk, when a flock of 30-40 sandhill cranes landed in the marsh where they planned to spend the night. The cranes didn't stay here all year, so this was a special treat to see them. They were on their way north, probably to somewhere much closer to the Arctic Circle than to Cedarville, Michigan. It was great to have them in one of my favorite marshes, even if it was just a short resting spot for them on the long, annual migration to their summer home.

They made an incredible racket as they approached the marsh, landed in it, and prepared to settle in for the night. It was a moving experience to see these magnificent birds with their six-foot wing spans and to hear the outrageously loud sounds they make. It was special music to me, almost prehistoric in nature and a sound that most nature lovers just can't get enough of.

Six months later, on this nice day in October, I passed by the marsh and recalled the crane music from the early spring. I pondered when the big birds would make their trip south again, this time with this year's younger birds who would see Brad's Marsh for the first time.

Just west of this marsh, I made it to an opening where I would hunt until dark. This was a good bow hunting spot – a place where dad and I had taken several deer with our bows. We had also killed lots of deer in this general area where we had several bow stands strategically placed.

As I settled into my seat fifteen feet high in a large, white pine tree, I prepared myself for an enjoyable evening of bow hunting. I was perfectly camouflaged, and I could sit motionless for long periods of time in this comfortable seat.

It was a picturesque setting, with large pines, aspens (poplars), evergreens, and spruces surrounding the small opening, with tall marsh grass on the south side. As I waited for deer to appear, I watched a small flock of chickadees fly around the opening. The little birds seemed to play tirelessly, and they fed all around me. It was fun watching them fly almost playfully around the clearing without seemingly a care in the world.

Some of the birds landed in my pine tree where I could watch them closely. One chickadee landed on my arrow as it lay across my bow in my lap, and then he flew up on my shoulder. After several seconds, he also jumped up on the bill of my cap and sat there for several seconds before he thought it wise to move. So far, I hadn't seen any deer, but boy, was I enjoying the front row seat I had for this spectacular bird show.

The chickadee is a gorgeous little bird who is a frequent companion to hunters in the UP woods during the fall. His colors are simple: black, white and gray, but they are such rich and contrasting colors that leave you thinking just how strikingly beautiful the little bird is.

As my little companions flitted about in front of me and on top of me, I marveled again at their beauty and simplicity. As I watched them, my thoughts wondered again to what a simple and peaceful life they lived.

Suddenly without any warning, a large Cooper's hawk burst into the middle of the clearing, coming right towards me, at breath-taking speed. Then, literally right in front of me, the hawk hit one of the chickadees in mid-flight as it crossed the opening. The hawk grabbed the tiny bird with his talons, using incredible timing as the unsuspecting chickadee had fluttered harmlessly across the forest clearing.

There was an explosion of feathers right in front of my face, only a few feet away. There was also a death cry from the tiny bird as he instantly died from the hawk's powerful and crushing blow. The whole thing happened so fast and with such surprise and intensity, that I thought about how unbelievably the fortunes had changed for both birds.

The hawk, in one graceful motion, landed on a bare limb in a dead poplar tree right next to me, just feet away from where I was perched.

He quickly tore off the chickadee's head with one movement of his powerful beak as he pinned the bird's body to the tree branch with his talons. He finished eating the chickadee in three more bites, tearing the small bird's flesh in morsel-size pieces and quickly devouring him. When he finished his meal, the hawk dropped down from his dinner perch and swiftly and silently moved on to another location. The whole event lasted less than a minute and then, the hawk also was gone, leaving only a Yooper deer hunter in the clearing.

Leonard Lee Rue III is one of my favorite wildlife photographers and writers. He also writes and does outstanding wildlife photography work for *Deer & Deer Hunting* magazine, one of my favorite magazines. Rue has written a great book, *Birds of Prey*, which I have in my wildlife library. He and other writers talk about the Cooper's Hawk as a woods hawk who can fly almost 60 miles an hour through the forest. This hawk haunts the forests, staying concealed in the heavy foliage and leaving the forest cover only to snatch a bird in an adjoining small opening out of thin air, usually with just one talon.

The big hawk I had seen did just that, and I got to see this rare life-and-death scenario play out in the forest at very close range.

In what seemed like a fraction of a second, I went from watching playful song birds peacefully feeding in a forest clearing to a dramatic death in the forest caused by a powerful predator. When life turned into death, the other song birds courageously scurried for cover as fast as they could, in a business-like fashion. As they fled the scene, I wondered whether they mourned the death of a companion. I also wondered whether they were thankful that the hawk had not selected them for his meal.

The hawk had probably watched the small birds feeding in the clearing from a nearby perch. He timed his powerful and graceful approach carefully, taking one of the many small birds for his evening meal.

The chickadees reacted to this incredible episode of violence and death by quickly moving on to another location. They left without one of their own who had the simple misfortune today of being in the wrong place at the wrong time. For the survivors, life would go on in another clearing somewhere in another part of this great forest.

As another hunter, it was hard for me to be angry at the hawk for killing the little bird.

After all, he did what was natural to him, what he had been taught to do and what he needed to do to survive in this rugged environment. He acted just as his ancestors have done for thousands of years.

What I witnessed in the forest opening that afternoon happens all the time, all day long and all night long. It is a very natural event. Death in the forest happens often and quickly, but many hunters and especially non-hunters, rarely, if ever, get to witness it as up close and personal as I did on this day.

While it was a bloody and gory sight to see what happened to this harmless, tiny chickadee, it is what nature is all about. It is the food chain at work, and it is the survival of the fittest.

In the forest, there are hunters and there are the hunted. There are predators and there are prey animals and birds.

And today, I felt privileged and honored to see another hunter, another efficient predator, at work. And I got to see him in an up close and personal way as I had never seen him before.

On this day, a Proud Yooper learned that sometimes in the wild, we can witness incredible acts of nature that involve everyday life and death situations. And on this

Life and Death in the Forest

day, a Proud Hunter learned that we always share the Yooper wilderness with other successful Proud Hunters of all kinds.

29

A Ten Day Hunt and Beginning QDM

Have patience.
All things change in due time.
Wishing can not bring autumn glory
or cause winter to cease.

-Ginaly-Li, Cherokee

In 1991, a huge change in my hunting tactics took place. Before the deer bow season began, my dad challenged me to an experiment that changed how I hunt and it changed my life.

In one of our frequent discussions about deer and deer hunting, my dad offered up that we should try a bold, new way of hunting.

"This year, let's make a pact that we will both pass up all the little bucks that we see and we won't shoot anything smaller than an eight or ten pointer," he suggested with a tone of seriousness.

I must have had a look of disbelief or skepticism because dad persisted in trying to convince me to try this new experiment.

"Look, we've killed lots of bucks the last few years, but almost all of them were small ones," he reasoned with me. "We're probably killing too many little bucks, and we're scaring off the bigger bucks, too. What do we have to lose by trying to shoot bigger bucks one year?"

After that analysis, I agreed that we might see bigger bucks if we let the little ones go.

I didn't know it at the time, but what we had agreed to do was a key component of a comprehensive deer management program called Quality Deer Management or QDM. We had not yet learned that there was a national organization called the Quality Deer Management Association (QDMA) that promoted the simple conservation practice we had discussed. At the time, the QDMA stood for many sound conservation principles, and its most famous slogan was "Let him go so he can grow!" The slogan meant that hunters should pass up small bucks so they could grow up into mature ones. With this program, the QDMA promoted using simple antler restrictions or other management techniques to reduce the excess harvest of young bucks, allowing a higher percent of younger bucks to grow up to maturity.

This simple challenge from my father was a defining moment in my life and one that would forever change how I would hunt and view the white-tailed deer.

Throughout that October's bow season, dad and I kept seeing signs of a big buck during our weekend trips to Hungry Hill, but we never saw the deer. We kept promising ourselves that there had to be one huge buck somewhere, and we thought we would see him soon.

A Ten Day Hunt and Beginning QDM

But as October wound down, I had only seen two bucks, one small spike and one six pointer. In accordance with our agreement, I had passed up both bucks. I let them go so they could grow up at least one more year.

As the month ended and the bucks were in rut, I was getting more frustrated because I had not yet seen the big buck – despite seeing the big tracks and rubs of a nice buck in our hunting area. Knowing that there was one nice buck in the area and not seeing him in a month of hunting had me feeling like a caged animal when I wasn't in the woods. While at work during the week, I couldn't wait to get back north to hunt for the big deer.

Finally, after helping my wife Susan hand out candy on Halloween night, I negotiated with her about heading back up to the UP. I told her I didn't want to return until I killed the big buck.

"I know I can kill that big buck if I can just get up there and totally concentrate on finding him," I reasoned with her. "I'd like to leave tonight and hunt until I kill him or ten days is up, whichever comes first."

"I understand," my wife said with the look I had become accustomed to in times like these. I knew I was pushing this, but the drive to get after that big buck was nagging at me like I was a possessed, crazy man. I counted my blessings that I was married to such an understanding woman.

My patient and understanding wife no doubt knew and accepted that she was married to a partially insane Yooper deer-hunting fanatic.

"Please call me every night to let me know you got out of the woods safely," she requested.

With that, I kissed her and told her to expect me in ten days unless I got lucky and brought her back a big buck early. I loaded up the 1975 Scout and headed the truck 300 miles north to Goetzville. I drove most of the night, but at the crack of dawn, on November 1, I was in Hungry Hill hoping to catch a glimpse of this mystery buck who had left so much sign in my territory.

For the next nine days, I hunted in the remote country of Hungry Hill, from daylight to dark, sitting in a portable tree stand all day long, in some of the most miserable weather I can remember.

It was snowy and cold most of those days, with harsh, unusual winter-like weather, something we didn't often have so early in November. That weather and those long days in the tree stand just made me that much more determined to hunt even harder.

After several days, however, I was literally exhausted from the long days in my tree stand and the cold temperatures and windy conditions. At the end of each day, I made the long walk out of Hungry Hill in the dark, and I made the long ride home to grandpa's house. Then I would make a supper for grandpa and me, and I would go directly to bed (after calling dad and Susan). Long before daylight, I would be up again so I could be in the tree stand before day break the next day.

Almost every day, I would see some sign of a huge deer in my area. Many times, he crossed near my stand, either just before I got there in the morning or some other time in the night after I had left the woods. I was so frustrated that I hadn't seen him anywhere, yet I felt like he was all around me. Did he know I was here? Had he seen me in my tree stand? Was he a nocturnal deer that would not come out in the daylight hours? Would I ever get even a glimpse of him? Was he a ghost?

Nine days into my ten-day stay, I was just about to give up and accept that I wouldn't see this mystery buck. But as it was getting dark, magic finally happened.

I was thinking about my hunt winding down when I heard a noise to my left. As I turned slowly, I immediately saw a huge rack of antlers on top of a very nice deer. There was no doubt this was one of the nicest deer I had ever seen. I thought he was a 12 point buck based on the look I had at him. The buck was coming along the ridge I was on, and it looked like he would walk right by me broadside.

As he stopped 28 yards away in the fading light, I drew my Jennings bow and sent an arrow toward him, hitting him just behind the shoulder, a little higher than I wanted. The deer actually went down when the arrow hit him, but he immediately bolted to the east, running along the edge of a marsh that I knew well.

I quickly got down out of the tree and went looking for signs of the hit. Almost immediately I found blood, and I began trailing the deer. For awhile, it was a good blood trail. I was confident that I would get the buck. I was pretty pumped up. Finally, all my persistence had paid off, and I would end up with a trophy buck – a buck worth waiting for and a buck worth passing up several smaller bucks.

Soon though, my excitement began to fade. The blood trail grew weaker, and I was having trouble tracking the deer even with snow on the ground. The buck quickly got to some major deer runways, and there were deer tracks all over. I had a tough job staying on him when he wasn't bleeding.

About a half mile from where I had shot him, the big buck had lain down, and I found some blood in his bed. It had taken me several hours to track him this far, and now my flashlights were on the verge of giving out. I was also getting concerned that grandpa would be worried that I was several hours late getting home. The buck was now headed into a thick cedar swamp, and I was confident he would lie down again and probably not get up from that bed if I left him alone over night.

All things considered, I decided to leave the deer and pick up the trail in the morning – the last morning of my ten-day hunt.

When a hunter wounds a deer, especially a nice buck like this one, it is an unsettling feeling to leave him in the woods or to give up on finding him. Because of these feelings, I had a hard time sleeping at all that night, and I couldn't wait for the alarm to go off so I could get back to the remote country of Hungry Hill to look for the big buck.

At daylight, I was closing in on where I had left off from tracking the buck the night before. But as I approached the area, I became concerned because I had cut several coyote tracks, and it looked like at least one coyote was tracking my deer.

I moved faster now, following the coyote tracks into the thick cedar swamp. In a typical eastern UP white cedar swamp, the thick cedars are the predominant vegetation and the terrain can be fairly wet. In some places, I was breaking through thin ice covering frozen water in the swamp. When I had gone about 100 more yards, I came to a small clearing among the cedars.

Here, I found a horrifying sight.

The snow in the clearing was completely covered in coyote tracks. There was bright red blood and hair from my deer everywhere. On the far end of the clearing was

A Ten Day Hunt and Beginning QDM

my beautiful buck. He had been killed in a savage fashion by a pack of hungry coyotes. All that remained of my magnificent buck was the bloody, red skeleton of his rib cage, his bare leg bones, about five inches of his neck and his head with an impressive set of antlers.

As I looked further around the clearing, I could see blood high up on one cedar tree on the outside of the clearing. It appeared that the coyotes had tracked my bleeding buck to this resting place of his. They may have found him while he was still alive, but he was in a weak condition from the wound to his shoulder and internal organs caused by my piercing arrow.

It looked as if he had put up one final stand by bracing himself against this big cedar tree, forcing the coyotes to attack him from only one direction where he had a chance to fight them off. Of course, I can't know for sure, but based on what it looked like, I imagined that the pack eventually wore him out and brought him down where they killed him and ate almost every ounce of meat on his body.

The pack of coyotes feasted and rested in this clearing all night until a lone hunter with a bow and arrow arrived at daylight to chase them away. These coyotes must have had an all-night party as if they were in coyote heaven. As I made my noisy approach, the well-fed and rested coyotes silently moved on to another part of the remote cedar swamp, content to sleep the rest of the day after gorging themselves all night on a gourmet treat of fresh venison.

As I pulled up the magnificent antlers of this beautiful animal, I proudly admired them as I thought hard about the horrible death I helped create for this deer. He was an 11 point mature whitetail, probably 4.5 years old or older. He wasn't a monster buck, but he had six-inch tines and a 15-inch spread. His one brow tine was split, giving him an extra point on his otherwise typical ten-point rack.

Had this deer not been wounded by my arrow, there is no way the pack of coyotes would have captured this healthy, big buck. He would have been more than capable of either running away from them or fighting them off with his antlers and hooves.

At first, I was angry at the coyotes, and I vowed to come back with my rifle. I wanted to wait for them to return so I could kill them like they had done to my buck.

Deep in the woods of Hungry Hill on a cold, crisp November morning, I had to accept that this Yooper hunter would have to share his trophy deer kill with the coyotes of the eastern UP.

My anger toward these other hunters had to be redirected. Deep down, I knew that these coyotes were hunters just like me. I knew they were doing what they were put on earth to do. They had killed a wounded animal that was in pain – an animal that was slowly dying. How could I be angry with them for doing what was so natural to them? How could I be angry at these coyotes because they got to this deer first and finished him off before I did?

I unpacked my camera and took a still photo of my buck, hiding from view, his ravaged, skeleton body as best I could. I tried to show only the antlers, his head, and what was left of his neck. Even in his ravaged state, he was a beautiful buck and I wanted to capture that picture. I wanted to remember him because I had never worked harder or hunted harder to kill a buck than I did for this one.

Proud Hunters Proud Yoopers

It was my last day of a long, hard ten-day hunt. Today, I had to go home, with or without the big buck of Hungry Hill. I would be going home with him, but not quite like I had dreamed about for weeks.

I couldn't help thinking about how incredible all of this was. I couldn't help thinking about what a terrible death it must have been for this beautiful deer I had pursued with so much passion. For years, this buck had eluded me and lived among these coyotes without any problems. All that changed with the flight of one arrow from a tree stand hunter.

Eventually, my coyote-ravaged buck would win the award for the biggest bow killed buck in the Soo Sportman's Club annual big buck contest. He would also qualify for an award and listing in the Commemorative Bucks of Michigan Big Game Records Book.

As I started the long, 300-mile drive home that night, I thought hard about the QDM "rules" dad and I had agreed to follow early in the season. We had a pact that we would let the little bucks go and wait for an older buck. I thought about the two deer I had passed up earlier in the season to wait for this great buck.

All these emotions made me reflect about what it means to be a hunter and to be the hunted in the land of the Yooper. The feelings I experienced made me appreciate my trophy all the more. I vowed that no matter how long I hunted or how many big bucks I killed, this buck would remain one of my most respected and honored trophies.

On this day, a Proud Yooper learned that sometimes Proud Hunters share their best trophies with the coyotes or "brush wolves" of the UP. And, on this day, a Proud Hunter recognized and accepted the life-changing experience of letting young bucks go while patiently pursuing mature Yooper bucks.

30

A Second QDM Buck

Free yourself from negative influence.
Negative thoughts are the old habits
that gnaw at the roots of the soul.

- Moses Shongo, Seneca

After retrieving my 11 point buck from the coyotes on Nov. 10, 1991, I returned home, driving 300 miles south to Holt, Michigan, where I waited out the next four days until the beginning of rifle season. I occupied my mind by working hard those four days, all the time secretly wanting to be back at Hungry Hill sitting in a tree stand.

I had another chance for a buck because Michigan's rifle season was about to start, and I could take any buck with three-inch spikes or bigger under Michigan's law. Four days after finding my 11 pointer, I was back in the Scout, driving 300 miles north to Goetzville for the Nov. 15th firearms opener.

Dad and I would hunt on the snowmobile trail where we watched for deer to cross the trail going north or south. We could each see almost 200 yards in one direction. Together, we were covering about a quarter mile of this stretch of the Hungry Hill wilderness.

As we drove in the darkness from grandpa's house on opening morning, dad wanted to make sure I was still going to live up to our pledge to let the little bucks go. After all, in his view, our plan was working.

"Now you're still going to look for a big buck, aren't you?" he asked me in a tone that gave a hint of what my answer should be.

"Dad, I'll see how it goes the first day," I hedged. "Even though I got a nice buck, the odds are good that he's the only big buck in the area. Besides, I didn't get any venison from him – the coyotes took it all. If I see a small buck, I might take him so I have some venison."

Dad accepted this, but I could tell he wasn't in total agreement.

"You might still see a big buck if you are patient," dad cautioned me. "I wish you would hold out for awhile and wait for another big guy. Why don't you wait and shoot one bigger than the buck you got with the bow?"

"Dad," I complained, "There won't be another buck bigger than the one I got. He's the mature buck around here, and it's really unlikely that there will be one bigger. Heck, the one I got is one of the biggest we've killed here."

I was arguing hard for the right to kill a smaller buck.

"Are you sure you don't have a good chance to see another big buck?" dad said with a gleam in his eye and slowly showing a big grin.

Proud Hunters Proud Yoopers

I knew my dad too well to not know something was up. "OK," I said. "Tell me the rest of the story."

"Well," dad said slowly. "I was out two days ago, and I saw another huge, lone track crossing between our two rifle seats. I think there is another big buck running around here somewhere."

"Wow, that sounds promising," I admitted. I thought about this development, and I reasoned that it wouldn't hurt me too much to let a few more small bucks go. After all, I already did have a great season, no matter what happened in rifle season.

"OK, I'll try and be patient for awhile this morning and see how things go. I'll let the little ones walk away, and I'll wait for a bigger one for a few hours," I committed reluctantly.

"Good," said dad. "Keep your eyes open, because we are going to see that big guy somewhere. I just hope we see him before someone else does."

Long before daybreak, we were hiking to our Hungry Hill rifle seats. It was a beautiful morning, quiet and peaceful, a perfect morning for an opener.

There were still close to 2 million deer in Michigan, and the UP was also loaded with deer. As the morning moved on, there were quite a few shots around me, and I surmised that lots of Prentiss Bay hunters were taking deer.

By mid morning, I had seen lots of deer, and three small bucks had walked by me. I could have shot any one of them, and I was tempted to take one. They all looked like healthy, chunky deer for being 1.5 year old bucks. Any one of them would have been good-eating venison.

In the next couple of hours, I didn't see any bucks. There had been several shots close to me earlier in the morning near the time I saw the three bucks. I imagined that those bucks that I had passed up were now dead, belonging to other hunters.

I took a break and walked 300 yards to dad's seat on the snowmobile trail. Dad hadn't shot yet, but he had heard the other shots too, and he told me he had also passed up two small bucks.

"We are wasting good venison, Dad," I teased him. "We could have several deer to hang on the meat pole tonight if we'd shot those little ones."

Dad was sympathetic, but he urged me to stay the course. "We've come this far with letting those little bucks go, and it's worked out because you already got a buck bigger than we usually kill. Let's be patient, and maybe we'll see another big one."

"I want to have some venison, and guys are killing little bucks all around me," I reported to him. "I'm going to kill the next little buck I see and fill my tag."

"I wish you would just hang in there a little longer," he encouraged me. "It's still early in the season."

After our update, I walked back quietly to my stand, thinking about my conversation with dad. Maybe he was right. Maybe I still should wait for a bigger buck.

The more I thought about it, the more determined I was that I was going to shoot the next little buck that walked by, no matter how small he was. I thought I had better get something before other hunters killed all the little bucks on Hungry Hill.

For the next two hours, I didn't see another deer. That made me all the more determined to kill the next small buck I saw. As time wore on, I reinforced to myself that I should have shot one of the small bucks I had seen in the morning. As I ate my

A Second QDM Buck

sandwich for lunch, I vowed to myself that I would shoot a little buck, if I were fortunate enough to see one.

I had now abandoned my promise that I made to dad early in the season. I felt guilty about this because dad seemed so determined that we should still hold out for a bigger buck.

In addition to watching the snowmobile trail, I was also watching a small opening in the brush 100 yards behind my seat in fairly heavy cover. Deer passed through that opening when they were traveling parallel with the snowmobile trail. To sweeten up the odds of seeing a deer in this opening, I had dumped some apples there near a large, burned out old stump, a relic from the old forest fires decades ago.

As I was finishing up my lunch around 1 pm, I looked behind me at the hidden clearing. I could see a large deer with a big rack of antlers coming to the opening. At first I didn't think he was going to stop. I thought he was scent checking the area for does that may have visited the apples. Initially, he looked like he was on the move looking for does in heat. But as he came close to my opening, he walked right up to the big stump, and he began munching on the apples.

I quickly raised my Remington .30/06 rifle and checked him out in the scope.

Unbelievably, he looked even bigger than the 11 pointer I had killed with the bow five days ago.

I immediately put the crosshairs on his shoulder and touched off a shot. At the sound of gunfire, he went right down like he was hit with a ton of bricks.

As I raced up to him, I could see his antlers clearly. He had longer tines that the 11 pointer, but it looked as if he had fewer tines. It also looked as if he had a larger spread.

Wow, I thought to myself, he is bigger than the other buck.

Just as I got to him and held up his antlers, I heard dad yelling, "Did you get him?"

He was on the snowmobile trail, near my stand and he couldn't see where I was. I stood up and yelled to him. He started down the trail toward me as I continued to admire this beautiful buck. Of course, I was thinking about how determined I had been that I should kill a small buck if one came along.

And, I was also thinking about how dad had insisted I might still see a bigger buck, even one bigger than my eleven-point bow kill. I had dismissed those odds as unlikely, and yet it happened.

As dad got close to me, he was smiling from ear to ear and his first words were, "I told you we'd see another big buck. Guess your old man knows a few things about deer, ha?"

We took some pictures, and I told dad how I had been ready to shoot the first little buck I saw.

I told him how easy it had been to kill this nice buck compared to how grueling it had been to get the eleven-pointer in bow season.

What a year. Two dandy bucks in five days, and I took them in two completely different ways. One came incredibly easy, and the other took so much work and effort. Even so, I was proud of both of them.

It was a great season. My rifle killed nine-pointer with seven-inch tines and a 16-inch spread just missed making the CBM record book, but he was a very nice buck nonetheless.

Proud Hunters Proud Yoopers

At the end of this season, I was a believer that there was something to this plan dad had about letting little bucks go and restricting our harvest to older, more mature bucks with bigger racks.

At the time, we didn't know anything about the Quality Deer Management Association or the practice of QDM, but we had now experienced its magic, and that would forever change my hunting practices, my views on deer management and the rest of my life.

In years following this experience, I would begin a search to read everything I could on deer management practices. One of the first books I read was *Producing Quality Whitetails* by Al Brothers and Murphy E. Ray, Jr. This is a classic deer management book first produced in 1975 and now in its third 1997 printing. A second great book was the 1995 edition of *Quality Whitetails – The Why and How of Quality Deer Management,* edited by University of Georgia wildlife biologist professors and researchers, Drs. Karl V. Miller and R. Larry Marchinton. The book includes research material by the UP's John Ozoga. Third, I read and really enjoyed a 1994 book, *A Practical Guide to Producing and Harvesting White-tailed Deer,* by Dr. James C. Kroll. A Texas-based researcher, Kroll would become a deer management consultant to many Michigan clients and a frequent speaker at Michigan deer management events.

From these classical books about quality deer management, I learned about the magic of these simple conservation principles and their profound impact on our deer herds and our deer hunting experiences.

These great books also confirmed for me the wisdom of the simple principle my father had encouraged me to experiment with in this landmark deer season.

On this day, a Proud Hunter vowed that from then on, he would do everything in his power to educate other Proud Yoopers about how much more fun hunting could be if we practiced QDM throughout the UP. On this day, a Proud Hunter also learned how much better our deer herd would be if we let more little bucks go so they could grow up to be mature Yooper bucks.

31

Surrounded by Coyotes in the Dark

The antelope have gone;
The buffalo wallows are empty.
Only the wail of the
coyote is heard.

-Chief Plenty-Coups, Crow

In early November, 1993, I was bow hunting deep in Hungry Hill country, about as far away from civilization as I could get. Dad and I had found this hot spot where a large white pine tree stood tall on the end of a ridge. Deer runways crisscrossed just south of the tree where the deer traveled the ridge.

I loved this place because I saw plenty of deer here, and I had taken a number of them, both bucks and does. All the time I had hunted here, I had never seen another hunter – a rare occurrence during hunting season, especially on state land.

On this nice day in November, I had not seen a deer, but near dark, I heard one moving in my area as I was preparing to leave. I stayed in my tree stand until long after dark and until I could no longer hear any movement. I did this so that I wouldn't spook any deer.

As I started the long walk out to my Scout, the temperature started to drop dramatically. There was no cloud cover, and I could feel the cold air thermals as I hiked along the trail.

I had a flashlight with me to guide my way, but the light was dim from weak batteries.

I was about half way back to the truck when I hit one of my ridges where I hunted with the rifle. As I approached an opening on this ridge, I paused to catch my breath. While taking a short break, I looked up at the sky, and I felt the cold temperature against my warm and perspiring body. It felt good to rest and cool down. In the opening now, I could see the rough outline of the ridge in the moonlight, and it was quite a sight.

Suddenly, off to my right, just a short distance away, I heard a coyote howl loudly. I stood perfectly still wondering if he knew I was here. Was he howling at me? Was he howling for another coyote? Was he trying to warn another coyote?

Right away, another coyote with a distinctly different tone howled just like the first one. This coyote was also very close, but it was to my left and behind me.

By now, the hair on the back of my neck had to be standing straight up. I was really on edge, being this close to not one, but two coyotes, in the darkness and with the dancing shadows of the moonlit night.

135

Proud Hunters Proud Yoopers

Just when I thought it couldn't get any scarier, I heard a third coyote howl out in front of me. By the tone of his howl, I was sure he was a different coyote than the first two.

All of a sudden, it occurred to me that I was surrounded by three coyotes, and all of them were close to me, closer than I had probably ever been to three coyotes before.

It was a bone-chilling and hair-raising event unlike anything else I had ever experienced.

Now, I was on full alert, waiting to see what would happen next. Would the coyotes attack me? I'd never heard of that happening before, but gosh, these wild dogs were really close.

I grabbed my Buck hunting knife in my right hand, and I removed an arrow from the quiver on the bow that I clenched in my left hand. I waited on this ridge where there was some light from the moon for about five minutes.

For the first minute, I thought I might have a run-in with one of the coyotes. For this minute, I thought I might be the hunted and not the hunter.

Visions ran through my head that the coyotes might slowly move in on me, surrounding me before they attacked. I imagined that one coyote might just appear out of nowhere and pounce on me, with the others joining him as he took me to the ground.

After the first minute had passed, I began to relax, believing that my worry about danger was all for naught. For the next few minutes, I never saw or heard a single sound. The woods were incredibly still and quiet, and I didn't move a muscle. The coyotes never appeared, and I made the rest of the hike back to the truck in an uneventful manner. Somehow, those coyotes disappeared into the still of the night just as quickly as they had stumbled unto me.

I love to hear coyotes calling. I've heard their legendary howling, barking and yelping hundreds of times over the decades I've hunted in the UP, and I never get tired of hearing their music. Each time is special, and each time I get a chill thinking about this group of wild dogs gathering together and starting their evening hunt.

I always believed their classic howling just before dark was an eerie warning to the small game animals and deer in the woods that the coyotes were beginning their evening hunt. It has always seemed to me that when coyotes begin this howling, they are taunting the other game animals in the forest with a "look out, we are coming to get you" warning.

On this night, when I was surrounded, the reality is that the coyotes were probably hunting rabbits in the lowlands around both sides of the ridge. I just happened to get between them. I probably startled one of them, and he howled as a warning to the others. In any event, they quickly moved away, avoiding contact with the Yooper bow hunter.

On this night, a Proud Yooper learned that we don't have to fear coyotes because they would never attack a human hunter under normal circumstances. And on this night, a Proud Hunter learned that sometimes we can feel as if we are the one being hunted when we are surrounded by coyotes in the dark, and that is an incredible Yooper experience.

32

To Bait or Not to Bait

*Do not judge your neighbor until
you walk two moons in his moccasins.*

- Northern Cheyenne proverb

In the late 1970s, we were hunting the Hungry Hill area hard and having moderate success. In those days, we did not use deer bait of any kind. We simply watched deer runways and places where we had historically seen bucks chasing a doe. Like many experienced and deer-savvy hunters, we often sat near places where bucks had rubbed their antlers or made scrapes.

In other words, we really had to hunt to see deer. We had to understand their habits and the motivation for their movements. To kill a deer, we had to find a way to intercept them when they were traveling from point A to point B.

In fact, most other eastern UP hunters also did not bait for deer in either the bow or rifle season. While a few hunters who owned land talked about limited baiting at their camps, only a very few hunters we knew bothered to bait for deer on state land.

The hunting was still great fun as long as you had realistic expectations and you were patient. In these remote parts of the UP where we hunted, we didn't often see lots of deer and getting close to one with a bow was a real challenge.

After deer hunting in the UP for ten years, my personal goal in the 1970s was to get within 20 yards of two deer a year with my bow. If that happened, I was confident that I could kill one of those two deer using archery equipment of that time period. That was my expectation based on hunting between eight and ten days a year in a typical bow season.

In rifle season, I hoped that I could see one buck within rifle range. I would put in about seven days hunting in rifle season, usually watching a different place than where I had bow hunted. If I saw a buck within rifle range, I could usually get him.

If one of these two modest goals was achieved, odds were good I could put my tag on a deer during the season. In those days, you were considered lucky if you periodically got a buck with either your rifle or bow. If you got a deer on regular basis, you were considered a pretty darn good hunter.

Compared to what hunters expect today when they buy a license, our goals in those days were humble. Today, hunters expect to see ten to twenty deer every time they go out. Many of them sit in a heated, wooden blind overlooking a regularly stocked bait pile. Because of these changes in expectations and hunting methods, some of our young hunters have little or no idea of how to watch a scrape line or find a runway coming out of a bedding area.

Proud Hunters Proud Yoopers

As the size of Michigan's deer herd exploded in the 1980s to over 2 million deer, so did baiting. With an increasing reliance on baiting, hunters lost the incentive to learn about natural deer movements. As a result, too many of today's hunters only know that if you put out a 50 pound bag of sugar beets or carrots (that you buy at the local gas station), the deer will come to you.

In short, we have a whole generation of new "hunters" who really don't know how to hunt.

James A. Lahde, Ph.D., is one of the UP's most eloquent spokespersons on this issue. In 1998, Jim wrote a provocative book called "*Dumbing Down Deer Hunting*," which was published by the Woodcock Press of Rock, Michigan. Jim is a founding member of the UP's Superior Deer Management association, and he's been one of the strongest champions in the UP for quality deer management principles.

In his book, Jim traces how we got into deer baiting, and he chastises the DNR for allowing it to happen. He also challenges hunters to end the practice and restore more ethical standards to our hunting methods.

One of the practical barriers to reducing baiting is that Michigan's agricultural and retail industries are also impacted by this huge increase in baiting. Today, Michigan hunters spend millions of dollars on $5 bags of carrots, sugar beets and corn. Michigan's agricultural industry, the third most important industry and employer in the state, distributes these deer feed products to thousands of Michigan gas stations and other retail outlets all over the state. There is tremendous profit to farmers and retail store owners in these bags of deer bait. It's become such big business that there's great pressure now from agricultural and retail lobbyists to keep the practices in place.

The state of Michigan charges the seven-person NRC board with establishing policies to properly manage our precious natural resources like our deer herd. The NRC, in carrying out its policy role, gives guidance to our DNR staff on the actual management of our deer herd and other natural resource issues.

Michigan's Governor appoints the commissioners to serve on the NRC. Over the last ten years, some of the DNR's top biologists have told the NRC that they should ban deer baiting throughout the state because the practice is not biologically sound. When hunters use significant amounts of bait in the same area, deer have extraordinarily higher odds of making contact with body fluids of other deer. This contact allows deer to pass communicable diseases between the animals.

Some experts believe it was this nose-to-nose contact among deer, as they fed at large baiting sites in northeast Lower Michigan, which led to deer contracting and spreading tuberculosis (TB) among the deer herd. When that happened, the NRC did stop baiting in several counties in this part of the state, and it reduced the amount of bait hunters could use statewide. The NRC, however, under what many believed was intense pressure from agricultural and retail interests, refused to totally ban baiting in other parts of the state.

One DNR biologist from the central UP, Terry Minzey, told me that he believes baiting should also be stopped because it has made Yooper hunters too efficient, allowing us to kill too many yearling bucks. One year, while I volunteered at the Mackinac Bridge DNR deer-check station checking the age of deer killed by successful hunters, Terry told me how we could kill two birds with one stone by stopping deer baiting.

To Bait or Not to Bait

"We give hunters three months to kill deer in this state, and, in most parts, hunters attract deer to the same location by baiting every day," he said. "I think our hunters have become so efficient with baiting, that we are killing many of the yearling bucks. With baiting, eventually, hunters will kill a young buck if he's in the area."

Because of my interest in QDM and passing up yearling bucks, Terry also told me that we would be saving more yearling bucks if we didn't allow baiting. "Many more yearlings would live to become two-year-old bucks without baiting, giving us many of the same QDM benefits without mandating antler restrictions," Terry said one afternoon as we measured antlers and aged the teeth of dead deer, with the beautiful Mackinac Bridge in the background.

I thought long and hard about what Terry had told me. Even though we didn't agree entirely on the benefits of mandatory antler restriction programs, I admired him as a knowledgeable and practical DNR biologist – a guy with common sense. I also liked him because he ran one of the largest deer satisfaction surveys throughout the eastern UP. Each year, he polled a number of hunting camps, including ours, on hunter success and satisfaction with the season. He used the data from the survey as one factor for recommending hunting season changes the following season.

I thought odds were good that Terry was right. We could reduce the number of yearling bucks killed and increase the number of older bucks in the herd if we stopped baiting. I thought this was especially true in the UP where we were so efficient and effective with baiting.

Our own early experiences with deer baiting may have been similar to how many Yoopers got into baiting. We weren't baiting at all when something unusual happened that changed our views on the issue. For us, that big change happened rather dramatically during a season in the late 1970s.

By the middle of the rifle season, we had not seen any deer at all – not a single one, even though we were hunting in the same old places that had produced for us for years. For some reason, it seemed as if the deer had just plain vanished from our area.

At the same time, a group of hunters we knew well were hunting just north of us. While they were only about a mile from us, they were seeing lots of deer and one of their hunters even openly bragged about killing three bucks from one seat when the limit was only one buck per year.

All of this was a mystery to dad, and when the hunters to our north were not in the woods one day, he suggested that we hike to where these guys hunted. Dad thought we should snoop around to see if we could find out why we weren't seeing any deer and why these guys were killing lots of bucks.

When we were near the Bedsprings area, dad found where one of the hunters had been sitting. He also found the gut piles of two recently killed bucks. When we examined the stomachs of the deer, we found that they were filled with wheat.

Dad was baffled by this development. He knew there wasn't a farmer's field within five miles of this remote place and there were no wheat fields that we knew of for more than 10 miles. These deer hadn't filled their bellies with wheat from a farm field – someone close by had to be feeding them.

We were pretty sure the other lucky hunters weren't hauling in huge quantities of wheat to use for bait. As a result, we made a wide, exploratory circle in the dense woods. Just west of where the dead deer were killed, we found a 50-gallon barrel in the middle of a small clearing that was filled with wheat. Someone had carefully cut holes in the bottom of the barrel, and wheat was freely falling out of the feeder as deer ate it.

While this wouldn't be an unusual finding today, in the 1970s, it was something we had never seen before. We were stunned that someone had made the effort to haul all this wheat and the custom-made grain feeder way back in the bush.

We also saw the results that this determined hunter and other nearby hunters had experienced. It appeared to us they had drawn all the deer from our area and concentrated them in this area. They saw and killed lots of bucks at the same time when we couldn't see a single deer.

The next year, we vowed that we would put out a small amount of bait to counteract this effort that had enticed the deer in our area to abandon their core area for a neighboring place with an easy food source. Early in bow season, dad and I each backpacked into Hungry Hill shouldering 50-pound packs of apples we had picked from a tree in the Sault. We called our effort "defensive baiting," and we promised ourselves we would put out just a small amount of bait in several areas to see if it would hold the deer in our area.

Our results were rather impressive. Right away, we started seeing far more deer, and we saw some nice bucks. My former goal of getting close to two deer a year was blown right out of the water. With our defensive baiting, I was seeing lots of deer at close range, and I was getting really good at killing them with a bow.

Somewhere along the line, we probably changed from "defensive" baiting to "offensive" baiting. And somewhere along the line, my views on baiting started to change.

I was now seeing lots more deer at close range and I had chances to observe deer behavior by as much as a tenfold increase. When I took a shot at a deer with a bow, it was a very good shot, and so I rarely wounded a deer. With the bait in place, I had time to wait for an almost perfect shot. If the shot was not a perfect shot, I waited, knowing that if I didn't get the deer this time, he would be back another time. Many of my kills were very clean kills, with arrows driven right through both lungs. The deer almost always died with 100 yards of my stand, and they were easy to find.

With baiting, archery season now became a very good time to take a deer. Our success rate shot up dramatically.

The baiting worked so well that dad and I put out more bait every weekend from early September to the end of rifle season. During the week, usually on Thursday nights, dad made a special trip alone to Hungry Hill to freshen up the baits so that there would be feed at our bow stands when I came up on Friday night for the weekend hunt.

We also noted that our deer were getting bigger and fatter. Each deer we harvested in late October or November now had a significant amount of fat on it. We knew that was good because deer need those fat deposits to make it through the harsh UP winters. It appeared to us that baiting helped better prepare the deer to withstand the hardship of winter.

Most important though, is that the baiting kept deer in the area. We had now neutralized the impact others had by baiting nearby. They could no longer draw all the deer away from us. Deer now hung around our deer seats all season long because they had a steady food source.

To Bait or Not to Bait

It is hard to describe just how much more fun this made the hunting for us. Not only were we seeing more deer, getting more shots at deer and killing more deer, but we were also getting much more time to observe deer behavior. With the bait near our bow seats, we had hundreds of chances to watch deer interact with each other. We could see deer fight with each other and assert their dominance or social order over other deer. We got to see how deer approached the bait so cautiously, looking, smelling and listening for danger signs. We also got to see bucks spar with each other and make scrapes and rub trees to mark their territory near the bait sites.

Some of my hunting friends, however, were not so enamored with all this emphasis on baiting. Like Jim Ladhe, they questioned how sportsman-like it was to watch for deer over artificial bait.

Because I was now living in lower Michigan, I had a few opportunities to hunt in places other than the UP. A co-worker at the Auditor General's Office where I worked offered me a chance to hunt on his large farm in the Ionia area. When I first got to the farm, I noticed that there were well-worn deer trails all along the edge of a large corn field. That night, my first hunt ever in Ionia County, I arrowed a nice eight-pointer that walked by me on the edge of that corn field.

I thought a lot about how I got that nice buck. I didn't have any bait, but I shot him as he traveled toward one of the most unnatural, man-made food sources in the area. This huge corn field was a major food attraction for deer, and it was completely unnatural. I thought it was funny that no one claimed this was a form of baiting.

A year later, I got invited to hunt with friends of dad's on public land in northern Lake County near Irons, Michigan, in northwest Lower Michigan. In the evening, we went to a heavily forested area that surrounded a clover food plot the DNR had cleared and planted. I was amazed at the incredible deer runways that were coming from the woods to that field. There were also dozens of hunters crowding each other out, trying to sit with their bows where they could watch those runways. There were almost fistfights among some hunters over who was going to sit at sites that were deemed the most likely for deer to use.

As darkness approached, there were deer running everywhere, trying to get to that field to feed. I didn't get any shots at deer, but I saw lots of deer, and I heard even more. I was impressed with how many deer were attracted to this spot. Several hunters, including one in our party, killed deer that night.

I didn't really enjoy the hunt as much as I could have because there were too many hunters hunting in a small area and there was a form of competition among the different hunters. Some of them defended the places they wanted to watch with a vengeance, physically threatening those who crowded them. The experience made me appreciate hunting in the UP all the more.

On the way home, I thought about how unnatural that field was in the middle of that big forest. Man had cleared the land and planted special food sources to increase the chances that deer would use that field during hunting season. Yet, no one complained that this field was a form of baiting.

When I returned to the Lansing area, just for fun, I challenged my friends to explain how much different it is to hunt over a food plot or a corn field in the lower peninsula than it is to hunt over a small amount of bait in the UP.

Proud Hunters Proud Yoopers

"Don't they all attract deer to the area using an unnatural food source?" I asked my good friend Mike Jackson of Dewitt, Michigan. "Hasn't Man been hunting animals over bait since the Stone Age?"

Of course, I was kidding Mike, but he got defensive just the same.

"Leon, it's not the same thing," Mike insisted. "I've killed my last deer over bait, and you should do the same thing."

Just to tease him, I proudly told Mike that I wasn't the baiting purist that he was and that I would keep baiting deer with small amounts of feed as long as it was legal. I also told him that I'd hunt over non-baited locations too, just to meet his approval.

And each year, thousands of other Yoopers do the same thing.

As the years passed and I began doing more work with the QDMA, I learned much more about land management for wildlife, including food plots, timber management and other techniques for attracting and helping wildlife. I hope that someday, these techniques will increase in popularity, minimizing the need or desire for the intensive deer baiting that is commonly practiced in Michigan today.

In late August 2008, the DNR found a positive case of Chronic Wasting Disease (CWD) in a Kent County deer raised on a deer farm inside a fenced hunting enclosure. This was the first confirmed case of the dreaded CWD in the state of Michigan. To prevent further spread of the disease, the NRC and DNR immediately implemented a deer-baiting ban in the entire Lower Peninsula. For the first time in decades, lower Michigan hunters would have to go through a full hunting season without any baiting.

At QDMA, our national association and our State Chapter in Michigan both supported the NRC and the DNR in this difficult decision. Some hunters, businesses and farmers were angry with the baiting ban and they lobbied hard to overturn the decision. These parties argued in the press, with legislators and in court that the action was harsher than it needed to be to adequately protect Michigan's deer herd. As we go to press with this book, hunters are still split over how to manage this issue.

Over the years, a Proud Yooper learned that Proud Hunters both love and hate deer baiting and the controversy over its ethics and its future rages on even among good friends and even among Proud Yoopers in the same deer camp.

33

Sometimes Big Ones Get Away

It is not good for people to have an easy life.
They become weak and inefficient
when they cease to struggle.

- Victorio, Mimbres Apache

Sometimes the best hunting adventures in the UP wilderness involve events where the trophy animal gets away and no animals are harmed, except maybe the pride of the hunter. That's happened to me more times than I can remember. These adventures are some of my favorites, and they are, in part, why I still have such a strong desire to hunt.

One of the first chances I ever had to kill a huge buck occurred on October 20, 1984. I was hunting by myself in Hungry Hill between two big marshes. I had selected a large white pine tree for my bow seat. In those days, we didn't even own a commercial tree stand, so I was actually sitting on a limb of the tree, 15 feet off the ground, resting my back against the trunk of the tree. The only improvement I had made was to cut a few twigs so I had two clear shooting lanes.

The set up was a far cry from the elaborate portable tree stands we have today, and yet it was much better than hunting from a ground blind that we often used in those days. While this arrangement was crude by today's standards, I actually thought the spot was pretty comfortable, and I had a great view of the surrounding countryside.

For the first two weeks of the season, I baited the area with apples I placed about 20 yards from the tree. Deer had found this food source, and the apples were gone when I got to the seat on this sunny, but very windy day.

I had not seen a single deer from this seat, and today didn't look like a good day either. I knew from my hunting experiences over the years that deer didn't like to move on really windy days, and the wind had blown hard all morning. At exactly 10 am, after three hours of sitting on a hard limb five yards up a big tree, I decided to call it quits.

That's when I heard a faint sound to my right as I was about to exit the tree. When I looked that way, I saw a beautiful 10 pointer with huge tines walking parallel to my seat, roughly 30 yards to the south. In all my years of hunting, this was the biggest buck I had ever seen this close.

My heart was pumping rapidly, and I starting breathing hard with excitement. "Wow, that's a great buck, and I've got to get him if he comes closer," I thought to myself.

Just when I thought it couldn't get any more exciting, the big buck stopped near a small balsam fir tree, lowered his head, and starting rubbing his antlers on the bark of the tree. He rubbed for about one minute, and then he pawed at the ground right near the base of the rubbed tree. He also seemed to bite or chew on the balsam branch near his eye level.

For the first time in my hunting career, I was witnessing one of the greatest sights a white-tailed deer hunter can experience. I watched the big buck mark his territory with an antler rub, and I also saw him leave a scented scrape for other deer. Incredibly, I had one of the best seats in the house to view this fascinating act of deer behavior that few hunters get to see.

It was a show that lasted several minutes in total. When the buck was done, he made a bee-line for the apples I had right in front of me. My heart was really pounding now because it looked as if the buck would walk right by me, giving me a broadside shot at about 15-20 yards. I thought I was in the perfect spot to kill this great buck.

As the buck got closer, I made a costly and rookie mistake. At the time, I hadn't killed many bucks, and I was still learning the ropes on killing deer with a bow. While the buck walked toward me, I raised my bow so I would be ready to shoot. Unfortunately for me, the deer saw this movement. He stopped dead in his tracks, focusing all his attention on the dark object sitting 15 feet up in the big pine.

As he watched me, I tried to remain perfectly still, praying hard that he would calm down and continue on his trek toward the apples. The big buck, however, was too concerned about the unnatural figure perched in the tree. He actually started to walk away backwards from his dangerous location. All the while, he never took his eyes off me. Then, he quickly turned 180 degrees, and he took off, snorting loudly at me as he jumped his way to the safety of the heavy cover. In several seconds, he was gone. I was left cursing at myself, thinking about what had just happened.

I had made a classic bow hunting mistake by moving before I was ready to shoot and moving while the deer could detect my movement. Had I waited for him to take a few more steps, I would have been ready to shoot, and he would not have seen my movement.

This was a painful lesson, but one that was a powerful teacher.

That night, I couldn't wait to tell dad about the big buck and my experience. We continued to hunt that spot hard and several other spots nearby, but we never saw the big buck again. I also never heard about anyone else ever killing him.

Following that experience, dad and I talked a lot about how big bucks rarely make mistakes. When they do, they rarely repeat the same mistake. We talked about the mistakes that hunters make too, and we talked about learning from them so we don't repeat them.

On Christmas Day, 1985, dad called me in the evening. He had hunted in the afternoon in the Gogemain, and he had seen three bucks, including one that he said was a ten-point monster. "He's got really big tines," dad told me over the phone. "You need to get up here as soon as possible so we get a crack at him."

I needed to work a few days after Christmas, but by Dec. 28, I was in the UP, hiking into the Gogemain to hunt for the big brute. Dad explained there had been some heavy snowfall and cold temperatures, forcing deer to migrate to the Gogemain sooner than they had in prior years. "There are deer everywhere," dad told me. "Come prepared for an exciting hunt."

Sometimes Big Ones Get Away

I had selected a stand in a big white spruce tree about a mile into the Gogemain, some two hundred yards from where dad had seen the big buck. I was confident he was probably using a heavily-used deer trail near my stand.

The first day, I had about 20 does and fawns come by my stand, just south of me. Near the end of the day, several more deer came through. The last one was the big buck. He was too far to shoot as he followed another runway through the heavy brush, just north of my seat. From my vantage point, it appeared he was a heavy-beamed buck with a big body. I guessed he was a 10 pointer. I was sure that he was the buck dad had seen.

For the next three days, I hunted for him morning and evening in sub-zero degree temperatures. I returned to the warmth of grandpa's house only at noon time and only for a brief break. While I saw lots of deer, I never saw the big buck again until the last day of the season, New Year's Day, January 1st. Dad had joined me for this hunt after working through the Christmas holidays.

At 11 am, on the first day of the calendar year, I was about to pack up and return to grandpa's for lunch with dad, when I heard a noise behind me. I turned to see three antlerless deer approaching me. The first deer was a large, muscular doe, followed by a young button buck fawn. The third deer, trailing the other two, was a huge-bodied deer that looked about one-and-a-half times again as big as the large doe. As this deer walked almost right under my tree stand, I saw two big, bloodied holes on the top of his head.

I immediately knew what this meant. The big buck that I had pursued so intensely had dropped his antlers for the season, probably in the last few hours, and maybe in the last few minutes. Those two large, red blood spots on his head used to hold his magnificent antlers.

As the big deer walked by me, it was tempting to shoot him with my bow, but I passed up the shot. Somehow, it didn't seem right or appropriate to end the life of this beautiful animal after he had survived another season and right after he had lost his antlers. With a reflective pause, I let him walk away to face another winter and hopefully another full year of life as a mature whitetail buck.

At the moment, I hoped that I would see him again next year in Michigan's late season archery hunt. I imagined how huge his antlers would be in another year. He would be a trophy that any Michigan hunter would be proud of.

Well, I never saw the big buck again - not in the fall and not in the next late archery season. He simply vanished from the Gogemain, and I never learned his fate. But I have always believed that some lucky eastern UP hunter killed the buck of a lifetime the next fall. And I always felt good about the small role I may have played in making that happen.

The next spring, dad found the left shed of the buck just 100 yards from my bow seat, right on the runway where the big buck had walked by me. We looked everywhere for the matching shed and could not find it. Later that fall, I found the other matching shed just 50 yards from where we had found the first one. A mouse had chewed on part of the antler beam, but otherwise, it looked identical to the other side. Even more strange, I found a smaller eight-point shed from the same buck (probably from the prior year) another 100 yards away under a spruce tree. The shed had the identical markings and unique, but smaller tines than the big sheds had.

145

Proud Hunters Proud Yoopers

At the time, this was the nicest set of sheds we had ever found. It appears the buck may have dropped the antlers just out of my sight on the last day of the late bow season. He was a perfectly symmetrical 10 pointer with high tines, and he was likely a 4.5-year-old buck or older, an old dominant buck of the UP forest.

Two years later, in late December, dad had been hunting in the Gogemain again, much deeper and further from the road. He had seen another huge buck, this one a 12 pointer, but not quite the impressive rack of the big 10 pointer. Dad had passed up a less than perfect shot to wait for another chance at the buck.

While dad worked the busy Christmas season in our sporting goods store, he urged me to get up north and hunt for the big 12 pointer. "Just don't miss him or spook him away if you see him," dad warned me. "I already passed up one chance to kill him, so make your shot a good one if he comes."

The first evening I hunted dad's bow seat, the big buck walked by me 20 yards away right near dark, just as dad had predicted, but he wasn't broadside. As he started to turn and walk away from me, I quickly raised the bow, making a small sound as I moved. The big buck heard the noise, but he didn't see me. He got quite nervous, and he quietly moved away from my seat. I could have almost cried to see that big buck walk away after being so close to him.

For a second, I thought about flinging an arrow at him, but it wasn't a good shot, and I wisely passed up the opportunity.

"Did he see you?" dad quizzed me over the phone that night as I relayed the story. "If he didn't see you, you will get him tomorrow night. Just don't miss him and don't scare him away. Remember, you are hunting in my seat!"

I was fairly sure, but not certain that the big buck had not seen me. I was hoping he had only heard the unusual noise, and his instincts had told him to move away from potential danger. I had to hope that tomorrow he would come again and forget about the danger he had avoided today.

I was pumped up the next day, hoping to get another look at the big buck. I hunted virtually the whole day in the wintery cedar swamp, but I never saw any sign of the bruiser. Then, as the sun started to set, I heard a familiar sound coming from the northern reaches of the Great Gogemain.

In a minute, I saw the outline of the deer coming down a trail that ran by dad's bow seat. Seconds later, I saw the unmistakable antlers of the 12 pointer. He was walking down the ridge right toward me.

My heart was pounding about as hard as the heart of a healthy "30 Something" year-old could take. When he moved into position, I was certain I could take him, so I started to slowly raise the bow and pull back on the arrow.

Like the night before, it was a perfectly quiet evening, so all sounds were magnified. Even moving my arms created a noise in my clothing that could be heard. This time, the big buck looked right up at me, marking me as a dangerous hunter. He immediately got tense and stiff, locking his eyes on my position, as he started to move away.

Believing I had nothing to lose now, I hurriedly raised the bow and started to draw back on the big guy. That's when he whirled and moved quickly to get back into the safety of the Gogemain. In a flash, he had turned directly away from me, and he was gone into the swamp. I never even got the bow pulled all the way back before I

Sometimes Big Ones Get Away

realized a good shot was hopeless. I had to accept that the big buck had gotten away again, and now he wouldn't be back here.

Once again, I just about cried. I had blown an opportunity to kill a huge UP whitetail, one almost every hunter would drool over. Dad had warned me about this possibility, but I scared this buck away despite my best intentions and my careful planning and preparation.

That's how unpredictable deer hunting can be, especially when big, mature bucks are the target. I had to accept that I was not meant to kill this beautiful buck.

In the mid 1980s, dad and I were hunting Hungry Hill in the rifle season without any luck seeing a big buck. There were lots of deer around, but we hadn't killed a big buck.

After the first week of the season, I had returned to work in the Lansing area, and I was planning to get back up right after Thanksgiving. While I was away, dad had stayed at grandpa's house and his sister, my Aunt Charlotte Firack, asked him over for Thanksgiving dinner.

"There are deer right here by the house," my Aunt Charlotte told the men at dinner, just like my grandmother used to say. "Why do you have to go so far away to hunt? Why can't you hunt right here by the house?" Like my grandmother, Aunt Charlotte didn't like it that we hunted in such remote country like Hungry Hill.

On this particular day, after a big Thanksgiving dinner, all the relatives decided to take my aunt's advice and do a deer drive of the cedar swamp by grandma's house. Dad agreed that he and my cousin David would be the drivers, and dad placed grandpa, my Uncle John and my cousin Dan all along the south hardwoods, where they hoped the deer would run.

When dad and David got into the swamp, they jumped the deer, chasing them toward the awaiting hunters. The drivers didn't know it, but there was an incredible buck in the swamp, and he ran hard right past my Uncle John. Johnny got off a quick shot at the big bruiser, but he missed him. The big buck continued on into the hardwoods.

When the hunters regrouped and went over what happened, Johnny told everyone that the buck was a huge 10 or 12 pointer.

"I don't know how I missed him, but I did," Uncle John admitted later that day.

When I returned to the UP after Thanksgiving, dad and I went back to hunting Hungry Hill. On Saturday night, the Firacks called us. They asked about our interest in driving the swamp again.

"We should do it," dad told me. "That big buck will probably be back in there, and maybe he will run out the same way because it worked for him once," dad thought out loud. "This time, I want you to be where he's going to come out because I know you won't miss him – you don't miss bucks when you see them."

Dad would drive the swamp himself, and my Uncle John, grandpa, cousin Dan and I would post up on the hardwood ridge. We were close enough to each other so that we had every inch of the hardwoods covered. If the deer ran out of the swamp and tried to cross the hardwoods, one of us would see him.

As the drive started, we got into position and waited on pins and needles as the minutes past. Thirty minutes went by without any action. I was thinking there weren't any deer in the swamp or that they had run out to the east, out of our sight.

147

Proud Hunters Proud Yoopers

Just when I thought this was a dry run, I heard a loud rifle shot from my right. It had to be my Uncle John or Dan. I was hoping they had killed the big buck, when I heard my cousin yelling at me.

"Get him, Lee!" Dan screamed.

I was franticly scanning the bottom of the ridge, looking for deer against the dark green of the hemlock and cedar swamp. Suddenly, I heard the sound of a running deer, and I caught a glimpse of a deer headed back into the swamp.

The deer had an enormous set of antlers on his head. There was no doubt this was one of the biggest deer I had ever seen. I raised my Remington semi-automatic and looked for him in the scope. He was running and making huge jumps. I had a hard time staying on him in the scope, and I couldn't get a good shot at him.

In what seemed like only a few precious seconds, he was gone into the thick swamp, and my opportunity was gone too. Dad had put me in the right place, and after all his bragging about my deer-killing skill, I didn't even take a shot at this monster buck that ran right by me.

We regrouped to go over what had happened. Dan said that he had a good shot at the deer and he was sure he had hit him. I reported that I didn't see the deer running like a wounded deer because he was going flat out when he went by me.

We looked high and low for blood or other signs that Dan had hit the deer. Unfortunately, we found nothing. That was the last we saw of the big bruiser that had lived by grandpa's house, right under our noses, while we hunted all over Chippewa County looking for a big buck.

The big buck had escaped us a second time, and it appeared that he was safe from the local Hank and Firack tribes. We surmised that after two close encounters with the two Polish families, this buck knew it was time to find another hiding place.

Even so, I will forever remember the sight of that big buck running away from me and my cousin, those huge antlers shining in the afternoon sun as he took huge leaps to get back to the safety of the Gogemain swamp.

In the off-season, when I am at home and reminiscing about pursuing big bucks, I love to read some of the best white-tailed deer books on the market. These great books allow me to remember those big ones I've taken over the years and those that got away. One of my favorites is *Whitetail – Behavior Through the Seasons,* by Charles J. Alsheimer. Alsheimer is an outstanding writer and photographer from upstate New York. He is also a field editor for *Deer & Deer Hunting* magazine, and his book brings the magic of the whitetail to life in front of you. The UP's John Ozoga does the same thing with his excellent four-part series of books on the whitetail, called *Whitetail Autumn, Whitetail Winter, Whitetail Spring,* and *Whitetail Summer.*

On November 7, 2002, I was hunting on our Neebish Island property, near a place where my friend Mike Jackson had picked out as a good bow-stand location. It was near a marsh and several nearby bedding areas where deer spent their days hiding from humans and predators. Mike had picked out a narrow band of poplars and brush where he predicted a buck would use as a travel corridor.

I had set up just north of Mike's favorite spot, and I had sweetened up the place with some apples and sugar beets. Our trail cameras confirmed there were a number of bucks in the area.

Sometimes Big Ones Get Away

On this quiet evening, one week before the rifle opener, a huge buck came from the area of the marsh and walked almost directly to the apples and sugar beets. I watched him approach my bow seat slowly and cautiously for a solid three minutes before he came within archery range. While I couldn't see the right side of his rack, it looked to me like he was at least a 12 pointer, with a beautiful, but asymmetrical set of antlers. He had one particularly unique antler point that was very distinctive out on the end of his rack.

I was perfectly calm as the big buck walked into my shooting lane. I was certain I was about to kill one of the biggest bucks of my life any second. After all his caution, the buck now seemed relatively relaxed, and he walked up to the apples and sugar beets. He lowered his huge rack of antlers to the ground and he began to feed.

When he looked away from me, I slowly and confidently raised my bow from my hiding spot 20 feet high in large white cedar tree. I took careful aim at the spot right behind the buck's shoulder. I was rock steady as I released my arrow toward the target.

Just like I've seen many times, the big buck whirled and ran hard after the shot. I lost track of the arrow, but I remained confident that I had made a good hit. I watched the big buck run at full speed back into the thicket from where he had come. He sure looked like a deer that was hit hard in the vital areas with a razor-sharp arrow. I quickly climbed down out of my tree stand to see if I could find this trophy of a lifetime.

As I walked over to where I had shot, I found my arrow lodged horizontally in a fallen spruce tree, at a height that looked taller than the deer. I found bits of deer hair on the ground where it appeared the arrow had clipped hair off the top of the shoulder of the big buck.

I was stunned. There was no blood on my arrow. It was clear that I made a simple miss on the deer by shooting just over his back, close enough to give him a haircut and scare the wits out of him, but not close enough to do any damage.

I was so confident I had killed the deer that it was difficult to accept that I just plain missed this gorgeous buck. But that was reality. Now I was worried that I had also scared the buck so badly that he wouldn't come back.

For the next week, I hunted as much as I could, hoping to see this big buck again. Two days before rifle season started, I saw him just before dark as he was running along a marsh just east of the same bow seat. He never even looked my way, so I knew he was on a mission going somewhere else.

Sometimes, though, Yoopers get lucky, and my luck was about to change. The next evening, a half hour before dark, a lone doe came waltzing through the woods toward the apples and sugar beets. Right behind her was my big buck. She was probably close to coming into heat because he didn't want to leave her side.

Lucky for me, she was more interested in food than sex, and she walked right into the apples and sugar beets. I froze against my white cedar tree, waiting for the big buck to follow her into my shooting lane.

"I won't miss you a second time; I've got you now," I told myself as I steadied my nerves and prepared myself mentally for the shot.

The buck took two more steps toward me. He had only two more steps to go before I could shoot him. Suddenly, he seemed to remember that this was a dangerous spot. For the moment, he forgot about his lady friend. He simply turned around and slowly trotted back into the thicket without his girl.

I marveled at his beautiful rack as he hustled away out of range and out of my life. I had come so close this time to getting him, and yet he was now so far away. After that evening, I never saw him again even though dad and I hunted hard for him in rifle season. We hunted all around the places I had seen him three times, figuring one of us would see him in the area nearby.

During the second week of season, I heard from my neighbors, Myles and Murray Meehan, that the neighbor east of them, Green Hamlin, had killed a big buck, a huge 12 pointer.

Dad and I stopped at Green's house that evening and asked about the big deer. Green had killed another big buck in Kentucky in 1966, one that scored 180.2, making it the Wayne County record – a record still on the books 40 years later. Green's story was featured in the July 2007 edition of the *North American Whitetail* magazine, another one of my favorite pieces of literature.

We asked Green about the buck he had killed. As he showed us the buck, I checked the top of his shoulder. I couldn't see exactly where I had shaved off the hair, but I was sure this was the same buck. He had that one unique antler point on the front of his rack that made me sure this was the buck I had seen three times and missed once.

Green told us that he had never seen the buck before the day he had killed him. He had gone to his stand about 3 pm on November 21, the sixth day of the season. He had just gotten ready when the big buck walked right in and started feeding on his bait pile. He dropped him with one shot. Dad and I congratulated Green on the beautiful buck, and we headed back to the cabin.

I couldn't believe how close I had come to killing this great buck. His presence and the adventures and thrills he had given me and a neighbor were confirmation that our QDM program to grow bigger bucks was working. I was confident that this monster buck had been living on our property for several years as a young buck. No doubt, we had passed him up several times in prior years. And while I didn't kill him, I had several chances to get him, and I had the thrill of being that close to a giant whitetail. Several times, I told myself that is what hunting is all about, and this is why it is a sport and not a sure thing.

From these four bucks, a Proud Yooper learned that sometimes we don't kill the biggest bucks we see, but these experiences form some of our most vivid and powerful memories of deer hunting in the UP. And from these adventures, a Proud Hunter learned that the big bucks that get away are the essence of why we keep hunting.

34

The Stalwart Slasher

*One has to face fear
or forever run from it.*

-Hawk, Crow

Over the last two decades, the Michigan DNR has done a nice job managing our black bear population. By making some evolutionary changes in how we hunt and manage black bears, DNR wildlife managers have dramatically improved and upgraded the status of bear hunting. In the process, they also expanded bear numbers at a time when overall bear habitat size was shrinking. Like many other states, Michigan's DNR has also kept the bear population at a size that minimizes human contact and unintended interaction with bears.

While some hunters, including me, have been critical of how the NRC has managed Michigan's deer herd, many hunters think we've done a much better job managing our bear population. In fact, the bear results really do speak for themselves.

While I wrote this book, Dave Bostick was one of the DNR's bear and furbearer management specialists during this period of sound, scientific bear management. Dave became the DNR bear specialist in March, 2004, and he had held other responsible resource jobs including a stint as a local biologist in Alaska, where he had lots of experience working with both black and grizzly bears. Some of those bears were problem bears with "behavioral issues," the kind of bears that make bear management an interesting profession.

Dave and his predecessors, including Tim Reis, have implemented programs in Michigan that have steadily increased our bear numbers during much of my hunting career. Tim was the DNR's bear specialist during much of this period, and now he's a DNR wildlife unit supervisor.

Just how much better has the black bear fared in Michigan in the last few decades under Tim's and Dave's leadership than it had in the past? Well, in the good ole days of the 1950s, bears were so scarce that hunters killed only 200-300 per year statewide. In the 1970s, we only killed between 350 and 850 bears in a given year. By 1989, there was an estimated population of just over 7,000 bears in the UP. Hunters were allowed to kill any bear on a gun deer license. Up until this time, we treated the black bear more like a menacing predator than a magnificent game animal that he is. And prior to 1990, the DNR didn't have a targeted number of bears to harvest each year. In effect, we weren't doing much at all to actively manage the bear population.

All of that changed in 1990 when the DNR implemented a new bear management program that required all hunters to apply for a special license in a lottery which was designed to limit the total number of bears harvested. This program allowed the DNR to expand the number of bears in Michigan by specific management areas, and it required mandatory registration of all bears. Registering every bear harvested gave the

Proud Hunters Proud Yoopers

DNR a wealth of biological data on the bear population. The program also established three earlier seasons for bear, beginning on September 10 and closing near the end of October at about the time bears hibernate for winter.

The DNR also stopped allowing hunters to kill bears during the last half of November, while the gun deer season was open. They ended that practice on the management theory that many of the bears killed in late November were sleeping in their winter dens. This was hardly a sporting end for the bears, and it was way too easy for the lucky hunters who happened to find a drowsy bear.

Like many wildlife management changes, at first some hunters criticized the "radical" change in bear hunting rules. After all, hunters do not like change of any kind, and, so some hunters didn't like the new bear restrictions. Over time, however, hunters accepted the DNR's new management approach. Today, bear hunters are really pleased with the increased number of bears and the opportunity to harvest very nice, mature bears.

In effect, both the bears and the hunters have it better today because Michigan took a proactive, science-based, wildlife management approach that by all measures today is highly successful.

In 2006, there were an estimated 15,000 bears in the UP and just under 10,000 bear tags were issued. That's a stable number of bears and a huge increase over what we had in the "good ole days." In 2006, the DNR registered about 2,500 bears, the most ever registered as killed in Michigan. Those 2,500 bears are almost ten times more than what we killed in the 1950s. In the eastern UP, bear numbers have increased 67% since 1989, to an estimated 5,200 bears today. In the western UP, bear numbers have skyrocketed by an incredible 150%, increasing from 4,200 bears in 1989 to 10,500 today. Clearly, our DNR bear managers are making the hunting and management of bears better and better each year.

The odds of drawing a bear license in the annual lottery are about 20% for the eastern UP. I can usually count on getting a bear tag every four or five years because of the NRC lottery point system. Basically, in years hunters don't draw a permit, they earn a preference point, which gives them two chances to win a lottery license the next year. The system has worked to ensure hunters eventually get a bear tag if they apply every year.

In the early 1990s, dad and I were lucky in drawing bear permits because one of us usually got one almost every other year. In one early fall deer hunting season, when we didn't have a bear tag, we had seen a very large bear in the Gogemain several times while bow hunting. We vowed we would get the bear the following year if we got a tag.

When I really decided I wanted this bear, it was on a warm October day when I was headed into the Gogemain to duck hunt one of my favorite ponds. On the way to the duck pond, I was going to drop off some apples at dad's deer stand.

As I left the main trail and headed towards dad's bow seat, I heard a loud noise right in front of me. I thought I heard a deer gasping and struggling, and then I saw a glimpse of a deer running through the brush. There were loud sounds of running game, and there was something else besides the deer making all the noise.

I got down on one knee to see through the thick brush, and I caught sight of the deer running away. As I watched the deer run off, I was startled because there was another animal just yards away from me in the brush, coming right for me. In an instant, I could see the outline of a large bear looking at me through the thick brush. The bear was stationery, but I could see the brush moving around him as he fidgeted in a nervous fashion. Several times, he grunted at me, less than ten feet away.

I was carrying my Browning semi-automatic shotgun, loaded with three rounds of no. 6 bird shot for any partridge I might flush on my trip to the duck marsh. I had some no. 4 magnum shells for ducks in my vest, and, for a brief second, I thought about reloading my shotgun with the more powerful shells in case the bear charged me. Then I realized that there was no time to reload. The bear took one more step toward me. Now he was close enough that I could almost touch him.

The bear continued to grunt at me as if to provoke me to attack him. He apparently didn't know just how afraid I was that he would charge me. I was prepared to shoot him with all three rounds of my shotgun at point blank range, and I mentally prepared myself for that event. At one point, I thought about how dangerous this encounter was and I noticed just how hard my heart was pounding.

Just when I thought it couldn't get any scarier, the bear moved again and turned slightly. I prepared myself believing that I was going to have to shoot him. I was only hoping I could survive this attack. I again visualized that I would shoot him three times in the head and chest with my shotgun at point blank range before he would tear into my flesh with his razor sharp teeth and claws. My only hope was that he would die from my gunshot wounds before he could do too much damage to me. For a second, I thought about how I would drag my bloody body out of the Gogemain to get help.

Suddenly, like a ghost, the bear was gone. As I waited for him to charge, I saw one movement of a sapling as he turned and silently retreated. In an instant, he vanished, and the horrifying fear of an eminent bear attack was over.

Incredibly, he had backed down and melted back into the heavy cover of his home territory in total silence and without a trace.

I breathed a heavy sign of relief and reflected on this close call, trying to calm my nerves. When I had regained my composure, I looked around to see how I had run into this startled bear.

I immediately spotted blood near where the bear had been and where the deer had run away. I tracked the blood back to our bow stand where we had been baiting with apples. From the evidence at the bow stand, I surmised that the bear had come upon the deer feeding on the apples. The bear had successfully attacked the deer, causing it to bleed, but not killing it.

The bear and the deer must have struggled, with the bear trying to bring down the deer and the deer trying hard to get away from the grasp of the bear. In the process, the bear either bit or clawed the deer, drawing blood.

I must have come upon the struggling animals just as the deer was getting away from the bear's death hold. I saw the deer as it ran away, and I startled the bear as he was chasing the wounded deer.

The bear didn't want to give up trailing the wounded deer, but he also didn't want a confrontation with another predator (a lone Yooper hunter), so he made a decision to let the deer go. He also backed away from an interaction with me in the thick brush.

Proud Hunters Proud Yoopers

Just to be sure the deer was not mortally wounded, I tracked the deer as far as I could. The deer bled moderately for several hundred yards and then only sparsely after that. I was able to track the deer for a considerable distance until I concluded the deer appeared to be in good condition. It probably had flesh wounds from the bear that would heal in time.

In any event, this was one of my most scary adventures, and one of my most unusual events that I have ever encountered in the deep woods of the UP. It has to be extremely rare for a black bear to catch an adult white-tailed deer. It has to be even rarer for a hunter to witness the successful attack and then to almost get attacked himself.

We didn't have a bear tag this year, but I was sure pumped up about the chance to hunt for this bear the next year, if we were successful in the permit drawing.

The next spring, there were reports all over Stalwart of a large bear terrorizing the area. Grandpa Hank's next door neighbor, Joe Zbiega, had the big bear raid his chicken coup two times, killing and eating 16 chickens one time and almost as many the second time. The bear tore into the chicken house, ripping off the door in the middle of the night to get his chicken dinner.

Four miles to the west, near the Stalwart fairground property, there were several reports in the *Sault Evening News* about a large bear that had attacked horse farms at night, leaving claw and teeth marks on several injured horses.

Dad and I wondered about this bear. He could be the same bear I had encountered the fall before. We labeled the menacing bear as the "Stalwart Slasher" because of his penchant for violence and destruction. We were pretty sure he was the bear we planned to hunt in the fall. Meanwhile, the DNR told local Stalwart residents that they would live trap the bear and move him somewhere else.

We sure didn't want the bear relocated somewhere other than his Gogemain home where we knew he hung out. As luck would have it, the DNR officials could not lure the bear into their traps, and soon the August bear baiting season was here. We baited up our favorite Gogemain bear hot spots, including the spot where I had seen the bear last year. Almost immediately, we had bears coming to our sites. We kept one trail to our favorite seat clear of brush, and we worked up the soft soil around the bait so the bruin always left a clear track. That method helped us confirm that we had a huge bear hitting our bait.

The next few weeks seemed to drag on like months, but soon the season opened, and I was in the woods, looking for the bear as often as my work schedule would allow.

In early September, I was deep in the Gogemain, miles from the nearest road, waiting for a big bear to return to my bear seat. For days, I went to the stand in the early evening, and I stayed until dark. I never saw a bear, and I was getting discouraged, thinking someone else may have killed my bear.

Then, one night, just as the sun was setting, I heard a familiar noise behind me in the swamp. I knew that a bear was coming to me. The bear slowed down his approach as he got close to the bait, as bears usually do. He cautiously circled the area, and then he waltzed closer to the bait area, stopping right underneath my seat. He was so close, I could almost touch him and I could see him breathing, yet he wasn't in a position that I could shoot.

The Stalwart Slasher

He stayed underneath me for what seemed like several minutes, looking around for signs of danger and lifting his nose to scent any nearby odors. Finally, he confidently moved forward, walking directly away from me to the bait pile of raw meat, donuts, rolls, and loaves of bread I had for him.

As the bear moved into position, I was sure he was the one I wanted. He looked like a huge male, with massive shoulders, legs, rear end and head. I was sure he would be a record book bear, and I imagined that this had to be the infamous Stalwart Slasher.

That's when I slowly lifted my bow and drew an arrow. I held for the kill spot, just behind the bear's shoulder. As I released the arrow, I saw it slice through the bear higher up than I intended.

The bear bristled and turned around, looking in all directions for the source of the pain in his shoulder. He slowly and almost defiantly left the bait site and walked back toward the swamp. He again stopped right underneath me, where he looked around again, not quite sure what had happened. Unfortunately, while I had readied another arrow, I was not able to get a second shot. After he surveyed the situation again, I thought he might walk back to the bait. Suddenly, he turned and walked back into the swamp from where he had come. I didn't have a chance to shoot again.

He sure didn't look like a bear who was seriously hurt from an arrow. I nervously waited in my tree stand until dad came at dark and I quickly told him the story. We both had flashlights, so we looked for blood on the trail the bear had taken.

We found blood right away and a considerable amount in several places. Bears are notorious for not leaving much blood because their thick hair absorbs and catches much of it. So, finding good blood right away was encouraging.

"Maybe you will get lucky," dad told me as we scanned the landscape for more signs of where the bear went.

Soon, however, our hopes began to fade as the blood sign grew sparse. I knew this was a bad sign. By now, it was pitch dark.

Dad and I continued looking for the bear in the dark, following specks of blood down a long, narrow game trail leading into the depths of the mighty Gogemain Swamp. As we followed the narrow game trail into the big swamp, we noticed that both sides of the trail were so thick, you couldn't easily penetrate the brush if you had to. That made us feel really insecure.

After about a half hour following the blood into the darkness, dad made an important observation.

"You know this is crazy," he said. "We've got two small flashlights and one bow – no guns. We're following a wounded, 400 pound fighting machine in the dark in the depths of his home territory, and we don't even know where we are. He could jump out at us at any time, and we wouldn't even have a chance to defend ourselves. We're totally nuts to be doing this."

I was going to kid him about Polish Yoopers not always having the common sense that they should have, but I decided this was not the time for humor.

We agreed to go just a little farther. If we didn't see more blood or other encouraging sign, we would postpone this recovery effort until tomorrow morning. As we went a little farther, we just about jumped out of our skin every time we heard a noise in the brush. We prepared ourselves to have the huge bruin attack us at point-blank range. There were times when I swear the hair was standing up straight on the

Proud Hunters Proud Yoopers

back of my neck in anticipation of a wounded, angry bear jumping out at us in the dark. I kept thinking about my earlier encounter with this big bear. He walked away from me once, but I wasn't sure he would do it again, especially now that he was wounded. After all, he probably was the "Slasher" bear.

But it never happened. And after another 30 minutes of tracking and finding no blood, we were disappointed. We faced the facts and agreed to give up the cause for the night. In a hurry, we got out of the Gogemain, returning to grandpa's house where I didn't sleep a wink that night thinking about a wounded animal I left in the woods.

I wish I could say that the next morning was productive, but it was not. We picked up the trail again, and we were able to follow the bear another couple hundred yards. There was no evidence that the bear was mortally injured. He had not ever lain down, and he had only lost a small quantity of blood. My visual view of the bear had also confirmed that I had hit him high in the shoulder, so I knew chances of any serious damage were minimal.

At a certain point, dad turned to me and said, "You know, we are not going to get him. He's only got a flesh wound, and we won't catch up to him. He's going to be all right, but unfortunately, he is going to get away."

With that, we gave up the search, and I had to give up on killing the Stalwart Slasher. I still hunted for him in the area, but he never returned to any of our bait sites, and we never saw him again. As far as I know, he lived a long life in the Gogemain, and he left the residents of Stalwart alone, never returning to feed on their chickens or harass their horses again.

At the end of this hunt, a Proud Yooper learned that there is no scarier moment in the deep woods of the UP than when you are tracking a wounded "slasher" black bear at night. A Proud Hunter also learned that sometimes big bears, even the legendary kind, can get away and live another day in the wooded jungles of the UP.

35

The Ultimate Deer Hunter Test

I will not lie to you.
I do not come to deceive you.
I come to lead you.

- Cochise, Chiricahua Apache

When I teach a deer management seminar to a group of hunters, I like to ask this question: If you come upon a clearing and a ten-point buck and a spikehorn are feeding, which buck would you shoot?

In every class, almost all hunters laugh and admit that they would shoot the ten-pointer without even thinking about it. A few argumentative hunters insist that they would shoot the little buck. Typically, they point out that the meat on the smaller buck might be better eating and not as tough. These few counter-cultural hunters and contrarians all have one thing in common: they are liars.

I, on the other hand, am a big buck hunting fanatic. I openly admit that I want to kill a big buck, and I make no apologies that I live to pursue and shoot mature bucks with big antlers.

The reality is that virtually all hunters love to see and shoot big bucks. The chance to take a truly nice buck (like the big ten-pointer in my theoretical test) is something all hunters dream about. Virtually no hunter on the planet would shoot the small buck given the chance to shoot a buck with big antlers. So, yes, those few smart alecks who say they would shoot the small buck are neither truthful with their classroom peers nor with themselves.

No matter how many times I ask the question in a large group of hunters, there is almost always a spirited discussion about the behavior and the deer selection of the hunter. The great thing about the dialogue is that the hunters realize they are all deer managers making decisions that impact their local deer herd where they hunt. One of my friends, Perry Russo of Clarkston, Michigan, the former Michigan QDMA Regional Director, calls this "trigger management." What he means is that we all exercise deer management decisions when we pull the trigger or release the arrow. Perry says that as individual hunters we actually have more impact on the deer herd than we think.

It is the second question I ask them, however, that is, for me, the most interesting. I like to ask the same hunters this question: If you came to the same clearing and there was a spikehorn buck and a mature doe, which deer would you shoot?

If I am asking hunters the question in the UP, it is almost certain that most hunters will say they would shoot the spike buck. Only a few brave souls will claim a preference to shoot the doe.

The reason for this response goes back more than five decades to an early 1950s decision by the NRC to allow a "doe season" in the state. In this hunt, 100,000 does and fawns were killed statewide (all of them in the northern lower peninsula) for the first time in years. In the same season, hunters also killed 75,000 bucks - an average number for the 1950s. For the prior ten years and as long as most hunters could remember, no one ever killed a doe. So killing 100,000 antlerless deer in one year seemed incredibly excessive.

In the 1960s, the DNR held a similar antlerless deer hunt in the UP, the first one in a long time where they issued thousands of "doe permits." This time, hunters killed thousands of does and fawns in the UP, too.

Hunters across the state were outraged at the DNR over these two seasons.

UP hunters remember this doe season as one when the landscape was red with the blood of dead deer dragged out of the woods – mostly does and fawns. Some older Yoopers refer to the season as the "the Big Doe Slaughter" that subsequently ruined our deer hunting for decades to come.

As a young hunter growing up in a strong hunting family, I listened closely to these discussions among the older, more experienced hunters. And like many young hunters, I was influenced by what the older hunters said, believed and practiced. Well into the 1970s, my own family members thought the DNR had virtually wiped out the deer herd with this hunt.

I can remember my grandfather, my father, and my uncles talking about a nearby family like they were second-class citizens because they shot does and fawns, something more disgusting than violators who shot big bucks out of season. These doe shooters were described in unflattering terms that made me think they were not real hunters and that they were not "manly" men. Based on what I heard, I believed these guys were unskilled hunters who weren't good enough hunters to kill a buck - a real man's deer with antlers.

And then there were the lessons I learned that anyone shooting a doe was killing two more bucks that could be born next year and two more every year after that. By killing that doe, I was taught, you were killing the goose that lays the golden eggs – and no self-respecting hunter would do that.

It was also considered a good conservation practice in the local hunting circuit to forgo shooting any does. When I would spend time in my dad's sports shop, dozens of local hunters would come in and talk about how they would be buying a doe permit, but not using it. "I'll burn mine before I will use it. I'm just getting one so I stop someone else from shooting a doe," hunters would say defiantly as they purchased doe permit applications from my dad's store. "The darn DNR, all they care about is the money and not the deer!"

With those attitudes and related camp talk, was it any wonder that many of us in the baby-boomer generation grew up believing we should not shoot does?

The reality is that the deer herd had built up significantly prior to that infamous 1950s hunt from years of protecting all antlerless deer and growing the size of the deer herd. The DNR intended to kill a significant number of does and fawns to reduce the size of the herd, and they got what they wanted. The problem is that many hunters never understood the issue. These hunters, my family included, never wanted to understand or accept this basic deer management concept. After these massive deer harvests in the 1950s and 1960s, the public made things so uncomfortable for the DNR staff members that they hesitated to have future antlerless deer seasons or they felt

The Ultimate Deer Hunter Test

pressure to significantly reduce the size of antlerless hunts because of the public outcry over the number of does and fawns killed.

To this day, there remains a tremendous bias in the UP against the killing of does and fawns.

Years later, I learned that killing female deer (does and young female fawns) is one of the best things hunters can do for deer management – even in my beloved UP.

Making that statement could get me tarred and feathered or get me permanently barred from ever crossing the Mackinac Bridge again. That's because some of my fellow Yoopers still believe it's a terrible sin to shoot a doe.

But the research that supports shooting reasonable numbers of antlerless deer as one part of an overall sound and scientific deer management program is overwhelming. Today, the QDMA and other outdoor organizations are making progress in breaking down the strong stereotypical beliefs among Yooper hunters that real hunters do not and should not kill does and fawns. In fact, an adequate (but not excessive) harvest of antlerless deer is one of the core values and guiding principles of the QDMA. As a part of QDMA herd management educational efforts, many QDM managers suggest trying to achieve an older buck herd and a younger doe herd. That is accomplished by harvesting more does.

Rod Clute is the DNR's Big Game Specialist in Lansing where he is one of the principle players responsible for the overall management of the state's deer herd. Rod tracks the total number of hunters in the state, whether they hunt with a gun, bow, or both, and whether they are willing to purchase an antlerless license. Rod knows from years of watching license sales that older hunters and gun-only hunters are less likely to purchase antlerless licenses. In all likelihood, many of them still hold on to the values that hunters should only shoot bucks. He also knows that the younger generations of hunters and bow hunters in general are more likely to buy antlerless licenses. Most of them will use the doe tags to harvest does and fawns, rather than burn them as a protest.

Now, as QDM disciples preach to the masses that killing some antlerless deer is good (and not the end of the world), we need to be careful. The DNR can and sometimes does issue too many antlerless permits. When that happens, hunters can kill too many antlerless deer, taking the total population down below the area's carrying capacity.

While this does occasionally happen, and it has happened recently in parts of the UP, the great thing about the white-tailed deer is that it can rapidly rebound in one to three years unless the herd has been seriously over-harvested.

But there's another important twist to this story.

The flip side of the over-harvesting issue is the most disturbing misconception about killing does. And very few Yooper hunters know how badly this lack of scientific management hurts the deer herd.

Because Yooper hunters take so few antlerless deer, in some years, more deer die from starvation in the winter deer yards than hunters kill during the prior hunting season. When Mother Nature tragically gives us a harsh winter, hunters lose big time, because we could have had more of those deer in our freezers. We also missed out on some high-quality hunting time. We could have enjoyed dozens of hours in the woods hunting for those does and fawns that died anyway. Unfortunately, because we didn't

Proud Hunters Proud Yoopers

kill more does and fawns, they will die a tragic and painfully slow death in a deer yard that didn't have the capacity to support and feed all those deer.

While managing deer in the winter in southern Michigan is a no-brainer, managing deer through the UP's unpredictable winters is a much more complicated challenge to the state's resource managers. These managers must decide how many deer should be shot so too many deer don't go into winter and die from starvation. In effect, they make a critical life-and-death decision for the deer. This decision is a delicate balancing act that is part art and part science. As a result, we should have great respect for our DNR biologists who must make these tough decisions every year.

The problem is, as hunters, we could have helped biologists prevent winter kill by humanely killing a few more does and fawns each year during hunting season.

But first, we have to overcome those incredible biases we have against killing antlerless deer.

At no time in history has this basic management principle been better illustrated than when the deer herd's population was building up to a 2 million level statewide in the mid-1990s. The UP population of whitetails was at an all-time high too. As the DNR began to aggressively reduce the size of the herd, Yooper hunters were being cooperative, and we killed 17,000 antlerless deer in 1994, 23,000 in 1995 and 46,000 in 1996.

In the winters prior to each of these seasons, the overall weather conditions had been very mild so that deer losses to winter starvation had been minimal and most deer survived. At the same time, Yooper hunters were also shooting about 20,000 more bucks than does in those seasons. As a result, lots of hunters were happy. It seemed as if there were deer everywhere in the UP. Record numbers of Yooper hunters took home venison.

All that changed with the devastating winter of 1996, when DNR biologists believe about 100,000 UP deer died in deer yards from starvation caused by the excessively long winter. The next season, harvest levels crashed to 29,000 antlerless deer and 43,000 bucks. In the prior year, hunters had killed almost 70,000 bucks, so this season was almost a 40% reduction in our buck kill! As terrible as this was, hunters weren't making the connection that they lost almost as many deer to a bad winter as they had killed in the previous season.

If that weren't bad enough, the next year's season saw a worse winter, and, this time, DNR biologists believed 200,000 more UP deer died in the deer yards from starvation. The size of that number is just staggering. In the history of the UP, we've never killed anywhere close to 200,000 deer in a season. Then in two consecutive years, we lose 300,000 deer to starvation from harsh, long winters.

As expected, deer populations crashed big time, and harvest levels of both bucks and does fell dramatically. The DNR estimated that Yooper hunters killed only 28,000 bucks and 13,000 antlerless deer in the 1998 season after those devastating winter losses.

There is a silver lining in every dark cloud. The huge starvation losses stimulated deer management discussions about what could be done to reduce those losses from harsh winters. Biologists and foresters began pushing for more preservation of critical winter habitat like deer yards. Respected biologists like John Ogoza of Munising made it clear that our wintering deer yards are our most important factor in determining the population of our UP deer herd. These discussions prompted DNR officials to look harder at the trends of deer yard ownership and harvest and regeneration patterns for large cedar and conifer swamps. Outdoor groups started asking questions too about whether we were doing enough to help the UP deer herd in the long term.

Antlerless deer advocates also got more respect and bigger audiences when they talked about the strategy of harvesting more antlerless deer so fewer of them would die of starvation. Some boldly asked, "Shouldn't we shoot more does and fawns if they are going to die in deer yards anyway?" QDMA members started preaching that it would be better to have the venison from more antlerless deer in our freezers than to let those deer die such painfully slow deaths in the cedar swamps. All these efforts and the attention from the two-year, massive deer die-offs made a dent in the armor of those with the traditional anti-doe shooting bias. More and more hunters began to understand and accept that it is OK to kill a doe or fawn, and that in fact, it might be a good thing for the deer herd.

While these bigger discussions were taking place, there was also strong support to educate more hunters about the advantages of letting young button bucks go when hunting for antlerless deer. Another principle of quality deer management is that hunters should forgo shooting the young bucks as another technique for helping more bucks grow older, creating a herd that is more natural and has a better balance of different age classes of deer, especially older male deer.

Boyd Wiltse, a retired auto manufacturer finance specialist from Brighton, Michigan, and a long-time QDMA member, had prepared a guide for how hunters could tell the difference between does, female fawns and button bucks (male fawns). Boyd was able to convince the DNR to include this educational piece in its annual hunting guide. QDMA members used this material throughout Michigan when we taught deer management workshops. The guides were one of the most popular parts of our seminars, and we got frequent questions about how to identify and protect BBs (shorthand for button bucks).

In my own hunting experiences, I made sure I was practicing what I was preaching. I made it my personal goal to shoot at least two antlerless deer per year to show everyone I wasn't afraid I'd devastate my local deer herd if I did that. I also encouraged all my relatives and friends who hunted with me to take at least one antlerless deer for every buck they killed.

Some of my QDMA friends had told me that harvesting more does actually encourages more young bucks to set up residence on your property. The logic is that older does are very territorial, and these does are very aggressive when it comes to defending the area where they raise their fawns. As a result, they chase away younger bucks who have just left their mothers and who are looking for new territory to begin their life as an adult buck. The logic behind more aggressively harvesting does is you might make it easier for more bucks to begin living on your land. From my own experience, it seems as if there is some truth to this theory. This belief gave me another reason to ensure I took a few does each year.

Many of our guests were also able to take antlerless deer, including some who killed their first deer with us. My biggest triumph, however, was converting my grandfather, the one who had refused to kill does for so many years, to take antlerless deer. In his last decade of life, grandpa became a doe-shooting machine, killing at least one doe a year and two in some years, including his last season, when he killed two female fawns at age 98, just two months before he turned 99.

I too, became a doe-shooting machine, killing them with bow, rifle and muzzleloader. I set a goal every year to take a certain number of deer from my property: a number I thought would be a good management harvest. If we harvested fewer bucks than we had hoped, I increased the doe harvest so we still met our population goals. Some years, we may have taken a few more deer than we should have, but amazingly, the deer came back just fine, in the same manner that the state's population rebounded from down years.

Deep down inside, I knew that if we were ever to overcome the biases against shooting does and fawns in the UP, we needed to celebrate when we do kill a nice doe or fawn just as we did for a nice buck. In fact, as hunters we need favorite doe stories just as we have favorite buck stories. And we need to make sure our next generation of hunters has the facts about basic deer management principles so that they are not biased against shooting reasonable numbers of does and fawns.

In the Charlotte area, the Eaton County QDMA Branch, lead by former branch president Tony Smith, sponsors a biggest doe contest each year to highlight and celebrate the importance of harvesting an adequate number of antlerless deer. Each year, this "doe pole" is a big hit in Charlotte.

My all-time favorite doe hunting story took place in the late 1990s on one of the last days of December. I was bow hunting at my grandfather's house near Goetzville, hiding out in an old hemlock tree where I have taken about a dozen deer over the years, many of them in the late archery season.

It was a crisp 20-degree day, with about six inches of snow on the ground, including several inches of fresh snow that had fallen over night. I had seen four deer early in the afternoon, two does, each with one fawn, traveling together through the edge of this deer yard. I could have probably taken a shot at one of those deer, but conditions weren't perfect, and I passed up the potential shots, hoping for something better.

Thirty minutes before dark, I saw a large deer coming toward me, walking down the edge of the hardwoods that bordered the cedar and hemlock swamp where I watched. The deer was so big I thought it might be a mature buck that had already lost his antlers. I didn't want to shoot a deer like that and rob someone else (or myself) of that possible future thrill next season. So, I carefully looked over the deer as she walked past me to ensure this was really a big doe.

As she passed by, I was sure she was not a buck who had dropped his antlers. By her sheer size, I knew she had to be a mature doe. I guessed her body size at about 150 pounds dressed, bigger than most bucks harvested that year and bigger than many bucks I had killed in my lifetime. She was one of the biggest does I had ever seen.

She was also alone, and there wasn't any sign of fawns following her. At that point, I decided to take her, and I drew my bow for the shot. When she stopped broadside at 22 yards, I released the arrow, and it was a perfect shot, passing directly through her heart area. The arrow had gone through the deer so cleanly, that I was not even sure that she knew she had been hit. She continued to walk past me for several seconds, and then she shook her whole body before she stumbled briefly and just fell over dead. It was one of the fastest and cleanest kills I had ever made on a deer with

The Ultimate Deer Hunter Test

an arrow. I was really pumped, and I thanked our Creator for letting me take such a special deer.

I quickly climbed down from the hemlock and stood in awe of my trophy. She was a huge deer, the largest doe I had ever killed, and I was tickled to have taken her so late in the season, just minutes before my season ended for the year.

After the season, I had a number of DNR biologists look at her jaw bone to predict her age. I have a collection of jaw bones and her teeth are more worn down than any other deer's teeth I have in my collection. Nearly all biologists predict her age at eight or more years old. Most of them claim it's hard to accurately predict the exact age once they get that old.

That information made my doe kill even that more special. As I think about this trophy, I have to wonder how many years she had lived in the eastern UP and how many fawns she had brought to life. I imagined that she made eight or more dangerous trips from her home ground to the edge of the Gogemain deer yard each winter, probably on the same migratory route. From radio-collar tracking experiments the DNR had conducted (with Tri-County Wildlife volunteers), we know some whitetails travel more than 30 miles to their winter deer yard. Had she traveled that far so many times? It is almost certain she had traveled over a great deal of the eastern UP getting to and from the deer yard. In the process, she must have led a dozen or more fawns to this same place so they could survive the savage winters. She also took those young fawns back to their spring feeding grounds after nurturing them through the winter and while teaching them all about the dangerous world they inhabited. I wondered how many times she had avoided other hunters in her long life and how many times she had narrowly escaped close encounters with hunters, wolves, coyotes, bobcats, cars, and other dangers she no doubt faced.

After I butchered up the deer and prepared her steaks and backstraps, I determined that they were as good as any I had eaten. While enjoying this venison, I scoffed at the old wives' tale about older deer not having tender meat.

Was this female deer without antlers a special trophy to me? You bet she was! And she will always symbolize to me the educational work we still have to do in the UP to improve our deer management practices.

On this day, a Proud Yooper learned to celebrate the life and death of a special doe he shot, and he marveled at the long life she no doubt led. And, on this day, a Proud Hunter learned that when faced with a management decision to take either a doe or a young buck, it's generally a good thing to kill the doe and spare the young buck.

36

Three Coyotes are a Charm

We are part fire, and part dream.
We are the physical mirroring of Miaheyyun,
the total universe upon this earth,
our Mother.

- Fire Dog, Cheyenne

On a hot, sunny August day in the mid 1990s, I was traveling in Hungry Hill country. I had several bear baits in the area, and I was checking to see if anything had hit them.

As I made my way to my next bear bait, I had a rare clear view in the distance for several hundred yards. I had a backpack of bear bait with me, and I had my Savage Arms lever action .22 High Power Rifle. The .22 High Power is an unusual cartridge because while it is a .22 caliber shell, it is also a center-fire cartridge. It has significantly more fire power than the typical rim-fire .22 caliber rifle, hence its name of "high-power."

The gun was one that both my Grandpa Ed and Grandma Mary Hank had used at different times. It was a light-weight gun, and the stock had been cut down to fit a woman or a kid. My grandfather had given the gun to my mother Betty Hank when she hunted with the group for a few years during the 1960s. Eventually, my dad and mom gave me the gun to hunt with when I began to rifle hunt for deer in 1968 at age 14, and I used it for several years. Unfortunately, I had never killed a deer with it or anything else for that matter.

The shells from the gun haven't been made for over 30 years, so we used them conservatively, and we always save the spent casings for reloading.

I have always believed you shouldn't own a gun that you don't shoot on a regular basis. As a result, I take this gun with me periodically, and I try to shoot it each year, even if I don't hunt with it. On this day, when I would be covering some mileage in this big country while checking bear baits, it seemed natural to me to be carrying this light-weight rifle.

As I approached this unusual vantage point in the normally heavy timber, a mature coyote ran from the brush on the west side and crossed in front of me going east.

The coyote never slowed down when it crossed my path, and it was gone before I could get the gun ready. I thought about how far it would be to shoot at the coyote. For humor, I even kidded myself that if I had been faster, maybe I could have gotten a shot at the fleeting coyote. On the chance that another coyote might cross with this one, I mentally prepared myself for this long-range shot with the .22 High Power.

Three Coyotes are a Charm

Amazingly, another coyote ran across the trail in the same place. I threw the gun up again, looking through the scope at where the two coyotes had crossed.

"Darn, if I had been faster, I may have gotten a crack at him too," I thought.

Then I challenged myself to estimate the distance and to guess at where to hold the gun to hit an animal that far away. I guessed that the coyotes were about 300 yards away. I estimated I would have to hold my rifle about eight inches over the back of the coyote to compensate for the drop in the bullet's flight because of the long distance.

All of this was really pure guesswork for an amateur long-distance shooter because I had never even practiced at this range. I also had never shot at a live animal anywhere close to this distance.

Because of the heavy cover in the UP, Yoopers rarely take long shots at deer or other game animals unless they are hunting in farm country or in an open meadow or other clearing. Generally, most Yoopers kill their deer at 100 yards or less. To this point, I had killed almost all of my deer at short distances.

"Maybe there will be a third coyote," I secretly hoped, recognizing that this was not likely.

Suddenly, the third coyote did magically appear on the trail where the other two had crossed. Unlike the first two, he saw me right away, and he turned and ran straight away from me for about 20 yards.

This time I was ready and waiting. As I was desperately trying to follow him in my 4X Weaver scope, he stopped, turned broadside, and looked back at me in a classic coyote pose just before he planned to run into heavy cover with his two companions.

I quickly pulled the scope eight inches over his back and touched off the trigger, never expecting to come even close to him. "I'll let him know I am in the area," I thought.

At the sound of the shot, the coyote dropped right in his tracks.

I don't normally swear, but I dropped the gun to my waist in a dramatic fashion and said out loud, "Holly sh--! I got him!"

I dropped my gear and sprinted to where the fallen coyote lay. He was a young male pup from this year's litter. The first coyote had apparently been his mother and the second smaller coyote was probably one of his siblings. Mother probably had them out on a late summer hunting exercise.

As I examined the coyote, I saw that I had made a perfect shot, hitting him in the backbone, right behind his front shoulder.

I paced off 283 yards for the shot distance. I couldn't believe it. I had never killed or shot at any game animal at any distance close to this. I couldn't believe that my little .22 High Power was so deadly at such a long distance. I was stunned and amazed at what had happened.

As I hiked several miles deeper into Hungry Hill to check my bear baits, I kept replaying the coyote shot over and over again in my mind. I accepted that this one shot was nothing but pure luck, and I accepted that I couldn't have killed another coyote under similar circumstances in another 100 tries, maybe a thousand tries.

I accepted that this was almost a one-in-a-million shot for me. I thanked my lucky stars and the Lord above for this thrilling and pure luck shot of a lifetime.

On this day, a Proud Yooper learned that sometimes as Proud Hunters, it's better to be lucky than good!

37

Lost in the Gogemain

This we know.
The Earth does not belong to man,
man belongs to Earth.

-Interpretation of Duwamish thought

From early on in my childhood, I developed a special appreciation and fascination for the great Gogemain Swamp.

To those in the eastern tip of the UP, the great Gogemain Swamp is simply known as the "Gogemain." In the 1960s when I first saw it, it was a huge conifer swamp south of the Munuscong Bay, running all the way from the bay to state highway M-48. The Gogemain was also a massive deer yard that was over 25 square miles of mostly conifer and cedar swamp with no roads running through it.

From the south side of the huge swamp, there are small spring-fed creeks that run together and form the Gogemain River. The chocolate-brown majestic river bi-sects the swamp and empties into Munuscong Bay.

On our weekend family trips to my grandparents' homes, we traveled down the north side of the Gogemain (on the gravel Gogemain Road) to my Grandma Florence's house in Raber. We traveled along the south side of the Gogemain (on M-48) to my Grandpa Hank's home in Stalwart.

Along both routes, we would often see animals like groundhogs, rabbits, partridge, squirrels, deer and even the occasional bear, coyote and fox. As a small boy, I used to stare out the car window hoping to see this wildlife. From our 1957 Chevy, I saw my first bear run across the road in the Gogemain. After that, I was convinced that this was a wild and wonderful place full of game animals of all kinds.

While dad didn't hunt in the heart of the Gogemain, he knew lots of hunters who did, and he had hunted around its southwest corner since he was a small boy.

One November day in deer season, dad came home from work and told my mother and me that the doctor who worked in the Sault Poly Clinic behind our downtown store was lost in the Gogemain while hunting. He explained that the county sheriff had called for volunteers to form a large search party to help find him.

My mother was very concerned, and she offered to help right away. "Why don't you join the search party and try to find the doctor?" mom asked dad that night. "I can work for you in the store until you get back."

The next day, my dad dressed in his hunting clothes and drove to the north end of the Gogemain to look for the lost doctor. He searched for him most of the day.

I could hardly wait to find out what had happened to the doctor. "Did you find him, Dad? I asked as he came to the door. "Did you see any sign of him?"

Lost in the Gogemain

I remember my father looking really tired as he slowly told us about his long excursion.

"There were lots of volunteers, and we searched in small groups. We tried to walk in a straight line, and we yelled out his name as we walked through the woods. We covered a large area, and none of us saw him," dad explained as I waited on his every word.

Dad couldn't go search again the next day, and he felt badly about that. He told me that a man cannot stay outside too long in the cold weather that we have in the UP, and a lost hunter cannot go too long without fresh water and food.

In those days, we didn't use the term hypothermia, but dad explained to me how a lost and confused hunter could work himself into a sweat trying to find his way out of the woods. He could keep going for awhile until he was exhausted, but then he would sit down, and his wet clothes would begin to freeze; at this point, his body temperature could drop to a dangerous level.

Dad explained to me how cold it would get at night and how dangerous that can be for a hunter left out in the woods without the proper clothing. He said he was worried about the doctor and his safety.

"Dad, could he die if he's not found soon?" I asked.

"Yes, Son, he could, and that's why I wanted to help look for him," dad explained in an honest way that sent shivers down my spine. "If they don't find him soon, he could die, and we might not find his body for a long time because winter and heavy snows are coming."

Dad explained that people from all over the area had joined the search party and that everyone was confident that they would find the doctor as long as he was OK. What he meant was that everyone had to hope the doctor wasn't hurt or already dead from the weather or an injury.

As good fortune would have it, after being lost for four days, the doctor walked out of the woods on his own to the safety of the main road, and he was no worse for the wear. He had spent three cold nights in the woods, and he had lost a few pounds, but otherwise, he was in good shape.

My mom and dad were happy when they heard the news.

Dad reinforced to me how this hunter had gotten lost and how he couldn't find his way out on his own, except by accident.

"First, he didn't know the woods he was hunting," dad explained to me several days later as I pestered him to learn more about the event. "You need to know the places you hunt before you go into them alone. Second, you never go into unfamiliar woods unless you have a compass."

Dad just shook his head over the thought that someone would go into a place as remote and rugged as the Gogemain without a compass. "The Gogemain is a huge swamp with no roads for miles and few landmarks," dad told me. "It's crazy to go in there without a compass – that's just asking for trouble. It would be so easy to get turned around and lost in there. You could walk around for days and never come out."

Dad also told me that hunters should always carry extra ammunition so if they become lost, they could signal those who are searching for them. "I don't think he had any extra ammunition," dad mused.

Proud Hunters Proud Yoopers

Finally, dad said that all hunters should carry a knife for survival to cut up an animal to eat if they needed food. He also said good hunters carry matches in a waterproof container. He didn't think the doctor had any of these standard survival accessories.

"If he had matches, he could have started a fire at night to keep warm, dry out his clothes and signal someone that he was alive," dad explained. "Sometimes, if you take the time to make a fire, not only will you warm up, but you might get your bearings again, too. You have to keep your cool if you get lost."

I was now just about infatuated with the Gogemain and the fact that you could be lost in it for days. Several years later, another hunter got lost in the big swamp. This time, the search party never found him. After several days of searching, they had to give up.

A year later, another hunter scouting for a new deer-hunting stand thought he saw something in the leaves in a dense part of the Gogemain. As he moved the leaves, he found the rusted gun of a deer hunter, and he found a human skeleton.

The skeleton and the gun belonged to the missing hunter. He had been found, but the Gogemain had claimed him forever.

This story both scared me and fascinated me. After these two lost hunter stories, I was totally in awe of the Gogemain.

From kindergarten on, dad started taking me on regular hunting trips with him, and we frequently hunted the southwest corner of the Gogemain. As we would drive to my grandpa's house on M-48, near the Michalski and Yegal farms, I would gaze in wonderment when I could see all the way across the Gogemain to North Raber and the Munuscong Bay. I was amazed at the size and the density of the swamp that stretched that far without a single road across it.

The landscape in the eastern UP is remarkably flat with few hills, but from this one location on M-48, you can see five or more miles clear across the Gogemain to the bay and to Canada. This view is a constant reminder of how vast the Gogemain is.

Over the years, dad and I killed hundreds of partridge, dozens of deer, lots of ducks, and one trophy size bear in the Gogemain. All the while, this magnificent land was owned by timber companies who allowed the public to hunt their lands under the State's Commercial Forestry Act (CFA).

And while the timber company owned this land, I felt as if it were my own special place. Very few hunters ventured into the Gogemain as dad and I did, and we almost always had it to ourselves during the hunting season.

Occasionally, other hunters showed up, but they never stayed long, and very few knew how to hunt this vast country like we did.

Over time, I really fell in love with the Gogemain. It became my own little piece of paradise. I hunted it from early August, when we first put out bear baits, until January 1, the last day of bow season for deer.

I was there in hot August and September days when the mosquitoes were almost unbearable, and I hunted it in late December when the temperatures were as cold as 20 degrees below zero. And I loved every minute I spent there.

One summer, the timber company put up signs that they were selling off the Gogemain land we had been hunting. Initially, I didn't worry about this development.

Lost in the Gogemain

For a long time, the land didn't sell, so I thought the timber company wasn't really serious about selling the land, or there were no willing buyers for this "swamp land."

While Kimberly Clark Corporation had owned the property for decades, they had sold the land to Champion, another large paper producer with significant UP land holdings and paper processing plants. As long as this property remained in the hands of some timber company, odds were good we could continue to hunt it as we had in the past. Consequently, I still wasn't worried about losing access to the Gogemain.

Sometime in the late 1980s or early 1990s, Champion sold the Gogemain to a firm called Christy Products. Christy Products wasn't a large or well-known timber company, but they immediately started logging the Gogemain right by grandpa's home where we hunted. After taking some easy timber near the main road, the company just disappeared from the landscape. Soon, Christy had transferred the Gogemain to a new company called Pickford Investments. I was never really sure who owned or operated these companies.

Christy Products and Pickford Investments appeared to me to be start-up businesses that no one locally knew much about. Both companies kept the land open to the public under the CFA program, but they also cut some of the easily reachable timber around the edges of the Gogemain. One summer, a timber crew cut down one of my favorite bow seats, one located just north of grandpa's house and up high in a huge balsam fir tree. Virtually everything else in the area around my seat was clear cut, too. Just like that, I lost one of my best December deer-hunting spots.

After several decades of hunting the Gogemain, it looked like there would be some changes coming. Different timber companies were buying and selling the Gogemain. It was hard to keep up with who owned the property. I feared that one day I would be shut out of the Gogemain. I began to hunt as if every day there were my last day.

One day, I saw an advertisement in the MUCC outdoor magazine about a condo-type arrangement where hunters could have access to thousands of acres of land to hunt in the eastern UP. I called the 800 number in the ad, and the telemarketer told me that this land was the same land I had been hunting. Suddenly, I had visions of hundreds of hunters owning the Gogemain, each holding a condominium share of the property. I asked about the price, and then I told the telemarketer that I was not interested. Apparently, there were no takers for the condo project because after a few months, the ads never reappeared. That was the last I heard about the Gogemain condo scheme.

Both John Griffin, the Cedarville-based owner of the Smith and Griffin realty firm, and Forbes McDonald of the McDonald Realty firm in Pickford were hired to split up and sell the Gogemain for the different timber companies. At first sales were slow, but soon the properties on the north side started to sell, and then the east side properties sold. Still no one appeared interested in the southern properties near grandpa's house where we hunted.

Dad knew the John Jorgeson family of Sault Ste. Marie who ran a beer distribution company in town. They told dad that they purchased several hundred acres of the Gogemain on the east side near Raber. While dealing with the timber company had been difficult, they were able to negotiate for a nice piece of property for a reasonable cost.

Proud Hunters Proud Yoopers

As I would see other hunters from the Stalwart area, we would talk about the property being for sale. Most local hunters quickly dismissed the idea of a sale for most of the land.

"No one would buy this property," one local hunter told me. "The Gogemain will always be here and open for us to hunt."

I wasn't so sure, and at one point, I thought I had better get at least a piece of the Gogemain, just in case it did all get sold to private owners.

From 1992 to 1997, I made almost a dozen different offers to the owners of the property to buy my favorite piece of the Gogemain. I worked with both John Griffin and Forbes McDonald to do everything I could to make an acceptable offer to the struggling timber companies that were trying to hang on to the property. In my offers to the timber companies, I offered virtually everything I owned and pledged to borrow every dime I could so I would end up with as much acreage of the Gogemain as possible.

I had a three-inch folder of my real estate offers, a timber appraisal of the property, DNR forestry maps of the timber, soil maps of the area and other material that I had accumulated in my quest to ensure I could still hunt the great Gogemain.

I would spend hours at my home in Holt trying to think of creative ways I could afford to purchase a large chunk of the Gogemain, trying to realize my dream to keep hunting the magnificent Gogemain.

Despite all this effort, I could never get the sellers to accept my offers. Meanwhile, others were being more successful, like the Jorgesons. By the late 1990s, nearly all the other Gogemain property had been sold to private individuals and no trespassing signs were going up all over the place. Slowly but surely, public access to the Gogemain was disappearing.

At one point, I walked over to the DNR offices in Lansing, and I told them about the remaining Gogemain property and the timber company's interest in selling large chunks of it. Forbes McDonald of Pickford also pushed me to get the DNR to buy what was left of the Gogemain.

"This is a very valuable deer yard for the eastern UP, and you should consider buying some or all of it to protect it as winter deer habitat," I told the DNR staffers. I wanted the DNR to use dedicated revenue available in the state's Natural Resources Trust Fund to purchase the land so it would remain open to the public and be protected as a perpetual and priceless deer yard.

"If an individual buys it and timbers it off," I warned, "it's gone forever, and we lose one of the eastern UP's best deer yards."

Despite my pleadings, I couldn't interest the DNR to contact the timber companies about buying it. I confirmed with the realtors that they never made a serious effort to buy it.

Somewhere in this process, there were also rumors that one timber company had defaulted on its business loan, and the company had not been paying its property taxes. Another new company, Sandridge Outback Corporation, now owned the Gogemain, and now another company was marketing it to the public.

Sure enough, when I checked, the Gogemain property was listed as delinquent in the tax notices published in the county's annual tax sale. While I had never been to a county tax sale, I went to this one, and on May 7, 1997, I paid $534.46 in back taxes on

Lost in the Gogemain

the Gogemain property for the timber company. Secretly, I was hoping the company wouldn't pay me back, and then I would get title to their property through the complicated tax lien process.

For several months, I held a tax lien on my favorite Gogemain property. To my disappointment, the timber company did eventually pay me off on the property taxes plus interest that they owed. This preserved their ownership rights in the property. I then lost my tax lien and any chance I had of acquiring the property through the tax lien process.

Finally, I got a call that I had hoped I would never get. One day at work, Forbes McDonald called me to tell me that a group of hunters from southwest Michigan had purchased all 2,300 acres of the Gogemain across the road from my grandpa. They had formed a company called the Cedarwood LLC to hold the property. Forbes said they had a plan to aggressively timber the property and manage it as a hunting club. Ironically, these same hunters also owned significant holdings of land on the Prentis Bay Road where I also hunted. Forbes told me they would start building access roads into the Gogemain as soon as possible. He said they were a reputable group of guys with the resources to complete the sale.

When I hung up the phone, I felt like I had gotten a phone call about a relative who had just died. There was a pit in my stomach, and I had a sense of losing something very important and dear to me. I now had to accept that someone else was buying my little paradise, my piece of the Gogemain. I knew what that meant – I would probably never hunt the Gogemain again, at least not in the manner that I had over the last four decades. And it meant that my children would never see it or hunt it as I had.

As soon as I could, I made one last trip into the Gogemain. I started out from my grandpa's house as I always did. I put on hip boots for all the wet spots I would encounter, and I took a lunch with me so I could stay the whole day. I walked straight north into the heart of the Gogemain from my grandpa's house, following as best I could, an old, grown-up trail that lead to a ridge of mature hemlock and white pine trees. It was the secret, mystical ridge that my Uncle John Firack had always talked about.

"There's a nice Hemlock ridge, way back in the Gogemain, near the river," my Uncle John had told me many times. "There's huge hemlock and white pine on the ridge, and they are big enough around that you could build a house with any one of them," he would joke. It was the ridge that very few people knew about and even fewer had ever seen. When I got there, I marveled one last time at the mature timber and at this isolated ridge rising up in the middle of this huge cedar swamp jungle.

As I approached the middle of the Gogemain, I encountered some of its most dense swamp land forest. I remembered the hunters that had been lost in this great wilderness, and I remembered the hunter who had lost his life in here. I paid a silent tribute to those hunters, and I thanked our Creator that I had always found my way out of this special place by nightfall.

I crossed the hemlock ridge, and I continued on through rugged country until I hit the Gogemain River. I sat on the bank and watched the brown water of the mighty Gogemain flow east and north toward Munuscong Bay. I thought about how beautiful this spot was and how few people in the State of Michigan even knew it existed. I

Proud Hunters Proud Yoopers

thought about my plans to build a cabin on this river someday and my plans to canoe up and down the river. There was sadness in my heart as I accepted that these were dreams that would never be realized.

As I walked away from the river, I looked back several times to say goodbye one more time. On my return trip out of the Gogemain, I circled around to visit the ridges and marshes on the south side where dad and I had hunted for over 40 years for bear, deer, partridge and ducks. I visited all my favorite deer stands, our lucky bear stand, and my favorite duck pond. I remembered the hundreds of times I had flushed partridge on the south logging trail.

I remembered how much I loved to hunt this land in late December when the deer migrated from as far away as 35 miles to spend the winter in the Gogemain. When Christmas was over each year, I couldn't wait to get up north again and trek into the Gogemain for one last bow hunt before the season ended the first of January.

I remembered all the deer (and especially those big bucks) I had seen in the Gogemain, the ten and twenty below zero temperatures I had braved to hunt here, and the sheer ruggedness of those late season hunts.

I remembered the bears dad and I had pursued in the Gogemain, the bear bait I had backpacked into the area, and the excitement of watching those curious black bears approach our bait while we waited for them with a bow and arrow. I remembered tracking the wounded "slasher" bear in the dark with dad, and I remembered my close encounter with the deer-attacking black bear.

Then I remembered the first hunt I had in the Gogemain with my dad when I was five years old. I walked by the area where I first saw the toadstool I wanted so badly. I remembered the lesson dad had taught me that day about landmarks hunters used to find their way out of the woods.

I walked out of the Gogemain 30 minutes later, having spent almost the entire day in these magnificent woods.

The long day had been a deeply satisfying and moving experience. I was physically exhausted and mentally drained, but I was so glad I had done this.

The next time I returned to grandpa's house, the "No Trespassing" signs were up, and the entrance to my piece of the Gogemain had a metal gate across it. The gate and signs were confirmation that my days of wandering the Gogemain were over forever.

I didn't hold any resentment against the new owners. They were, in fact, doing what I would have done if I had purchased the Gogemain. I was just so sad that they had achieved what I had worked so hard to accomplish. I had a feeling the new owners would do good things with the land and that they would be good stewards of the great Gogemain. I wished them well in their ownership of the property I loved so much.

It was time to move on. While I would never hunt the Gogemain again, a Proud Hunter had etched in his brain almost forty years of memories spent hunting in a great and wondrous place.

This short story would have ended here, except that in May 2006, I got an e-mail from my friend Mike Jackson who attached a DNR press release, announcing that the DNR had just purchased 2,300 acres of an eastern UP deer yard in the Gogemain Swamp. I reread the press release several times to make sure it was the same piece of property. I made a quick call and confirmed that this was the Cedarwood LLC piece of property – the Gogemain property that dad and I had hunted for so long. I had tears in

Lost in the Gogemain

my eyes when I realized that, the Good Lord willing, I would hunt the Gogemain again. I wrote an emotional e-mail to the leadership of the DNR, thanking them for the good thing they had done.

And I made plans with my son and father for another December bow hunt in the Great Gogemain.

On this day, a Proud Hunter realized the power of public land ownership over critical natural resources like the Gogemain. A Proud Hunter also recognized that because of a single land purchase by the DNR, another generation of Proud Yoopers could start their own adventures in the Great Gogemain.

38

The Perfect Yooper Deer Camp

When you begin a great work
you can't expect to finish it all at once,
therefore, you and your brothers press on,
and let nothing discourage you
till you have finished what you have begun...

- Teedyuscung, Delaware

By age ten, I was wandering around alone on my Grandpa Ed's 40-acre parcel in Goetzville, carrying my BB gun and hunting for squirrels, chipmunks, frogs, starlings, sparrows and similar targets. And I was gaining an appreciation for just how big a 40-acre parcel was. At my Grandma Nutting's place in Raber, I was exploring the wild and remote Pointe Aux Frene property.

I didn't know it yet, but I was building a strong desire to own a large block of hunting land. By now I understood that Grandpa Ed lived on 40 acres that was actually only a small part of a square mile of mostly vacant land. One day, my dad took me on a four-mile car ride around the entire square mile. When we had circled the property, I was amazed at how much land one square mile was – a whole 640 acres, my dad reinforced. I thought grandpa's 40 acres was large, and I thought a square mile of hunting land was huge.

Soon after that, I walked around the entire square mile with my cousin Dan and my sister Linda. That really confirmed for me just how big a square mile really is.

Sometime in this era, I started dreaming of owning a square mile of land myself that I would hunt intensely whenever I wanted. In my boyhood dreams, this land of mine had perfect habitat so that lots of wildlife used it. On my dream property, there were lots of deer, bear, rabbits, partridge, ducks, squirrels, chipmunks, and other game.

Some time after that, I heard my dad and the other hunters discussing a story about the DNR having a one-square mile fenced in wooded area where they had a private deer herd inside the fence. The DNR studied the deer herd inside this protected enclosure for research purposes. These UP deer were safe from hunters and coyotes, they never got hit by cars, and they were protected from violators and poachers. The DNR also knew exactly how many deer there were.

Most important to hunters, the DNR knew there were exactly seven bucks inside the enclosure. In the legendary Yooper story about this place, the DNR had invited the best hunters in the area to go inside the fence to hunt the bucks. The way I heard the story, those excellent hunters didn't even see a buck until the third day, and no one killed a buck until several days later. Some hunters never saw a buck in their entire hunt.

Even though the bucks were enclosed inside a fence and couldn't get away very far from the hunters, most of the bucks survived and were not killed. The purpose of

The Perfect Yooper Deer Camp

the unusual, organized hunt was to illustrate that there are more deer than most people think living in every square mile of Michigan. The story also proved that deer can hide and stay away from hunters better than most hunters think they can.

I was in awe of this story, thinking that those deer could hide so well in one square mile so that even outstanding hunters couldn't find them, let alone kill them.

I didn't know until years later that this story was, for the most part, a true story. It happened at the UP's Seney Wildlife Research Center in Shingleton, Michigan. One of the country's most respected deer biologists, the UP's own John Ozoga of Munising, Michigan, was the DNR's deer researcher at the facility for years. Ozoga published dozens of research studies on deer behavior based on what he learned in the facility.

These events made me more determined that one day I would own a whole square mile of prime hunting property that I would manage for wildlife.

Ten years after I started my career with the State of Michigan, I went to an out-of-town seminar where the speaker had all audience members write down their secret goals of what they wanted to accomplish in life. The speaker told us that one thing all millionaires had in common was that they had all developed a written goal that they wanted to make a million dollars (a lot of money in those days!). He was trying to convince us that whatever our key goals were, we needed to get them recorded on paper into a "Life Plan" of what we wanted to accomplish in life.

He promised us that if we recorded our goals, our odds of achieving them were far greater.

Near the end of class, we shared some of our goals with each other. Almost all my co-workers in the class wrote down that they wanted to be millionaires or make a million dollars. That was by far the most popular, personal goal. There were also goals written about family, faith, good health, nice homes, fast cars, and similar goals.

I was the only one in the class who recorded that he wanted to own one square mile of deer hunting real estate.

This experience probably best explains why I worked so hard to buy the Gogemain property. I knew the Gogemain opportunity was my best chance to get my square mile of deer habitat in the UP.

After losing my bid to get a major chunk of the Gogemain, I had to accept reality and adopt a new goal that I should look for hunting property somewhere else. I wasn't giving up on buying something like the Gogemain, but I needed to keep my options open.

After hunting on state and CFA land for decades, I also accepted that things were changing rapidly for UP public land hunters. There were fewer lands enrolled in the CFA program as major timber companies implemented their corporate strategies to sell off their large land holdings. The new owners, usually private landowners who bought the property for hunting purposes, quickly put up "No Trespassing" signs. They did not participate in the CFA program, and their land was not open to public hunting.

And the hunting on public land was not the same high quality that it had been either. While I still enjoyed the vastness of Hungry Hill, the large blocks of unspoiled wilderness areas were being carved up and invaded by new armies of hunters who used All-Terrain Vehicles (ATVs) to gain access to the formerly remote areas.

After hunting for decades and rarely seeing any other hunters on state land, I was now not only seeing more hunters, but sometimes hunters were riding right by my bow and rifle stands in ATVs and sometimes in pick-up trucks or Jeeps. The privacy and seclusion of Hungry Hill seemed as if it were slipping away.

On one hand, I couldn't totally blame these hunters. After all, we used ATVs to get close to where we hunted, and we used them to take out our deer. We also used them to haul in feed for deer. The hunters that followed us were, in one sense, only doing what we had originally done. Like us, they were searching for a more remote, secluded and high-quality place to hunt.

These hunters had as much right to be there and to explore new horizons as I did.

At the time, I owned 40 acres of property, a very nice parcel that my parents had owned prior to their divorce. After the divorce, my mom had offered me the property - land in Raber close to the house where she had lived as a youngster growing up. The property had a nice grove of sugar maple trees, and it had a few mature apple trees. It also had about 15 acres of a vacant field.

This property had been in our family for three generations, but for as long as we owned it, dad and I had never hunted it. I decided that since I owned this piece of property, I should work harder to make it better deer habitat, and I thought I should hunt it occasionally.

In November 1993, I had hired a professional land management consultant, David Neph of the Grossman Forestry Company, to complete a Stewardship Incentive Plan for me on the Raber 40 acres. Grossman's offices are in Newberry, Michigan, and they are the largest forestry service company in the eastern UP. Dave lives in the Cheboygan area, and his wife Julie works as an engineer for the Mackinac Bridge.

In his management plan, Dave recommended that I thin the hardwoods to let more sunlight hit the forest floor so I would get better regeneration of the maple forest. He also recommended that I plant 1,700 pine trees around the vacant field so that wildlife would feel more secure living in this woodlot.

Under the rules of the Stewardship Incentive Program, I also had to get approval for this work from the DNR and the Chippewa-Mackinac Conservation District (CMCD). Bob DeVillez of the Newberry DNR office and Dusty King and Lynn MacArthur of the CMCD approved the plan for me. Along the way, Bob also gave me approval to plant several thousand oak trees on the property.

This program got me turned on to planting trees for wildlife habitat. On the Raber property alone, I planted about 4,000 trees of almost every variety, but with heavy emphasis on red oaks and red pines, two fast growing UP trees.

A few years later, another state worker in Lansing, Don Niemi, asked me if I might be interested in buying 40 acres on Neebish Island that he had owned for years, land which he no longer hunted. "I know you go up to the eastern UP all the time," he told me one day in front of the State of Michigan's Ottawa Building. "Why don't you look it over and see if you are interested."

"You know, Don, I lived within 15 miles of Neebish Island for 22 years, and I have never been over there," I told him. "Maybe I will look at it this weekend."

Now I wasn't really looking for 40 acres, especially if it were on a remote island. But on a lark, dad and I headed over to Neebish Island to look over the property. Our first challenge is that we had to take a ferry boat ride across the St. Mary's River to get to the place. The ferry boat operators, Bob and Mary Schallip, charged us the standard fare of $10.

The Perfect Yooper Deer Camp

At that point, I defiantly said to dad, "I don't like this place already, and I haven't been there yet. Who in their right mind would pay $10 every weekend to get to their deer camp?" I hadn't yet learned that there was a much cheaper "commuter" rate for frequent travelers that would lower my costs to get back and forth to the island.

When dad and I got to the Niemi place, there were two small cabins as Don had described except that someone had broken into both of them and literally destroyed everything of value in each of them. The nicer cabin had been exposed to the elements for so long that the ground floor had almost completely rotted away so that the living room was falling into the basement. I didn't think there was really anything that was salvageable.

The second cabin had also been severely damaged. Vandals had blasted the front door open by shooting off the door hinges. Once inside the cabin, the vandals had shot out every window, they blew holes through every wall, and they destroyed the refrigerator, stove, furnace, and every shelf by shooting shotgun shells through them. Worst of all, they shot multiple holes in the roof so that the rain and snow poured through the cabin.

"What a mess," dad said to me. "Can you believe that someone would do this to another person's place?"

I wrote off the two cabins as complete losses. I was sure there was no value in either one of them.

I thought to myself, strike two against the Neebish Island property.

Dad and I checked our compasses and headed into the woods. Just behind the cabin were 25 junk cars and what looked like the unauthorized island dump. There were old, broken down appliances of almost every type scattered about a wetlands area.

"What a sickening place this is," I said to dad. I was just about to claim "strike three" and write off this place as a wasted afternoon.

But as we got beyond the wrecked cabins and the junkyard, we started seeing well-worn deer trails and some very nice deer country. There were beautiful ridges of mature white spruce, poplars, balsam fir, and even some huge white pines. In between the ridges, there were small marshes that were excellent deer bedding and cover areas. The mix of the land looked like outstanding deer habitat.

"Dad, this is a deer factory if it is managed right," I boldly proclaimed.

"This is nice looking country," he agreed with me. "Maybe you should buy it, and we could use it for bow hunting in October. You can hold it while you look for a better piece of property. It should be a good investment even if you find something else."

Not long after that, I made an offer to Don Niemi, and I bought the 40-acre parcel with the two destroyed cabins.

Dad and I bowhunted Neebish Island that fall for the first time. Almost immediately, dad and I started seeing a number of bucks, but most of them were small, one-and-a-half year-old bucks. Even so, we were intrigued by this enchanted and remote island. One day, while we were exploring the south end of our property, dad grabbed my arm and whispered to me to stop and look to the right.

There in the late afternoon shadows was a huge 10-point buck looking at us from the security of heavy cover. Somehow, dad had spotted him hiding in the bush.

Proud Hunters Proud Yoopers

Just a year later, a large piece of property directly behind the 40 acres came up for sale. The Dwight Hitchcock family of Bellevue, Michigan, owned the property. It was 136 acres that included almost a half mile of frontage on a cove that bordered the main shipping channel of the St. Mary's River. The huge great lakes freighters went by this place so close you could almost touch them. At the edge of the St. Mary's River, the property had a huge outcropping of limestone that looked like property on Drummond and Mackinac Islands.

"This is a unique piece of property," dad said to me one day as we looked over the place.

I made an offer on the Hitchcock property through the McDonald Real Estate Office, and we closed on the property. I didn't have my entire square mile of hunting property, but I now had hunting property a mile long, from the 15 Mile main road on Neebish Island to the waterfront.

I now set out on a mission to buy the rest of the property in the area. Over the next few years, I was able to purchase four other contiguous pieces of property, giving me 270 total acres of choice hunting property. I used every creative financing tool I knew to buy the properties, sometimes leveraging my finances to the limit. Despite the financial stress, I convinced myself that this would be worth it – and it was.

As I thought about the turn of events that lead me to Neebish Island and my successful efforts to acquire 270 acres, it occurred to me that I was almost halfway to my boyhood dream of owning a square mile of hunting country.

Now I turned my attention to the land itself. I began work with the DNR and CMCD on another Stewardship Incentive Plan for the Neebish property. Working with those agencies, I would line up more federal grant money to help me cover about 50% of my costs to make some major improvements to the wildlife habitat on the property. Over several years, I would plant hundreds of oak, pine, spruce and apple trees to make the deer habitat even better. I also dug three one-acre wildlife wetland ponds, using the services of Ken Norris, a former state trooper, and his excavation company, Norris Contracting, of Sault Ste. Marie. We used a huge bulldozer and an excavator to dig the ponds to a depth of about 24 inches, perfect for ducks and geese. Those ponds would become important nesting and resting stops for both migrating and local waterfowl. I also cleaned up the dump and got rid of the junk cars, turning a wasteland into useful wildlife habitat.

While working on improving the habitat, dad and I also needed a place to stay on the island. As we contemplated tearing down both busted up cabins, dad made this famous statement: "You know, with a little bit of work, we could save this one and make something out of it. We need a place to stay anyway, so why don't we keep this one and fix it up a little at a time?"

That infamous statement would formulate our work plans for the next ten years after I agreed to keep the "little red cabin" as we affectionately called it. That cabin had a floor littered with spent shotgun shells, every window blown out, every appliance blasted, and multiple holes in the roof. And, oh yes, it didn't have a front or a rear door – they had been blown away, too.

But each weekend, dad and I would tackle a new project, in many cases, doing something we had never done before. We put on a new roof, we installed new doors

The Perfect Yooper Deer Camp

and windows, we gutted the interior, we replaced the plumbing and the electrical wiring, we paneled and finished the interior, and we put on new outside siding.

Over a ten-year period, we restored a destroyed cabin (and a visual eye sore) into the perfect Yooper hunting camp. From this modest camp, we would hold an annual Opening Day family hunt every November 15, with all four generations of our Hank family participating.

I received lots of help from my hunting friends along the way. My CMU track teammate Jeff Reynolds of Lake City and his boyhood friend Ed Davenport of Holt spent a long weekend with me to rebuild the busted up cabin foundation. Ed runs one of the largest masonry contracting companies in Michigan, so having these guys come up was a godsend. They had all the right equipment and know-how to restore my foundation in quick order. To return the favor, I needed to take these two QDMA supporters on a good workout with their pointers and retrievers for some grouse and woodcock hunting, a price I gladly paid. Jeff and Ed run a 200-acre deer camp in the Lake City area where they have taken some mature whitetails after starting an aggressive QDM program in the mid-1990s.

Our Canadian hunting friend and licensed electrician, Ron Kay, helped me rewire the house and perform all the technical electrical hook-ups I needed. Ronnie is a moose and deer hunter who really lives to fish every day he can.

One of dad's friends, Walt Sterling of Sterling Plumbing, completed our plumbing work. Walt is an avid Yooper bear and bobcat hunter, and he's run a guide service, using his dogs to tree the bears and cats he chases in the eastern UP.

And every time I brought someone up north for a weekend hunting trip, they usually got a chance to help improve the cabin. Dozens of great guys got a piece of that action, and they really helped dad and me with the ten-year restoration project.

Now that most of the work is behind us, the best thing I like about the cabin is that I can walk out the front door and immediately be hunting for deer or small game. I love the idea that wildlife lives right around the cabin and that I could see game right out my windows at any time. That made the camp even more special. And I love that during the spring grouse mating season, I can be awakened in the morning by the drumming of a nearby male grouse.

Those kinds of alarm clocks are the best, and they are priceless.

I also like that the cabin is not nice enough that I have to take off my muddy boots when I come in from a hunt. Who cares if there's a little mud on the floor of a cabin that was destined to be torn down?

On the inside of the cabin, we left room to display the antlers of all bucks 2.5 years and older that we harvested. Our south living room wall is almost covered with an impressive display of bucks we have killed on the property since starting a QDM program. My friend Mike Jackson of DeWitt calls it our "Wall of Fame."

Our cabin is still tiny, with an outside frame of only 16 feet by 24 feet, and it gets pretty cramped when we have four to six guys for opening day. Even so, having your own hunting cabin is almost every Yooper's dream, and those cabins are filled with special memories. I am blessed that I have been able to fulfill my cabin dream – even if it did take ten years and "a little bit of work."

From these experiences, a Proud Yooper learned that a young boy's dream of acquiring a large tract of wildlife habitat can come true, especially if he makes a

Proud Hunters Proud Yoopers

written plan. And a Proud Hunter also learned that many other Proud Hunters will lend a hand when it comes to fixing up your special, fix-it-upper Yooper hunting cabin.

39

A Son's First Deer

My heart is filled with joy
when I see you here,
as the brooks fill with water
when the snow melts
in the spring;
And I feel glad as the ponies do
when the fresh grass starts
in the beginning of the year...

-Ten Bears, Commanche

In November, 1995, my son Jeff was 14 years old, the age when he was now old enough to hunt deer with a rifle for the first time. Because of school, sports and other commitments, he couldn't get up north with me to hunt on the critical opening day weekend. So, after spending Thanksgiving Day at his Grandma Sternhagen's house in Saginaw, Jeff and I were headed up to Grandpa Ed's house where we would hunt Hungry Hill with my dad.

I had my gear ready from previous weekend hunts, but I needed to pack Jeff's heavy clothes and my Remington bolt action .30/06 rifle that he would use.

All the way to the UP, we talked strategies about deer hunting, and I explained how he might see deer that he could shoot. He had both a doe permit and a buck tag, so he could shoot any deer he saw if he wanted. Most important, I talked to him again about gun safety, and I explained to him that I had promised his mom and my wife, Susan, that I would not let him hunt alone with a gun.

Jeff would sit with me in my blind or with my dad, his Grandpa Lou, in his blind.

He wanted to hunt alone, but he accepted that these were the ground rules, set by his loving mother, until he was a little older and more experienced.

We arrived in the UP after dark, and we talked with Grandpa Lou and Grandpa Ed before heading to bed.

The next morning, we ate a big breakfast, packed our lunches, and loaded up dad's old blue Chevy pickup for the trip to Hungry Hill.

When we arrived at our parking spot in the bush, we grabbed our gear and our guns. That's when dad said to me, "Leon, what gun did you bring for Jeff?"

"He can hunt with my Remington," I told him. "What's wrong?"

"Well, we have a problem, because you brought the wrong gun for him," dad explained. "You brought your .22 instead of the Remington .30/06."

Now in Michigan, it's not legal to hunt deer with a .22 rimfire rifle, and, even if it were legal, it's probably not a good idea.

I was distraught. How could I have made such a stupid mistake on something this important? I had wanted my son to have a great experience on his first rifle hunt, and

181

now I had really screwed it up by bringing the wrong gun. Now he didn't even have a gun to hunt with.

I could have cried. I tried to think through what I had done and how I had made this terrible mistake. The .22 and Remington do look a little bit alike, and they both have similar bolt actions and scopes. In my haste to pack, I must have grabbed the wrong gun.

Dad and I did the only thing we could have done. We promised Jeff that he could use either of our guns, depending on whom he was sitting with.

"Jeff, my blind is a better two-person blind than your dad's blind, so maybe you should hunt with me," dad offered.

Then dad kidded me. "Maybe you should give Jeff your gun, and you should sit in the woods today with the .22! After all, you are the one who brought the wrong gun for your son's first hunt."

"Thanks a lot, Dad, I am already feeling bad enough," I said as I again apologized to Jeff.

After this friendly razing and consoling, we left the .22 in the truck and headed to our blinds, three hunters with two rifles.

We saw no deer in the morning, and Jeff spent several hours watching the Hungry Hill snowmobile trail with both dad and me. To keep his interest, I moved him several times from my seat to dad's seat and back again.

By early afternoon, Jeff was with dad when a doe came to feed on some apples dad had spread out about 60 yards from his blind on the north side of the trail. As the deer began to feed, dad coached Jeff on how to get the gun ready for a shot.

Because the deer was relatively close and a young doe, dad told Jeff to try shooting the deer in the head so he didn't ruin any meat.

I don't think Jeff was too excited about this, and I had schooled him long and hard about how a perfect killing shot is to shoot a deer just behind the shoulder.

Nonetheless, he followed his grandfather's advice and put the crosshairs on the deer's head. I don't know exactly what happened, but Jeff missed the deer, and the deer, probably scared out of its wits from the bullet flying by its head, took off immediately for the Canadian border.

Hearing the shot and confident my son had killed his first deer with a rifle, I headed up to see the grandpa/grandson duo. When I got there, they weren't cleaning out a deer as I had expected. After hearing the story, I asked Jeff if he wanted to come back to my seat for the last couple of hours before dark.

"No, I think I've got a good spot here with grandpa, and I think I will get the next deer I see," Jeff said confidently.

My dad agreed. "I probably shouldn't have told him to shoot the deer in the head," dad admitted. "That's a tough shot for an experienced hunter, let alone for your first hunt."

"He'll get the next one that comes along!"

After I left, my rookie deer-hunting son also told his grandpa that he wanted to shoot the next deer in the shoulder.

An hour later, I heard another unmistakable shot from dad's seat. I headed up there right away.

A Son's First Deer

This time, Jeff and dad were cleaning out the deer. Jeff had killed a female doe fawn with his grandpa's .30/06 Browning Automatic Rifle. He had hit the deer perfectly in the shoulder, and the deer had run straight away from the blind. The deer dropped about 60 yards from where Jeff shot it.

He and grandpa had followed the brief, but prominent blood trail to the deer, and now dad was showing Jeff how to clean out his first deer. I came along just in time to help.

Now Jeff wasn't too excited about pulling out the insides of a warm deer, so I did much of the honors, showing him how it was done.

When we were finished, we tucked the deer under a tree until the day's end. At dark, we dragged the deer to the ATV, and we hauled the deer back to Grandpa Ed's place.

That night, we ate the tenderloins out of the deer. Jeff loves a good steak, and he really thought it was cool that he could be eating the deer he shot just several hours earlier.

Tenderloins from a new hunter's first deer tasted just great to me too, especially knowing they came from my own son's first deer.

Near the end of this season, dad and I decided this would be our last rifle season hunting on Hungry Hill.

The remoteness of Hungry Hill had started to disappear. Each year, we were seeing more and more hunters. Some of them came on ATVs coming down the snowmobile trail that they had traveled on their snow sleighs in the winter. One day, a group of guys in a huge four-wheel drive truck drove right up to my blind.

We now had our Neebish Island property, and we had started to manage it for deer and as a deer hunting camp. It was good deer country and big woods country like Hungry Hill. East of our property were almost 2,000 acres of private hunting land without a single road crossing it. Just north of our property was another four square miles of public land owned by Michigan State University. No roads crossed this property either.

Gradually, dad and I talked about leaving the increasing crowds at Hungry Hill and converting all our hunting to our Neebish Island camp. Soon we also realized that we were two aging hunters, and we came to accept that we were no longer able to easily hunt the vast, remote Hungry Hill country that we once hunted as if it were our own homestead.

As dad and I explored this move, I remembered how we had left Springer Road and the Burning area to come to Hungry Hill. I remembered the different parts of Hungry Hill we had hunted as we evolved to our stands on the snowmobile trail. And I remembered the dozens of Hungry Hill bucks we had shot over the last 25 years. I remembered the dozens more that had gotten away.

On a cold November day, I remember looking at my Hungry Hill deer blind one more time and realizing that this was the last time I would hunt this country the way I had for so many years.

The hunt that dad and I had with Jeff on his first rifle hunt, when he killed his first deer, was to be our last successful hunt on Hungry Hill.

The next fall, I took Jeff to Neebish Island after our Thanksgiving dinner at Grandma Ginny's place in Saginaw.

Proud Hunters Proud Yoopers

When we arrived at our small cabin on Neebish, we took off on foot behind the cabin down a narrow trail. About 600 yards south of the cabin, I put Jeff in a makeshift seat that another hunter had used years before. I showed him an opening to the north where he could watch.

I asked him if he were ready to hunt on his own with his rifle for the first time.

"I am ready, Dad, and I will be careful," Jeff promised me. "Besides, you won't be far away, and I can call you if I need you."

We went over the safety instructions one more time, and I looked favorably at the Remington .30/06 bolt action rifle that Jeff was holding. This time, I had packed the right gun. He would be using the same gun that my dad had given me to hunt with, a gun that both my grandfathers had used.

It was a gun that I had used to kill lots of deer.

Confident now that my son was ready to hunt on his own, I promised him that I would be right down the trail, over the next ridge, looking south where I would be shooting away from him. I told him that I expected he would shoot away from me, too.

With those instructions understood, I took off on a hike, expecting to go only a few hundred yards away, well within hearing distance of Jeff. But as I got around the next bend on the trail, it seemed like the best place to sit was always just around the next bend.

As I kept looking around for a place to sit, I kept heading south until I came to a hardwoods forest on the southern border of our property. This looked like a good spot and I stayed there until dark. Being new to the property, I didn't realize just how far away from Jeff I really was.

Several times I heard shots that I thought might have been Jeff, but I didn't make a move to go to him, because the shots sounded too far away. I imagined that the shots were from hunters hunting on the public land to our north.

Shortly after dark, I came walking up to where I had dropped Jeff off. It was a lot longer walk than I had thought it should have been. That was when I realized that I had drifted farther away from him than I had planned.

"Dad, where have you been?" Jeff shouted, shining a flashlight at me as I approached. "I've been yelling for you for over an hour."

"I guess I was one or two ridges too far away," I explained sheepishly. "What's up?"

"Well, I shot a deer, a big doe, right after you left," Jeff said rather calmly.

"I didn't go look for it because you told me not to take off tracking a deer in this big country unless you were with me."

"I've been waiting here for several hours to see if I got the deer!" Jeff said.

Jeff took me to where the deer had crossed, and sure enough, he had hit the deer well. As we started following the blood trail, I knew the deer wouldn't go far. I put Jeff in the lead tracking the deer, and I followed him, while we used our flashlight to highlight the bright red blood on the white snow. Seventy yards into the timber, Jeff came upon the large doe he had taken cleanly with another perfect shot right behind the shoulder.

As we examined the deer, we noticed that the mature doe had very unusual markings on her. All four of her feet had pure white hair around her hooves. Two of her hooves were also almost pure white (when they should have been pure black), and two of them were partially black with distinctive white marking on them.

Obviously, the deer was a partial albino, with very attractive markings on an otherwise very typical looking deer.

This was one of the first deer we were to kill on Neebish Island, and one of the most special ones, because it was also Jeff's first deer on his own.

When we got the deer home, I saved the unusual feet, and I had them mounted on an oak board in the form of a gun rack with the four feet used to support two guns. It was a very cool looking accessory in our trophy room.

Now another generation of hunters was with us, and now we would begin hunting seriously in another remote stretch of vast deer country in the UP. And this Yooper could hardly wait to get started exploring and developing this new wildlife paradise.

On this day, a Proud Hunter learned about the joy of his son shooting his first deer on his own, and a Proud Yooper learned that another generation had joined our special hunting fraternity.

40

Wounded Bucks and Second Chances

The path to glory is rough,
and many gloomy hours obscure it.

- Black Hawk, Sauk

In October 1996, I found a large, mature white spruce tree with long, draping limbs that could provide excellent cover for a camouflaged bow hunter hiding in this tree. The tree was along the southwestern border of our Neebish Island property, close to the shoreline of the St. Mary's River.

I brushed out a spot in this tree about 20 feet up from the ground, and I placed a bow seat in the tree where I could shoot either in front of me or to my left. Right below me were two frequently used deer runways. This location was the perfect ambush spot for whitetails, because deer had trouble seeing you and they also had trouble smelling a hunter. My human scent was often blown harmlessly down the edge of the river by the prevailing winds. I could also get to the stand easily without spooking deer. All in all, this was a great bow hunting spot.

To sweeten things up more, I regularly baited up the small opening to my left with a few apples or sugar beets. Soon, lots of deer in the area knew they could find their favorite foods 20 yards from the big spruce that served as my bow stand.

In the first few weeks of the season, I didn't see any deer I wanted to shoot. But on Sunday of the third weekend, I was determined that I would see a good buck, and I arranged with dad to hunt until dark. That might not be unusual for mainland deer hunters, but for me, it was a bit trickier, because by staying until dark, I would miss the last ferry to the mainland.

Because I needed to work in Lansing the next morning, that meant dad and I would hunt until dark and then take our canoe across the swift current of the Neebish Island channel in the dark. Once on shore, we would pick up our vehicles, which we had taken to the mainland earlier in the day.

All this was a lot of work for two determined bow hunters, but we knew we would need to do this if we were to maximize our quality hunting time in the woods.

So, on this nice fall evening, I was enjoying the beautiful day, sitting in my remote elevated bow seat near the St. Mary's River. My scenery was a gorgeous opening surrounded by conifer trees and colorful red maples in the heavily forested country, close to the peak of the fall color season.

As darkness approached and the "witching" hour came, I was about to pack up my gear to leave. I was mentally going over all the preparation and packing we had to do to ensure dad and I got everything in the canoe. I was also thinking about the long drive home and how tired I would be tonight during the drive. I also thought about how exhausted I would be all day Monday, going to work with only a few hours sleep.

Wounded Bucks and Second Chances

While other hunters were focused on their quarry, these were the broodings of a Yooper hunter, who spends his weekends on a remote island.

Just as I was about to call it a day and exit my tree stand, I heard a distinct noise to my right. The noise snapped me back to reality and reminded me why I was hidden in a spruce tree. There was a deer approaching me as darkness was quickly setting in.

As the deer came into the opening, I could see antlers on his head and a good size fork. He looked to be at least a decent six-point buck and maybe he was bigger. In the fading light, I couldn't be sure.

The deer walked slowly across my opening. He browsed on bits of vegetation as he moved to my left, where I would have a clear shot at him.

All the time, I was urging him on, knowing that darkness was coming on fast. Soon, it would be difficult to see through the peep sight on my bow. I carefully turned on my lighted sight pin on the bow so I could at least see the pin clearly.

The deer kept move methodically to my left where I would have a clear shot at him. I needed him to turn slightly so I could get the perfect shot at his vital organs near his shoulder. As the seconds passed by like minutes, he finally turned so that I had the shot I wanted.

I gently raised the bow, looking for him in the sight. In the fading daylight, I now had trouble seeing him through the small, round hole of my peep sight. I pulled the sight off of the buck and tried to get my bearings. I wanted to be sure I could see his shoulder clearly. I didn't want to blow this shot and miss, or worse yet, wound the animal.

I knew this might be my best opportunity this year to take a nice buck, so I did everything in my power to ensure that I had a good shot at the buck. Confident now that I could kill the deer, I raised the bow again, drew it back and put my sight on his shoulder. When I was confident that I had a good shot lined up, I released my arrow at the unsuspecting buck.

As the bow launched the arrow, the deer lurched and ran hard from the clearing into the heavy cover. I had a good idea of where he had gone.

I had a good feeling that I had buried my arrow in the buck's shoulder area. I was confident it was a good shot.

I got down from the tree stand and began looking for my arrow. I couldn't find the arrow anywhere, so that meant that I had probably hit the deer and the arrow had likely stayed in the deer.

I started looking for signs of blood along the trail where the deer had exited, and soon I found a few drops that shortly turned into a good blood trail. By this time, dad had joined me, and I told him the story of how I had shot the deer.

Now my dad is an excellent tracker, so I was glad to have him along. While I might stumble through the woods looking for a wounded deer, dad was meticulous when tracking a deer. He would look at all the signs again and again. He was always looking for where the wounded deer was headed. He would analyze why the deer was headed in a certain direction. To him, the whole tracking experience was like finishing a massive jigsaw puzzle. He was always looking for sign that others like me would overlook.

As with many things in life, there was a little bit of science and lot of luck in this process. Overall, I was happy with our success rate in tracking wounded deer. We were always careful with the shots we took at deer. Dad had taught me to not take shots unless I was fairly certain I had a good, clean killing shot at the deer. With the bow and arrow, this was especially important. He had taught me early in life that it is better to let a deer go when presented with a bad shot than to shoot at him and wound him, maybe never to find him.

As we tracked this buck, I thought back to a prior wounded buck experience I had that still left me feeling almost ill.

In the late 1980s, I had one very bad experience while we were bow hunting in the Hungry Hill area. It was early November, and dad had taken the day off from work to hunt with me. It was a perfect day for bow hunting, with cool temperatures, a beautiful fall day with lots of sunshine and a light breeze, and the rut in full swing. Dad and I had a hunch that deer would be moving because the mating season was right around the corner.

At about 8:00 am, just minutes after I had arrived at my bow seat in a tall, white pine tree, a very nice ten-point buck came by my stand and gave me a broadside shot. I let my arrow go, and it looked as if I hit him six or seven inches behind the shoulder with what should have been a fatal shot. I was excited because I was sure I had taken a very nice deer.

I got down from my seat, and I ran to get dad right away. I could hardly wait to tell him the story and to show him this trophy buck. Soon we were tracking the deer and the blood trail was good. After about 200 yards though, the blood trail started to get weaker. Soon there were only specks of blood every 20 yards. A short distance later, we lost the trail completely. During our tracking experience, the deer never did lie down, and I knew that was a bad sign. We continued looking hard for several hours, and we found nothing – not a trace of the deer.

My tracking partner, the guy who I thought could track a lizard across the barren desert, couldn't believe we lost the deer. We were both sick about it.

"That was a beautiful buck, Dad," I said to him in a highly disappointed tone. "I can't believe we can't find him. I'm sure that was a good shot, but I may have been a little behind him."

"You must have been too far behind his shoulder," dad explained. "You probably just missed his vital areas, and you probably hit him in the intestine area. I don't think there is anything else we can do right now. If we don't push him any further, maybe he will lie down and die soon. We can look for him again this afternoon or tomorrow."

With that advice, I headed back to my seat and dad to his. It was now almost 11:00 am, and I didn't expect to see anything else this late in the morning. I needed to settle down though and forget about my bad morning experience. Dad had one last piece of advice.

"Just to be sure we don't lose another deer, why don't you try one of these new deer tracking strings," dad suggested, pulling one out of his pocket. He helped me hook up the device on my bow and tie the string to the arrow head.

"Now, if you shoot another deer, we can track him more easily because he will leave this string behind him," dad predicted.

With my new string attached, I left him and prepared to hunt for several more hours until we broke for lunch. Incredibly, I had only been in this stand for several

Wounded Bucks and Second Chances

minutes when a very nice eight-point buck, with a high rack and long tines, came along the same run way as the first buck.

As he stepped into the same position as the first buck, I raised my bow and made sure that I aimed closer to the deer's shoulder. I wanted to avoid another gut shot deer. As I released the arrow, there was a loud thud when the arrow slammed into the deer in what looked again like a good shot.

At the shot, the deer headed for the hills, following the same path as the earlier buck. As he ran, he pulled out 400 yards of fine, orange-colored string from the device mounted to my bow. It was as if my buck were a huge fish, ripping off line from a spinning reel.

In only a few seconds, all 400 yards of the line were gone, and I could see the line still being dragged by the deer through the woods. Soon, the deer, my arrow and 400 yards of line were gone.

I got down out of my tree, and I went to get dad again. He couldn't believe it. "You've gotten two shots at big bucks this morning?" he asked. "That's incredible. It sounds as if we will get this one."

With this optimism from my hunting partner, we started the search for the second deer. There was a blood trail that eventually led to the end of the string. Now we could easily follow the buck's path because we had both a blood trail and the trail of the string for the next 400 yards. Dad, however, was now getting pessimistic about our chances of finding this deer.

"I don't like that he's already run well over 400 yards," dad said somberly. "He's also not bleeding much anymore, and he hasn't lain down yet. If he is hurt, he should have bedded down by now. We should have seen that sign."

After another quarter mile, we ran out of string, and we found my arrow which had worked its way out of the deer's shoulder. There was little blood and no sign of the deer. Soon, we were out of places to look for the deer.

We looked for much of the rest of the day, combing over the area and trying to find any new sign of either deer. We found nothing. Eventually, dad told me that we would have to give up.

"We are just not meant to find them," he concluded for me.

I was sick to my stomach. How could I possibly have wounded, not one, but two very nice bucks in one morning? How could we have not found either deer? I was so depressed, that it was hard to imagine hunting again. I didn't even want to tell anyone about this day.

"What will happen to these two beautiful bucks, Dad?" I asked as we left the woods for home.

Dad gave me his best assessment of what might happen.

"Well, I would guess the first buck may die with 48 hours," dad said. "You probably shot him through the stomach or intestine area. He will probably get sick from the internal bleeding, and he will lie down and die in the next day or two. That's what normally happens to gut shot deer. I think the second buck will survive because you hit him directly in the shoulder blade, and the arrow only made a flesh wound. He will have a very sore shoulder, but I think he will survive. Maybe we will even see him again. Sometimes that happens."

It gave me some comfort that at least one of the bucks might live.

Proud Hunters Proud Yoopers

"We can keep this our secret, if you would like," dad offered. "No one has to know that you wounded the two bucks. This does happen to good hunters. It is a part of hunting that is sometimes hard to accept. But you have done everything you should have done, and now we have to move on. Whatever happens to those deer happens to them."

All this good advice from my father and hunter partner made me feel a little better, but I was still reeling from the experience. There was something about the whole event that made me feel irresponsible as a hunter. I vowed that I would never take another shot at a white-tailed deer again unless I was completely confident that I could and would kill the animal cleanly.

Eventually, I did get over the pain of this day, and I recovered as a hunter. I accepted that sometimes, despite the best preparation and best shot selection, good hunters will wound and not find beautiful white-tailed deer. I came to accept that even the very best hunters would sometimes lose a deer they had shot. Nonetheless, I knew there were things hunters could do minimize these events, and I vowed to do everything in my power to ensure that I didn't wound another deer again.

Back on Neebish Island in 1996, I was thinking again about the two big bucks I had not been able to find after wounding them in the 1980s. Our Neebish Island blood trail was running cold. After the initial optimism that we would get this buck, it was now looking like our chances were sinking fast. We were occasionally finding a new speck of blood here and there, but soon we ran into a dead end, and we couldn't find a trace of the deer.

Still, I felt like I had made a good shot, one that should have been fatal to the deer. I didn't want to give up.

As we were thinking about calling off the search, the terrible day on Hungry Hill came back to me in a vivid fashion. I remembered all too well how badly I felt after wounding those two big bucks. As the blood trail evaporated, and our odds of recovering the deer dropped, it looked like the bad Hungry Hill experience was haunting me again.

"Let's leave the trail here and come back in the morning," dad said. "We can see better in the daylight, and we might pick up something we are overlooking in the dark with our flashlights. The deer might also lie down and die over night if we quit pushing him."

This sounded like a plan and we made arrangements to spend the night. I had to call my boss, the State Controller, at home and tell him I wasn't coming in the next day because I had to look for a wounded deer. He wasn't happy with that news because I had planned to give a presentation on Monday to lots of people we had invited to our offices. My boss had to scramble to find someone else to cover for me. From our discussion, I speculated that he wasn't happy that I would choose to spend time looking for a deer over spending time doing my job.

"Obviously, he's not a deer hunter," dad quipped when I told him of my boss's displeasure with my priorities.

Early the next morning, we were back on the trail, picking up from where we had left off the night before. Maybe I should have gone to work that day, because dad and I spent most of the day looking for this buck and we never found him. We did find an

Wounded Bucks and Second Chances

occasional sign, a tiny speck of blood, here and there, but we never found the deer, and we never found any encouraging sign that he was mortally wounded.

"I don't know where you hit him, but we are not going to get him," dad concluded as we headed out of the woods and toward our jobs.

"I know I hit him good, Dad, and I can't explain why I didn't get him," I said in a disappointed tone.

It was a long drive back to Lansing that evening. I had lots of time to relive how I could have wounded another buck and not killed him. I had lots of time to revisit my horrid Hungry Hill experience of losing the two big bucks.

Almost one year later to the day after wounding the Neebish Island buck, I was back in my big spruce tree on Neebish Island, waiting for the last few minutes of daylight to expire. I had hunted for several weeks and not yet seen a deer I wanted to shoot. Just as darkness was falling, I heard a familiar sound of a deer approaching me.

Slowly, the deer came closer. Soon I could see a nice rack of antlers through the brush. My heart was pumping hard, but like last year, I was nervous that daylight might run out before the deer gave me a good shot.

As luck would have it, he walked across my opening with only minutes of daylight left. When he stepped to my left, I had a perfect shot, so I released an arrow.

The big buck lunged as the arrow hit him in what looked like a good hit. He ran hard down the same trail that the buck had used last year. This time, however, the outcome would be different as the big buck crashed 80 yards away where I could see him. He was stone dead by the time I got down from my tree.

He was a beautiful nine pointer and he weighed 180 pounds dressed. He was a very nice deer, the kind I loved to hunt. He would be the largest archery buck killed in the Soo Sportsman's Club Big Buck contest that year. I was really proud of him and considered myself lucky to get him.

Soon dad came to pick me up, and I had a nice surprise for him.

"Wow, you did well, Son," he beamed proudly. "That's a nice buck. Congratulations."

We hauled the big buck from the woods, away from my bow stand, and dragged him near the edge of the St. Mary's River beach where I began to field dress him.

After I had removed most of his organs, I was cutting away the excess tissue from inside his body cavity. Dad was holding the flashlight for me and offering me unsolicited advice on how to clean out the deer.

Suddenly, while I had my hands inside the deer's body cavity, I hit my hand on something very sharp. I pulled my hands out and I felt a pain in my left hand. As I wiped away the deer's blood from my hand, I could see that I had a large cut on my hand and my own blood was gushing out of the cut.

I cleaned my hand and told dad to shine the light inside the deer again. "There's something very sharp in there," I said. "Maybe it's a broken rib bone, but it's really sharp."

Inside the deer's body, just below his back bone and near his front shoulder, was an embedded arrow head. The arrow head was encased in a small mass of scar tissue that had formed around this wound, which had completely healed over.

As I examined the arrow head closely, I was positive that it was my arrow head from one year ago. This was the buck I had wounded almost exactly one year earlier.

Proud Hunters Proud Yoopers

The buck had come by me the same way, at the same location and at the same time one year later. He was completely healed from my almost deadly shot last year, and he was an even bigger buck this year. I was amazed at how he had survived the shot from last year. I wondered where he had been all year since I hadn't seen this deer at all before today. I wondered how he had survived the wolves and coyotes that must have chased him while he was in a weakened condition. I wondered how he had survived the severe winter we had this year – a winter that killed 100,000 healthy deer across the UP. I was amazed at the recovery power of this magnificent animal.

Dad looked closely at the arrow head and the healed over wound. "Wow, that is your arrow head. This is the same deer you shot last year. He's recovered completely from the wound, and he's as healthy as any deer. Somehow he hid from us and everyone else for a whole year while he recovered. He's a beautiful and a very special buck."

I said a special prayer on the beach of the St. Mary's River that night and I thanked our Creator for letting me have this experience with this amazing animal. And I also thanked the Good Lord for second chances at wounded bucks.

On this special night, a Proud Hunter learned that sometimes we do indeed get second chances to redeem ourselves for wounded deer. A Proud Yooper also learned that wounded deer sometimes do recover in amazing ways to be hunted by Proud Yoopers another time.

41

The Season I didn't Fire a Shot

Honor age!
Even an old blind man
may guide you to a rainbow.

-Micmac proverb

The UP's 2001 rifle deer season was a very special season for me and one that I might consider my greatest ever, even though I never killed a buck nor even fired a shot.

I started the year volunteering as project director for the eastern UP's Quality Deer Management (QDM) proposal. Under a new NRC regulation in Michigan, outdoor groups could sponsor proposals to establish experimental, mandatory QDM programs for five years. The QDM program allowed hunters to determine whether they preferred QDM over traditional deer management. The EUP's largest outdoor group, the Tri-County Wildlife Unlimited club, agreed to sponsor the program and help with the public relations and hunter education effort.

Our goal, as required by the NRC regulation, was to convince 66% of the hunters and landowners that we should only kill bucks with three antler points on a side or bigger. Generally, this meant we would pass up spikes and four-pointers, letting them live to grow up one more year. The experience would also allow hunters to practice a part of the QDM hunting philosophy and deer management program for the next five years.

So at a time when I should have been scouting deer and preparing for the fall hunting season, I was deeply involved in what my dad affectionately called "deer politics." For nine months before deer season, I spent much of my free time giving speeches about QDM and deer management, I met frequently with DNR personnel, I held public hearings on QDM, and I talked to everyone I could about our QDM program. Whenever anyone called for information on QDM, I would go and make a presentation, sometimes asking local DNR biologist Rex Ainslie of Sault Ste. Marie to join me for the event.

Rex was an avid hunter himself, and he had considerable knowledge about deer management issues. He was told by his DNR superiors to not be an advocate for QDM because of the DNR's neutral position on the subject. Even so, he often helped the general QDM cause when he spoke on the subject because he worked hard to educate those present on general principles of deer management. For his presentations, he was always well prepared, he was an excellent speaker, and he had very cool graphics in his presentations that helped show complex topics in easy-to-understand ways. Rex also pushed UP hunters to more aggressively harvest antlerless deer. He liked that QDM also opened a dialogue about that. In 2006, Rex got promoted to Wildlife District Supervisor in Newberry, Michigan, when Tom Wiese retired. Erynn Call replaced Rex as area biologist at Sault Ste. Marie in 2007.

Proud Hunters Proud Yoopers

In the middle of this deer education activity, my dad, and my lifetime hunting partner, had a heart attack. For the second time in his life, he needed open heart by-pass surgery. His doctor told him it would take months to recover from the surgery. He predicted my dad would miss much of the 2001 deer season.

"I'll be ready to hunt when the time comes," my 65-year-old dad said firmly when his doctor was out of earshot.

I knew dad had the will to get ready and hunt if he could. He loves to hunt and fish, and he's about as tough and physically strong of a man his age as anyone I have ever known. If anyone could recover quickly, I knew it would be him. He's also one of the best competitive archers in the area and one of the better ones in the state for his age. If there were a way to be ready for the hunting season, he would find it.

There's another reason I knew dad would be ready to hunt. For the last few years, he and I have had the unique pleasure of having both his father (my Grandpa Ed, age 95) and my son (Jeff, age 20), to hunt deer with us each rifle season. We think we are one of the few four-generation families in the UP, in the state, and probably in the whole country, who hunt together each year from the same deer camp.

We had tried our first four-generation hunt together several years earlier, and amazingly all four of us got a deer that year. Dad got a six-pointer, I got a seven-pointer with the bow, Jeff got a big doe with the bow, and Grandpa Ed got a doe on opening day. When word got around about our feat, we were featured in several newspapers in different parts of the state. I told John Schneider, columnist (and avid deer hunter) for the Lansing State Journal, about our hunt, and he ran a full column story on our experience. After that exposure, I had people calling me and e-mailing me from all over about our hunt.

Getting all of us together again this year looked to be an ominous task. Leading up to opening day, I wasn't sure we could pull it off.

But, when November 14th came, dad was feeling good and getting stronger. He was ready to hunt, so I picked up my grandfather and made arrangements with Jeff, my Michigan State University sophomore, to get to deer camp.

Grandpa was especially excited this year. He'd taken a doe each of the last two years, but he had not even seen a single buck. This year, he told me he wanted to get a buck. Because we practice voluntary QDM on our 270-acre family hunting property, we were already letting one-and-one-half (and sometimes two-and-one-half) year-old bucks go so they can grow one more year. We had an informal rule that we only shoot bucks with three or more points on the side. Grandpa, a big-time buck hunter in Michigan for over eight decades, understood our management "rules." In the 1940s, he had killed a huge 22-point non-typical buck that scored 190.4 and ranked as one of the top 100 biggest bucks ever killed in Michigan. He's killed lots of other big bucks too, but he never really practiced QDM until we started it in the 1990s.

"This might be the last year I am around, and I want to get one more buck," he told me matter-of-factly as we drove to deer camp. Then he asked quietly, "Can I shoot a spike or four-pointer this year if I see one?"

For a fleeting second, I thought I faced an ethical dilemma. After all, I was asking everyone in the area to consider letting all spikes and four-pointers go. I had preached this message all over the county, and I had asked hundreds of other hunters to make this sacrifice. We would be voting on the mandatory antler restriction program I was

The Season I didn't Fire a Shot

promoting within one month. How could I now authorize my grandpa to shoot a young buck? I could only think about one thing: how would I explain this one to those who opposed our antler restriction program?

Now at age 95, it's remarkable that grandpa is physically fit enough to hunt. It's even more incredible that he's taken a deer the last two years, both with a one-shot kill. In an area of Michigan where there is a long-standing bias against shooting antlerless deer, he's been an effective QDM supporter, taking an antlerless deer when others won't. Like many older Michigan deer hunters, he was originally taught that we don't shoot does because we don't kill the females that deliver next year's bucks. Years ago, he passed the same lesson on to my dad and to me.

The cultural bias against killing does in our area is so great, that in our county, many years we kill three times as many bucks as does (the vast majority are 1.5-year-old bucks), and we let more does die from starvation and winter kill than we harvest in some years. It's a tremendous challenge for those who support QDM and sound deer management to overcome this long-standing bias that forbids the harvesting of does and encourages us to harvest almost all our yearling bucks.

It's common in voluntary QDM programs to give exemptions to young and senior hunters, allowing them to take a smaller buck. In many mandatory QDM programs, the Michigan DNR program included, these exceptions are not encouraged. By requiring everyone to follow the same rules, we minimize law enforcement problems, and we instill QDM principles and values in both the youthful and senior hunter. The practice, however, remains one of those frequently debated.

For a brief second, I thought about whether this could be grandpa's last hunt. I also thought about how important it was to him to shoot a buck.

I made my mind up quickly and decisively.

"Grandpa, you've done your part for QDM," I told him. "If you want a young buck, you go ahead and take one, but please shoot a doe too, if you get the chance. If our vote for QDM is successful, next year, you will have to wait for a bigger buck like everyone else."

With those ground rules in place, and feeling better about my conscience, we prepared for the next day's hunt.

Opening morning was about as quiet as any I could remember in all my years of hunting. There were very few shots. Grandpa, as he does each year, elected to sleep in and skip the early morning commotion of hunters scurrying around to get ready.

By early afternoon, however, grandpa (with help from dad) would make his way to his heated blind on a clover food plot near a heavily wooded area behind our cabin.

Four years ago, I had brushed this field to remove fast-growing poplar trees, I blasted the plant vegetation with Monsanto Round-Up three times, and then I planted the field with three brands of clover and some birdsfoot trefoil as instructed by Ed Spinazzola, former President of the Mid-Michigan QDMA branch and a QDMA National Board Member. Ed had published his no-till food plot instructions on the Mid-Michigan Branch's web site (www.QDMA.net), and I had followed them to the letter. He's also experimented extensively with different types of seed and planting techniques in Michigan, all designed to help hunters improve the habitat and prepare better forage and nutrition for healthier whitetails. To many of us in Michigan, Ed is Michigan's "Mr. Food Plot."

Proud Hunters Proud Yoopers

For the last three years, I've had lush green clover all year long in this field. I had also been monitoring the field day and night with our Trailmaster Photo Hunter game camera, and from those deer photos, I knew we had lots of deer feeding on the clover, even in mid-November.

At 2 o'clock that afternoon, I heard a shot come from what I thought could be grandpa's field. At 4 pm, I heard another shot from the same location. As darkness came, I could hardly wait to get to grandpa's blind. As I approached it, my dad was already there and he had a huge smile on his face. Grandpa was grinning too, and he was about as excited as any 14-year-old kid with his first deer. He couldn't wait to tell me the story.

"Just after I got here, a four-pointer came to feed on the clover, and I dropped him right there," grandpa said as he pointed to the dead buck lying in the clover. "Then at 4 o'clock, three does came running across the field, so I picked out one, and I took her, too."

My dad and I examined the two deer. Grandpa had used his Savage Arms Model 99 lever action rifle in a .243 Winchester caliber rifle to make clean kills on both animals. Dad and I field dressed the two deer, and we had fresh venison tenderloins for dinner to celebrate our success.

During dinner and afterward that evening, I couldn't help but think about grandpa's feat, and I wondered to myself, how many 95-year-old guys had put two deer in the freezer today or at any time during this hunting season? Heck, how many 95-year-old guys were even hunting this year?

Dad, Jeff and I continued to hunt the rest of the season, but we hadn't seen a nice buck, despite putting in some long hours. On the last weekend, however, I heard a shot near dad's blind at 9:30 in the morning. One minute later, I got a call on my Motorola radio. "Better get up here quick; I think I shot a Muy Grande buck. I won't even go to see him until you get here, because we should be together for moments like this."

I left my radio and gear at my seat, and I covered the three-quarter-mile distance between us as quickly as I could. When I arrived, dad re-enacted how the big buck had been sneaking along an edge when dad hit him through the chest with a bullet from his .30/06 Browning Automatic Rifle. As we walked up to the mature eight-pointer, we reflected on how many times we may have passed him up over the last two or three years.

"We have let lots of small bucks go the last few years, and that's why there are a few mature bucks like this big guy around," dad said, smiling just like the 95-year-old kid earlier in the season. I had photographed a big buck like this one earlier in the year with the Trailmaster camera, but we had never seen him before today. Dad and I knew we were lucky to get him this late in the season, but we also knew that passing up all those little bucks gave this one a chance to grow older. After the season, DNR biologist Dick Shellenbarger, would age the deer for us at four-and-one-half years old.

The buck dressed out at 185 pounds, a huge buck for our area, and he had a nice symmetrical rack, even with one broken tine which he probably lost in a breeding rights battle to another big buck. Later that night, the old buck's tenderloins tasted just as sweet as the tenderloins we had from grandpa's young deer on opening day.

The Season I didn't Fire a Shot

There's something very special about hunting with your family and especially with four generations in the same camp. There is also something special about celebrating the philosophy of QDM and the success that can come from it.

Now while my son Jeff and I didn't take a buck this year, we still laugh about the thrills we had with grandpa and great grandpa. We're not at all embarrassed that the older generations showed us up this year. We just can't decide whom we are more proud of, the buck and doe combo of a 95-year-old deer slayer or the recovering heart-attack hunter who took a mature buck on the last weekend of the season.

And like all Proud Yooper hunting families, we just hope we have these two Proud Hunters in camp for a long time to come.

On this day, a Proud Yooper learned that there is pure joy in a hunting camp when you can have outdoor experiences with your family. And on this day, a Proud Hunter learned that sometimes, the best hunts are those where you never fire a shot.

42

The Birth of the EUP Wildlife Coalition

Peace...
comes to the souls of men
when they realize their relationship,
their oneness with the universe
and all its powers...

-Black Elk, Oglala Sioux

In late December, 2002, I got a call from Lou Kurtis, a retired dentist and die-hard deer hunter from Detour, Michigan. Lou asked me if I could come to a deer management meeting in Cedarville at the Great Outdoors Sport Shop. He clued me in that a number of dedicated hunters would be present to talk about doing something serious about our deer herd.

"Leon, you've got to come and hear how angry people are about how badly the DNR is managing our deer herd," Lou told me over the phone. "We're going to take some action, and we'd like you to help us."

I reminded Lou that I had just tried one antler restriction project with the Tri-County Wildlife Unlimited association, and we hadn't been successful. I wasn't excited about another attempt. I told Lou, in no uncertain terms that I was burned out from "deer politics."

For the last two years, I had done everything in my power to do something constructive with our local deer herd by implementing an experimental, five-year antler restriction program. To the core of my soul, I believed this would be one of the best things we could do to improve deer hunting in the eastern UP.

In this process, I didn't think other involved parties had treated us fairly. As a result, I didn't have a warm, fuzzy feeling for the NRC's antler restriction program. Actually, I was fuming mad about the whole process.

In fact, after working for two years on this initiative, the DNR wouldn't even give me a courtesy phone call to tell me the results of the survey we had paid for and they had conducted on our behalf. I had to attend a public meeting to hear for the first time whether our effort had had been successful.

In March, 2002, I attended a meeting of the NRC on the campus of Michigan State University, where I received the very bad and disappointing news. At the meeting, the DNR staff told the NRC that we (the Tri County Wildlife Unlimited) had failed to show support for the experimental mandatory antler restriction project, based on the results of our deer management survey. While a clear majority of hunters and landowners supported implementing a mandatory antler restriction program, we were told we failed to get a 66% approval rating in both categories.

The final result showed that 57% of all landowners supported the QDM initiative and 53% of all hunters supported it, too. The DNR had surveyed 3,200 landowners

The Birth of the EUP Wildlife Coalition

and hunters from the eastern UP, and almost 2,500 of them responded to the survey. Despite this high level of support for the program, the NRC and DNR would not manage the deer herd in a manner that most of the hunters and landowners in the eastern UP wanted.

I was thoroughly discouraged by this turn of events. My foray into deer politics had left a bad taste in my mouth. I wasn't anxious to get back into deer politics right away.

By this point, I knew as much about the NRC's QDM process as just about anyone in the state. I thought the whole QDM procedure was designed so that it would be virtually impossible for the public to have a fair opportunity to change from traditional deer management to QDM. It sure felt to me like the deck was clearly and intentionally stacked against those who wanted a change in deer management. I also thought that the deer management "power brokers" were determined that this unfair process would stay in place.

Why was the process unfair?

For instance, the NRC required survey takers to vote one of four options: "yes" for support of the proposal; "no" for not supporting the proposal; "don't care" for willing to support either option; or "no opinion" for those who had no preference. In tallying these results, the NRC counted "no opinion" votes like they were "no" votes. This rule had the impact of reducing support for the proposal by about three to five percentage points. Effectively, that meant we really had to have in excess of 70% support for the proposal to show that there was a "clear majority." That rule baffled just about everyone outside of the DNR staffers. One former DNR employee told me that provision had been put in place intentionally as a part of an overall plan to make it harder for QDM proposals to pass. That information really made my blood boil.

The DNR also insisted that we had to follow certain rules for how we communicated with the public and we had to be accurate in putting information out about the benefits of the proposal. In contrast, those who opposed us didn't have to follow any rules, and they could publish any outrageous lies or misinformation they could think of. According to DNR staff, the NRC wouldn't allow the DNR to respond and state that this information was false. Consequently, some individuals and some organized groups worked against our proposal using information they knew was false or misleading. We hit rock bottom when one individual accused me and our deer management proposal of being an organized stealth campaign with a hidden agenda to take away our hunting guns. That's the kind of nonsense misinformation some groups and individuals used to ensure our proposal did not pass.

At one point, it occurred to me that the NRC was actually encouraging one hunting group to work against another hunting group with this process. In fact, the way the NRC had structured the process, it actually pitted landowners against public land hunters. In the middle of public relations efforts to pass the proposal, one outdoor group told me they knew we had strong support among landowners to pass our proposal. They told me they would defeat our proposal by rallying public land hunters against us. I thought this splintering of hunting groups was bad for the future of hunting. I also thought the anti-hunting movement must be pleased to watch different hunting groups fighting among themselves.

Proud Hunters Proud Yoopers

As a result of this mismatch, I was just about ready to take a vow that I would never work with or for the benefit of the DNR ever again in my life. I felt that betrayed by how the eastern UP survey had been handled. I felt like the "power brokers" had really done a number on the eastern UP and on me personally.

I was ready to walk away from deer politics and never lift a finger to help the DNR again.

In fact, one of my hunting friends told me we should totally abandon Michigan and its deer management fiasco. We talked often about the DNR managing the deer herd as if it were still the 1970s.

"Let's sell our hunting properties and use the proceeds to finance hunting trips to the best places across the globe," he suggested one day.

"Guys like you and me are breaking our necks to manage habitat for the deer and the damn DNR doesn't care at all about how we like to hunt," he continued. "They won't raise a finger to help us, so why are we working our fingers to the bone to help them? Let's bag this and enjoy ourselves for the rest of our hunting years."

His offer sounded pretty convincing. If we sold our hunting camps, we could go on some of the best hunts around the country and even around the world, just using the investment earnings from the proceeds. And we wouldn't have to work anywhere near as hard as we do now managing our Michigan properties for deer that will be slaughtered by nearby hunters who don't share our values.

"We could sheep hunt one year and go for moose and caribou the next. We could also hunt the whitetail rut for trophy bucks all around the country in the other states where they value the deer and where they don't shoot everything that moves," my friend continued.

The offer made sense on the surface, but somehow, I couldn't abandon Michigan and the UP. I wasn't ready to leave everything behind here just yet. I wasn't ready to throw in the towel.

Back in the UP, Lou Kurtis tried to convince me that we had come this far and that we couldn't turn back now. "The DNR is just hoping you will go away after this survey," Lou told me. "Don't let them think they can win. We've got to keep fighting for more control over our deer herd."

"I know you've already done your fair share, but you have to come and see how many dedicated people we have who are willing to work hard to make some changes," Lou promised. "Please come and then decide if you can help us."

Lou had twisted my arm hard enough that I agreed to show up for the January 2003 meeting. "It will be a great way to start off the New Year," Lou said tongue-in-cheek.

When I got to the Great Outdoors Sport Shop, there was a good turnout with some very strong emotions from individuals who promised to work hard for deer management reform. Many of those present were angry and ready to do almost anything to get some reform. Before the night was over, we had formed a new group called the Eastern UP Wildlife Coalition. We also elected officers and established a charter to get the DNR to reduce antlerless permits to more reasonable levels and to enact a three-point antler restriction.

Dale Batka of Hessel would serve as our president and Bill Lamoreaux of Cedarville was elected vice-president. I agreed to be project director and spokesperson

The Birth of the EUP Wildlife Coalition

for the group on the antler restriction proposal. Outdoor writer Dwaine Starr of St. Ignace, Mike Rudd of Cedarville, and Lou Kurtis would also be board members and key players in helping to mobilize us and coordinate our meetings across the eastern UP.

Over the next two years, the Eastern UP Wildlife Coalition would sign up 250 dues paying members, raise money to conduct a deer management survey, and present deer management changes to EUP hunters and landowners in seminars at town halls, churches, and schools all over the eastern UP. Along the way, we also picked up other great helpers and supporters like Fred Gregg of Bruce Township, Leo Barens of Rudyard, Pat Meehan of Kinross, and dozens of others.

At certain times, it was an exhausting process. Frequently, I would ask myself why I was doing this again. I was giving up hunting opportunities and taking time away from my family, my job and my other hobbies, just to have a remote shot at changing deer management.

When I would get discouraged, someone in the Eastern UP Wildlife Coalition would give me a bit of encouragement that we would be successful and that we were doing a good thing. Usually, Dwaine or Lou would keep me pumped up and remind me that we had to do this.

"No one else is speaking up for the deer, and we have to do it," Lou would say periodically.

"The eastern UP is becoming the Dead Zone," Dwaine would say to me. "We've got to change that. We can have good hunting here again if we are successful."

We didn't know it, but at the same time we were meeting to plot our deer management reform strategy in the eastern UP, dozens of other hunters in the central and western UP were planning the same thing.

We would soon get word from the DNR that the Superior Deer Management group was also sponsoring a mandatory three-point antler restriction for the whole UP, including our area. While we didn't know these guys, we would soon learn that this dedicated group wanted the same things we did.

Before long, we were talking and meeting with Bud Norman, Jim Lahde, Jeff Sturgis, and other central and western UP Yoopers responsible for passing the central UP antler restriction changes in four deer management units. In the next few months, we would combine forces and even hold two joint meetings for area hunters on the antler restriction process. It was reassuring and comforting to know that Yoopers from across the UP were united in the cause to change the way we manage our deer herd.

By November, 2004, we had done most of what we could do to be successful. For two years, we had reminded hunters we had two goals. First, we wanted to restrict the harvest of young bucks so that 75% of yearling bucks lived one more year. We chose a three-point on one side antler restriction rule for our experimental, mandatory proposal, a potential change in the law for five years to see what a difference sparing these young bucks would make. To start the experimental program, we had to again show that 66% of hunters and landowners supported the change. This initiative would be almost identical to the one we had tried three years earlier with the Tri-County Wildlife Unlimited sponsored program.

Second, we wanted to get the DNR to slow down the harvest of antlerless deer. While it was important to kill reasonable numbers of antlerless deer each year, for one of the rare times in history, we had actually killed too many antlerless deer recently (and more died in winter kill) so that the population was actually below the area's carrying capacity.

No one was seeing anywhere near the deer they had been seeing several years ago. We knew the herd had been significantly reduced from two bad winters and from an excessive doe harvest.

Area hunters were fuming mad at the DNR because they had offered 7,500 doe permits in the 2002 hunting season for our 800 square mile deer management unit. That number of antlerless permits was so many, that the public wouldn't even buy that many at $7.00 a piece, half the cost of a regular license.

By the time the buck rut was on in early November, we had done all the preparation work for another vote on the issue, and we were now waiting until the DNR surveyed area hunters in December.

Very soon, all this work and our hope for deer management reform would come down to a simple survey or "vote" on what hunters and landowners supported.

All the time I was hunting, I was also thinking about how to get this deer hunting referendum passed. I was always looking for opportunities to get free publicity for our cause and save our small budget.

On November, 5, 2004, I had a great day in the woods in the morning, and I immediately recognized that this was a good opportunity to promote our cause. I couldn't have asked for a better way to contrast our views on deer hunting with those of traditional deer management than with what had happened on my simple morning hunt.

In the afternoon, I had to go to St. Ignace as a part of my job with the Michigan Department of Transportation to help cut the ribbon and open the new M-134 snowmobile crossing over I-75. While I was there, St. Ignace News reporter Amy Polk saw my buck in the back of my Chevy pickup, and she took my picture for her paper, telling people about the benefits of shooting older bucks. The Soo Evening News also published this complete story in late November:

On Friday, November 5, I shut off the alarm at 6 am and I stepped outside my deer hunting cabin on Neebish Island to feel a strong northwest wind and rainy drizzle greet me in the doorway. I've hunted long enough to know that deer don't like windy days and hunters don't like rainy days, so it was tempting to go back to bed.

This season, I've hunted in so many rainy and windy days that I thought I may as well go out and try hunting in this lousy weather. I put on my rain suit and grabbed my gear, arriving at my treestand just as daylight was breaking.

By 7:30 am, the clouds disappeared, and the wind died out completely. Suddenly, it was a gorgeous day to be deer hunting in the eastern UP, and soon I heard the sound of deer walking toward me.

I was watching the edge of a long ridge adjacent to a large deer-bedding area. On my right was a fresh buck scrape, and on my left was a huge rub (one of the largest I have ever seen), on a five-inch maple tree. These were classic signs that mature bucks were in the area and they were leaving their calling cards for female deer that would soon be ready for breeding.

The Birth of the EUP Wildlife Coalition

I was hunting in a place where local hunters have voluntarily agreed to stop shooting spike and four-point bucks, letting them grow up one more year. The "Let him go, so he can grow" practice is called Quality Deer Management or QDM for short. It is working all over the country with dramatic results on both public and private land.

On my property, we've been voluntarily passing up the yearling bucks for ten years, and we have shifted the annual deer harvest from 110-pound average yearling spikehorns to very nice bucks that are usually mature, eight or ten pointers with dressed body weights from 150 to 180 pounds. The bucks we kill today are usually 2.5, 3.5 or 4.5 year-old bucks, the kind of bucks that almost every hunter dreams of seeing during hunting season.

The beauty of QDM is that you have the same number of deer in the herd, but you have significantly more bucks (twice as many as we have now), and you have more older bucks. We still shoot the same number of deer, but we just have more fun because those that kill deer may get bucks that are almost twice as big as we killed before QDM.

Many experienced hunters know that, next to an orphaned fawn, the yearling buck is the dumbest deer in the woods and one of the easiest to kill. This buck has only been away from his mother for about five months, and his survival skills are still in the amateur stage. As a result, it makes good management sense to let him live one more year.

When hunters practice QDM and let yearling bucks live to grow up another year, a remarkable thing happens to the survivability of the buck herd. In the extra year of life, bucks gain another whole year of experience in learning how to avoid hunters and how to survive in their dangerous environment. With just one more year of life, their odds of surviving to become a 3.5 or 4.5-year-old buck increase significantly.

As I heard the sounds of deer moving toward me, I quickly picked up the outline of small spikehorn coming toward my ridge from out of the bedding area. At the same time, there was a larger buck approaching me from the south. The larger buck made a run at the smaller buck as a sign of his dominance just as the two deer got close to each other.

When there are more bucks in the herd, it's easier to observe some of this incredible social behavior of deer while hunting. Seeing all the scraping, rubbing, sparring, and fighting action of the different bucks as they prepare for the breeding season is just another benefit of QDM. Having a chance to see different bucks of different maturity levels enhances the quality of the hunt for many hunters who practice QDM. Until I started practicing QDM, I never saw this interaction between the deer. Now I experience it all the time, and I see things I've never seen deer do before.

While other states around the country are managing some or all of their deer, elk, sheep and moose herds using the principles of antler restrictions and quality deer management techniques, Michigan's game managers have resisted those practices.

As a result, hunting and outdoor groups in Michigan have demanded a process where they can experiment with QDM programs like other states. To meet this hunter driven need, the state's Natural Resource Commission (NRC) established a QDM process where local hunting groups need to demonstrate that 66% of the landowners and hunters in the area want to manage the deer herd using QDM. The procedure places a significant educational and promotional burden on the outdoor group. In effect, the outdoor group has to run and win a public referendum on deer management with odds that are almost impossible.

In the EUP, local hunters formed the Eastern UP Wildlife Coalition for the purpose of promoting the benefits of QDM to hunters and landowners. In mid-December, hunters and landowners in the EUP will get a chance to determine whether they would like to practice QDM for the next five years. The DNR will conduct a mail survey to determine the level of support for QDM.

Because we practice so little QDM in Michigan, our deer herd is one of the most manipulated and unnatural deer herds in the country. In fact, in Michigan, we've become so efficient at killing young bucks, that we kill almost all of them each year giving us an unbalanced deer herd that is a far cry from what nature intended. This happens because our hunting seasons are three months long, and there are no incentives or restrictions to stop the harvest of all young bucks. No other state in the country manages its deer herd this way.

The UP's own legendary DNR biologist, John Ozoga (now retired), from Munising, Michigan, says we need to quit managing our Michigan deer herd as if it is a large cattle ranch. Ozoga says the NRC and DNR need to make tough decisions and implement QDM principles statewide while we still have a deer herd worth managing.

Ozoga is critical of the NRC and the DNR for not doing more to stop the excessive harvest of yearling bucks. He wants to have a more balanced deer herd with more equal numbers of bucks and does and higher numbers of older deer in the population. The NRC's 2001 survey of 5,795 hunters also determined that 59% of hunters wanted antler restrictions and QDM practices followed. Only 25% of hunters opposed those practices.

Everywhere in the country where QDM has been started, the majority of hunters has always wanted to continue that process. A majority of hunters has never wanted to go back to shooting spikes and four-pointers after trying QDM.

I thought about all this as I watched the young spikehorn walk by my tree stand after his run-in with the bigger buck. I could have easily shot him, but he's a deer I've seen several times all ready this season, and I hope to see him several more times this year. As I passed him up again, I wished him luck in becoming an older buck.

Now the bigger buck was getting closer, and I clenched my bow, readying myself for a shot. The buck was an eight pointer with a semi-rare, partially palmated rack of horns. I had missed him earlier in the season, and he sneaked past a friend of mine, too (*MDOT's Wayne Roe*). He was a mature, 3.5-year-old buck, weighing about 190 pounds on the hoof. He was a buck almost every hunter in Michigan would be proud of.

When he turned broadside to me at 18 yards, I raised my Hoyt bow and released an Easton 2216 Gamegetter arrow with a 100 grain Muzzy head. The arrow went clean through both lungs, and the big buck was down only thirty yards away.

As I reached the beautiful, mature buck, I thanked our Creator for giving us such a magnificent animal to roam our Michigan forests, and I thanked him for letting me take another big buck.

The Birth of the EUP Wildlife Coalition

This December, you may be one of the 3,000 plus people surveyed by the DNR to determine if you would like to practice Quality Deer Management in the Eastern UP. Your Eastern UP Wildlife Coalition urges you to understand this important conservation issue and hopes you will vote "YES" for responsible deer management.

This is your opportunity to speak up for our deer. Make your choice a wise one for wildlife.

In April, the NRC released the results of our QDM survey. Over 59% of the landowners and 58% of the hunters voted to support mandatory antler restrictions that would spare young bucks with less than three points on one antler. For the overall UP vote, Proud Yoopers voted to support mandatory antler restrictions by 61% for hunters and 63% for landowners.

Despite this overwhelming support for restrictions to reduce the decades of over-harvesting young bucks in the UP, the NRC again refused to enact any deer management changes to protect more young bucks.

Shortly after the vote and the NRC's inaction, world renowned wildlife biologist Gary Alt of Pennsylvania would be quoted as saying our method for managing the white-tailed deer was one of the worst game management decisions in the history of modern wildlife management. By this statement, Alt chastised game managers like those in the DNR (and some other states, including Pennsylvania) for growing the deer herd to such huge levels and promoting hunting practices that encouraged the over-harvest of so many young bucks while protecting too many does.

I can't describe how disappointed I was that so many Yoopers wanted this simple, common-sense deer management change, and yet, our own NRC wouldn't work constructively with us to see something implemented to accommodate the will of the people of the UP.

In letters I wrote on deer management forums on the Internet, I challenged the DNR staff to show me any deer management practice that had a 66% approval rating. I challenged the NRC to prove that 66% of the general public approved of its deer management oversight. I knew that there were low approval ratings for both the NRC and the DNR regarding deer management. In fact, some believed their approval ratings were at all time lows. So, I couldn't believe that the NRC wouldn't embrace a management change that 60% of the public wanted when deer hunters, as a group, rarely agree on anything.

After a period of mourning and complaining about the state of our deer herd and how out of touch our NRC was with the Yooper deer hunting community, I decided it was time to quit moping and start working even harder for change.

At that time, we terminated the Eastern UP Wildlife Coalition, and I began to work much more closely with the national QDMA and a newly formed state chapter of the QDMA. I had learned that we would need a much more robust and politically influential QDMA if we were to ever get any meaningful deer management reform in the UP and throughout the rest of Michigan.

I was more determined than ever that I would do everything I could to ensure Michigan wasn't the last state in the nation to embrace the common-sense management concepts of QDM.

Proud Hunters Proud Yoopers

On this day, a Proud Hunter learned the painful realities of deer politics, and on this day a number of Proud Yoopers rededicated themselves to change how the deer herd in Michigan is managed, no matter what the cost or how long it takes.

43

A Mother-In-Law and a Last Hunt

We do not want riches,
but we do want to train
our children right.
Riches would do us no good.
We could not take them with us
to the other world.

-Red Cloud, Sioux

The 2004 deer season should have been a time of great celebration, but as I look back, it was one difficult year.

First, I had planned to go to our Neebish Island camp for an extended archery hunt in early November, hunting the last few weeks of bow season and staying through the first week of rifle season.

I had to change my plans when my mother-in-law, Virginia Sternhagen of Saginaw, needed some extensive medical attention. Susan's father, Mel Sternhagen, an avid deer hunter himself, had passed away earlier in the summer on July 4, 2004, at his Torch Lake cabin at age 77. Mel had been taking care of Ginny the last two years, as she battled some serious health problems. Following his unexpected death, she was on her own, struggling with these health issues and working hard to keep her mobility while her general health declined.

Ginny's most serious medical problem flared up while I was on a bow hunting trip in the UP. My daughter Sarah and wife Susan were visiting Ginny in Saginaw for a few days, and they were planning on a three-generation Christmas shopping weekend. On the first night of their stay, Ginny, who was recovering from a bout with pneumonia, was getting ready to go to bed. She told Susan that she felt as if she didn't have any energy. Moments later, she began to have difficulty breathing and speaking. Susan instructed Sarah to call 911 as Ginny's condition worsened and she collapsed. Susan grabbed her as she passed out.

As Sarah described Ginny's condition over the phone to the emergency personnel, she relayed instructions to Susan on how to help her mother until the paramedics could arrive. Susan was able to successfully perform the CPR breathing procedures which helped revive her mother. For a mother-daughter duo that had never had any emergency training, the two of them did an incredible job by keeping Ginny alive until the paramedics took over.

After the paramedics assessed the situation, they stabilized Ginny and then immediately transported her to Saginaw's Covenant Hospital. The next morning, the hospital personnel determined that Ginny needed a delicate heart surgery procedure that only the University of Michigan in Ann Arbor and Henry Ford Hospital in Detroit could perform. Because the U-M Hospital was full, the doctors decided to airlift Ginny to Henry Ford. Susan and Sarah immediately drove to Detroit with Susan's brother Paul to meet Ginny at the Detroit hospital. Susan's other brother John and his wife Andy soon joined them.

Once there, doctors told the family how risky the surgery was. Doctors needed to repair a torn aorta near her heart. At her age, the surgery was risky and recovery would be long. The doctors prepared the family for the worst by telling them that many patients don't survive the complicated surgery.

But Ginny, an avid slot machine player, beat the long odds.

Following eight hours of this high-risk medical procedure, Ginny emerged with a repaired aorta and she had won this gamble – something that didn't surprise those of us who knew just how tough she was.

She would now face months of recovery when doctors warned us that other things could go wrong. By now, I had returned from the shortened UP hunting trip and I joined Susan in Detroit. In the week that followed, Ginny appeared to be gaining strength and her recovery looked more promising. When she was recovering and I was able to visit her at Henry Ford, she couldn't speak, but I knew she was pleased that I had returned from the hunting trip to visit her. I, however, worried that she knew things were serious because I had returned from my annual lengthy hunting trip before it was over.

When I first saw her, I remember grabbing her hand as she lay in her hospital bed, unable to speak or move. Susan and her brother Paul announced to her that Leon was here, back from his hunting trip. I thought I saw her begin to tear up as she saw me, and she held my hand. I was glad I had made the long trip to Detroit from the UP.

Over the next few days, Ginny seemed to get even stronger, and her recovery was clearly underway. Her children, my wife included, were still not sure what life would be like for her when she recovered enough to be released. She would probably need a significant amount of nursing care. Prior to the surgery, she had been losing much of her mobility, and she had needed some care and assistance for many of the common tasks we take for granted every day. With additional health restrictions following the surgery, her children, John, Paul and Susan, would have to work out how to care for her.

As she got better though, Susan told me it would be OK for me to go back up to the UP for the opening day of rifle deer season. "Mom is out of the critical danger point now, so why don't you go back up for a few days?" she offered to me.

Thinking that Ginny was in better shape, I agreed with Susan. I left the Detroit area where we had been staying at the hospital, and I went back to work in Lansing for a few days. After that, I was on my way back to the UP for the last few days of the bow season and the beginning of the rifle season. All the time, I was assuming Ginny was on the recovery road.

Meanwhile, dad had checked with his sister, my Aunt Lorraine Schremp, and learned that she would bring Grandpa Ed to the Neebish Island ferry dock in the early afternoon on November 14. I would then pick him up at the ferry and transport him to the cabin. The plan worked well, and soon I had grandpa and his gear in my pickup truck as scheduled. After the short ferry ride, the 98-year-old hunter was ready for his deer hunt the next day.

A Mother-in Law and a Last Hunt

November 14th is about the busiest day of the year for sport shop owners in northern Michigan as last minute hunters are buying gear and deer licenses. It is just about non-stop chaos at our sporting goods store on the day before the rifle season opener. As a result, dad and his wife Judy work long hours getting hunters ready for the big opening day. That year, at about 6 pm, dad left the store and headed for Neebish Island in his truck packed with hunting gear. He made sure that he was on the last 7-pm ferry.

When dad got to the island, we had a big steak dinner and a traditional shot of whiskey with grandpa as we were organizing our gear for the next day.

We hit the hay early that night so we could get up early the next morning as we always do on opening morning. As grandpa always does, he planned to sleep in and hunt in the afternoon.

Back in Detroit, in the late afternoon, Henry Ford doctors told Susan and her two brothers and Ginny's sister Barb, that Ginny was stable. All three children had some business to attend to at home. The medical staff reassured the family members they could go home for a few days to tend to their business. The children were relieved to hear this. Paul had to return home briefly but planned to return to the hospital in a couple of days. Susan planned to return home to her teaching job and come back three days later for an extended stay through Thanksgiving. John also planned to return as soon as possible. Following their advice, Susan said good night and goodbye to her mother, her two brothers and her aunt. Shortly after Susan got home, she got a call that her mother had taken an unexpected turn for the worse. The hospital recommended that she return at once to see her mother.

The family members returned to the hospital as soon as possible that evening. Right after midnight, Ginny passed away with her three children by her bedside.

Susan called me on Neebish Island to give me the bad news. We had been in bed for several hours already, and I was sound asleep when she called. It was about 1 am, and there weren't any ferries returning to the UP mainland until 7 am. I told her how sorry I was to hear about her mother, and I said I could be on the 7 am boat to come home so I could be with her.

"No, why don't you hunt in the morning with your dad and grandpa and come home later in the day." she suggested. "There's really nothing you can do right now and my mom would want you to hunt opening day with your family."

I thought about it for a minute, and then I suggested that I would hunt only in the morning and leave on the 12 pm ferry. "If you are OK with that, I will stay and hunt for a few hours. I'll be home by 5 pm, and then we can go to Saginaw to be with your family and to start preparing for the funeral," I offered.

With that plan, I went back to bed, but I didn't sleep the rest of the night, knowing that Susan wasn't sleeping either and knowing the sadness that I would never see my mother-in-law again.

In the world of comedy, there are a thousand jokes and funny stories about mother-in laws. They almost always talk about bad relations with a mother-in-law or unpleasant experiences with your wife's mother. Funny, but I never thought about my mother-in-law that way at all. In fact, I had been blessed in life to have a highly supportive mother-in-law my entire adult life.

Proud Hunters Proud Yoopers

Ginny was one of the kindest and most caring persons I had ever known. She was an exceptional person who was an outstanding cook, a great junior high school English teacher for almost 20 years, and someone who loved life to the fullest. She had a wonderful sense of humor, and she always tried to involve everyone in conversations. Ginny was also an outstanding golfer and bowler – she was strong and athletic. She was an incredibly thoughtful person who cared so much about others. It was sad to think of all she had been through in the last two years, losing her husband of 55 years and facing all these health problems.

It was with mixed emotions that I got up several hours later when the alarm went off. Dad and I quickly got ready and tried hard not to wake grandpa. We ate a big breakfast, grabbed our gear and headed to our spots before daylight came.

As I watched the magic of daylight come to another opening day and I listened for the first shot of the morning, my wandering mind spent most of the time thinking about Ginny and how good she had been to me during her life. I also spent a lot of time thinking about my wife and how tough it must be to lose your mother and one of your best friends, one of your closest companions. Ginny was all those things to Susan. I also thought about John, Paul, Ginny's sisters, and Ginny's friends, many of whom I would see at the funeral home in the next few days. Then I thought about how difficult it had to be for my wife to lose both her father and mother within five months. Finally, all of this made me think about my family, my mother and father and sisters and others. I thought a lot about how short life is and how quickly it can come to an end for us.

As I was pondering all of these heavy subjects about life, at about 10 am, I heard one rifle shot from a familiar place. I grabbed the Motorola radio and called dad. Sure enough, he had killed a nice buck.

He described the buck to me, telling me he was sure it was a seven-point buck we had captured on camera. It was likely a buck that my MDOT co-worker, Matt DeLong, had seen several weeks earlier on a bow hunt.

"He's a nice deer," dad told me. "Do you think we should get him out of here now so you don't miss your noon ferry?"

One of the charms and curses of living on a remote island is that the ferry doesn't run all the time. Our ferry only runs at noon and then not until 3 pm. If I missed the noon ferry, I'd be three hours behind the schedule I promised Susan.

I took dad's advice and headed to his stand so I could help him with the deer. When I got there, we admired the nice buck, and I thanked the good Lord that my 69-year-old dad had taken another dandy whitetail. Dad was pumped up, and I was glad that I was there to share another moment like this one with him.

We cleaned out the deer, and then we struggled like crazy trying to get the big buck on the back of our Polaris 250 ATV. I was thankful again that I had been here to help dad with this work. I wondered to myself, "How would dad have ever gotten this big buck loaded himself if I hadn't been here?"

I then looked to the heavens and said a little thank you to my mother-in-law. "I know you and the good Lord had something to do with the timing of this Ginny. Thank you!" I prayed in silence.

Dad and I then navigated our ATVs back to our cabin, and I started mentally preparing for everything I had to do in the half hour before the ferry left. I quickly

A Mother-in Law and a Last Hunt

threw the gear I would need for the week in my truck. Dad also decided that I should help him load up his buck in his truck right away so he could take it for processing.

In my last few minutes, grandpa joined us in admiring the freshly killed buck. "Oh, that's a nice buck," grandpa said as he lifted up the buck's antlers.

Later I learned that, if I had paid more attention, I would have noticed that grandpa was feeling no pain as he looked over dad's opening morning buck. Dad would later tell me that after I left on the noon ferry, he learned that grandpa had finished off the entire bottle of whiskey we had opened and sampled lightly the previous night.

After I left the island, it turns out, my 98-year-old grandpa had one of the worst hangovers of his life, and he was in no shape to go on an afternoon deer hunt.

Dad did the only thing he could under the circumstances – he told grandpa to go to bed and sleep off his hangover.

Grandpa did as he was told, and he missed his first afternoon deer hunt on opening day. Dad was quite upset that grandpa would do something like that, but I tried to lighten up the event with humor by offering dad a bet that my grandpa was the only 98-year-old deer hunter in the country to miss opening day because of a whiskey hangover.

That got dad to laugh a little and I think he forgave our over-indulging special guest.

To make up for his behavior, the 98-year-old deer slayer went out the next afternoon and shot a doe just before dark. Dad took his buck and the doe to the meat processor, and the two old hunters went home for a few days until I returned the next weekend after Ginny's funeral.

That next weekend, grandpa came to camp again, and he filled his second doe tag by killing another doe at about 4 pm in the afternoon. This time, my cousin Dan Firack, another one of Grandpa Ed's grandsons, was also with us.

To make sure things went well, dad and I hid the whiskey bottle, keeping it under our strict control.

That night, the four of us celebrated the only 98-year-old deer hunter in the country to shoot two does that hunting season. Of course, we couldn't be sure, because somewhere else in the USA, there was probably another great grandfather who was also a deer-shooting machine, but because we hadn't heard of him, we toasted our special hunter with a shot of whiskey.

And when we were done, we again locked up the whiskey bottle so a certain 98-year-old party animal couldn't find it.

The next summer, my generally healthy grandfather broke his hip and took ill. He was hospitalized and, like Ginny, he had to have some risky surgery done. The nurses told us most people never left the ward where my grandfather was.

"I'll be honest," one nurse told me. "Most patients in this wing will die here in several days or several weeks. There's something different about your grandfather that has all of us pulling for him. He may be one of the few who walk out of here."

Like Ginny, grandpa initially beat the odds. He survived the surgery, and he got a little stronger each day. It looked as if he might fully recover.

Right after his hip surgery, I was with him in the hospital as he was coming out of the anesthetic. While the drugs were wearing off, grandpa was hallucinating about big bucks running by him, and he was raising his arms as if to line up his scope so he could

Proud Hunters Proud Yoopers

shoot the running deer. He was talking about all kinds of hunting adventures he had in his lifetime as the drugs worked through his system.

As my aunts and I listened to his stories, we couldn't be sure if they were the true adventures of his past or tricks his mind was playing on him. I could only think to myself, "He's a hunter's hunter. At a time like this, he's still thinking about hunting."

While grandpa recovered from that surgery, he took a turn for the worse several weeks later, and he died on August 24, 2005, my son Jeff's birthday. Grandpa's 2004 deer hunt with us would be his last.

And that last 2004 hunt, when he killed two deer, would be our last four-generation family hunt.

At his funeral, I was one of the grandsons who had a chance in his eulogy to recall our grandfather. As his many friends gathered to pay their last respects, I told them about the Proud Hunter I had known and the lifetime Proud Yooper who had the spunk and the spirit to kill two deer and drink too much whiskey in deer camp, all at the young age of 98 years.

On this day, a Proud Yooper learned that many Proud Hunters and Proud Yoopers will gather to say goodbye to one of their own, especially a very successful and dedicated Yooper deer hunter; and they will wish him luck one last time chasing UP whitetails in a new special place. And on this day, a Proud Hunter learned to remember special mother-in-laws who support us in our hunting adventures.

44

The Magical Yooper Bird

The sky is round,
and I have heard that the earth is round
like a ball and so are all the stars.
The wind, in its greatest power, whirls.
Birds make their nests in circles,
for theirs is the same religion as ours.

-Black Elk, Oglala Sioux

One of my favorite birds, and a favorite of Yooper hunters across the UP, is the ruffed grouse or Pat, as he is often called. His most common Yooper name, however, is the partridge. That's how I was taught to call him and that's how I think of him. No matter what he's called, he's a great bird that Proud Hunters love to see and pursue.

My first official, licensed small game hunts were for partridge, and that's what I cut my teeth on. When I look back on it, while I was carrying the BB gun and chasing small birds, chipmunks, frogs and squirrels, I was actually training to hunt partridge.

As a young hunter, I rapidly came to respect just how fast and crafty this bird was. At a tender age, I learned that partridge would not sit still if they heard or saw you coming. If you spooked the birds, they were on the move quickly, walking fast or running at a slow, but steady pace to get away from danger. I learned that these birds really didn't like to fly unless they had to. They really did prefer to get away on the ground – they were, after all, "a bird of the ground."

As I got older, I came to appreciate just how sophisticated a flyer this bird was when he was pursued hard enough. Hunters had to be ready, and they had to shoot fast when the birds flushed. If you weren't ready or didn't shoot quickly, the birds flew at such great speed that they were often out of range before you could get your gun up.

Perhaps the greatest thing I enjoy about partridge hunting is how the birds explode when you least expected it. When they burst into flight to escape, they jump into the air, flapping their wings so rapidly against their bodies that it sounds like a big engine starting up beside you, almost like a tractor motor firing up. It sometimes scares the daylights out of hunters when they are not expecting a flushing partridge at their feet or right in front of them. I love that explosion of sound and the sight of blurring wings disappearing into the brush, especially when you are completely surprised. It is a feeling and a sensation that grouse hunters live for.

This fine eating bird also has an incredible knack for flushing just as you are about to crawl under a log or take one hand off your gun to climb over a deadfall. As they fly away, they are also masters at putting trees and brush between themselves and a hunter so you can't get a clear shot at them. How they do those things mystifies hunters and makes the bird that much more magical to those who pursue him.

Proud Hunters Proud Yoopers

Most avid grouse hunters use highly-trained dogs, either pointers (like a German short-hair) or flushers (like a yellow or black Lab), to help find the birds. Those using pointers walk behind them while the dogs find the birds by scent. The dogs then go on "point," freezing in place and "pointing" to the sitting bird. The hunter walks up on the pointing dog and flushes the bird for the shot. Having a pointing dog makes it much easier to find the birds, and it helps minimize the number of surprise flushes – sometimes.

Hunters who use flushing dogs walk behind their dogs while the dogs run through the brush. When the dogs spot a bird or scent a bird, they will flush the bird out in front of their owners for a shot. Hunting behind flushing dogs can also improve the odds of killing grouse because the birds can't as easily escape by running away. Hopefully, the birds will flush in front of the hunters, giving them good chances for killing shots. Both pointers and flushing dogs are effective in hunting partridge.

Dad used Peanuts during my first few years of hunting as a flushing dog, and later we had another cocker spaniel, named Cindy, who also flushed partridge for us. After Cindy died, we got a German short-haired pointer, but she didn't work out. After she bit her second person, we gave her away to a Dafter farmer. After that, dad and I relied on each other to flush birds. That method too is effective for killing partridge, and it's a lot of fun because you usually don't know when the birds will flush.

When I was a young hunter, I sometimes killed birds on the ground, shooting them while they stopped briefly before they flew or ran away. The shooting was easier and the technique allowed me to kill more birds. Somewhere along the line, I stopped shooting grouse on the ground. Dad had encouraged me to enjoy the challenge of shooting birds in the air, and I began to read more about avid grouse hunters, many of whom never shot birds on the ground. Some serious hunters even thought it was a sin to shoot a grouse on the ground.

Anyway, for the pure challenge of it, I eventually wanted to flush a grouse before I shot at him. Just like the conservation practice of passing up young bucks, this is one of those decisions that responsible and educated hunters need to think about.

Much like in my youth, I don't begrudge any young hunters who want to kill their first few grouse on the ground. I think that is OK – for a while. But as the young hunter matures and becomes more sophisticated as a hunter, and more educated about wildlife management, that hunter can graduate to a more advanced hunting level. That means accepting the challenge of shooting grouse on the fly and resisting the opportunities to make easier kill shots on the ground.

After all, this is a great bird of the UP forest. He is a beautiful bird with rich colors, including jet black feathers around his neck that he occasionally fluffs up. During mating season, he will "drum" for hours, beating his wings against his body while standing still on a special "drumming" log. He drums like this to attract a willing female for breeding purposes. While strutting and drumming, he may fan out his beautiful tail feathers in an awesome display of color. That behavior belongs to this special bird of northern Michigan who is also such a challenge to hunt.

Partridge are dependent on man for proper forest management if they are to thrive in the heavily forested country like the UP. In fact, there's a great deal of art and science involved in intensely managing grouse management. The hunters who

The Magical Yooper Bird

understand this the best are a dedicated group called the Ruffed Grouse Society, an active wildlife management association with about 3,000 Michigan members.

Like white-tailed deer, the grouse cannot thrive in a mature forest. The grouse needs a younger, predominantly Poplar or Aspen forest for its best habitat. Ideally, the bird needs a diversified, good mix of age class forest types to provide it everything it needs throughout its life. That's why the most intense grouse managers cut timber every five to ten years in grid patterns on a rotating basis so they always have clear-cut, 10-, 20-, 30-, and 40-year-old aspen forests next to each other. Then grouse can access and grow up in these different age structures of aspen forest. The Ruffed Grouse Society has a great resource book for this management practice that maximizes habitat for this wonderful bird of the forest.

One of the interesting things about the ruffed grouse is the almost predictable ten-year cycle of good and bad times for grouse. While from a scientific point of view, we still don't understand exactly why this happens, it's been well documented that grouse do exceptionally well every ten years (usually in years ending in 9 or 0 like 1999 or 2000), and then they decline in population until they bottom out in years ending in 4 or 5, like 2004 or 2005.

My own hunting experience seems to bear this out. During several years around 1999 and 2000, I could see dozens of grouse on Neebish Island during the hunting season. It was also relatively easy to shoot one or two partridge for dinner if you spent about two hours looking for grouse in good habitat.

As a result, it became a routine to have a special grouse dinner every Saturday night during hunting season. But as the formula predicted, the grouse hunting started to decline during the early years after the new millennium occurred. During 2002 and 2003, the number of birds was down substantially, and it was no longer easy to kill birds for our Saturday night feast.

By 2004 and 2005, the low point of the population cycle, I saw so few birds, that I stopped shooting them entirely, because it was so rare to see any. As I get ready to publish this book in 2009, I can easily see that this year will be better than last year. That's the great thing about this incredible partridge. He will come back in greater numbers and be back strong for the next five years.

While hunting for partridge, I often also encounter a great little bird who is just a bit like a smaller cousin of the ruffed grouse – the American Woodcock. I love hunting woodcock almost as much as partridge, and I think they are even harder for hunters to kill because they are better at weaving through the woods as they escape hunters.

One of my favorite events in the springtime is to watch woodcock (often called Timberdoodles by some Yoopers) as they conduct their mating rituals in openings in the forest. Woodcock fly around openings in daredevil flight patterns that are fun to see right at dusk.

Al Stewart is the DNR's Upland Game Bird Specialist, and he's spent a lifetime working around and studying the legendary ruffed grouse. Al told me that Yooper hunters kill a lot more birds when the cycle is at its high point versus when the birds are in decline. Al can track these changes in population based on counts of birds drumming in the spring and extensive hunter surveys he conducts.

Proud Hunters Proud Yoopers

"The ruffed grouse is one of our most popular game birds in the state," Al told me as I was getting ready to publish this book. "The bird should come back over the next three to four seasons, and hunters should have lots of flushes and see a lot more birds than they did just 2-3 years ago."

In 2005, Al's data from hunter surveys shows that the average grouse hunter killed only 2.3 birds in the season. And ruffed grouse hunters, volunteers who keep accurate records of bird sightings while hunting, reported 1.5 flushes per hour of hunting. By contrast, at the peak of the cycle in 2000, the average hunter killed 4.6 birds, twice as many in 2005. Data from the late 1980s and 1990s also confirms this cycle of reduced partridge numbers roughly every ten years. It's still something we don't fully understand, and, to me, it just makes this bird that much more special.

The thrill of making an incredible shot on a partridge is something that old proud hunters never get tired of.

On a sunny and warm early October day in 2006, I was driving my ATV to my stand for an afternoon bow hunt when a lone partridge ran across the trail in front of me. I had my shotgun handy, so I stopped my bike, loaded up the Browning, and took off in the direction of the bird.

As I walked carefully and quietly through the brush, I only caught one glimpse of the bird on the run. I couldn't seem to get close to him, and I was about to admit defeat when I noticed a small clearing ahead that was the only open space around all the thick cover of poplars and spruces that engulfed me.

Just then, the bird exploded and took off across the narrow opening. I pulled on the bird, and feeling a little desperate, I squeezed off a quick shot just as he entered the thick brush on the far side of the small clearing. I assumed I had missed the bird on the first shot, so I hopelessly tried to line up a second shot. It was no use. There was no sign of the bird after my first shot, and I knew I couldn't see him behind the heavy screen of trees, brush, and a wall of leaves.

I hadn't heard the bird fall nor had I heard him continue on after he exited the clearing. Had I hit him? I just wasn't sure. It would have been a great shot if I had connected, but I surmised odds were low I had.

As I walked in the direction of where the bird had flown, I heard the sound of rapidly beating wings on the ground in the distance. I knew that sound well. It meant that I had hit the bird in the head and he would be dead in a few seconds. I quickly ran ahead to the sound where I found a beautiful, mature partridge who had been downed with a couple of shotgun pellets to his head. He would be a perfect bird for a grouse dinner tonight.

As I picked up the bird and admired his gorgeous plumage, I was thankful for this great bird of the Yooper forests and the challenging shots he presents. I had to chuckle to myself about whether I had made a super, skillful shot at this fleeting ball of feathers or whether I was extremely lucky to have gotten him. For the moment, it didn't really matter – all that mattered was I was quite proud to take him home for dinner.

On this day, a Proud Yooper was thankful for a great bird that runs the forest floors of the UP, and a Proud Hunter was thankful for a partridge who presents challenging shots when he flies.

45

Taking Good Care of the Land

We first knew you as a feeble plant
which wanted a little earth whereon to grow.
We gave it to you.
And afterward, when we could have trod you under our feet,
we watered and protected you.
And now you have grown to be a mighty tree,
whose top reaches the clouds,
and whose branches overspread the whole land,
whilest we, who were the tall pine of the forest,
have become a feeble plant and need your protection.

-Red Jacket, Seneca

Not long after I bought my Neebish Island hunting camp, I became more interested in habitat management and land stewardship – taking good care of the land and making it productive and attractive to wildlife.

After 40 years of hunting, suddenly it seemed more important than ever to do something good for wildlife. Now I wanted to create a new food plot for deer, to plant an apple or oak tree, to grow a grove of pine and cedar trees, or to dig a wetland pond – all to benefit wildlife. Overnight, it seemed as if I needed to do something good for wildlife, and that work became almost as satisfying as killing big bucks.

There is a theory in the hunting community that lifetime hunters become more attuned to the land and to wildlife in general as we become older. When we are young hunters, in our teens, twenties, and thirties, we focus on how much game we kill – we are into "taking" wildlife. The same theory says that once we've experienced a healthy share of "taking," and as we gradually age, we start thinking more about what we are giving back to the land and to the wildlife that it supports.

As I hunted in my forties, suddenly it didn't matter as much any more if I killed a buck every year. For years, I was obsessed with killing every buck I legally could. And so it came as a bit of a surprise, when after age 40, there came a point where that didn't matter as much as it once did. I still loved to hunt and to be outdoors in pursuit of deer, but now I was getting a deeper meaning and satisfaction out of doing anything that helped wildlife. Suddenly, I became more aware of the land and how it could be more productive for wildlife if I helped it. That help would take a commitment from me, but that was a commitment my heart and soul told me to make.

Soon, I was reading every thing I could about land management, timber management, food plots, wetland creation, and other wildlife improvement projects. I

Proud Hunters Proud Yoopers

spent time talking to farmers trying to pick up tips about farming techniques I could use for food plots on my property. I pressed other hunters for information about their experiences with land management experiments they had tried. I also learned all I could about government programs that encouraged land management experiments. I talked to timbermen and foresters every chance I got, trying to learn more about managing for healthy forests.

From these readings and discussions, I eventually knew I needed a habitat plan designed around four land management improvements: (1) establishing food sources like food plots, apple and oak trees, (2) providing cover and safe sanctuary areas for deer, (3) actively managing timber, and (4) creating wetlands. If I could complete these improvements, then I knew I would be giving back to the sport that meant so much to me. I also knew I would finally have the wildlife paradise I had dreamed about since my childhood if I completed this plan.

"Completion" became the key and illusive word. Would I ever complete this ambitious plan?

And so, I took off on a new mission in life. Now I spent almost all my free time making progress on my habit improvement plan.

Not long after I started, I realized that I might never finish this work nor could I do too much habitat improvement work. I came to accept that many of my projects would forever be in a work-in-process state. No matter how hard I worked, the projects were never done, and there was always more work to do. Even so, the work was highly satisfying even in an emotional and spiritual way.

For the first land management improvement technique, I studied food plots and their importance to a heavily wooded and mature forest like what we had on Neebish Island. From my QDMA acquaintances, I learned much about how to create food plots in the middle of the woods without heavy farm equipment. I was thrilled to learn that I could do that work myself with only small hand tools as long as I was willing to perform some back-breaking labor.

I was most impressed that a simple one-acre clover food plot could create 4,500 pounds of food for wildlife in a single year. If the same acre of land had remained as a mature forest, it would produce only 100 pounds of food. I thought an improvement of 45 times more food per acre was awesome. This discovery drove me to make food plots in the middle of my forest.

Dad and I were now spending whole weekends clearing out quarter-acre to one-acre spots among the mature Neebish forest. We would run chainsaws for hours cutting trees and brush so we could open up the forest canopy and let the sunlight hit the forest floor. Then I would spray the cleared area three times on three different weekends with the chemical Round-up, a non-selective glyphosate-type herbicide, to kill any remaining vegetation.

Sometimes, in the middle of summer, when we were drenched in perspiration from cutting timber and hauling brush all day, dad would say to me, "You know, son, we could be fishing right now and taking life easy!"

I would just smile, knowing that he was right, but also knowing that it was satisfying to know we were doing good things for wildlife.

The following late winter or early spring, I would plant clovers or other food plot seed mixes in the cleared landscape so that new shoots of tender, nutrient-rich plants would grow in the middle of the forest where deer and other wildlife could easily and safely feast on them.

I learned about food plot basics and more advanced techniques from the QDMA's Ed Spinazzola every time I saw him and every time he wrote something about food plots. Ed has given hundreds of presentations on food plots throughout Michigan, and he's written two books on beginning and advanced foot plot techniques. He also maintains much of his food plot advice on the Mid-Michigan QDMA's web site. I followed Ed's advice to the letter, and I had good success with his techniques. I kidded him that he had developed the perfect "food plots for dummies" book series because I could prove his methods worked even in the remote UP.

In addition, QDMA branches were sponsoring "Food Plot Days" all over the state, spreading the word about how to create food plots. These events were heavily attended by deer hunters anxious to learn more about the wonders and challenges of food plots.

The proof was everywhere that food plots worked as a valuable land management improvement technique. Most convincing were the game cameras that dad and I put out. They were filled with pictures of deer feeding on our food plots.

In 2006, I started a new Forest Stewardship Program with Will Bomier, a Soil Conservationist with the federal Natural Resource Conservation Service in Sault Ste. Marie. Will helped me put together a plan to cut additional openings on the Neebish property, creating new wildlife openings in dense forest cover. The natural vegetation growing back in these openings also provided huge amounts of food sources for wildlife that were almost as good as food plots.

In early November one year, my neighbors on Neebish Island were complaining about the lack of deer. No one was seeing any bucks and, in addition, no one was seeing large groups of does and fawns. On a cool evening just before rifle season opened, I set up a bow seat on a clover food plot I had planted five years earlier. Just as the sun was setting, I was amazed that eight different does and fawns came to feed on the small field. It was a great feeling to see that many deer feeding on a field I had created out of nothing. It was almost as satisfying as if I had killed a big buck that day. I was tickled to know I had provided these deer with highly nutritious food just before they went into the harsh winter season. I even had a hunch that this nutrition might be the little extra that would carry one or more of the young fawns through a devastating winter, if we had one. That thought made me feel really good.

One day, when I was alone on Neebish Island, I took a nice eight-point buck. When I made it back to my cabin, my neighbor and friend Bob Nowak and his son Adam, stopped for a visit. They helped me take pictures of the deer and hang him up. As we admired the nice buck, Bob took a minute to reinforce with his son, the importance of improving habitat for wildlife.

"If you take good care of the land, Adam, the land takes good care of you," Bob lamented as we looked over the nice buck now in the deer camp. Wow, I thought to myself, that was right on point, and it was a powerful message to a youthful hunter.

Along with food plots, I also became an apple tree planting fool. I knew from years of baiting deer that deer love apples. So, I set out to give them a smorgasbord of apple trees. I decided I would create a bunch of small apple orchards of all varieties that would benefit and delight the local deer herd.

Proud Hunters Proud Yoopers

I didn't yet know just how much tender loving care apple trees growing in the wild would need to survive in their harsh UP home. My first lesson came when I didn't fence in the young trees. Late one April afternoon, I planted ten trees along the edge of a large food plot in the middle of the woods. I had plans to come back the next day and put up deer-proof fences around the new apple trees. There was only one problem. The deer found my apple trees that night, and they ate off enough of the buds that they killed some of the trees and set back the growth several years on the others. My poor seedlings never got a fair chance to get used to their new environment before my local deer herd devoured them.

From that day on, I never planted an apple tree without immediately putting up a five-foot high deer-proof fence of rebar around my new seedlings. I supported the rebar fence with three six-foot T-Posts so that I had a solid, protective cage around my trees. Now, the deer could not browse on the seedlings until they were more mature trees. This construction technique added $10 more to the planting cost for each tree, but it was worth it.

To keep my apple trees growing, I also had to learn the art of pruning apple trees in the spring. In March or early April, I had to visit every apple tree, pruning some of last year's growth and planning for this year's growth with more strategic pruning. Soon, I was as comfortable carrying around a pruning tool in a holster on my belt as most people are carrying around a cell phone.

I also learned to battle bugs, mice, rabbits and bears to protect my apple trees.

The mice and rabbits could easily go through my rebar fence, and they ate all the bark around the base of my trees. This girdling process killed the tree within several months. To stop the mice and rabbits, I had to buy and install a special bark wrap for the trees. The flexible plastic bark wrap covered and protected the bark all the way to the ground, making the mice and rabbits eat something else in the winter.

The bears were another challenge. On both the Neebish and Raber properties, there were two mature apple trees that I rescued and revitalized by killing off the surrounding vegetation, cutting down bigger trees that shaded them, and pruning them to encourage more new growth. Once I got the trees reproducing great crops of apples again, the Neebish bears paid me a visit. The bigger bruins climbed up the trees and broke off some of the best limbs when the heavy bears tried to shake down more apples. The first time they did this, I just about cried when I saw the damaged and broken limbs. The second time it happened, I was determined to save the apple trees.

I stopped the bears by putting more rebar around the tree trunks and weaving barbed wire in the rebar. The bears didn't want to climb the trees once the barbed wire was in place.

I lost track of the number of times I replaced dead apple trees. I replanted new ones in the same places time and time again. But I was determined that I wouldn't give up until I had apple blossoms in the spring and juicy apples in the fall all over the property.

In 2006, I turned the corner when a few trees started to have apples and my older, rehabilitated trees were just loaded with apples. I used a game camera to photograph deer coming to feed on the apples, and it was great to know that deer were feeding regularly. The bears visited too, and they stayed out of the trees. As I looked at the

Take Good Care of the Land

brilliant red colors against the skyline, it was a satisfying feeling to know that I was providing dozens of deer and a few rowdy bears with one of their favorite foods.

One of my favorite habitat improvements for deer is planting oak trees. I have always admired majestic oak trees. From the time I was a small boy hunting with dad on the big oak ridge in the Burning, I have loved mature oak trees and the acorns they produce. Deer and other game animals also love acorns. In fact, acorns are also one of their favorite foods. Deer in the UP need acorns in the fall to help them put on layers of fat reserves so they can survive the tough winters.

Just like the apple trees, I had only three oak trees on both my Neebish and Raber properties. As a result, the two land management consultants I hired to complete my Stewardship Incentive Plans told me to plant large numbers of oak seedlings.

To learn more about trees that would grow in my part of the UP, I bought a great book I saw advertised in the MUCC's *Michigan Outdoors* magazine called *Trees of Michigan and the Upper Great Lakes* by Norman F. Smith. Smith's book is a must read for anyone who is serious about planting trees and managing his or her land for timber.

Before long, I was an oak tree planting fool too, planting hundreds of red, white, and bur oak every year. Deer also eat oak seedlings like candy, so I needed to protect the young seedlings with four-foot commercial tree shelters. The shelters are a relatively new technique for protecting tree seedlings in areas that are heavily browsed by deer. Tree shelters are about four inches in diameter, and they are made of plastic-like material that allows the sunlight to penetrate through their sides. Because the seedling grows inside the shelter, out of the wind and cold, the climate inside the shelter is like a greenhouse, allowing the seedling to grow safely and much, much faster.

To protect my oaks, I purchased about a thousand tree shelters from four different commercial vendors. Soon, I had tree shelters all over my land. I also wrote a story about how to plant oak trees and use tree shelters. I published the story of my oak tree planting adventures on the Mid-Michigan QDMA's web site, highlighting the expensive mistakes and mishaps I had over the years.

Almost a decade later, I am now the owner of some nice young oak trees. It might still be thirty or forty years before they produce heavy crops of acorns for foraging deer, but eventually they will. In the outdoor community, there's an old conservation saying, "You don't plant oak trees for yourself. You plant them for the next generation." That's been my experience to date. It has been satisfying to know that some day down the road, my children and my grandchildren may look at a mature oak and remember that a Yooper tree planting fool tenderly placed that beautiful tree in the ground when it was a young seedling.

For the second land management improvement technique, I learned that planning for "cover" or shelter areas for deer was really important if you were to keep deer on your land and provide them with safety or "safe havens." Ideally, deer should have large cover areas of thick vegetation or conifer trees, where they feel safe from danger. Cover areas should be located near food plots or other food sources so deer can get to them easily from their daytime hiding areas. Some land managers referred to these areas as "sanctuaries" or areas where humans never enter. Resisting the temptation to never enter these areas allows the deer to feel super safe in them. These areas will become prime deer bedding or resting areas if humans stay out and don't scare off the deer.

In 2002, I met Tony LaPratt of Coldwater, Michigan. Tony has killed more Pope & Young record bucks than anyone else I know. He's killed most of them on his own 52-acre piece of property in Branch County that he intensely manages for whitetails. Tony taught me and thousands of other hunters that you can actually encourage big bucks to stay on your property if you create safe bedding areas for the deer and then leave them alone by staying out of the sanctuaries. Today, Tony makes his living teaching deer management courses and giving hunters on-site, hands-on advice about a concept he calls "Ultimate Land Management" (ULM) principles. His ULM program focuses on teaching hunters how to aggressively manage small parcels of property so that deer use and stay on your property during the daylight hours. Tony encourages hunters to provide for all the needs of the deer so they are self-sufficient on your property. He has had amazing success with this program on his own piece of property, and he has the P&Y bucks to prove it works.

In the UP, Jeff Sturgis of Munising also teaches hunters and landowners about similar concepts. Like Tony, Jeff has killed some impressive bucks using his land management concepts that emphasize sanctuaries. Jeff specializes in land management techniques for small properties and he's written extensively about how small property owners can best manage their land to attract wildlife.

I was so impressed with what I learned from Tony and Jeff, that I started paying really close attention to the deer bedding areas on my property. I began working hard to create additional cover areas for deer by planting more pines, spruces and cedars for them.

I started really thinking about where deer bed when they are on my property and where they will move when they want to feed. To improve my hunting, I made a vow to stay out of the sanctuaries.

I also learned to pay attention to how deer approach my food plots and other spots we hunt. Tony and Jeff taught me that it really mattered how I approached my stand and how much human scent I left around the stand. While this didn't always matter to small bucks and young does, it did matter to the mature bucks and older does. Leave a lot of scent around a food plot or your seat, and a big buck might just figure out that he had better avoid that place during the daylight hours, especially during hunting season. That's how the big ones survive once they get several years of life experiences under their belts, and that's one reason why older bucks are so hard to kill.

One technique I learned about creating bedding areas is "hinge cutting." Jim Strader, a QDMA member and former state chapter president from Charlotte, showed me how to cut halfway through the trunks of 3-6 inch trees at heights 3-4 feet from the ground, leaving the trees alive, but with their tops now growing on the ground. Hinge cutting a bunch of trees in a small area creates a jungle that is a perfect deer bedding area.

I also noticed that deer like to bed in marshy areas, particularly when there is a high, dry spot in the marsh. If there isn't a high, dry spot, creating one by hauling in some sand or clean dirt will almost always assure that a deer beds there.

It's a real kick when a deer starts bedding in a place you created and declared a sanctuary.

Take Good Care of the Land

For the third land management improvement technique, I focused on developing a formal plan for managing my timber. I didn't know it, but my timber had considerable value. Several foresters told me that my timber had not been properly managed, and in fact, it needed immediate treatment because I was losing mature, dying timber everyday. DNR Forester Pat Hallfrisch of Sault Ste. Marie told me about the DNR's program where one of their professional foresters provides free general advice to landowners about their timber. He recommended I spend some time with DNR Forester Richard Stevenson of Newberry. Richard came to my property just before the 2005 rifle deer season, and we toured the whole Neebish place. He helped me size up my timber, and he gave me ideas for what I should do to manage it more aggressively for wildlife. His most important advice was to hire a commercial forester who would help me balance my desire to both earn money from the timber and to keep the forest in good shape so it would support more wildlife. He told me about several area foresters that did both well. After this discussion and a little research, I hired Todd Miller from Newberry's Grossman Forestry to develop a comprehensive timber management plan for me. Grossman Forestry is one of the most respected timber management firms in the UP, and Todd is one of the most respected foresters in the area.

In 2006, my family learned just how valuable timber can be. My father and his sisters sold some timber they owned on land they inherited from my grandfather. They created a plan to harvest some of the timber on a single 40-acre parcel in Goetzville. One timber buyer paid them $80,000 ($2,000 an acre) for a select cut of mature sugar maple trees they had. Interestingly, the market value of the property was only about $60,000 for the whole 40 acres ($1,500 an acre) before the timber was harvested. After the timber was harvested, the land still had a similar market value. This example, while not typical of most properties, speaks to the untapped and sometimes unknown value of timber to landowners today.

This timber harvest taught me that many Yooper landowners can make a very good second income from our timber if we make an effort to manage it. If we are lucky, we might even see economic returns that are outstanding from our property. On top of that, we are also usually doing good things for wildlife too when we harvest the timber. This phenomenon is one of the best kept secrets of wildlife land management.

Today, when I teach land management and deer management programs for QDMA, I try to point out the value and importance of timber and its management. I tell landowners that they might get 30-40% more money from their timber if they actively manage their timber and follow the advice of their foresters.

One year, Gerry Nettleton of Detour harvested some maple trees I had on the Raber property, and Joe Rogers of Rudyard clear cut aspen, evergreen and spruce trees on Neebish. Both jobs generated significant amounts of cash that I used to help pay for other land management projects, and they also helped me better manage my timber.

The timber industry is the largest employer and the largest industry in the UP. It is also the fourth largest industry in the state of Michigan following manufacturing, agriculture and tourism. Harvesting timber for a living is hard work, and it can be incredibly dangerous. We should all have high regard for our Proud Yoopers (men and women) who make their living in the timber industry.

Proud Hunters Proud Yoopers

In a stark contrast, some environmental groups want to stop all timber harvesting in our state forests. Many of them are anti-timber people who protest the removal of any timber from public lands.

Rather than protest against cutting timber, I usually celebrate timber harvests. Substantial research has shown that timber harvests help support higher levels of wildlife, especially deer and grouse. I've seen this personally on my own lands, and I've seen the power of nature to renew and replenish the tree resources that are cut.

Make no mistake about it, the timber industry is a friend of the wildlife community. They keep our forests young and healthy. Cutting timber in Michigan provides incredible amounts of food for wildlife while the timber is being cut and for several years afterward when young trees and other plant life regenerate in the cut-over area where sunlight now hits the forest floor.

After I had cut timber on some of my land, I became a pine and spruce tree planting fool too. Over the years, I have planted as many as 3,000 trees in one week each spring, always by hand. I usually select the last week of April to complete this work. That's the same week in which Earth Day falls. To celebrate the wonder of Earth Day, I take the whole week off and dedicate it to a week of intense habitat management. I don't just celebrate Earth Day; I celebrate my own Earth Week, working myself 15 hours a day to improve my land so it becomes better wildlife habitat. It's probably hard for some hunters to imagine, but this week is now almost as important as Opening Day of deer rifle season.

When I reached a point in life where habitat work became almost as big a deal as Opening Day, I knew my life was changing. I knew there was something important about this habitat stuff.

My fourth and final land management improvement technique was to create wetland ponds for waterfowl and other wildlife species. There were no running streams, lakes, or ponds on the Neebish property, except for very small seasonal ponds that dried up in the summer months, and of course, the mighty St. Mary's River at my property's edge. From my days on Hungry Hill and the Gogemain, I knew wildlife loved beaver ponds in the middle of a forest. Those ponds were also duck hotspots that I loved to hunt in the fall. I wanted some ponds on my property so I could have water magnets and so I could hunt ducks and geese on them. As a result, I decided to create several ponds on Neebish.

Roger Parr and Joe Johnston own 160 acres on Neebish Island, southeast of my place. They are avid and dedicated hunters who have done a considerable amount of work to make their land more productive for wildlife. They had also received a Stewardship Incentive Plan grant, and they used it to create a beautiful wetland pond in the middle of their property. Dad and I studied their pond carefully and talked with Roger and Joe about how they developed it.

Greg Stoll, a Manistique land management consultant, helped me develop a Stewardship Incentive Plan. I told him about my interests in ponds, and he included three ponds in my plan. The DNR approved the plan, and I applied for permits from the Department of Environmental Quality to dig the ponds. In May, 1998, I had Ken Norris of Norris Contracting of Sault Ste. Marie and his crew lined up with the mother-of-all big bulldozers to dig the ponds. The large dozer was almost idling in the

Take Good Care of the Land

driveway when I got a startling letter from Lori Sargent, who was an endangered species specialist for the DNR at the time.

Lori told me that there was a rare Michigan flower, called a Calypso Orchid (or fairy slipper), recorded in the DNR's data base. Someone had reported finding the flower on the mainland near the Neebish Island ferry. Because my land was near this property, the DNR required me to get someone knowledgeable about the orchid to search for this flower before we could dig the ponds. The DEQ wouldn't now authorize me to do the excavation work until this was cleared up. I needed to prove to them that we wouldn't hurt this flower when we created our wildlife ponds. Eventually, a DEQ employee helped me conduct a survey of the property for the rare flower. We never found any orchids, and finally I was able to begin digging.

There were challenges in digging the ponds. Initially, two of them would not hold water. We needed some design changes to keep 18 inches of water in each one. When digging the last pond, we really had trouble keeping water in the pond. Then heavy rains came, turning the site into a slippery mess of mud and clay. Now the big dozer had a hard time pushing the dirt. And the DEQ had insisted that we push all the excess dirt to the west side of the pond. On the other two ponds, we had pushed dirt to both sides of the pond, and that was much more efficient. Dumping all the spoils on one side of the pond quadrupled the dozer work and my costs.

I consulted another Neebish Island pond digging neighbor, Russell Tyner, about my options. Russ was an avid deer hunter and he was known on Neebish Island for his ability to call in big bucks by rattling antlers and using a grunt call. In 2006, Russ called in a large buck that his young son Hunter killed with a rifle. The deer was one of the biggest killed in the eastern UP that year.

Russ and his father Cliff had constructed ponds on their family's land on the southern tip of Neebish Island. I asked Russ to look at my pond, and tell me if he knew from his experience why we could not hold water in the pond. Russ surmised that we were on a gravel vein in the soil and that this porous bottom allowed the water to leak out of the pond, probably seeping back into the water table. Russ figured the pond might be OK if we dug a little deeper until we hit a clay bottom.

At one point, I was about to give up and abandon the pond. That's when Ken Norris suggested we use an excavator to work in tandem with the dozer. It was going to cost me more money, but Ken thought we would get the job done right with more equipment.

Wow, Ken and Russ called that one right. Once we got the excavator on site, we started moving some dirt - big time. We hit a nice clay bottom (as Russ had suggested) and the pond quickly filled up with water that drained in steadily from a nearby marshy area whenever there were heavy rains. I asked the dozer operator to leave a few islands in the pond, and he nicely carved out two small islands with big black ash trees growing on them. As we shut down the digging operation, I was pleased. I was going to have three very nice ponds.

It didn't take long for Mother Nature to clean up the signs that an excavator and dozer had been pushing mud all over the place. Before long, new vegetation was growing around the pond edges. Soon, deer, raccoons, otters and other animals were regularly using the ponds and traveling those fertile edges.

Proud Hunters Proud Yoopers

The next spring, a pair of Canadian geese took up nesting rights on one of the islands we had left in the last pond. For four years in a row, those geese came back and nested in the same place.

Over the next few years, there were more and more ducks and geese using the ponds during the spring, summer and especially the fall when I could hunt them. Every year, I killed a number of ducks on the ponds, and sometimes I got action on geese, too.

I built and installed a number of wood duck boxes, and I also installed protected mallard nesting boxes in all three ponds.

There was a feeling of satisfaction that I had done something really good to the land simply because I had modified it slightly so there was open water. Now a number of animals, birds, reptiles, and insects could use these ponds and their productive edges – edges that were teaming with life and food sources. There wasn't any question that I had improved the habitat with these changes and the land could now support more wildlife.

I was also pleased that I could observe more wildlife from spots overlooking the ponds. I had a feeling of great fulfillment whenever I saw a heron or sandhill crane or other waterfowl, turtles, or other wildlife in the ponds. I grew to love the ponds and the wildlife that they attracted.

But like all my habitat and land management improvement projects, I knew this one was also not finished. While some would have been satisfied to quit now that the ponds were attracting more wildlife, now I could not wait to plan for more ponds and a series of ponds that connected to each other, just like the connecting beaver dams I had hunted in the vastness of Hungry Hill and the Gogemain. I was determined to do more to improve the land and build upon my success.

From these experiences, a Proud Hunter learned that there is great satisfaction in making the land more attractive and productive for wildlife, almost as much satisfaction as taking a big buck. And a Proud Yooper learned that the work of land and habitat management for wildlife is never done until we are pushing up daises.

46

Taking a Stand for Deer Management

The longer a problem is allowed to exist,
the harder it is to return to peace of mind.

-Twilab Nitsch, Seneca

Sixty or more years ago, Michigan was the hot spot in the country for a white-tailed deer hunt. Hunters from all over our nation came to northern Michigan for a chance to kill a big buck, one with massive antlers and a huge body.

In fact, Michigan's reputation as a great deer hunting state was so good, that the rich and famous often planned their vacations around Michigan's deer hunting season. Many of them traveled to the UP to hunt for the big bucks that lived in our forests in good numbers.

My grandfather and other local hunters in the eastern UP made some good money when times were tough, guiding and catering to these hunters.

"They would say to you, 'Take me to where the big ones are'," my grandpa would fondly tell us with a big grin and a laugh, when describing the rich hunters who traveled to the UP. "I would take them to my favorite spots and hope they would see a nice buck," my grandpa would report when I pressed him on what it was like to guide the visitors.

In the 1940s and 1950s, a period of time often referred to as the good ole days, there were actually only about 100,000 deer in Michigan, and hunters only killed about 20,000 bucks each year. The difference was that there was a good cross section of each age class of bucks, and there were far fewer hunters. Consequently, hunters didn't kill the majority of the bucks each year, so there were lots of 2.5-year-old, 3.5-year-old, 4.5-year-old, and even older mature bucks. In fact, the deer herd was much like the balanced deer herd that Mother Nature had intended, with male and female deer of all ages in the herd.

As a result, hunters (like the ones my grandpa guided) did see lots of older bucks when they were in the UP woods, and these bucks had big antlered racks because many of them were allowed to grow to maturity. The combination of few hunters and a short hunting season meant we didn't kill all the young bucks, so many of them could grow older. Similarly, that is what happens in the states of Illinois, Iowa, Kansas, Indiana, Ohio, and other states where the deer herd is more natural because those states manage the deer herd differently than we do in Michigan.

Years of "traditional" deer management in Michigan, with its focus on killing mostly young bucks and protecting antlerless deer, changed Michigan's deer herd significantly to what we have today.

For decades during the 1950s, 60s, and 70s, the DNR changed deer hunting in Michigan by minimizing the harvest of antlerless deer so the deer population soared. While the deer population significantly increased, so did the number of hunters. The DNR, like some other states, focused almost exclusively on killing antlered deer. They

Proud Hunters Proud Yoopers

didn't really worry about the impact on the herd while the populations soared and when we began shooting a majority of the young bucks each year. As long as we sold lots of licenses, had lots of hunters, and killed lots of bucks, resource managers didn't focus on what we were doing to the overall quality of the habitat or the age structure of the deer herd.

In 1971, the DNR's Wildlife Division boldly adopted a new initiative to double the number of deer in the state from 500,000 to one million by 1980. Not only did the DNR accomplish that goal, but by 1990, they reached another stunning milestone when they produced a population of two million deer in the state.

By most measures, the DNR and the public thought this was an incredible accomplishment. Almost no one recognized the enormous problems that would accompany this increase in the size of the deer herd.

By the late 1980s, hunters were no longer killing large numbers of mature bucks in the state. Instead hunters had a very good chance of killing a small, yearling buck. Hunters became very proficient in killing these young bucks as archery, muzzleloading and other outdoor equipment improved and as elevated seats and comfortable hunting blinds became the norm. Heavy baiting in the northern two-thirds of the state also made hunters significantly more efficient in killing young bucks. We were now harvesting very high percentages of our yearling bucks and the percentage of older bucks in the herd steadily decreased. The DNR promoted this deer management strategy as good public policy because it provided for "maximum recreational opportunities."

When these changes happened, hunters from other states stopped considering Michigan as the place to go to kill a nice buck. Now, other states were taking our place as the best places to hunt for nice deer. These states recognized that years of traditional deer management could give them an unbalanced and unnatural deer herd. They put strategies and hunting restrictions in place that ensured their hunters did not kill high percentages of their yearling bucks. As a result, those states produced more natural deer herds, with older age classes of mature bucks.

Today, when major outdoor magazines do preseason stories on where to hunt for big bucks, Michigan no longer even merits any attention in their articles. Outdoor writers identify lots of places to hunt for big bucks – Kansas, Iowa, Illinois, Kentucky, western Canada, Texas, and others. Michigan never even makes these lists. In the eyes of many, we have gone from being one of the best deer hunting states in the country to being one of the worst, all because our hunters are now obsessed with killing small bucks every year.

Why hasn't the DNR acted more aggressively to manage our deer herd for a more natural deer herd? Many in the deer management movement believe the DNR has no incentive to change their management methods because they know that some hunters don't want to give up the only form of deer hunting many of them have ever known.

And some in the outdoor world believe the DNR staff is petrified that it might have a revenue reduction and be forced to reduce its staff or cut programs if it changes how it regulates the deer herd. After all, deer license revenue is the major revenue source that helps fund the department's wildlife programs.

By the 1990s, the deer population in Michigan had really exploded. There were now so many deer that they inhabited places in Michigan they had never been before,

Taking a Stand for Deer Management

places where the habitat was generally too marginal to support deer. But with a population so high, deer moved into these areas, and suddenly, people were seeing deer everywhere and lots of them.

At this point, some foresters believed we had so many deer that you couldn't grow a single maple tree seedling anywhere in the entire state because deer would eat it shortly after it germinated. There were that many deer over-browsing our forests and eating literally 100% of some plant species.

The damage our deer did to the overall state forest habitat is hard to measure, but some professionals have argued that the long-term damage to our forests is extensive. Some experts believe that certain forest plant life has been so devastated that it will take up to several decades to restore our forests to what they were before the deer population peaked.

Eventually, DNR officials realized that two million deer was way over the capacity that the land could support without causing extensive, long-term damage to our native habitat. They had to begin lowering hunter expectations and lowering the number of deer in the state. This change in policy, while desperately needed, was generally not supported by hunters who had become accustomed to seeing deer everywhere in the woods.

At the 2006 National Convention for the Quality Deer Management Association, former Pennsylvania Deer Management Director Gary Alt said it was a horrible mistake to greatly increase the size of the deer herd. He said this decision and the relentless harvest of young bucks for so many years, was one of the worst wildlife management decisions ever made by resource managers in modern times.

While Dr. Alt's comments weren't aimed just at Michigan, some of us in the deer management movement believed they certainly applied directly to us.

Alt knew what he was talking about. He had lived through some of the most radical deer management times in the history of Pennsylvania. Alt had been a well-liked and widely-respected black bear researcher and director of Pennsylvania's black bear program for the Department of Natural Resources. He gave up that comfortable job to take on the thankless and most difficult job of significantly changing Pennsylvania's deer management program.

In the late 1990s, Pennsylvania's deer population was much like the Michigan herd. This deer herd was way over its carrying capacity and it had destroyed major parts of the PA forests. Like Michigan, Pennsylvania hunters killed a high percentage of the young bucks each year, giving it an unnatural and unbalanced deer herd, almost devoid of older age classes of bucks.

Dr. Alt changed all of that when he challenged Pennsylvania hunters to adopt a program of statewide antler restrictions. Alt convinced hunters to harvest only bucks with three points on one antler in the heavily wooded areas of PA and four points on a side in the farm country where the bucks were bigger because of better nutrition. He wanted hunters to give up killing spikes and four-point bucks all across the state. He wanted young bucks to live at least one more year. And he also told hunters they had to start killing a lot more does and fawns to significantly reduce the overall population.

Alt gave hundreds of speeches about deer management all over the state to win acceptance of this significant change. In fact, he gave an educational deer management presentation within 20 miles of every hunter in the state. He also distributed 25,000 free copies of a video about deer management basics to hunters. His effort was one of the largest wildlife management educational programs ever conducted in the USA.

Unfortunately, not everyone in Pennsylvania wanted to hear Dr. Alt's message. He so threatened some traditional deer hunters that they made death threats on his life. These hunters hated the thought that they could no longer kill spikehorns if Alt was successful. Like Michigan hunters, this vocal minority of Pennsylvania hunters didn't want to stop their annual ritual of killing small yearling bucks. When Alt spoke in front of deer hunters, he had to wear a bullet-proof vest, just in case the death threats were carried out.

To many of us in the deer management movement, Dr. Gary Alt is our symbol of courage and leadership. He is a true deer management champion. He is a man who put the deer in front of his own public safety. He put the "deer" back in deer management. He is a man who had the attitude and persistence that he would change deer management for the better in this state no matter what the personal cost is to him. He is a man who wasn't afraid to educate average hunters about the options for deer management strategies. He is a man who made a difference in the lives of hundreds of thousands of deer hunters and millions of deer in one of our largest deer hunting states.

Eventually, the personal cost to Dr. Alt was too high. The vocal minority in Pennsylvania that opposed his historic efforts eventually made enough noise that he chose to leave his post as deer management point person and go into private wildlife management consulting work in California. His departure, however, didn't change the state's management of the deer herd. He had set the tone, and he had forever altered the direction of deer management in the state. Even after he left, the state continued to reduce the size of the herd by harvesting more antlerless deer, and they significantly stopped the slaughter of young bucks, creating a more natural and balanced deer herd.

By 2007, major outdoor magazines were singing the praises of what Alt had started in Pennsylvania. His experiment had been a tremendous success in reshaping the herd in the state, and most hunters had accepted the deer management changes. The number of record book deer killed also skyrocketed. After a couple of rough years, hunters were now enjoying the increased quality of the hunt and the chance to kill a really nice buck, a buck that they would have never seen just five years earlier. Outdoor magazines were now ranking Pennsylvania as a great place to hunt deer again.

The 2007 deer kill numbers told the story. Pennsylvania killed 213,900 antlerless deer and 109,200 bucks in 2007, a huge reversal in kill rates from the pre-Gary Alt days. They were now killing almost twice as many antlerless deer as they are bucks, and that kill pattern had now transformed their herd back to a more natural deer herd with buck and doe ratios like Mother Nature had intended.

In contrast, in Michigan, DNR officials estimated in their preliminary study that we killed 267,400 bucks and only 209,200 antlerless deer in 2007. Assuming 20% of the antlerless deer kill were male button bucks, we killed over 300,000 male deer and only 170,000 female deer. We can't keep doing that in Michigan and expect to have a natural deer herd like the other states.

As this drama with Dr. Alt was unfolding in Pennsylvania, I changed from being an avid deer hunter who happened to dabble in "deer politics" with the Quality Deer Management Association to someone who was now almost obsessed with changing how Michigan manages its deer herd.

Taking a Stand for Deer Management

I became convinced that Michigan had the most manipulated and the most unnatural deer herd of any publicly managed deer herd on the planet. I was convinced that almost every other state was willing to do something proactive to protect a few younger bucks so they had more older bucks in the herd– everyone except Michigan. I came to believe that some in Michigan thought of deer as a commodity to be bought and sold. It seemed as if some were entrenched with Michigan being a "numbers" state, or Michigan being a "brown, it's down" state. I thought the way we managed the herd in Michigan was demeaning to an animal that is one of nature's greatest creatures.

I was also concerned that we had developed two classes of hunters in the state. First, there were those of us who were fortunate enough to own land. Landowners like me could band together and practice QDM in large co-ops. As word spread about the changes in the deer herd when neighbors cooperated, QDM co-ops exploded throughout Michigan. These hunters started to experience hunting again as other states had. They had very high-quality hunting experiences because of their voluntary QDM practices.

Second, on public land, another trend was occurring. As the quality of hunting improved on the intensely managed private lands, the quality of hunting on public land plummeted. These hunters had no food plots to draw and hold deer; they had enormous pressure from other hunters who chased deer to the more peaceful private land; they couldn't erect permanent blinds; they had few deer and even fewer doe permits; and their success ratio was much smaller than private land hunters.

I was a proud hunter who had hunted public land almost exclusively for thirty years when the hunting experiences were higher quality. I was saddened by this transformation on our public lands. I was now convinced that the DNR had managed our deer herd into two classes of hunting experiences. We were now the "haves" (those with hunting land in QDM co-ops) and the "have-nots" (those hunting on marginal public land). I came to believe the DNR had unintentionally, but effectively, split our hunting community into these two factions.

Along with many in the QDM movement, I was now determined that we would do something positive to change how we managed our deer herd on both public and private land if it was the last thing on earth I ever did.

The frustration level among other QDMA members was also at an all-time high. Some of our most dedicated members were angry because we were still killing a high percentage of our year-and-a-half old bucks. This practice was even worse in the UP where it seemed like we were still killing a very high percentage of our 1.5-year-old bucks with our three-month hunting season and all the baiting that went on over the three-month period. We had worked so hard for changes, but we questioned whether we had accomplished any meaningful, long-lasting changes in our ten-year history.

Despite all the QDMA educational efforts and the modest progress we had made, hunters were still killing more than half of all the young bucks we had each season. Our national QDMA biologists believed that we were one of the only states still doing this. And yet those of us who were practicing QDM on our own properties could easily see the positive changes in our local deer herd when we stopped pummeling all the young bucks. We knew QDM would work and transform the deer herd. We had learned that other states were more effective in protecting their young bucks so that they had more bucks in the herd, they had a better balance of deer among all the age classes, and they had a more natural deer herd.

In fact, by the year 2005, many states used some form of restriction that helped protect younger bucks so that more of them advanced to the older age classes. Some had point or spread restrictions on the size of antlers. Some closed the hunting season during all or part of the breeding (rutting) cycle when many bucks are most vulnerable, making them harder to kill. Some had shorter seasons than Michigan, which reduced opportunities to harvest bucks.

I had taken a private vow that I would learn all I could about deer management techniques in Michigan and other states. I began reading everything I could find about deer management, and that included more than 100 books and major research papers on deer management concepts. My basement library of deer management books started to look pretty impressive.

I thought long and hard about how effective we had been with the Eastern UP Wildlife Coalition (EUPWC) and with the local branches of the QDMA. We had done some very good things with the EUPWC, and I was proud of them. Even those who disagreed with our efforts to establish mandatory antler restrictions acknowledged that we had done a good job raising awareness about deer management concepts through the many seminars we had conducted.

As proud as I was of what we had done in the EUPWC, I was also convinced that small, local organizations like the EUPWC and local QDMA branches couldn't be as effective as a larger, better-organized and better-financed state or national organization.

One night, I spent the entire evening on the telephone with Lou Kurtis, Dwaine Starr, and Brian Harrison talking about the future of the EUPWC. In the end, we decided to disband the EUPWC and merge it into the UP's Superior Branch of the QDMA. I also called Superior Deer Management Branch President Jeff Sturgis of Munising and made the arrangements to close down EUPWC, transferring the members to the Superior Branch. From then on, I would work exclusively with the QDMA on deer management issues.

In one sense, it was a huge relief. It had taken tremendous work (and lots of my personal time and money) to keep the EUPWC going. From now on, I would have significantly more resources to help with deer management issues – resources the national QDMA could provide throughout Michigan.

I was looking forward to working more closely with the state chapter of the QDMA. I was convinced that this organization could become a more powerful and influential group in shaping deer management in Michigan. Two key leaders who had this view included Eaton County QDMA Branch President Tony Smith and QDMA Regional Director Perry Russo. Those two, along with Jim Strader, got the QDMA state chapter of Michigan off the ground and they put the structure in place to ensure we could become a more effective organization. They had the "vision" of what we could become – the voice of sound decision-making for deer management in Michigan.

Some dedicated QDMA members told me that we had to become much more politically astute and we had to build more alliances with the "deer management power brokers" who controlled the deer management decision-making process in Michigan. I knew who these "power brokers" were, and I knew they were the key to making some positive changes in Michigan. Some of them had a bad taste for the QDMA and our efforts to establish mandatory antler restrictions. I knew that was something we would have to deal with.

There is an old saying that effective people "stay close to friends and stay closer to their enemies." Some of us thought this saying applied directly to QDMA and the deer management movement. We knew we had to stay closer to those who didn't share our views.

Because I was committed to make changes in the deer management process, I decided to run for president of the state chapter of QDMA when Jim Strader and Tony Smith announced they would step down from the State Chapter. In January, 2006, I got the job when the new QDMA 12-member board elected me. I now hoped that I had the best part-time, no-pay job in the world. I hoped and prayed that the state chapter board of directors could be effective in helping lead QDMA so that we could get management changes in our Michigan deer herd.

When I got the QDMA presidency (and no one else was interested in the position!), I knew I was surrounded by great people who would impact this important public-policy initiative. There were tremendously dedicated men and women on the QDMA board. Larry Holcomb, a former DNR employee, served as our Vice President. Larry is the author of *For the Love of the Outdoors.* He also headed up our quarterly meetings with the DNR's Rod Clute, a Big Game Specialist for the DNR, whom Director Becky Humphries had tapped to meet with us to discuss deer management issues.

Dan Timmons, a successful insurance executive from Novi, had agreed to be the QDMA board secretary. Dan is a dedicated and patient deer hunter who had turned an old farm in Hillsdale County into a wildlife paradise. His habitat work on the farm had been featured in *Quality Whitetails,* and his knowledge of whitetails was superb and widely recognized around the state. Often, he would spend his evenings trading barbs and whitetail statistics with other hard-core whitetail enthusiasts on the *Michigan Sportsman* chat room forums where he was affectionately known by his internet handle of "FarmLegend."

With all the challenges we had financing our projects, we needed a strong financial guru to handle our treasury duties. We were fortunate that Dave DeHaan, a young CPA from Hastings, agreed to be our treasurer. Dave hunted Barry County, and he helped form and operate the Barry County QDMA Branch, which had been selected as the best new branch of the year – an award the branch had received at the 2006 Annual QDMA Convention in Valley Forge, Pennsylvania. QDMA also honored Dave's branch in 2007 for being the best fundraising branch in the country.

The rest of our board was rock solid too. We had Marsha McKee, one the best fundraisers I had ever worked with on the non-profit scene. Marsha raised more money for us every year than anyone else. She worked with our flagship branch, the Mid-Michigan Branch, which supported and funded most of the QDMA statewide initiatives. She was an expert at getting businesses to donate valuable items to us for fundraising purposes at our banquets. Right with Marsha in fundraising capability was another board member, Eric Howard. Eric ran the Illinois Trophy Outfitters group (and later the Trophy Buck Outfitters), and he was well connected in the whitetail community, which helped him become a tremendous fund raiser and organizer for us. He had unlimited energy and enthusiasm for deer management issues, which we often

Proud Hunters Proud Yoopers

tapped. QDMA's national office named both Marsha and Eric as the top Volunteers of the Year in the country for promoting sound deer management.

We also had a public school teacher, Mike Myers, who headed up our operations in Montcalm County, where he had developed a large co-op. Mike and his young son had both taken mature bucks in 2006, with his son being successful in the youth hunt. Mike and his son represented what we thought the future of hunting in Michigan would be – involving our children and youth in hunting and focusing on harvesting older deer. We had Joel Malcuit, a researcher by background, who had a great mind for analyzing difficult policy issues. Joel also headed up our Eaton County branch, and he often provided us with great videos of big bucks that were using his property which he managed in a large co-op with his neighbors in the Charlotte/Vermontville area. Joel was also active in helping us partner with other outdoor groups like MUCC.

We had a newcomer, Alex Giftos of Cadillac, a businessman who ran retail stores in Cadillac and Traverse City. He took over our state chapter newsletter duties, and he provided us with some keen desktop publishing skills that we needed to jazz up our newsletters. Alex had done some good things to improve the habitat on 80 acres he hunted and owned in northwest Lower Michigan. Chad Thelen was also a key contributor on our board. Chad ran the Stoney Creek Habitat Company out of the Portland area, so he was hands-on helping hunters and landowners improve their property. Chad had formed one of the largest QDM co-ops in the Pewamo-Westphalia-Portland area, and the local farmers were raving about the tremendous improvement in deer hunting quality they now had. After two years of following Chad's advice on letting some small bucks go and harvesting more does, they were seeing huge bucks, which they hadn't seen in years.

We had James Holliday on the board, too. James worked with me at MDOT where he was a skilled tradesman who had a special gift when it came to working with wood. James designed and built a magnificent "QDMA Wall" for us that was 10-feet tall and 32-feet long. We used the wall at our outdoor shows and major events. Because of James and his handiwork, we had a first-class drawing card wherever we went to promote QDMA. Phil Andres also joined our board in 2006. Phil and his wife Illona run a bed-and-breakfast operation north of Detroit. Phil is also a leader in the successful Mid-Michigan branch where he has used his business skills to help make that branch one of the best in the country.

In 2008, we added four new board members, including Boyd Wiltse, a retired General Motors finance specialist from Brighton who had done extensive work with the Mid-Michigan branch and who had helped form a QDM co-op in southern Jackson County. John Knevel, of Parma also joined our board, bringing his leadership skills from his long association with Commemorative Bucks of Michigan to QDMA. John, who runs two insurance agencies, also was active in a QDM co-op in Jackson County. Third, Mike McGuire of Fowlerville stepped up to help us, too. Mike was a logistics expert with a national transportation company, and he managed QDM property in northeast Michigan. Mike had great skills in analyzing and solving business problems. Fourth, Jerry Gordenier, a businessman and avid white-tailed deer enthusiast from the Jackson area, joined us. Jerry managed a large track of southern Michigan land for whitetails, and he was active in supporting any marketing efforts we did.

Taking a Stand for Deer Management

Some of our branch presidents, while not serving on the state chapter board, were also effective in promoting QDMA throughout Michigan. These guys really made things happen on the ground and they were our connection with our members and the hunting public. Some of the most influential presidents included Paul Plantinga from the Thumb Branch, Jason Perry from the Southeast Michigan Branch, Jeff Brown from Northeast Michigan Branch, Richard King of Gladwin's Mid-Michigan Branch, Ryan Ratajczak of the Northwest Michigan Branch, and Brad Madalinski of the UP's Superior Branch.

On the national level, we got world-class help in Michigan from the QDMA executive director Brian Murphy, a wildlife biologist who had built our association from a one-room office in the 1980s to the multi-million dollar organization we had become. Like all outstanding leaders, Brian had a great vision for where we needed to go, and he had exceptional people skills. He could also take the most complicated scientific studies and make them understandable to the average deer hunter. One of Brian's best moves was to hire another talented biologist, Kip Adams, who would serve the northern states. Brian assigned Kip to work closely with us in Michigan as we went about crafting our plans for improving deer management in Michigan. We added a local player in 2006 when we hired Bob DuCharme, one of our branch presidents, to be our new full-time regional director, with responsibility for building our membership and assisting our branches in their development. Brian, Kip and Bob would become outstanding resources to help us change deer management in Michigan.

It was a great honor to work with such a dedicated group of people who wanted strong, scientific deer management in the state. Every member of this group had volunteered significant amounts of time and donated money to help us be successful. I knew that over time, we would be.

As a board, we made a commitment that we would work closer with the NRC, the DNR and other outdoor groups to get some of the deer management changes we wanted. We acknowledged that this would be a long-term project. It would be more evolutionary in nature than the revolutionary approach we preferred.

We knew we wouldn't agree with the NRC and the DNR on all things. We accepted that we would look for small victories and that we would move forward, one step at a time.

We started to realize what our strengths were. Of all the outdoor groups in Michigan, we provided the public with the most educational materials about deer management concepts – bar none. No other group came close to the educational effort we put on each year. We were good at getting hunters together to learn about deer and habitat management issues. Hunters seemed to trust us, and they believed we had a plan to do something about our deer herd. Hunters knew we would speak up for the deer and for the future of deer hunting.

We knew that education was the key to changing deer management in Michigan. Too many hunters didn't understand the principles of deer management, and many of them had no idea how other states managed their deer herds to ensure they protected more young bucks. We knew we could change that by educating more hunters about basic deer management principles. We knew if more hunters understood what other states were doing and what hunting was like in other states, they would demand changes.

Proud Hunters Proud Yoopers

We also knew that changes in deer management could help Michigan's struggling economy. As the quality of Michigan's deer hunting suffered, more Michigan hunters began hunting in other states. When they did that, they returned with incredible stories about the number of bucks they had seen and the quality of those bucks.

One Neebish Island hunter, Rob Ware, is probably typical of many Michigan hunters. Rob lives in Barbeau, Michigan, near where he works with the Michigan Department of Corrections. He loves to hunt deer, and he spends several weeks and weekends hunting with his family on their property on Neebish Island, near my camp.

One year, Rob tried deer hunting in Iowa with some friends. He saved up all year long so he could afford the hunt. After his first few days in Iowa, he couldn't believe the difference between this deer herd and what he was used to in Michigan.

Almost every day, he spotted up to ten different bucks, and each day, one or two of them were mature four-, five- or six-year-old bucks with huge racks.

"Our hunters in Michigan don't have any idea what we are missing or what we could have if we managed our deer herd differently," Rob told me one day as we waited to cross on the Neebish Island ferry.

"I'm going to do whatever I have to do to keep going back every year," Rob explained. "I'm missing some hunting time here in Michigan with my family, but this experience is so intense that I can't wait until I can go again. I have already made plans to go again next year."

In 2008, Rob traveled to Missouri with other Michigan hunters. He brought back a 140-150 inch buck with 13 inch tines that he killed with his bow. The quality of this hunt and his other hunts in previous years are on a scale most of our hunters in Michigan cannot even dream about because they have never experienced anything remotely close to what Rob experiences in other states.

Each year, more and more hunters I know are making similar changes in their hunting practices, just like Rob. They are reducing their Michigan deer hunting time and they are seeking opportunities to hunt in other states. They go to those other states seeking a higher quality deer hunting experience, and they return, raving about the difference they saw. When they go, they don't spend money in Michigan, and they spend it in another state.

How long will it be before even more Michigan hunters figure out what they are missing in other states?

How much is this change in preference for hunting experiences costing our economy in Michigan? How much money do we lose when hunters like Rob travel to hunt in Iowa or Missouri, forgoing a hunting trip in Michigan?

Many northern Michigan small businesses who service deer hunters have figured out that the number of satisfied deer hunters is down, and they know that has hurt their businesses. At more QDMA meetings, members brought up concerns about how deer hunting was changing for the worse. They also reported that this was having an adverse impact on the economy of northern Michigan.

When QDMA members with a business background talked about this development, most of us thought the DNR was significantly underestimating just how much they were hurting the economies of northern Michigan with their deer management policies. It frustrated many of us on the one hand, that the DNR could justify using (or misusing) the principles of social science to move in just about any

Taking a Stand for Deer Management

direction they wanted, but on the other hand, no one was pushing to recognize the negative impact on the economy that traditional deer management caused. And no one was pushing to manage the deer herd differently so that hunters would return to northern Michigan. I found this difference in philosophies fascinating despite how painful it was to watch it develop.

At QDMA, we knew we could make a difference, and we wanted to see that happen. We established a four-point strategic plan to get the reforms that we wanted.

First, we needed to establish ourselves as a voice to be heard on deer management issues. If the power brokers were ever to recognize us and listen to us, we needed to let them know we had the numbers behind us and the expertise in our ranks. We needed to demonstrate that we represented lots of Michigan deer hunters. Goal number one was to increase our membership every year by a significant amount. We set a goal of 20% growth a year, a phenomenal growth rate, but it was an ambitious goal we thought we could achieve.

We were right. In 2006, we grew at a 20% growth rate in Michigan, and QDMA also grew at a rate close to 20% on the national level. At a time when other outdoor groups were struggling with membership, we were signing up new members at record rates. At a 2007 state chapter meeting, QDMA national executive director Brian Murphy gave us the good news. QDMA had the highest growth rate of any outdoor group in the country, and Michigan had the highest growth rate of any state. Brian also reported that QDMA had the highest member retention rate of any outdoor organization in the country at 75%. Those statistics confirmed for us that our members liked our message and what we stood for. To say we were proud of those accomplishments would be an understatement.

Second, we needed to be active in every major deer management issue. As a result, we established a goal that we would present the NRC and DNR our formal position on the key issues. We set up a committee of knowledgeable members who could write position papers and testify on deer management proposals. From 2006 on, QDMA in Michigan would let the public know what we thought about managing our deer herd. We now had a process where we researched each issue and developed a proposed response; then we had our national association review it for content. Deer Biologist Kip Adams of Pennsylvania was our national QDMA representative to help us ensure we had national support for the positions we took. This effort gave us a solid foundation for providing the NRC and DNR with our science-based feedback. Every time we testified before the NRC, we reminded them that we had more deer management researchers and related wildlife professionals in our organization than any other outdoor group in the country. And we told them we represented more than 50,000 hard-core deer hunters.

Third, we realized that we needed to strengthen ourselves by intensifying our educational efforts and reaching out more to all hunters, not just deer hunters. We knew we needed to hold more educational events about food plots, land and habitat management, and deer management practices for hunters and the general public. We knew we needed to demonstrate that we cared about all wildlife and not just the deer. To accomplish this, we started sponsoring more events to teach others about wildlife, and we started reaching out more to other groups like Pheasants Forever, the Wild Turkey Federation, Michigan Bow Hunters, Whitetails Unlimited, MUCC, and other deer groups to see what we could work on together. These coalitions would help us gain more credibility and recognition across the state.

Fourth, we had a small handful of dedicated QDMA supporters who would do literally everything they could to support our organization. The problem was that this small group did virtually everything for us so that we didn't seek out and grow other leaders in the organization. We took a new approach where we started to grow leaders throughout the organization. We knew we had to mentor future leaders and attract more people to commit to doing something in the organization so they owned and bought into our mission. Slowly, but surely, we got more people involved in helping and building QDMA. Some of our early leaders even stepped aside and let new leaders take over. The new leaders have thrived, and the older leaders keep involved by promoting us in new ways too, primarily by helping with QDM co-ops and speaking engagements. Tony Smith was a good example of a former leader still engaged in helping us with our mission.

For me, I took on this new challenge to grow and strengthen our association as one of my top challenges in life. I dedicated myself to doing all I could do to ensure that we would be successful in growing this small, grass-roots association into a full-fledged educational and politically-wired machine that could change the way we managed deer.

Little by little, we started seeing signs that we were gaining recognition and status among the deer management decision makers. Each time we got some recognition, I felt a little validation that we were on the right course and just a small step closer to achieving our goal.

In late 2006, NRC commissioner Frank Wheatlake of Reed City chaired a large workgroup of outdoor groups that reviewed funding issues at the DNR. The work group concluded that the DNR had serious long-term funding problems, and that significant funding increases were needed to ensure the DNR could continue its programs at acceptable levels.

At the January 2007 NRC meeting, I testified that QDMA supported the fee-increase package that the DNR had requested. The package had generated reams of controversy among outdoor groups because it basically doubled license prices, including increasing deer licenses from $15 to $30 each. At a prior meeting, a number of outdoor groups, including the powerful National Rifle Association, had vigorously opposed the increases, saying they would end hunting for many families.

On behalf of QDMA, I challenged that assessment as unreasonable and reported that we believed the license increases were necessary and reasonable. After all, most hunters spend more than $15 on gas to get to their hunting grounds each trip. I questioned whether they would quit hunting just because their license went up $15.

Following our testimony, Keith Charters, the chair of the NRC thanked us, and Commissioner Wheatlake also thanked us for our support. Then we heard the kind of news we were hoping for. NRC Chair Charters asked me if he could switch subjects. He told me that he had heard great things about how well the antler-restriction program in Leelanau County was working. He said that hunters were raving about the differences in the bucks they were now seeing and killing. He concluded that he would want to talk more with QDMA about this program.

Taking a Stand for Deer Management

Our QDMA members at the meeting felt as if we were on cloud 9. For the first time in a long time, someone at the NRC had said something positive to us publicly about managing the deer herd for older bucks. It felt as if we were finally moving in the right direction.

We also knew that it was premature to celebrate. There would still be strong resistance from some corners against efforts to change from the status quo. We knew we still had a long, uphill battle to manage the herd the way we thought we should.

But a few kind words from a supportive NRC chairman gave us hope. Maybe someday soon, young bucks in Michigan would finally get a chance to grow up and become the majestic, mature animals nature intended for them to be.

In March, 2008, we got some more great news. The five-year, antler restriction experiment in Leelanau County was officially declared a huge success. A QDMA member and DNR conservation officer, Mike Borkovich, had helped lead this massive effort behind the scenes. Leelanau County hunters and landowners had witnessed the magic that happens when you don't kill all your young bucks. In the 2007 deer season, Leelanau County hunters killed 24 record-book bucks – a phenomenal feat for a county where most hunters never shot anything other than a spike or a four-pointer. This time, 72% of the hunters and landowners had approved of the program after the five-year period. Now, the NRC authorized the county to continue to operate under the antler-restriction provisions into the future. As QDMA members celebrated this great day, we pondered our future, and other opportunities and barriers that lie ahead.

With this momentum, could we finally change the face of deer management in Michigan?

In late 2007, a lone hunter from Marquette, George Lindquist, also started a one-man crusade to change deer management in Michigan. George worked for the Empire Mine in the Marquette area, and in his spare time, he crafted a plan to find an antler-restriction program that more hunters could support. He was a board member of UP Whitetails, and he got eight chapters of UP Whitetails to support a proposal he called the "Hunter's Choice" proposal.

Under this plan, a hunter could choose to purchase a single buck license, good for any buck with three-inch spikes or bigger (the current regulation). If a hunter chose to purchase two buck licenses, however, the hunter would have to kill a buck with three points on a side for the first license (likely a six-pointer) and four points on a side for the second buck (likely an eight-pointer). In effect, the hunter who purchased two licenses would be practicing a modified antler-restriction program - one important part of a quality deer management program - forgoing the killing of yearling bucks (spike horns and four-pointers).

The beauty of the Hunter's Choice proposal was that it gave hunters the choice to either try antler-restriction principles if they wanted two buck licenses or they could shoot any buck if they opted for a single buck license. The proposal was supported as a plan that gave everyone a little of what he or she wanted, and it took away many of the arguments against a pure, mandatory antler-restriction program for everyone.

Over the next six months, Lindquist spent much of his own money and his own vacation time to sell the idea to the NRC, the DNR and the major outdoor groups. Along the way, QDMA members did everything we could to help him, including giving the NRC a letter of support.

Proud Hunters Proud Yoopers

But at an April 10, 2008, NRC meeting, the DNR staff spoke against the proposal and laid out plans to see that it stayed on the shelf for several years.

QDMA and other groups protested the DNR approach, pushing to have the proposal given more consideration. NRC commissioner John Madigan asked Lindquist to scale back his plan to include only the UP.

The same day, the *Marquette Mining Journal* ran a very favorable story about the proposal.

As I watched these developments, there was a sense of satisfaction that deer management issues in Michigan were finally getting their day in court. And now, maybe, just maybe, we would see some changes in how we managed the public's deer herd.

During the April meeting, however, I was so mad, I was about ready to throw in the towel again. While I had deep respect for the DNR staff, I was really disappointed in how biased their presentations to the NRC had been with regard to antler restrictions. In particular, it appeared the DNR staff was positioning itself to deep-six the Hunter's Choice proposal. They had also made a statement about there being no science to support that deer herds improved with an older buck population when managed under QDM principles. I was so angry about the message from these presentations, I had to leave the NRC meeting so I could calm down. Our other QDMA members in attendance were livid, too.

At the public comment portion of the meeting later that evening, I tried to diplomatically express my anger and disappointment. I asked the NRC commissioners if QDMA could come back and give them a presentation about other deer management alternatives and how other states managed their deer herds. I told them they needed to hear "the rest of the story" as Paul Harvey reports in his radio broadcasts. I promised them we would bring in a national expert, and that our presentation would be science based.

Over the next month, the DNR staff did a big reversal and proposed the Hunter's Choice program in a Wildlife Order presented at the May 8, 2008, NRC meeting. The DNR staff also postponed our presentation to the NRC until after they could get this policy reversal in front of the NRC.

On June 5, 2008, QDMA was back in front of the NRC with Kip Adams giving a tutorial on QDM principles to the seven NRC commissioners. During his presentation, the commissioners asked good questions about deer management alternatives. They seemed to grasp that we were killing a very high percentage of our young bucks. They understood that we couldn't have adequate numbers of bucks in older age classes if we killed them when they were yearling bucks. They understood that other states were not doing this and that those other states made efforts to ensure only a small percent of their yearling bucks were killed each year.

The commissioners also understood very well that the DNR's own data showed that 72% of Michigan hunters wanted the herd managed so we had more bucks and older bucks. It also helped that at the April NRC meeting, NRC commissioner Mary Brown (a former state representative) stunned the QDMA members in attendance when she challenged the DNR staff to think "outside of the box" on how to meet this need. After we got over the shock of her strong support, we wanted to hug her and thank her for setting this kind of tone. Clearly, things were starting to change.

Taking a Stand for Deer Management

At about 6:30 p.m. on June 5, 2008, the NRC voted 7-0 to accept the Hunter's Choice proposal and implement this modified antler-restriction program for the entire UP. I couldn't stay for the vote, but Boyd Wiltse called me with the news as soon as it happened. I had tears in my eyes when we hung up. I had waited about ten years for this day, and now I wanted to savor the simple pleasure of it.

My first phone call was to George Lindquist to tell him that after all this time, we had finally been successful. I thanked him for all his work and for never giving up on our deer. And I reminded him and our QDMA members that we should never underestimate the power of a few dedicated citizens to make profound public policy changes.

Several days later, the *Sault Evening News* ran a front page story on the deer management changes. They even came to my father's sport shop so they could get a picture of a big buck to have alongside the story. The *Evening News* reporter Scott Brand reminded me that some would love this change and some would hate us for it. "You will be a hero to some and a goat to others," he predicted with a hearty laugh. I laughed with him, and told him that was a role QDMA members were accustomed to.

On this day, a Proud Hunter learned that well-laid plans can help lead to major policy and social changes when a few talented individuals dedicate themselves to effecting the change, even in the rough world of "deer politics." And on this day, a Proud Yooper learned that deer hunters need patience when expecting to turn around something that has been ingrained in the culture of the hunting community for a long, long time.

47

The Boots of an Old Hunter

We respected our old people above all others in the tribe.
To live to be so old they must have been brave and strong, and good fighters
and we aspired to be like them.

- Buffalo Child Long Lance, Sioux

In March 2005, Susan and I went to her parents' home on Lindsay Drive in Saginaw, Michigan, to help her brothers and their wives clean out the house. We were preparing the house for an estate sale following the death of both Mel and Ginny Sternhagen, Susan's 77-year-old parents who had both died in the last year.

It was sad to sort through the belongings of two people I had known so well for so many years. It was particularly hard on Susan and her brothers, John Sternhagen of Riverdale and Paul Sternhagen of Freeland. The entire family had been very close, and we spent all major holidays, birthdays and other special events together.

The Sternhagens had lived in this three-bedroom suburban home for over 40 years, and they had, like many of us, accumulated their share of "stuff." While their three children worked upstairs on the ground floor splitting up the furniture and cleaning out the bedrooms, I worked in the basement with my two sister-in-laws, Andy Sternhagen and Kim Sternhagen, helping to sort out boxes of stored items and miscellaneous belongings, some of which none of us had ever seen before.

At one point, Paul asked me to go through his father's file cabinets and purge most of the material, saving anything of sentimental value. He also asked me to shred all the old financial documents that permeated the file cabinets.

It was a dirty job, literally and physically, but someone had to do it, and I was up to the challenge. To claim that Mel and Ginny had a bit of a packrat in them was probably an understatement. As I skimmed the 12 file drawers, I found a potpourri of paperwork that documented the life and times of my in-laws through six decades, interspersed with outdated records and documents that no longer served any useful purpose.

In my detailed review of the large file cabinets, I found lots of old papers and documents that could be pitched, and I quickly disposed of them. Occasionally, I found something really interesting that I was sure one of the kids would want to keep. Along the way, I uncovered first job offers from the 1940s, love letters to each other, report cards from college, retirement papers, and other information that documented the life and times of these two special people.

After several hours of going through old, routine financial records, I came across an old journal tucked away amid a bunch of old bank statements. As I opened the journal, I saw the handwriting of Mel, and I immediately recognized the writings of a man describing his hunting adventures and mishaps. My interest perked up when I confirmed I had discovered Mel's hunting journal from long ago.

The Boots of an Old Hunter

I sat down in the middle of a mound of papers I intended to throw away, and I read about how my father-in-law hunted. I was amazed at how similarly he and I looked at things in the wild. In his journal, he talked about the weather conditions, he recorded where he and his friends were hunting, and he, of course, wrote about how much game they saw and what they shot that day. He recorded the shots he had missed and the game that had gotten away, just as I did. I was touched to see how similarly he and I had recorded our observations about our daily hunting routines.

I knew Mel had loved to hunt when he was younger, but I had known Mel for more than 30 years, and I only now knew just how much hunting had meant to him. It was a deeply moving experience to read about his experiences and to visualize him enjoying himself on his hunting excursions. I tried to picture him sitting down at home and writing these details in his journal.

I spent more than an hour going over his journal notes, reading his thoughts about chasing rabbits and pheasants and deer, and remembering other stories he had told me over the years.

I tried hard to remember how he had described to me deer hunting in the vast hardwood "hills" around the Rapid City area. He had hunted there extensively in the 1950s through the 1970s with Susan's grandfather, Maurice Guy, who lived at Torch Lake after his retirement from Saginaw Public Schools. I remembered how Mel would get excited telling me about the bucks the Guy family would chase in the rugged, hilly country northeast of Traverse City.

He had a number of good stories about bucks they had killed and bucks they had missed in the "hills." He had special stories he would tell about some family members (in-laws and outlaws) who might not always follow the law in the pursuit of whitetails. I remembered how he and I would laugh about these incidents.

I recalled him telling me about all the rabbits he and his friends in the Saginaw area used to kill in the early winter each year near Pinconning and Hemlock. There were certain beagles that were the best dogs of the bunch, and he would tell me about special adventures they had with each of them. There were certain special friends that he hunted with too, guys like Herb Ditmar of Saginaw and others Mel would fondly remember as he retold the stories of days when they would shoot boxes of shotgun shells at running rabbits – rabbits that would often fill their car trunk by the end of the day.

I remembered him telling me about the big flocks of pheasants they used to see right around the outskirts of Saginaw and the surrounding area, places now developed into subdivisions or commercial establishments. Mel used to point out these locations when we were driving. He would subtly mourn that no more pheasants would be hunted in those places. But then, he would chuckle, and say, "Did I ever tell you about all the pheasants we used to kill here?" Whether he had told me or not, I enjoyed his tales of the old hunts so much, that I would let on like I hadn't heard, just so he would tell me again.

I recalled a special place along the Tittabawasse River on the way to Freeland that he would always point out to me, reminiscing about the time he and some friends shot a dozen or so pheasants in the marsh grass along the river. "The pheasants were everywhere, and we really got into them on that day," he would say with a huge smile on his face.

Proud Hunters Proud Yoopers

My mind thought back to the one time he and I had hunted together in the Upper Peninsula. It was in 1975 when I was dating his daughter and getting serious about her. Because he and I often talked about hunting when I would visit Susan on the weekends at their Saginaw home, I had thought it would be nice to invite him to the UP to try hunting Yooper style. So, braving freezing cold temperatures, Mel, his older son John and I joined my dad for a rugged hunt in Hungry Hill.

The three of us made a long trip to the UP to meet my dad at my grandpa's house just before opening day. The next day, the four of us hiked into Hungry Hill and spent the day hunting that wild country that I had told Mel about so many times.

Unfortunately, none of us saw any bucks that weekend, and we went home empty-handed. The highlight of the trip, however, was when the four of us had gathered on a big rock near the Bedsprings for lunch the second day. While eating lunch, Mel told us a joke about being in the army and not having enough toilet paper. Thirty years later, I can't remember the punch line, but I do remember that all four of us laughed so hard at his joke that it was a miracle we didn't fall off the rock. We made so much noise from laughter that we probably scared away all the deer within four square miles. Mel was that kind of guy and that kind of a storyteller.

As I read more of his journal, I remembered how we used to hunt together with his son John near John's home in Riverdale. Mel even had his own seat that John had carefully built for him so his dad could get to it easily and so John and Mel could be close together. I remembered the last buck that Mel had killed in Riverdale, a deer that I had come close to killing with a bow earlier that year. I remembered how happy I was when he told me that he had gotten that nice buck that John and I had been after in archery season.

I reflected back on how John had worked so hard to custom build a warm and comfortable blind for his dad on their hunting land near Rapid City. The blind had allowed Mel to continue hunting late in his life with his two sons and now one of his grandsons. I thought about the preparation that John and Paul had put into hunting with their dad each year, trying to maximize his chances of seeing a deer.

And then I remembered the non-hunting things that I loved about this guy. I remembered how he had taken me under his wing when I had gotten a job working as an auditor for the State of Michigan right out of college. I remembered how he helped teach a Yooper how to dress for success in that day's work environment – something I had no clue about.

I had fond memories of how patiently he worked with me to teach me how to tie a dress tie – something I had never learned but needed to know right away for survival in my new urban environment. I thought about him spending several hours going over and over how to tie those silly knots so I had the perfect tie in place when I arrived for my first day of work the next day.

I remembered how he had given me so much good career advice over the years, little private chats that we would have in the basement of his home. It was often how he reached out to me, to connect with me in other ways besides hunting – in ways that would help me in life.

As I was reflecting on the life of this man I had admired so much and as I was gaining new-found information about his life as a hunter, his children came to the

The Boots of an Old Hunter

basement. I took a break from the file cabinet duty, and we began going through the items in another closet.

This closet was filled with old shoes and boots. The three children split up those shoes and boots that one of them could wear, but most footwear was tagged for disposal or donation to a homeless shelter.

One pair of boots, however, stood out to the two boys. Paul grabbed them first and showed them proudly to John. "These are the ole man's boots," Paul said with great reflection. "They are old and torn up. Look at how often he patched them up," he said, referring to the dozen red patches on the greenish-brown, calf-high rubber boots.

"He wore these boots everywhere, and he wouldn't ever throw them away," John said, turning away in sorrow.

The boys knew that Mel had worn these boots on hundreds of hunting adventures with them, including their last outing together.

Paul turned to me. "Here, I can't do anything with these. Can you please take them and do something with them," Paul said, with tears in his eyes and his voice trembling and tapering off.

Fighting back my own tears, I took the boots and told the boys I would "take care of them."

As I drove home that weekend, I thought long and hard about how I would dispose of the boots of an old hunter – a man I admired and loved so much. It would have been easy to just throw the boots away and forget about them. No one would know the difference.

Instead, I hatched a different plan. I decided that it would be fitting to spread the ashes of these boots around the different places where Mel hunted. That way, some part of him – a meaningful part – could always be in those places he had loved to hunt so much.

A month later, while I was at my cabin on Neebish Island, I set Mel's boots on fire so I could have a pile of ashes to spread around in his favorite places.

There was an immediate problem. The boots wouldn't burn cleanly. Instead, much like burning an old car tire, they smoked like an out-of-control fire, creating a huge, thick cloud of pitch-black smoke that raced off toward the horizon. The boots, however, were still intact and were not breaking down into ashes as I had planned.

I had to laugh at myself as I pictured Mel in heaven looking down on me and yelling at me that I should know better than to try to burn up a pair of rubber boots.

Nonetheless, I persisted, and with a little help from some kerosene, the boots eventually got hot enough to burn up. When I put out the fire, I had a small container full of boot ashes.

Over the next six months, I distributed those ashes to the places where I thought they should go.

First, I left some ashes at my favorite hunting spots on Neebish Island, a place I had always wanted Mel to see, but a place that somehow, because of schedules and his health, we had never arranged. His two sons and two of his grandsons had hunted here, so I thought it was fitting that some ashes be sprinkled here in the places I had wanted to show him, the places I had wanted him to hunt with me, and the places his off-spring had hunted with me.

Proud Hunters Proud Yoopers

Second, I left some ashes on the trails of Hungry Hill where we had first hunted together and a place where we had first connected as future father-in-law and son-in-law. This was a place that I was proud of and a place that I was sure he would appreciate.

Third, I hiked into the hills above Rapid City that he had told me so much about and where he had deer hunted so much of his adult life. I left a few ashes there in places that I found the most beautiful and in places that sounded like spots he liked to watch for deer.

Fourth, I dropped off some ashes in the marsh grass along the Tittabawassee River near Freeland, in that magical spot he always liked to point out to me where he killed so many pheasants one day.

Finally, I walked around his property near the Rapid River just southeast of Torch Lake where he hunted out of the custom blind his son John had built for him. I sprinkled the remaining ashes around his blind – the last place he ever hunted.

It would have been easy to just take those old, tattered boots and throw them in the garbage container. It took a little more effort to spread a few ashes in some remote locations. It was more work, but the special tribute was worth the effort.

On this day, a Proud Yooper learned what Proud Hunters do to honor great men and other Proud Hunters who have touched their lives in many ways.

48

A Special Buck for a Special Season

There will be happiness before us.
There will be happiness behind us.
There shall be happiness above us.
There shall be happiness below us.
Words of happiness shall extend from our mouths.
For we are the essence of life.

- Navajo Prayer

On December 4, 2005, *The Sault Evening News* published this story that I wrote about the 2005 deer season. I am really grateful to editor Kenn Filkins and reporter Scott Brand for running the story on their Sunday Outdoor Page:

On August 13, 2005, I stood in line at the photo counter at a local store, waiting to pay my bill for the latest roll of film I had developed from a motion-detector deer camera. I use these cameras on our Neebish Island property to determine how many deer and how many bucks live on our property. As I casually flipped through the pictures of spotted fawns and does, I almost had a heart attack when I laid eyes on a huge eight-point buck we had caught on film.

We've taken almost a thousand pictures of deer with these wildlife cameras, but we had never captured a buck this large or this beautiful. While he was "only" an eight pointer, he had huge tines that I thought might be ten inches long, and his antlers were almost perfectly symmetrical. The big buck's antler spread and overall mass of his antlers made him a trophy almost any hunter would cherish. He was a large-bodied animal that I estimated might weigh close to 200 pounds by fall.

I quickly returned to my father's business to show my dad, Louis Hank of Sault Ste. Marie, the buck. "Now that's the buck we have to get this year," he told me when he saw the pictures. Following that challenge, my dad and I began planning how we would hunt this buck in both the archery and rifle deer seasons that would soon begin.

Two weeks later, our preparations would be interrupted when my 99-year-old grandfather, Ed Hank of Stalwart, passed away. While some would say that might have been expected at his age, this was a very sad event for us because this healthy 99-year-old guy also hunted with us every year at our deer camp.

For years, my grandfather, my father, my son and I have hunted from the same camp on Neebish Island. As far as we know, we are one of the few families in the country to have four generations of hunters hunting out of the same camp. Some years, we were even lucky enough for all of us to get our deer. What we experienced was very special – and it was a unique, family-oriented hunting event.

My grandfather had hunted throughout the eastern UP his entire life. He had shot some huge bucks including a 1940s deer that scored 190.4 and was one of the top 100 biggest deer ever taken in the state of Michigan. Just last year, grandpa, at the age of 98, had killed two deer at our camp. That kind of passion for deer hunting flowed through our veins.

By October 1, 2005, the beginning of the archery season, my dad and I had not seen the big buck nor had we captured him on camera again. During the next 45 days of archery season, I criss-crossed the Mackinac Bridge six times to hunt this special, mystery deer, and I put 4,000 miles on my truck riding back and forth from my home in Holt, Michigan. I used almost three weeks of vacation time and spent 28 days hunting this buck, sometimes staying in the woods all day long.

In our efforts to find this deer, dad and I hunted in 12 different tree and ground stands, we hunted using bait and without bait, we rattled antlers and used grunt calls, and we watched over real and fake scrapes the buck had visited. My dad even gave me an early Christmas present, a $400 Scent Blocker high-tech hunting suit, to minimize the chance that the deer would smell me.

Despite all that effort, not once did we ever see this special deer. Worse yet, we couldn't capture him on our game cameras either. All of this made it seem as if this deer were a ghost.

But the signs of him were around, giving us hope. Almost every weekend, we would see his massive tracks in the mud, and we would find freshly rubbed trees and scrapes on the ground under balsam fir trees where he would mark his territory, telling other bucks that he was the king of this area.

On the evening of Nov. 12, our luck finally changed when my dad saw the big buck. He almost got a shot at him with his bow as the buck chased a lone doe, trying to mate with her. The big buck though stayed 45 yards away from my dad and eventually just walked away.

That night, dad could hardly wait to tell me the story. "He's here, and he's a huge, beautiful buck with long, white tines," dad reported. "We'll get him now that the rut has started and he's chasing does."

In the next few days, our luck turned bad again as we were hit with a devastating wind and rain storm that made for lousy hunting and we lost our electricity for two days. During that time, I had no heat, water, phone, or electricity. I lived at our cabin like a hermit, hunting all day in miserable weather and cooking on a gas grill at night, using candles and lanterns for light. At night, I hunkered down in a sleeping bag trying to stay warm.

My bad luck continued as I damaged my rifle scope and I was not able to shoot the gun accurately. My father graciously gave me his rifle to use and he used his back-up gun.

All these hardships led up to the opening day of rifle season and our hopes again were high. For the first three days of rifle season, we hunted hard all day long, never leaving the woods until dark, but we still didn't see any sign of the big buck. I did see several spikehorns and a four-pointer, but I passed them up because I wanted a mature buck. It was fun to see the young bucks chasing does trying to breed with them and the does resisting, knowing that bigger bucks were in the area.

The fourth day of the season, November 18, was my father's 70th birthday. Again, I had high hopes that this would be the day we would get the big buck we had pursued with so much passion.

A Special Buck for a Special Season

At 9 am, I got impatient, and I had a strange feeling that I should go for a walk, something I rarely do early in the season. I followed this impulse, and I walked into the middle of a large marsh. There I jumped a lone, bedded deer that I only got a glimpse of, but my instincts told me he was probably a mature buck. I returned to my stand, angry at myself that I had chased away a bedded deer only 200 yards from where I intended to watch.

A short time later, I caught a glimpse of a lone, large deer coming from the back side of the big marsh. The deer crossed in front of me at about 70 yards. I immediately saw the large, white high tines of the great buck that was obviously out looking for does in a breeding mood. "Oh my gosh, it's him," I thought to myself as I quickly raised my father's Browning .30/06 rifle. When the crosshairs of the scope met the buck's front shoulder, I fired a shot.

The buck immediately stopped and seemed to be looking for where the shot had come from. He didn't look like a deer who had been hit. I frantically tried to line up the scope for a second shot, but the buck was hidden behind two trees. I could only see his large antlers and his tail. I was fearful that I had missed the big buck and that he would bolt from his hiding spot any second. When the buck finally moved away from the trees, I shot again, but this time there was only a click. I looked down to see that my dad's gun had jammed.

I couldn't believe my bad luck. After all this time hunting so hard for this deer and never seeing him, how could my gun now jam when I finally got my chance? How could I mess up this opportunity after working all season to prepare for this moment?

As I unclogged the jammed gun, I looked up again for the buck. In just a few precious seconds, he had seemingly vanished, and he was no where in sight. Somehow, it appeared, he had eluded me. I was about ready to cry.

I rushed from my stand to where I had last seen him. As I got close, I saw the outline of a deer on the ground and a huge set of antlers. As it turned out, I had hit the deer well, and he died right where I had shot him, while I was fixing the jammed gun.

I immediately ran to get my dad so we could celebrate this great buck together. This was our 40th deer season together, and this was the first time I had ever killed a deer on his birthday.

My dad has been my hunting partner since I was five years old when he began taking me with him on hunts in the eastern UP. We've always been a great team, hunting together, helping each other in every way we can, and enjoying each other's success just as much as our own.

As we approached the big buck together, dad was excited. "Yes, that's him for sure," he said as we admired the beautiful buck.

"Your grandpa would be very proud, and he would tell us what a nice buck this is," dad lamented.

That day, we celebrated the joy of a family hunting together and later that night we called my son who had been unable to be with us because of law school commitments. When we spoke, we talked of the hunt for a great buck, and we remembered an old hunter now chasing whitetails in a special place. It had indeed been a special season full of special surprises, special challenges, and special memories. It was another great deer season in the eastern UP and one that I will never forget.

Proud Hunters Proud Yoopers

Dawn Garner, my co-worker and a communications specialist with the Michigan Department of Transportation, published the story in an MDOT electronic newsletter. My friends in the State Quality Deer Management Association also published the article in the association's quarterly newsletter that was sent to 3,000 Michigan hunters. The national office of the QDMA in Bogart, Georgia saw the article, and *Quality Whitetails* editor Lindsay Thomas also asked me to run the story as their *Firepot Stories* feature article. That meant another 40,000 deer hunters saw the article. After the article was published in these places, I received over a hundred e-mails, phone calls and notes from people telling me how much they enjoyed the story.

I got a lot of satisfaction out of writing the article, and it was a great way to get closure on my grandfather's death. It was my special tribute to him, someone who had always enjoyed hunting with me and teaching me what he had learned over the years. I was sad that I would never be able to hunt with him again. It was also a tribute to my father, who has hunted with me since childhood, and to my son, who is my hope for the future of hunting in the UP. I hope I am able to hunt with him for the rest of my life.

In his song, *Fred Bear,* rock singer and hunting advocate, Ted Nugent, sings about the great Fred Bear after Fred has died. Ted sings about Fred whispering signals to him in the wind as Ted is pursuing a big buck. Ted is unsure whether he should go up on the ridge or down in the swamp to intercept the buck. Ted says that the moment of truth is at hand and he must decide which way to go. He asks Fred Bear to talk to him. As the wind blows, Fred tells Ted to go down into the swamp. Ted follows the "signal," and, sure enough, he gets the buck.

I love that song and I have played it hundreds of times even before my grandfather passed away.

A number of spiritual people have asked me whether my grandfather gave me a signal to go into that marsh on Nov. 18 and roust out the big buck.

Was my grandpa in heaven, watching over dad and me as we hunted, and did he know where the big buck hid from us? Did my grandfather believe that I had worked hard enough for that buck and did he believe that it was time that I should get him?

Did my grandfather whisper in the wind, "Leon, go into that marsh and get that big buck!" Did he "talk to me" like Fred Bear talked to Ted Nugent?

Was my boyhood hero Fred Bear along side my grandfather in heaven, watching over my hunt, and were they working together to help me?

So, did I or didn't I get a signal from another world or from an old hunting partner?

On this day, a Proud Yooper learned to listen to the wind for whispers from Proud Hunters who watch over us from a special place.

49

Living with Wolves

Even if the heavens were to fall on me,
I want to do what is right...
I never do wrong
without a cause.

- Gero

I remember one of the first times I saw a pack of wolves on a television show. The small pack was chasing a mature cow moose in the deep snow. The wolves ran behind the moose until one wolf caught up to the moose and grabbed the back of her thigh with his powerful jaws. As the wolf buried his teeth into the animal's leg, she slowed down, reeling from ripped flesh in her leg and dragging the weight of the 100-pound wolf behind her.

The tendon severing bite and the shear weight of the first wolf was all that was needed to slow down the moose. Now the opportunistic trailing wolves caught up and helped finish the job. In a flash, they closed in on the moose and systematically attacked her, too. In a matter of minutes, they had her on the ground, with one of them tearing into her throat, a fatal bite which started her slowly bleeding to death.

Before she was dead and while she was still struggling for life in the clenches of the wolves, some of the wolves began tearing away and eating her intestines, one of their favorite meals. That's right, several wolves were feeding on her before she was even dead while other wolves held her in place. There were a few more seconds where the moose hopelessly struggled for life, but soon she breathed her last breath. Now she was dead, and all the wolves began feverishly and savagely pulling away at her flesh. Their faces were completely covered in dark, red blood, and the snow around the fallen moose would soon be solid red in color, too.

For the next few hours, the wolves would feed on this freshly killed carcass, gorging themselves on the meat, hide and bones. And while a pack of coyotes would have left the large leg and rib bones behind, the wolves would use their much more powerful jaws to crush and devour many of the large moose bones. Crushing the bones allowed the wolves to get at another favorite delicacy: the bone marrow. After several days of feeding, there will be virtually nothing left of the unfortunate animal. Only blood and hair will remain on the snow to mark the life of the prey animal.

The suffering endured by the moose at the end seemed cruel and painful, but it was relatively short. The graphic portrayal of a large wild dog eating another harmless grazing animal before it is even dead can be repulsive to those not closely connected to the outdoors. I've even seen people turn away while watching videos of wolves tear away mouthfuls of flesh, while an animal like the moose was still thrashing in its last moments of life. It made them sick to watch this highly brutal form of Mother Nature at work in the wild.

Proud Hunters Proud Yoopers

While vivid kill scenes like this one are periodically shown on television, they are not images that most Michigan residents have never seen in the wild nor do they comprehend, appreciate or understand. Unfortunately, many Michigan residents know little of the violence and viciousness of this prey-and-predator relationship that occurs in nature.

The image I described is also one that most wolf proponents do not want seen on television or shown in other media forms. Those who are passionate about successfully reintroducing the wolf in Michigan (or protecting him against all forms of hunting) do not like the image of the wolf as a savage killer, one who kills often (sometimes just for fun), and with great violence. To achieve their protectionist agenda, wolf proponents want these images kept from the public so there is stronger support for returning the wolf to Michigan. Yet, this vivid television broadcast is an accurate portrayal of how the wolf kills and feeds on large mammals like moose, deer, elk and even cattle and sheep.

When it comes to wolves and their management, I will not generally be supportive of the wolf until we have reasonable management controls in place so wolves don't decimate our deer herd. Some of my hunting friends, on the other hand, absolutely despise the wolf and what he does to our Yooper deer herd. Other hunters I know are a little more tolerant of this animal that, in many ways, is a predator much like human hunters. These hunters generally are OK with a few wolves around.

In the mid 1960s, my Grandpa Ed Hank and my Grandma Mary took me to the Game Haven ranch in Wolverine, Michigan. This tourist attraction was a relatively new, large game ranch in northern Michigan, just below the Mackinac Bridge. The ranch had advertised that it had a large population of elk and other animals on its premises that were easy to view. At about the same time, there was a lot of talk about the DNR holding its first hunt for elk among the small wild elk herd that had been reintroduced in the Wolverine area. As a result, there was lots of interest about elk in the Michigan hunting community.

I remember this being an exciting day for a young hunter who rarely left the UP. I had a great time during the trip, given my love for hunting and the outdoors. As we toured the facility, I was seeing all kinds of game animals for the first time and the elk left me feeling really impressed. They were beautiful animals. My grandpa told me how he hoped to get a DNR permit to hunt elk in this area some day.

Despite all this excitement, there was one exhibit that made me feel incredibly sad and helpless.

Near the end of our trip around the Game Haven property, I was walking with my grandma when we came to an exhibit that had a Canadian timber wolf in a small cage. We were able to get really close to the wolf, and I was surprised to see how big this animal was. He was huge with long legs, big feet and a large head full of big teeth!

While the elk and other animals were behind fences with lots of room to roam, this lone wolf was in a small cage that I remember being about eight feet wide and 16 feet long. While we gazed in wonderment at the wolf, he just kept pacing nervously from one end of the 16-foot cage to the other end. He walked continuously back and forth at the same pace with a worried and sad look on his face.

Soon, my grandfather caught up to us. That's when my grandmother turned to me and said, "Leon, that's some life for this poor wolf, isn't it? He just walks back and

Living with Wolves

forth all day long thinking about getting out of this cage. He should be free in the woods where he was meant to be."

I can't put into words how that impromptu reaction by my grandmother impacted me. I've never forgotten the image of that caged animal looking so helpless and longing to be free. I've also never forgotten the image of dozens of star-struck tourists staring at him in such an unnatural setting. Based on what my grandma had said and what I had seen first hand, I felt so bad for this lonely wolf. And I secretly wished that someone would break into the ranch and set him free.

Years later, I would learn even more about the wolf, his impact on our deer herd and the art and science of wolf management.

While taking an ecology class in my junior year at CMU, I would read *Sand County Almanac* written by the great conservationist, Aldo Leopold. This is a book that everyone who cares about wildlife should read. In this classic book, Leopold describes in detail his encounter with a wolf that he kills. After the shot, he ends up eye-to-eye with the wolf just as the wolf is dying. Leopold says the wolf looks at him helplessly as the life goes out of his eyes. Following the dramatic experience, Leopold, who is an avid hunter, vows that he will never kill another wolf.

The DNR estimates that there are about 500 wolves roaming the UP and that the population, which was thought to be stabilizing, is still growing steadily each year. Some knowledgeable Yoopers believe the DNR estimate is low and that there may be up to twice that many wolves in the UP. Others believe that whatever the current population, we have reached the population pinnacle of society's acceptance of the wolf in the UP.

The DNR says that we may be reaching "our social carrying capacity for the wolf in the UP." That's fancy wildlife management talk for saying that UP residents may not tolerate any further increases in wolf population without a revolution like what occurred sixty years ago when we killed the last wolf in the state.

One of my prized possessions is a 1939-1940 Michigan Department of Conservation hunting season poster. The Department of Conservation was what the DNR used to be called back in the good ole days. My 1939 poster states that there is no closed season on wolves, coyotes, foxes, owls, and hawks. In those days, it was common to have a year-around season and no bag limits on varmints and predators. The wolf was clearly in the varmint and predator category. For most of the time, there was also a bounty paid on wolves. In general, people shot wolves on sight in those days. These policies and a general intolerance for and a fear of the wolf eventually lead to the disappearance of the wolf from Michigan.

The wolf that once roamed all of Michigan was systematically eliminated by hunters and landowners, with the last one thought to be killed in the 1940s, shortly after my poster was created. In effect, we shot the wolves indiscriminately until we killed them all. And almost no one cared that he was gone. In fact, most landowners and hunters didn't want any wolves around.

The return of the wolf to Michigan after being gone for decades is the source of more than a little controversy and a long history.

Brian Roell is the DNR's wolf coordinator. In a presentation before a hunting group in Munising, he told the audience that we really don't know how many deer each wolf kills in the UP, but it is at least 20 per year. Thus, the 500 wolves are killing a

Proud Hunters Proud Yoopers

minimum of 10,000 deer per year in the UP. Most remarkable, the DNR knows from tracking wolves in the snow, that each small pack of wolves kills at least one deer each day during the winter! While DNR biologists don't think that the wolves keep up this pace at other times of the year, the truth is we really don't know how many deer wolves kill once the snow melts.

Around the UP, individual deer hunters and some outdoor groups believe we have too many wolves. They also believe these wolves are killing too many deer.

During the 1995 season, Yooper hunters killed a record number of bucks and does, taking 68,000 bucks and 45,000 antlerless deer, for a total deer kill of 113,000. Today's wolf kill of 10,000 deer a year is about 8% of this record kill – a significant number.

In 1997, after two of the worst winterkills on record, Yooper hunters only killed an estimated 30,000 bucks and 13,000 does, for a total deer kill of 43,000. Today's wolf kill of 10,000 deer is almost 24% of the kill that year – clearly a significant number of deer.

When the wolf starts taking one out of every four deer killed (and remember, the DNR wolf numbers and deer numbers admittedly may be low), hunters are going to get hopping mad. And some of them are going to take action.

In the last few years, hunters have grown increasing critical of the growing wolf population and its impact on the Yooper deer herd. All over the UP, farmers, landowners and hunters have complained about wolf damage. Sometimes they asked to be reimbursed when it hurts their pocketbook.

In 2002, I was conducting QDM presentations across the eastern UP. In almost every meeting, some hunter would want to talk about what we can do about wolves. One landowner was from Goetzville, Michigan, and he told the group he had lost over 20 sheep to wolves in the summer. Another Rudyard man told those in attendance that a wolf was coming to his yard every day and eating the dog food from his back porch. Others reported that their pet cats and dogs were missing, and they suspected they were victims of wolf kills.

Dwaine Starr of St. Ignace, Michigan, accompanied a DNR biologist into a cedar swamp deer yard in 2002. What Dwaine saw in that deer yard was horrifying. He found the carcasses of several dozen dead and partially eaten deer, most of which appeared to be healthy deer, but deer confined to a small cedar swamp because of the deep snow.

Dwaine, an experienced hunter, who has hunted throughout Michigan and around the world, was certain that wolves had killed the deer. And the wolves clearly killed more deer than they could eat. They killed all those deer just for fun, just because they could kill them. The key question for hunters and game managers is whether this was an unusual winter deer kill or do wolves kill at this level in all our winter deer yards across the UP all winter long?

My own Neebish Island neighbor, an 87-year-old farmer named Walt Sanford, has lost several young calves to wolves over the years. One year, he asked for my intervention when he was having trouble getting government reimbursement for his wolf-killed calves. In short, Walt was fed up battling the Lansing red tape over the wolf payments.

Living with Wolves

"They want clear proof that wolves killed the calves, and sometimes the wolves carry off the calf into the woods," Walt explained to me one day. "It might take me several days to find the kill sight, and, in a matter of hours, the wolves can eat the entire carcass. The DNR takes several days to get out here, and by that time the evidence is gone. When that happens, how can I prove that a wolf killed my calves?"

I talked to several DNR and Department of Agriculture officials about Walt's complaint, including DNR Wildlife Director Becky Humphries (prior to her promotion to department director). The Lansing officials were sympathetic, but they insisted that they couldn't pay out cash to everyone who complained they had a wolf kill. "Some of the kills are from coyotes," one official told me. "We only pay for wolf kills, and we have to see evidence of wolves."

Walt was confident that he was being victimized by wolves, and I believed him. He was totally frustrated by the DNR position on the issue. He couldn't understand why the state of Michigan wouldn't reimburse him when they were so late getting to his property after he reported calf kills.

Earlier, Walt had taken the law into his own hands. One day, a wolf came right into his yard and was harassing his cattle near his barn. Walt brought out his rifle and killed the wolf right on the spot. He then called the DNR to report the kill. If there were ever any doubt about whether there were wolves attacking his cattle, those doubts should have ended with a dead wolf in his barn yard.

The DNR gave Walt a pass for shooting the wolf. They never prosecuted him and just warned him to not take the law into his own hands a second time.

When I met with the DNR to discuss freeing up some wolf damage payments for his losses, they were quick to tell me about Walt's history with them.

"We know he's frustrated with this process," one DNR official told me. "Please help us make sure he doesn't kill any more wolves. We'll arrest and prosecute him if he does it again."

I talked with Walt more about the process, and I offered to help him make sure the DNR officials got to his place promptly when he had a wolf kill. We also had a talk about Yoopers who practice their own version of wolf control.

Yoopers call it the 3-S Wolf Control Plan. The three S's stand for (1) Shoot, (2) Shovel, and (3) Shut up. The Yooper version of wolf control is to take things into your own hands, shoot wolves on sight, bury the carcass where no one will find it, and keep your mouth shut about what you did.

I have had several dozen UP residents and hunters tell me they will practice the 3-S program until the DNR gets a better handle on how to control and moderate the wolf numbers. Those who practice 3-S include some of my friends and neighbors.

Almost every year in the eastern UP, there is at least one report of a wolf shot and abandoned by a hunter who may also cut off a radio tracking collar from the animal, if the DNR had attached one. In a recent Chippewa County wolf-kill case, the DNR only found the collar and not the animal because the hunter allegedly disposed of the carcass and separated it from the radio collar so the kill couldn't be traced to him.

In the DNR's defense, it has tried to be more aggressive in dealing with problem wolves that attack farm animals. In the past, when there was movement by the federal government to turn over more control of wolf management to the DNR for state control, out-state environmental groups and anti-hunting groups have sued the federal government and the DNR to stop or slow down DNR efforts to control wolf damage.

For many years, the environmental groups kept the federal government and the DNR at bay. That action angered Yooper hunters and galvanized more of them to take the law into their own hands by practicing 3-S. By 2007, however, the federal government had succeeded in transferring more wolf control oversight to the state. Yoopers would now have to wait to see how much more effective this process would be. What frustrated average hunters, however, is that the anti-hunting interest groups again tied up the federal government and the DNR in court, preventing more reasonable wolf control plans from being implemented. Those anti-hunting environmental groups don't get it that they encourage a more aggressive 3-S program by their actions.

Roell and other DNR employees can trap and relocate problem wolves, and before the latest lawsuit the DNR could also shoot and kill wolves causing damage. While trapping wolves is considered one of the most difficult of trapping skills, Roell is a skilled and successful wolf trapper. In fact, in 2008, the Safari Club International recognized him as the Biologist of the Year, in part because of his skills in trapping problem animals.

At an April 10, 2008, meeting of the Michigan Natural Resources Commission, the public got a glimpse of what the future of DNR wolf control might look like. At this meeting, the DNR staff presented its latest data on wolves, and it talked at length with the NRC about its proposed wolf-control plan. DNR staff reported how difficult it had been to reach consensus among wolf proponents and opponents on how to manage and control wolves during a wolf roundtable established to review the issue.

NRC commissioner and wildlife committee chair John Madigan asked the DNR staff why it wouldn't set a ceiling for the maximum number of wolves it would allow in the state. He was worried that the population had grown so fast over the past five years, that the 500 wolves we had today could be 2,500 wolves in another ten years.

"Where do we draw the line?" commissioner Madigan asked the DNR staff. Acting assistant wildlife chief Patrick Lederle told Madigan that there was no agreement (between the wolf lovers and those who want meaningful wolf controls) on the "social carrying capacity" of wolves in the UP.

Madigan, a Yooper commissioner from the Munising area, continued to press the DNR staff on why it wasn't a good thing to set a limit on how many wolves we should have in the UP. He wanted to know what was wrong with having a target on the number of wolves and having a goal where we would reduce wolf numbers if wolves exceeded that number. Madigan thought it was reasonable to have a certain number of wolves based on the number of square miles in the UP. During the discussion, the DNR staff continued to rationalize why it wasn't necessary to cap the number of wolves in the UP.

At that point, another NRC commissioner, JR Richardson from Ontonagon, weighed in, too. He told an overflowing audience that "we have wolves per square inch in the western UP." While he was intentionally over-exaggerating for the sake of effect, he was making the point rather emphatically that hunters and the public in the western UP are tiring of having so many wolves in their part of the world. It appeared he was backing commissioner Madigan's effort to pursue establishing a maximum number of wolves we would allow before reducing the wolves through legal hunting or other means.

At that point, someone in the audience asked, "How many deer do wolves kill?"

Lederle answered that wolves can kill 40 deer per year at the high end of the estimated kill rate. That rate is twice what the DNR had been saying about deer kills by wolves. If each wolf does kill 40 deer a year, that means they could be one of the most influential forces in determining overall deer populations in the UP. And it means that following bad winters, they theoretically could kill up to 50% of the total Yooper deer herd kill.

When I heard this presentation on the wolf control plan and the DNR's answers on deer kills, I could only think that we were unknowingly signing the death warrants for a lot more wolves under the 3-S plan. It seems so obvious to me that without some overall controls on the number of wolves, hunters and landowners will more often take the law into their own hands because they will sense the DNR is not serious about keeping wolf numbers under control.

I left the meeting thinking this was bad wildlife management policy and poor decision making by people who didn't live with wolves like many UP residents, hunters and landowners do. I was grateful that Commissioners Madigan and Richardson understood this issue, but that wasn't enough to ensure we implemented common-sense wolf management policies.

Several years earlier, one Yooper who represented a UP outdoor club affiliated with the Michigan United Conservation Clubs, drafted a resolution for the MUCC annual meeting. In the resolution, he proposed that the DNR should live trap some UP wolves and reintroduce them in the suburbs of southeast Michigan. He knew the resolution wouldn't pass (and it didn't), but he made a point that people in southern Michigan don't appreciate or understand how wolves impact the UP.

His point was this: southern Michigan residents wouldn't stand for wolves living in their backyard, yet they have no problem raising and protecting wolves in someone else's backyard in the "wild" UP.

Several years ago, someone in the eastern UP killed a wolf and allegedly cut off the radio collar, dumping the collar in the Munuscong River just south of Pickford. When DNR staff got the radio signals that the animal was not moving, it set out to find the wolf. Its radio signals told them the collar was at the bottom of the river. The DNR had to get the State Police dive team to recover what they thought would be an illegally killed wolf. All that they found at the bottom of the river was a radio collar – no wolf. Speculation was that the wolf was killed and the collar separated from the animal. It was another incident of the Yooper 3-S Wolf Control Program being carried out.

To this date, no one has ever been arrested in the case.

In late April 2008, I was planting trees in Raber, and I took a break for lunch at the Raber Bay Bar. Just like the Goetzville Bar, the Raber Bay Bar is the only commercial business (other than cabin rentals) left in the once booming town of Raber. And the bar sits right on the edge of the road, just like at Goetzville. Rich and Mary Lou Harmon run the Raber Bay Bar today.

There were only two customers in the Raber Bar that day, another hunter and me. My new friend in the bar told me he had driven by the Munuscong River when the

Proud Hunters Proud Yoopers

State Police dive team was recovering the collar from the dead wolf. He was amazed at the resources and expenses the law enforcement officers were directing toward solving the mystery of who killed this wolf.

"Can you imagine spending that much effort and cost to work a wolf-kill case?" he asked me. "When I saw all those police cars at the river, I thought we must have lost a child."

Several years earlier, I was working in Marquette where I gave a short presentation on transportation issues as a part of my job at MDOT. Following the meeting, one young man approached me and told me that he knew I was active in deer management issues. He explained that he was an avid deer hunter himself.

We exchanged some small talk about the deer season and our success. At one point, he talked about all the wolves that area residents were seeing and how the deer numbers were down, in part because of the wolves. Then he told me in a very matter-of-fact way that he had killed two wolves the prior muzzleloading deer season. He described in graphic detail how he shot the first wolf from his blind. When he approached the dead wolf, a second wolf walked toward him with his head down, growling in a low voice. He told me how he quickly reloaded his muzzleloader and shot the second wolf, just feet away from the first one, after the wolf wouldn't run away when he yelled at it. He then told me how he hid the two wolves in two separate areas to avoid getting caught.

During the discussion, it occurred to me that he could be making all this up. After all, he might be just bragging and telling an outright lie. But given the great detail of his story, I was fairly certain that he was telling the truth. What amazed me the most was that he wasn't uncomfortable at all telling a perfect stranger about the incident.

To him, he did a good thing for all deer hunters by killing these two wolves.

Now I didn't know his name and he didn't give me any specific information I could have turned over to a law-enforcement agent. Even so, I thought his attitude about wolves reflected that of many otherwise law-abiding UP residents. Many deer hunters will kill a wolf if they get a chance and if they are reasonably sure they can get away with it.

For all these reasons, I hope that someday we can have a legal wolf-hunting season in Michigan. That may be our only way to stop or slow down the 3-S program.

On the other side of the coin, one of the most interesting stories I've heard about wolves and their impact on the deer herd came from one of the DNR's most senior leaders. His sighting in 2006 may give us hope that not all wolves are successful when they attack healthy deer.

Until his retirement in 2008, Jim Ekdahl was the DNR's UP deputy director. As deputy director, Jim served in one of the DNR's top leadership positions, and he was the "top dog" in the UP's DNR hierarchy. Jim is one of the most respected DNR officials in the state, and he's had an outstanding career of service to UP residents. During his several decade career with the DNR, he held many different positions, including time as a Conservation Officer in the eastern UP. In fact, when Jim would see me at NRC meetings, he liked to tease me about the times he arrested some former Neebish Island neighbors of mine for multiple game violations on two opening days, two years in a row, in the same location in the 1970s.

Living with Wolves

"I always wondered what would have happened if I had showed up on opening day that third year," Jim kidded me.

Following the 2006 deer season, Jim told me that he was watching a spike buck feed one day while hunting the central UP in rifle season. Suddenly, he witnessed a mature wolf attack the deer. Jim said the deer and the wolf struggled, with the wolf looking like it was going to kill the deer. He wouldn't have predicted it, but somehow the deer escaped. Later, Jim saw the same buck, and it appeared to be in good condition, no worse for the wear from its close encounter with the wolf.

While I am not much of a wolf supporter today, I still am in awe when I see a wolf or even a wolf track. They are awesome animals when you see one, and the sight of even a fresh track can start your heart racing.

Near the end of the 2004 muzzleloading deer season, I was approaching my blind near the St. Mary's River on Neebish Island. I was a little late getting there, and it was just breaking day. As I hiked the last 400 yards to my blind, I came across a huge wolf track in the fresh snow that had just quit falling. The tracks were about four inches long and they were remarkably crisp and clear in the freshly fallen new snow. Most amazing, the striding distance between the tracks was almost five feet. The wolf had walked down my trail the entire route to my blind before he ducked into the brush of a cedar thicket. Incredibly, a wolf has a nose that is 20,000 times more sensitive than a human's nose. This wolf probably smelled me only minutes before I spotted his track. His tremendous sense of smell probably told him I was about to meet him, allowing him to coyly by-pass me without incident.

I never saw a deer that day, but I thought about the huge wolf who circled my blind just before I got there. It was an eerie feeling to know that he and I hunted the same area at the same time. As I sat in my deer blind, I thought about how this wolf hunted Neebish Island. I wondered whether he killed 20 deer a year or more.

In my lifetime, I've had several opportunities to hunt wolves in Ontario, but I have only killed one wolf. She fell from one bullet from my Remington .30/06 rifle following a 70-yard shot. I ran to her quickly, and, just like Aldo Leopold wrote about in *Sand County Almanac*, the wolf looked up at me. At that point, I saw the life go out of her eyes as she expired. Like Leopold, I did feel some sadness at her death, but I was also proud that I had taken this magnificent predator, a true hunter like me. When this happened to Leopold, he vowed he would never kill another wolf. Unlike Leopold, when I killed my wolf, I knew that I would hunt and hopefully kill another wolf some day.

And if things go well with the DNR's wolf management plan, maybe Yoopers like me will someday be allowed to legally hunt wolves in our state. And maybe that will minimize the need for the underground 3-S wolf control program.

If there is a future for wolves in the UP, it may lie with the younger generation of hunters who are more tolerant than baby-boomers like me. In early March 2008, the *Sault Evening News* carried a front page picture of a wolf running through the snow on Sugar Island, just a few miles from our hunting camp on nearby Neebish Island. I sent the web link to my son at his law office in Jackson, Michigan, with some snide comment about the wolf being a savage deer killer this time of year, when the deer were in such weakened condition from the long winter.

Proud Hunters Proud Yoopers

My son Jeff wrote back, saying, "Dad, I know these wolves kill some deer, but I still think it's cool that we have a few around."

Sometimes, there is nothing like the statement from a youngster to make you reflect on your own emotions. That sentiment coming from my own flesh and blood made me think again about my tolerance for the timber wolf. Maybe there was still hope that someday, I, too, would welcome the wolf back to Michigan.

On a cold winter day, a Proud Hunter learned what it was like to hunt in the same woods with one of nature's greatest predators, the mighty timber wolf. And from years of wolf experiences, this Proud Yooper knew he would continue to speak up for reasonable wolf management throughout the UP to protect our deer herd from excessive wolves, but maybe with just a little more tolerance for the wolf.

50

Reflections on Opening Day's First Shot

To be a great people is not just to be fine hunters and famous warriors.
The Great Spirit thinks it is far more important for us
to be good and kind to one another,
so that we don't look down on other people,
but help them with love and understanding.

-Sweet Medicine, Cheyenne

This chapter is slightly out of sequence, but for reasons I hope are obvious, it had to be the last chapter of this book. After thinking about this hunt, I knew this story would have to be the final chapter in a book about proud hunters and proud yoopers.

It was November 15, 2002, my 35th rifle hunting season in the eastern UP. Three generations of the Hank family, Louis, Ed and Leon, were in camp at Neebish Island, and we were excited for the season to start. Son Jeff would be absent this week because of a college exam, but he hoped to come up soon to join the four-generation family hunt later in the season.

The weatherman had predicted that this would eventually be a nice day. But first, we would have to wait out a heavy fog that blanketed the area and limited my view as I stared out of my elevated deer blind by the St. Mary's River, one of my favorite Neebish Island hunting spots.

The fog was so thick that I could barely see 30 yards down the 125-yard shooting line I had cut through a marshy area to the south east. I also looked out the front of my blind to the west, at an overgrown food plot that dad and I had created in this heavily forested area four years earlier. The deer used this food plot to forage for clover and other tender plants we had planted. I squinted at the small field in the early morning light, but I couldn't even see the edge of the food plot.

I had arrived at the blind well before daylight as had been our custom over the years. There is something really special about the opening day of rifle season. No matter how many opening days I celebrate, each one is special and unique. And each one must be celebrated by being in the woods when the day breaks. If you are there at day break, maybe you will be the lucky one to fire the first shot of the morning. The first shot is almost right at day break. Every year, it seems, somewhere, some lucky hunter always manages to shoot a deer right at daylight – the first one in the area to fill his tag.

Every year, there is something magical about that first rifle shot on opening day. Every year, I hope it will be me or one of my hunting partners.

At no other time in my 34 hunting seasons have I been that lucky one to fire the first shot of the morning. As another season opened, I had high hopes that maybe, just maybe, I would fire the first shot this year.

Proud Hunters Proud Yoopers

Dad and I had left the cabin plenty early enough so that we would get to our blinds long before daylight. Little did we know that we could have slept in a lot longer this year and still not missed much action because of the fog.

On this morning, I knew it might be quite a while before someone fired that magical first shot. As daylight came, the thick fog looked like it might stick around forever.

Some mornings on opening day, it sounds like a war, with all the gun shots concentrated into the early morning hours. This year, however, it was remarkably quiet. There wasn't a noise to be heard in the woods anywhere. There was no wind and I swear, I think you could have heard a pin drop from a mile away. It was so still and quiet that it was eerie.

There also seemed to be little game movement. I had not seen any birds or squirrels or any animal activity as I should have seen. Instead, there was just this dead calm silence as the heavy fog engulfed the area.

It was really weird, but at the same time, it was very cool. It seemed as if I were on another planet, it was just that strange.

The first few minutes passed by like hours, and, soon, it had been a full hour since the morning broke. Now the sun was peaking over the horizon and rapidly climbing higher. The warm sun was now slowly burning off the thick fog.

This was also almost surreal. It looked as if the fog was actually evaporating in some spots as the sun rose in the sky and the temperature climbed from the early morning chilly conditions. Gradually, I could see further and further down the line (a shooting lane) I had so carefully cut just months before. Dad and I cut this line so we could see deer crossing the line on their way to the food plot or even if they were just passing through the area.

It was a very nice ambush spot for a white-tailed deer hunter.

When we had cut the line last summer, dad and I had a serious debate about how wide to make it. Generally, I would have cut the line wider to give the hunter more time for a shot at a crossing deer. Generally, dad would have liked the line cut narrower so we minimized changes in the landscape and so we didn't scare the deer away from crossing the line.

There was one large, dead birch tree on the west edge of the line, 80 yards from the blind. I wanted the dead birch cut down. As I surveyed the line from the blind during the summer, I had instructed dad to take it down.

"No," he told me. "This birch isn't bothering you, so let's leave it. I think you can shoot around it if you have to."

I muttered something to myself about a stubborn, old Polish Yooper, and I vowed to return another day to take out the tree.

One week later, with my dad absent from deer camp, I returned with my chain saw, and I cut down the old, dead birch. "There, now I can shoot through where that birch was if I need to," I told myself.

Now as the first hour passed on opening day, I suddenly realized that I had not yet heard the first shot of the day. It was incredible that no one in the area had shot yet.

By now, I could almost see to where the old dead birch had once stood. With the sun now higher in the sky, the fog was beginning to fade away, but the landscape still had that smoke-filled, eerie, dead-planet, sci-fi look to it.

Reflections on Opening Day's First Shot

All at once, I heard a tremendous noise that I knew had to be deer running hard. From inside my deer blind, I couldn't tell where they were, but I was sure they were coming my way and that they would probably appear on my right at any time. Just when it seemed like they were directly behind me, there was only silence.

I strained with all my might to hear another sign, to catch a glimpse of the animals moving through my area. I couldn't see or hear anything.

Suddenly, I could hear the deer running again, and this time they were very close to me. I was sure the deer would pop into view on my right any time. Precious seconds went by, and I didn't see any thing.

I was getting flustered. Where were the deer? They had to be close.

When I heard one more sound, I glanced over to my left, and there was one deer crossing my line just about at the edge of the fog. As I threw the gun up, the deer disappeared into the brush and the fog on the far side of the line.

I had considerable trouble seeing the deer in the scope. First, there were hazy, foggy conditions everywhere, and, second, I was looking almost straight into the low-hanging, but very bright sun on the horizon. I only got a fleeting glance at the deer with the scope, but I was pretty sure the deer wasn't a big buck. Even so, I thought about how tough it was to see the deer under these conditions.

I settled back down and put the gun back in my lap. In the next second, a large buck appeared on the line closely following the first deer.

I instantly threw the gun to my shoulder, and I strained hard to find the deer's vital organs. For an instant, in the hazy conditions, plus looking almost directly into the morning sun again, I had trouble locating the deer in the scope. I was extremely frustrated, knowing that the big buck was on the move and that he would be out of sight in the blink of an eye, just like the doe. I had that sinking feeling that an opportunity for a big buck was quickly slipping by.

In the next second, something magical happened, as I found the cross-hairs perfectly on the deer's shoulder just as the buck was crossing the line behind where the old birch had been. For only a second, I could see through the foggy haze, and the glare of the sun was not blocking my view.

Human nature would have been to be more cautious and to make sure that the scope was truly lined up on the deer. Human nature would have been to double check this and triple check that.

To kill this big buck, there wasn't any time for double or triple checks. It was now or never.

As the great Fred Bear used to say, this was a hunter's "moment of truth."

For me, it was like I was on auto pilot. I was on cruise control. It seemed as if there was a machine inside me taking over. There was no time at all for hesitation. The seasoned instincts of an experienced hunter took over, and I instantly pulled the trigger just as the big buck moved into the heavy brush.

The remarkable stillness of the morning was abruptly shattered by the incredibly loud blast of a 180 grain .30/06 shell exiting my Remington Model 742 rifle.

For the first time ever, I was the first shot of the morning on opening day!

At the recoil of the shot, I lost sight of the deer. I wasn't yet completely sure I had hit the buck. Maybe I hadn't been on the deer as I had so confidently thought. Maybe I did shoot too fast. As I desperately scanned the horizon with my scope for a running

Proud Hunters Proud Yoopers

deer and a possible second shot, I could see one tail jumping through the heavy brush. I couldn't tell for sure, but I thought that deer that was probably the first deer, a large doe.

As I pulled the rifle to the right, I caught a glimpse of a second deer with large antlers. That had to be my buck, I thought. As I struggled to get the cross-hairs again on the deer's vital area, I thought I saw the deer go down. Suddenly, in the fog, haze and bright sunlight, I couldn't see anything.

I slumped back in my chair in my blind and tried to compose myself. As I did, for a moment, I could still see glimpses of the one deer running off into the distant, heavy timber. Then there was no movement and only silence where I had last seen the image of the deer going down – a deer I thought was a big buck.

I took a deep breath, and I left my blind, hurrying to where I had seen the buck fall. When I arrived, I was stunned to see a 180-pound, nine-point buck on the ground, dead from a perfect shot right behind his front shoulder. He had run only about 50 yards from where I had shot him – right over the freshly cut stump of an old, dead birch tree.

I instantly threw my hands in the air and said, "Yes!" out loud. I kneeled down next to the magnificent animal and stroked the fur on his upper body and I admired the massive shoulders and swollen neck he had. I looked over his antlers carefully. He was a great buck, and I was incredibly proud to have taken him.

For a solid minute, I sat there in awe of what had happened over the last few seconds, and I recounted how this event had played out.

I shook my head in amazement of this great kill, and I said a thank you to our God for letting me take another beautiful whitetail in such a dramatic and classical fashion.

I pulled my Motorola radio from my jacket and I called dad.

"Hey, did you hear that first shot of the morning?" I asked in an excited manner that gave away my secret.

"No, I didn't hear one yet," dad replied in a baffled tone. "Did you shoot? I can't always hear well in this blind and with my bad hearing."

"Yes, I did shoot, and you should come and see the buck I got," I told him proudly.

"I'll be there in a flash," he said.

Ten minutes later, dad's ATV came down the trail. He had a big grin on his face as he approached. I stayed cool and tried to not show any emotion.

"Well, take me to him," dad said, still grinning ear-to-ear.

We walked over to the buck, and I started telling dad the whole story.

Dad was really impressed with the deer, and he helped me field dress him, all the while admiring the mature buck with the nice antlers.

"You did well, my son!" he said as I finished the story, and we completed the field-dressing work. "Your grandpa will be proud too, and it's too bad your son isn't here, because this is probably where he would have been sitting! He might have gotten your buck!"

"This is what it is all about!" he said proudly to me.

After dad gave me a congratulatory hug and handshake, he headed back to his seat, and I went back to mine.

Reflections on Opening Day's First Shot

There was a warm glow in my body as I returned to my hunting blind. There was a sense of deep satisfaction in this particular hunt. I spent the rest of the day thinking about how lucky a guy I was and how good life had been to me.

I thought a lot about how lucky I was that I had been born in the UP and that I got to spend my childhood in the UP, with all the richness of the experiences that I had with this unique culture, living in this special place, and living among the people that would be my friends for life.

I reflected on how I got to spend my fall days hunting in the eastern UP where I had hunted from Hulbert to the Sault to Detour to Cedarville and everywhere in between.

I thought about all the great hunting experiences I had enjoyed in four decades of hunting all kinds of game in this area.

In my daydreaming, I went back to my childhood, and I even remembered the frogs I had chased in a small tributary of the Gogemain River at age seven. I thought about the chipmunks I had hunted as a kid with a BB gun in a Detour hardwood forest. I remembered the years I had hunted in Raber, Stalwart, Hulbert, in the Gogemain, on Hungry Hill and now on Neebish Island. I thought about the lessons I had learned from those experiences and how they had prepared me to kill the nice buck I got today.

I recalled the more than one thousand trips I had made across the Mackinac Bridge – trips I had made every weekend to return to my roots so I could hunt in the eastern UP. I thought about the long 600 mile journeys I made every weekend so I could wake up in the UP and go to a deer or duck blind – blinds I had hunted in for decades.

I reflected back on this hunting land I owned on Neebish Island and the work I had done to improve the habitat of this place so it was a paradise for wildlife. I thought about my boyhood dream to own a piece of hunting property like this. I remembered the sacrifices I had made to acquire this property and the thousands of hours of work that had gone into improving the property. I went over in my mind everything I had learned about the concept of stewardship of the land and leaving the land better than you found it for the benefit of the next generation.

I contemplated the classic opening day hunt I had experienced today. I thought about the first shot of the morning and the annual ritual of a rutting buck chasing a doe through the woods, hoping to mate with her. I reminisced about the excitement of hearing running deer in the woods and the excitement of waiting for a possible shot.

My wildly racing mind considered that ten or twenty years ago, I would have never killed the deer that I killed today. I thought about all the hunting skills I had accumulated and fine-tuned over the decades while chasing frogs, chipmunks, grouse, ducks and deer. I thought about flock shooting and buck fever and other rookie mistakes that young hunters make. I recalled how all these adventures and youthful experiences had prepared me so that today, I could make a split second decision and take a beautiful buck that would have eluded almost all other less skilled and seasoned hunters.

I thought about the magic of opening day and all the opening days I had enjoyed over the years. I reflected on the magic of hunting with your family – especially four generations of them. I thought about how my family celebrated hunting with so much enthusiasm all year long. I thought about how great it was to grow up in a family with such a rich hunting heritage and where hunting was so important to us. I relished how

Proud Hunters Proud Yoopers

close my father and I were and how much time we had spent hunting together over the years. I thought about the bond we had and the adventures we had shared over many decades. I thought about my son and the effort I had made to see that he enjoyed some of this heritage, too. I enjoyed good thoughts about my mother, my wife, my daughter, my friends and my co-workers and how supportive they had been of my hunting experiences over so many years.

That day, when the sun set on my deer blind on Neebish Island, I thought one last time about the great deer I had taken in the morning, and I thought one last time about the richness of my hunting experiences in the UP.

"I am a blessed man to have had these experiences," I told myself over and over.

As I left my deer blind for camp, I knew that no matter what happened with the rest of my life, I knew how proud I was to be a hunter, and I knew how proud I was to be from the UP.

Yes, I knew that I was now and always would be a Proud Hunter and a Proud Yooper.

On this day, a man who had spent his lifetime hunting in the UP realized that he had become a very Proud Hunter and a very Proud Yooper. He knew in his heart that he shared a unique kinship with many Proud Hunters and Proud Yoopers throughout the land. And he hoped in his heart that the magic of the UP and its strong hunting heritage would live on for many generations!

A Proud Hunter and a Proud Yooper

May serenity circle
on silent wings
and catch
the whisper of the wind.

- Cheewa James, Moduc

Ordering Information

The book retails for $12.95, plus $0.78 for Michigan state sales tax, and $5.00 for shipping and handling charges.

Order copies of *Proud Hunters Proud Yoopers* by sending a check or money order for $18.73 to:

Big Buck Ranch, Inc.
    P.O. Box 285
    Holt, MI 48842

Or use your credit card and order from our web site:
www.proudyooper.com

On the Front Cover

Top right side: Louis Hank (left) and Leon Hank with two nice bucks the Hanks killed on Neebish Island in 2005. The hunt for the bigger buck is covered in chapter 48.

Bottom right side: Leon Hank with Jennings bow and backpack ready to enter Hungry Hill in the 1980s. Hungry Hill bow hunts are covered in chapters 28 and 29.

Left side: Uncle Fred Hank (left) and Grandpa Ed Hank as young boys with their guns in the Goetzville area in the1920s. Read about Uncle Fred in chapter 18.

On the Back Cover

Top left side: Uncle Fred Hank (left) and Grandpa Ed Hank with a large 10-point buck Fred killed around 1940.

Top right side: Grandpa Ed Hank and the record book buck scoring 190.4 he shot around 1945. This is one of the top 100 biggest bucks ever shot in Michigan. Read about his last buck kill in chapter 41.

Bottom left side: Four generations of the Hanks (Grandpa Ed (far left), Louis, Leon, and Jeff) stand by their Neebish Island buck pole in the 2003 season. Read about our four-generation hunts in chapter 41 and Grandpa Ed's last hunt in chapter 43.

Bottom right side: Grandpa Ed Hank with two nice bucks taken by the Hank family in the 1930s.

About the Author

Leon E. Hank was born in 1954 in Sault Ste. Marie, Michigan, in the eastern UP, where five generations of his family have lived.

He is an avid deer, duck, goose, grouse, coyote, and bear hunter who hunts almost exclusively in the UP. While he works in the Lansing area, Leon has made over one thousand trips across the mighty Mackinac Bridge to hunt in the UP over the last 36 years.

Leon is a lifetime member of the NRA and he currently serves as president of the State Chapter of the Quality Deer Management Association. He has also been active in the UP's Superior Deer Management association, the Tri-County Wildlife Association, the Sault Sportsman's Club, Ducks Unlimited, the Raber Area Sportsman's Club, and the Michigan United Conservation Club.

Leon manages 310 acres of free-ranging deer habitat in the UP. In 1998, the Chippewa-Mackinaw Conservation District gave him the Eastern UP Conservation Steward of the Year Award for his work in habitat management. He has given dozens of seminars on deer management and how to create wildlife food plots, build wildlife wetland ponds, and plant oaks, apple trees, and conifers for better deer and wildlife habitat.

Professionally, Leon is a certified public accountant who serves as the Chief Administrative Officer for the Michigan Department of Transportation.

Leon and his wife Susan live in Holt, Michigan. They have two children, Jeff and Sarah.